Skills for Preschool Teachers

Ninth Edition

JANICE J. BEATY

Elmira College, Emerita

Boston   Columbus   Indianapolis   New York   San Francisco   Upper Saddle River
Amsterdam Cape Town   Dubai   London   Madrid   Milan   Munich   Paris   Montreal   Toronto
Delhi   Mexico City   Sao Paulo   Sydney   Hong Kong   Seoul   Singapore   Taipei   Tokyo

Vice President and Editor in Chief: Jeffery W. Johnston
Senior Acquisitions Editor: Julie Peters
Editorial Assistant: Tiffany Bitzel
Director of Marketing: Margaret Waples
Senior Marketing Manager: Christopher Barry
Senior Managing Editor: Pamela D. Bennett
Senior Project Manager: Mary M. Irvin
Senior Operations Supervisor: Central Publishing
Operations Specialist: Laura Messerly

Senior Art Director: Jayne Conte
Cover Designer: Suzanne Behnke
Cover Art: Stock Connection/SuperStock
Full-Service Vendor: Aptara®, Inc.
Composition: Aptara®, Inc.
Printer/Binder: Courier
Cover Printer: Courier
Text Font: 10/12 Optima

Photo Credits: All photos by Janice J. Beaty.

Credits and acknowledgments borrowed from other sources and reproduced, with permission, in this textbook appear on appropriate page within text.

Every effort has been made to provide accurate and current Internet information in this book. However, the Internet and information posted on it are constantly changing, so it is inevitable that some of the Internet addresses listed in this textbook will change.

Library of Congress Cataloging-in-Publication Data
Beaty, Janice J.
   Skills for preschool teachers / Janice J. Beaty.—9th ed.
      p. cm.
   Includes bibliographical references and index.
   ISBN-13: 978-0-13-038840-7 (alk. paper)
   ISBN-10: 0-13-038840-8 (alk. paper)
   1. Child development.   2. Education, Preschool.   3. Preschool teachers—Training of.   I. Title.
   LB1115.B325 2012
   372.21—dc22

                                                                      2010034542

10 9 8 7 6 5 4 3   V 0 1 3

www.pearsonhighered.com

ISBN 10:   0-13-038840-8
ISBN 13: 978-0-13-038840-7

*To Head Start teachers and teacher assistants
across the nation
for making a lasting contribution
to the lives of young children
and their families*

About the Author

Janice J. Beaty, professor emerita, Elmira College, Elmira, New York, is a full-time writer of early childhood college textbooks and a consultant and trainer in early childhood education from Cape Coral, Florida. Some of her textbooks include *Early Literacy in Preschool and Kindergarten: A Multicultural Perspective,* 3rd Edition, with Dr. Linda Pratt; *Observing Development of the Young Child,* 7th Edition; and *50 Early Guidance Strategies* (also in Chinese). Dr. Beaty is also involved in an early literacy training program with Foster Grandparents in schools and Head Start centers in Columbia, Missouri.

Preface

Skills for Preschool Teachers is fast becoming a classic in the field of early childhood education. For more than two decades it has prepared teachers, teaching assistants, college students, classroom volunteers, and CDA candidates to work with children 3 to 5 years of age in preschools, center-based child care, Head Start programs, and prekindergartens.

The skills for working with young children are presented in 13 easily readable, fact-filled chapters, each of which is based on one of the CDA "functional areas": safe, healthy, learning environment, physical, cognitive, communication, creative, self, social, guidance, families, program management, and professionalism. Information on obtaining a CDA certificate is presented in Chapter 13 and Appendix A. For students working in infant and toddler programs, a new observational tool, "Teacher Skills Checklist for Infant and Toddler Programs," is presented in Appendix B.

To gain the greatest value from this program, the student should have access to an early childhood classroom setting to apply the skills with young children.

 ## NEW FEATURES IN THE NINTH EDITION

This ninth edition of *Skills for Preschool Teachers* has been completely revised with special emphasis on tying learning activities to the latest early childhood research and to the NAEYC Early Childhood Program Standards. Here is a sample listing of the new material to be found in this edition:

- Use of the text and the Teacher Skills Checklist for in-service training.
- Appropriate NAEYC Program Standards listed within the chapters.
- New children's picture books continue as lead-ins to children's activities in every chapter, with 100 new books out of the 230 books described. In addition, 70 multicultural books are also featured. (Important books are in boxes.)
- A discussion of bullying in the classroom and on the playground with suggestions on how children and teachers can respond.
- In the health chapter, a discussion of excessive sun exposure, of attention deficit/hyperactivity disorder (ADHD), and of autism spectrum disorder (ASD).
- Expanded discussions of walking, running, galloping, and new information on skipping.
- Expanded discussion of brain research describing neurons, dendrites, and synapses, and how cognitive development can be promoted in preschool.

v

- An important section giving critical information on helping "dual language learners" who are learning to speak English while learning their own home language.
- How teachers "taking dictation" of children's oral stories helps children emerge into writing and reading.
- How coaching children on how to relate to their peers through communication helps resolve problem behavior.
- What social skills are learned through dramatic play.
- How teacher modeling helps children with mild disabilities enter group play.
- An expanded discussion of child involvement in rule making.
- An expanded discussion of methods for two-way communication with families, especially using digital photos.
- Under "Families of Different Makeups" a discussion of gay and lesbian families with children's picture books to use.
- In Chapter 13, on professionalism, how to create a professional portfolio.

Observations of Students and In-Service Teachers

Students and teachers should begin the program with a self-assessment of their present skills using the revised, strengths-based Teacher Skills Checklist found in the Introduction.

Observations of Children

Strength-based observations of children are an important part of this program. The following checklists found in the chapters can be used by students and teachers:

Large-Motor Checklist (p. 101)
Small-Motor Checklist (p. 111)
Creative Movement Checklist (p. 118)
Children's Curiosity Checklist (p. 128)

Cognitive Concepts Checklist (p. 137)
Self-Concept Checklist (p. 215)
Social Skills Checklist (p. 232)
Learning Center Involvement
    Checklist (p. 307)

Observations of the Environment

To make the environment as safe, healthy, and as learning-effective as possible, the following checklists from the first three chapters can also be used:

Learning Center Safety Checklist (p. 18)

Bathroom, Stairs, and Exits Safety Checklist (p. 20)

Outdoor Playground Checklist (p. 21)

Classroom Cleanliness Checklist (p. 51)

Classroom Eye-Appealing Qualities Checklist (p. 65)

ACKNOWLEDGMENTS

My special thanks for the new edition of this book go to the directors, teachers, parents, and especially the children of the Tiger Paws and Park Avenue Head Start Programs and Trinity Lutheran Child Learning Center in Columbia, Missouri, with thanks to its director, Gail Schuster.

My thanks also go to Ann Gilchrist, director of the Central Missouri Foster Grandparent Program, for allowing me to participate with and photograph the grandparents who have given so much of themselves to the young children in these programs; to Vicky Rathbun, volunteer coordinator of the program; to Mernell King, Head Start director; to Darin Preis, executive director of the Central Missouri Community Action Program, for his cooperation and support; to Elaine West, executive director of the Missouri Association for Community Action, Inc., for allowing me to use children's art created for the annual MACA calendar; to the young artists and their parents in Joplin and Southwest Missouri; to faculty members from Polk Community College in Lakeland, Florida, for the Infant and Toddler Checklist found in Appendix B; and to Pearson editor Julie Peters for her creative ideas and support.

Finally, many thanks are extended to the following reviewers: Jane Bobay, Lansing Community College; Pamela Briggs, McLennan Community College; Ronda Hawkins, Sandhills Community College; and Karan Marshall, Eastfield College.

Brief Contents

Contents

2 Maintaining a Healthy Classroom   38

3 Establishing a Learning Environment   64

4 Advancing Physical Skills   99

7 Advancing Creative Skills   184

8 Building a Positive Self-Concept   208

9 Promoting Social Skills   231

10 Providing Guidance   256

11 Promoting Family Involvement   278

12 Providing Program Management   305

13 Promoting Professionalism   335

Appendix A   Becoming a CDA: Child Development Associate   359

Appendix B   Teacher Skills Checklist for Infants and Toddlers   367

References   372

Index   379

Introduction

WELCOME to the exciting world of early childhood education. Whether you are a student, teacher, teaching assistant, or volunteer you will find this rapidly expanding field offers unlimited opportunities to work with those fascinating humans: young children, 3–5 years of age. The training and credentials you may need to enter this field are described in Chapter 13, Promoting Professionalism. Most training is offered in colleges, universities, or the programs themselves. This textbook serves as an introduction to such training. The text also offers another option: the In-Service Training Option for program personnel who need to upgrade their skills of working with young children or for volunteers new to preschool programs.

THE IN-SERVICE TRAINING OPTION

The In-Service Training Option is a unique approach for teachers, assistants, and volunteers to upgrade their early childhood classroom skills. Although this text can be used in a traditional college course, learners also have the option of using the text independently for in-service training. The program consists of 13 chapters that can be used separately or in any combination or sequence to meet the individual's training needs. For college students in preservice training, the entire text can provide them with the basic skills necessary for preschool teaching. For staff personnel already in preschool programs, they may need to work on one or two of the skills at a time. What are these skills?

Skills Based on Child Development Associate Training

The skills in this text derive from the original six competency goals developed by the federal Council for Early Childhood Professional Recognition for the Child Development Associate (CDA) training program (see Appendix A). These goals represent basic competencies for persons with primary responsibility for groups of young children 3 to 5 years of age. From these competency goals, 13 key words or phrases known as Functional Areas have been extracted to serve as focus for teacher training.

Textbook Chapters from Functional Areas

Each of these 13 CDA Functional Areas serves as the basis for one of the 13 chapters of this textbook. Each of these 13 Functional Areas also appears as a heading for the items appearing on a self-assessment tool, the Teacher Skills Checklist. Thus, *Skills for Preschool Teachers* has integrated the recognized CDA competencies into a college-based teacher preparation program, as well as an in-service training program for teachers, assistants, student teachers, and volunteers already in the classroom.

CDA Goals, Functional Areas, and Book Chapters

1. Establishing and maintaining a safe, healthy learning environment

SAFE	Chapter 1 Maintaining a Safe Classroom
HEALTHY	Chapter 2 Maintaining a Healthy Classroom
LEARNING ENVIRONMENT	Chapter 3 Establishing a Learning Environment

2. Advancing physical and intellectual competence

PHYSICAL	Chapter 4 Advancing Physical Skills
COGNITIVE	Chapter 5 Advancing Cognitive Skills
COMMUNICATION	Chapter 6 Advancing Communication Skills
CREATIVE	Chapter 7 Advancing Creative Skills

3. Supporting social and emotional development and providing positive guidance

SELF	Chapter 8 Building a Positive Self-Concept
SOCIAL	Chapter 9 Promoting Social Skills
GUIDANCE	Chapter 10 Providing Guidance

4. Establishing positive and productive relationships with families

FAMILIES	Chapter 11 Promoting Family Involvement

5. Ensuring a well-run, purposeful program responsive to participant needs

PROGRAM MANAGEMENT	Chapter 12 Providing Program Management

6. Maintaining a commitment to professionalism

PROFESSIONALISM	Chapter 13 Promoting Professionalism

True learning occurs when students have opportunities to make practical applications of theoretical ideas. Therefore, the classroom skills to be acquired should be performed in actual preschool settings. If already serving as a teacher, assistant, or volunteer in a Head Start program, child-care center, nursery school, private preschool program, or prekindergarten program, you can use the children's classroom as the location for completing the prescribed chapters. If enrolled in a college or university early childhood program, you will need to volunteer in a nearby preschool classroom.

This ninth edition of *Skills for Preschool Teachers* presents a comprehensive program for training primary caregivers in early childhood programs. It will also help those already employed in programs to assess their areas of need and strengthen their skills. It will help those preparing to work in such programs to develop entry-level skills in a classroom setting.

Teacher Skills Checklist

This checklist was developed and field tested by the author for use as an initial assessment instrument and training tool by college students and CDA trainees and candidates. It is based on the previously mentioned Competency Goals and Functional Areas developed for CDAs.

Each item of the checklist stands for one Functional Area and contains three representative indicators that demonstrate competence in the particular skill area. Each chapter of the text then discusses one of these Functional Areas, with the indicators serving as specific objectives for the chapter and as subheadings within the chapter. Thus the *Teacher Skills Checklist* serves not only as an initial assessment tool for teacher training but also as an outline for this text. It is important to refer to the particular chapters of the text to clarify or interpret any checklist items in question.

ASSESSMENT FOR IN-SERVICE TRAINING OPTION

You will need to arrange for a trainer to make an initial assessment of your skills using the *Teacher Skills Checklist* in an early childhood classroom. If you are employed in an early childhood program, a master teacher, educational coordinator, or director may be your trainer. It is important that the trainer be someone experienced with young children who can evaluate your classroom skills objectively and support you throughout your training.

You yourself must first make a self-assessment using the Checklist, checking the items you have performed and writing down the evidence. Your trainer will do likewise, visiting you one or more times to complete the Checklist. Then the two of you should meet and compare the results. After reviewing the data gathered, the two of you can decide on which of the 13 chapters you should read and complete the Learning Activities at the end. In the days to follow the trainer can revisit your classroom to see how you have improved.

Some trainers use the Checklist differently by scheduling an in-service training workshop for the entire staff based on one of the Functional Areas, asking everyone to read the appropriate chapter and complete the Learning Activities before the workshop takes place. Afterwards, the trainer visits with each classroom to see how the learning has been applied.

Teacher Skills Checklist

Name _____   Observer _____

Program _____   Dates _____

Directions

Put a "×" for items you see the student perform regularly.

Put an "N" for items where there is no opportunity to observe.

Leave all other items blank.

Item	Evidence	Date

1. Safe

_____ Promotes toy and material safety within each learning center. _____

_____ Plans and implements necessary emergency procedures. _____

_____ Provides a safe classroom atmosphere through teacher behavior. _____

2. Healthy

_____ Encourages children to follow common health and nutrition practices. _____

_____ Promotes and uses materials to ensure children's health and cleanliness. _____

_____ Recognizes unusual behavior or symptoms of children who may be ill and provides for the children. _____

3. Learning Environment

_____ Sets up stimulating learning centers in appropriate spaces. _____

_____ Provides appropriate materials for children's self-directed play and learning. _____

_____ Promotes a high-activity, low-stress environment where children can play and learn happily together. _____

4. Physical

_____ Assesses children's large-motor skills and provides appropriate equipment and activities. _____

_____ Assesses children's small-motor skills and provides appropriate materials and activities. _____

_____ Provides opportunities for children to engage in creative movement. _____

5. Cognitive

_____ Helps children develop curiosity about their world through sensory exploration. _____

_____ Helps children develop basic concepts about their world by classifying, comparing, and counting objects in it. _____

_____ Helps children apply basic concepts about their world through high-level thinking and problem solving. _____

6. Communication

_____ Talks with individual children, including dual language learners, to encourage listening and speaking. _____

_____ Uses books and stories to motivate listening, speaking, and emergent reading. _____

_____ Provides materials and activities to support emergent writing. _____

7. Creative

_____ Gives children time, opportunity, and freedom to do pretending and fantasy role play. _____

_____ Provides a variety of art materials and activities for children to explore on their own. _____

_____ Encourages children to create and have fun with music. _____

8. Self

_____ Accepts self and every child as worthy and uses nonverbal cues to let children know they are accepted. _____

_____ Accepts and respects diversity in children and helps children to respect one another. _____

(Continued)

(Continued)

_____ Helps every child to develop independence and experience success in the classroom.

_____

9. Social

_____ Helps children learn to work and play cooperatively through sharing and turn-taking.

_____

_____ Helps children learn to enter ongoing play without disruptions.

_____

_____ Helps children learn to find playmate-friends.

_____

10. Guidance

_____ Uses positive prevention measures to help eliminate inappropriate behavior.

_____

_____ Uses positive intervention measures to help children control their inappropriate behavior.

_____

_____ Uses positive reinforcement techniques to help children learn appropriate behavior.

_____

11. Families

_____ Involves families in participating in children's program.

_____

_____ Recognizes and supports families of different makeups.

_____

_____ Builds teacher-family relationships through family meetings.

_____

12. Program Management

_____ Observes, records, and interprets the needs and interests of children.

_____

_____ Plans and implements an emergent curriculum based on children's needs and interests.

_____

_____ Assesses outcomes and arranges follow-up.

_____

13. Professionalism

_____ Makes a commitment to the early childhood profession.

_____

_____ Behaves ethically toward children,
           families, and coworkers.
                                                    _____

_____ Takes every opportunity to improve
           professional growth.
                                                    _____

Permission is granted by the publisher to reproduce this checklist for evaluation and record keeping.

DEVELOPMENTALLY APPROPRIATE PRACTICE (DAP)

In addition to the material presented in this text, students and trainees need to be aware of national guidelines for teachers of young children as spelled out by our professional organization, the National Association for the Education of Young Children (NAEYC), and being implemented by early childhood programs across the country. These guidelines for all teachers of young children are called *developmentally appropriate practice (DAP)*. How you teach and what you teach should be in accord with these guidelines.

Copple and Bredekamp (2009) explain, "Developmentally appropriate practice (DAP) requires both meeting children where they are—which means that teachers must get to know them well—and enabling them to reach goals that are both challenging and achievable" (p. xii). That's the main idea: getting to know the children well. Three fundamental considerations help teachers to decide what is developmentally appropriate:

- It must be *age appropriate.*
- It must be *individually appropriate.*
- It must be *socially and culturally appropriate.*

The material in this text, *Skills for Preschool Teachers,* has been developed according to these guidelines. How you as a student, trainee, volunteer, or teacher apply the information and ideas should also be governed by the three preceding principles. What teachers must do to enact the DAP principles are further defined by five key aspects of good teaching:

1. Creating a caring community of learners
2. Teaching to enhance development and learning
3. Planning curriculum to achieve important goals
4. Assessing children's development and learning
5. Establishing reciprocal relationships with families (pp.16–22)

The book *Developmentally Appropriate Practice in Early Childhood Programs* (Copple & Bredekamp, 2009) is fast becoming a standard for program practices throughout the country. It spells out in detail what developmentally appropriate practice means and how it should be used with children and families in early childhood programs.

NAEYC EARLY CHILDHOOD PROGRAM STANDARDS

In addition to following the developmentally appropriate practices described above, students, trainees, volunteers, and teachers need to be aware of program standards that have been developed by the NAEYC to ensure high-quality early childhood education. The extensive list of the standards is available online at http://www.naeyc.org or in the booklet *NAEYC Early Childhood Program Standards and Accreditation Criteria* (2005). Such standards are used by early childhood programs as accreditation criteria. They cover the following areas:

Relationships	Families	Community Relationships
Curriculum	Health	Physical Environment
Teaching	Teachers	Assessment of Child Progress
Leadership and Management		

This text uses a sampling of appropriate standards throughout the chapters asking readers to describe how they would meet the standards listed. Assessment of child progress is discussed more fully in this author's companion text: *Observing Development of the Young Child* (Beaty, 2010). Teaching is serious business. Teaching young children is more than serious; it should also be a happy business and great fun for you and the children involved. Enjoy!

Maintaining a Safe Classroom

☐ **General Objective**

To be able to set up and maintain a safe classroom environment and to reduce and prevent injuries

☑ **Specific Objectives**

____ Promotes toy and materials safety within each learning center

____ Plans and implements necessary emergency procedures

____ Provides a safe classroom atmosphere through teacher behavior

SAFE ENVIRONMENT

First and foremost for young children in your classroom is how they feel about the environment. Do they feel safe and comfortable? Schiller and Willis (2008), who create environments using brain-based teaching strategies, have this to say about safety: "Safety and well-being come before anything else. The brain attends to these needs first. A child who comes to school hungry, ill, or frightened will find it difficult to focus on what is going on in the classroom. Children will struggle with learning if they feel afraid because a classroom setting is too restrictive, a home environment is too demanding, or a classmate's behavior is aggressive" (p. 53).

It is up to you as a teacher to make sure the physical environment is free of anything that could frighten the child. Do you have snakes or spiders in your science center? Some children are just not comfortable with the feeling that these animals may escape. You may need to plan your science activities differently. Use yourself as an example. How do you feel about coming into this setting, knowing you will be staying most of the day? Is there plenty of room and enough interesting-looking activities to pursue? The classroom should project an atmosphere of "caring spaces, learning places" as Greenman's (2005) book describes.

In addition, you must check the condition of the bathroom, the exits, the stairs, and the outdoor play area daily to be sure they are clean, clear, and safe. Although a maintenance person may have the responsibility for cleaning and repairing the building and grounds, it is also up to you as the leader of a group of young children to see that the environment is truly safe.

PROMOTES TOY AND MATERIAL SAFETY WITHIN EACH LEARNING CENTER

The learning centers found in early childhood classrooms are the heart and soul of every program. It is here that teachers set up activities for children to engage in on their own, for the most part. These centers usually include art, block-building, books, computers, cooking, dramatic play, large-motor, manipulative/math, music, sand/water/sensory, science/discovery, woodworking, and writing activities. How safe they are for the children's use depends on how you as a teacher have set them up.

Are there slippery floors around the water table? Expect unwary youngsters to slip and fall. No safety goggles for the sand table? Expect crying when sandy fingers rub unprotected eyes. Dramatic play area too small for all who want to use it? Then expect lots of pushing, shoving, and loud complaints. Fye and Mumpower (2001) tell us: "A warm, nurturing, stimulating environment tells children that they are valued and that they, and their ways of learning, are understood and respected. Safety and accessibility are also essential when designing any learning environment. Make sure that all equipment and furniture are suitable and safe for young children. Furniture is arranged to enable children, including those who use mobility aides such as wheelchairs or braces, to move about freely" (p. 16).

Art Center

The art center should be located near a source of water so brushes and hands can be cleaned easily and water for painting is not so easily spilled. The center may consist of one or more easels for painting, one or more tables for flat painting and crafts, and shelves at children's level for youngsters to select and return art materials on their own. Teachers' art supplies are better stored in cabinets inaccessible to children.

Sharp scissors are less dangerous for young children to use than dull ones, which may slip and cut a child. Small sharp scissors can help young children develop manipulative skills safely. A nearby adult should keep a watchful eye on children when scissors are out, however, and have children put the scissors away in scissors holders on nearby shelves when not in use.

NAEYC Early Childhood Program Standards: Safe

Describe how your program meets the following standard:

2.A.08 Materials and equipment used to implement the curriculum provide for children's safety while being appropriately challenging.

Replace art materials that are hazardous with nontoxic materials. Some sidewalk chalk contains lead (National Association for the Education of Young Children, 2004, p. 49). Contact the Art and Creative Materials Institute to check for certified safe materials (http://www.acminet.org). Use water-based nontoxic paints and glues. Even rubber cement is toxic if inhaled. Instead, use white glue. Avoid using powdered clay, powdered tempera paints, or instant papier-mâché. When using modeling sand, be sure children wear safety goggles to prevent them from wiping their eyes with sandy fingers. When using glitter, have children apply it from a shaker and keep hands away from it. If glitter gets on fingers, be sure children wipe or wash it off because glitter can be dangerous to eyes, which children tend to rub. All art materials for young children should be nontoxic, nonflammable, and water-based. Do not use tiny craft and collage beads, buttons, and gems that the youngest children may put in mouths, noses, or ears.

Block-Building Center

Blocks should be stored lengthwise on shelves for easy selection and return. Be sure the block shelves are steady, against the wall if necessary, so that someone bumping against them will not tip them over on children playing in the center. The principal safety feature of block-building areas is the height of constructions. Some teachers permit children to build with wooden unit blocks or large hollow blocks only as high as a child's own height. Others allow children to climb on chairs to build towers as high as they can reach. The danger is that the tall building may fall on another child or that the climbing child may fall and be injured. You must decide if this situation poses a problem with your children. If this is a safety priority with you, you will want to establish block-building rules with the children at the outset.

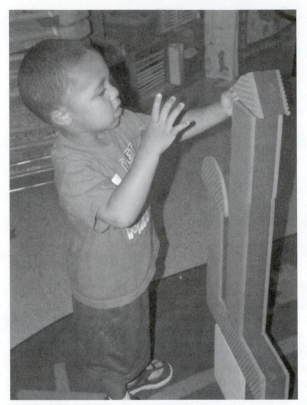

Height of buildings is a safety consideration.

Because preliterate children are not able to read written rules, why not post illustrated rules for them to follow? You can draw an outline of a block building next to the outline of a child to show the allowable height and another that shows a building that is too tall. Underneath each picture write a simple rule such as "Just Right" or "Too Tall." Most children will soon figure out what the words as well as what the illustrations mean.

Block accessories such as small trucks, cars, figures of people, animals, and dollhouse furniture should be free of broken or jagged parts. Flat carpeting in the block area makes a most appropriate building space. Riding trucks do not belong here where they may crash into buildings or their builders.

Book Center

Your library or reading corner should be a comfortable place for children to stretch out on the floor or curl up on a soft couch to read. Make sure the floor is covered with a rug to keep it warm enough in cold weather, and place the reading corner in a location that is free from drafts. Be sure that floor pillows or beanbag chairs do not accidentally cover heat vents. If you have a rocking chair, help children learn to control it. Children tend to get carried away with child-size rockers and may tip over or rock on someone's fingers. Keep bookshelves low enough so that children are not tempted to climb up for out-of-reach books.

Computer Center

Young children can teach themselves to use these powerful interactive learning tools if teachers set up the area for their convenience and safety. Children should sit and not stand when using this valuable piece of equipment. Two children at a time can be seated in child-size chairs in front of one computer with the monitor screen on a table at their eye level, not on an adult-size computer shelf high above them. Electric cords should be plugged into a wall outlet behind the machine and out of the children's reach. Do not use long extension cords that people will trip over. Instead, plug computers into surge bar outlets. Keep water and sticky fingers away from the computer keyboard. Children should wash their hands before using the computer. When it is not in use, cover the keyboard or move it out of reach to prevent children from playing with keys or inserting tiny objects.

Cooking Center

Most states have licensing and insurance regulations governing safety in child-care centers. You also need to learn the local safety regulations governing hot food preparation in schools and child-care centers. Some schools do not allow electric appliances, microwave ovens, hot plates, or blenders in the classroom. Some require only special kitchen areas for hot cooking. Food preparation without heating can be carried out within the classroom. Whatever the case, an adult should always be in the area during food preparation. Electrical equipment can be plugged into countertop outlets that are otherwise covered when not in use. Young children can learn to use knives and scrapers safely, but an adult should supervise.

Dramatic Play Center

The dramatic play center can be sectioned off for children's pretend play with child-size cupboards, refrigerator, stove, and sink. Toy safety is a particular concern in the dramatic play area. Check dolls for small parts that a child could twist off and swallow accidentally. Remove dolls with buttons, glass eyes, and beads that are sewed or wired on. Be sure that earrings are large and that strings of beads are unbroken. Tiny objects sometimes find their way into young children's noses or ears. Also remove toys with springs, wires, or sharp parts. Look for a nontoxic label on all painted toys.

If you use plastic dishes, knives, or spoons, make sure they are not broken. Cutting knives, of course, should not be used for play. Ensure that mirrors are shatterproof and that breakable dishes are used only in carpeted areas. Remove drawstrings on dress-up clothes (Wellhousen & Crowther, 2004). Be sure hooks for hanging dress-up clothes are not at children's eye level.

Large-Motor Center

Indoor climbing equipment and the tumbling area should be cushioned with pads or other materials thick enough to prevent injuries in case a child falls. Thompson and Hudson (2003) suggest: "Use several four-inch landing mats secured so they will not move when children land on them." Or: "Use surfacing tiles or mats that are permanently secured to the floor and of a thickness proportionate to the height of the equipment" (p. 111). Establish safety rules for climbers at the outset. If you have wheeled riding vehicles, establish safety rules with traffic signs and safety games. This is how young children learn safety rules—through games and fun activities.

Choose equipment appropriate for young children for indoor play. Teeter-totters are too difficult for most preschoolers to use without injury. Lofts should be no higher than 4 or 5 feet off the ground. A sturdy railing around the top is important. If the railing contains slats, they should be spaced close enough that children's heads cannot be entrapped. How do children get up onto the loft? Fye and Mumpower (2001) suggest: "A loft with a removable ladder makes it possible for an adult to control access to the area. Lofts should be monitored at all times and the number of children playing in them limited" (p. 22).

Inclusion

Children with physical limitations should be involved in all of the activity areas of the classroom, including the large-motor center. Find ways to give them safe access to large-motor experiences. Children in wheelchairs can throw and catch soft balls or inflated balls. True *inclusion* means that all children are included in all classroom activities. Use your ingenuity to accommodate everyone. For example, in a catch and toss game, have everyone sit in chairs just as a child who uses a wheelchair does.

Manipulative/Math Center

If you have 3-year-olds or younger children in your program, be sure the stringing beads and counters are large. Three-year-olds often put small objects into their mouths, noses, and ears. Use large counting and sorting items whenever possible, and keep them stored in clear plastic containers on nearby shelves. Check games and toys for broken parts and discard anything with splinters, wires, or peeling paint.

Inclusion

Tables for children with minimal mobility should be sturdy enough to support their weight. Otherwise a carpeted area may make manipulative play easier. Select large versions of manipulative toys. Use trays or cookie sheets with raised edges to contain small pieces of games. Glue knobs onto puzzle pieces for easier handling (Wellhousen & Crowther, 2004).

Music/Listening Center

Cords on record players, tape recorders, and electronic keyboards should be out of children's reach. Children should not be allowed to plug or unplug the equipment. Better to use battery-operated players when possible. However, avoid equipment with small mercury-type batteries that could be swallowed accidentally. If children use headsets for listening to records, tapes, or CDs, be sure to control the volume on the player in a permanent manner so that children's hearing is not damaged if the volume is too loud. Cover control buttons with green and red tape so children have a visual clue for starting and stopping equipment.

Sand/Water/Sensory Table

When playing at the sand table, children should wear safety goggles to keep sand out of their eyes. Spilled water and sand around tables are slippery and should be cleaned up. Spilled rice from a sand table is especially slippery. Keep a child-size mop, broom, and dustpan in the area so that children can help with cleanup. They will not

To prevent spills, keep ingredients at low levels.

only take pride in themselves and their classroom by performing this adult-type task but also learn safety practices useful in other settings. To prevent spills in the first place, keep ingredients at low levels in the play tables. Children can have just as much fun and learning with a few inches of water as they do with a filled water table—and they will stay drier.

Be sure toys and implements for sand and water play are not broken, rusty, or sharp-edged. Glass containers such as baby food jars or glass eyedroppers should not be used. Replace them instead with plastic cups, containers, bottles, funnels, droppers, and basters.

Clean and sanitize the water table with a bleach solution at least once a week before filling with water. Also clean and sanitize toys to be used. Have the children wash their hands before water play. Avoid using sponge toys, which may harbor bacteria. When play is finished, discard the water.

Science/Discovery Center

Display children's collections of seeds or beans under clear plastic wrap instead of leaving them open for handling. As mentioned previously, some young children put such items in their mouths, and certain seeds or beans may be poisonous. Be sure animal cages are cleaned daily and food and water are provided.

Certain houseplants are highly poisonous if ingested and thus pose a hazard to young children who may be tempted to eat a leaf or berry. If you have plants in your classroom, keep them out of reach. Rather than warning children against eating such leaves or berries, it is better to remove the temptation. If you stress "no eating," certain young children who had no notion of eating a plant part will try it just because you mentioned not doing it! Figure 1.1 lists some of the more common poisonous plants. If a child has ingested a poisonous plant, immediately call the local Poison Control Center whose number should be posted on the wall next to a phone (1-800-222-1222 nationwide). Follow their directions before treating the child. Current research does not support inducing vomiting outside of a hospital (National Association for the Education of Young Children, 2004, p. 49).

Woodworking Center

In woodworking, as in playing with sand, children should wear safety goggles, and most love the experience. Use small-size adult hammers, saws, pliers, and screwdrivers. Most children's toy sets are not made for use with real wood and nails.

Figure 1.1   Common Poisonous Plants

Source: From *Caring for Our Children, National Health and Safety Performance Standards: Guidelines for Out-of-Home Child Care Programs* (p. 434) by the American Academy of Pediatrics and American Public Health Association, 2002. Reprinted with permission.

Poisonous Indoor Plants	
Philodendron	
Mistletoe berries	
Dieffenbachia	
Poinsettia leaves	
Amaryllis	
Poisonous Outdoor Plants	
Holly	Yew
Mustard	Lily-of-the-valley
Hydrangea	Mushroom
Buttercup	Bittersweet berries
Azalea	Black locust tree
Castor bean	Rhubarb leaves
Rhododendron	Cherry tree
Datura	

Children can learn the safe use of real tools by having a staff member or a parent demonstrate how. An experienced child can also show a beginner. Limiting the number of children in the area will also reduce safety hazards.

Woodworking generates much interest for both boys and girls. Roofing nails and ceiling tiles are easier for beginners to use successfully. To cut down on noise, put rug squares under the pounding materials. Pick up nails not being used and keep them in covered containers so they don't fall on the floor. Have children help make rules illustrated with stick figures to be posted in the center: "Two children at a time"; "Tools used only when teacher is present"; "Wear goggles at all times." You or a staff member should model how tools are to be used.

Inclusion

Use golf tees and Styrofoam for children with weak muscle tone to help them learn to hammer (Flynn and Kieff, 2002, p. 21).

Writing Center

This is a most important learning center these days with the focus throughout the educational system on promoting literacy. It can be set up simply with a table, chairs, and nearby shelves for writing materials. But a more interesting arrangement, such as an office, invites more children to participate. A desk with pigeonholes, desk lamp, file cabinet, in-basket, pencil sharpener, toy telephone, and cell phones make the center more realistic. Pens, pencils, markers, pads, tablets, stationery, envelopes, stamps and stampers, paper clips, and paper punchers can be stored in containers on shelves or in the pigeonholes of a desk. Fye and Mumpower (2001) have this to say about the furniture: "Child-sized furniture and safety are primary factors in the selection of pieces, all of which should meet current safety standards. Comfort and convenience are necessary because furniture in early childhood classrooms is expected to be moved often and may have many different uses" (p. 18).

Place the desks against the wall with wires from lamps plugged into a socket directly behind the desk without extension cords. Any wall sockets not in use should be covered. Encourage children to use the materials only in the center. Pencils with sharp points, for instance, can accidentally stab someone when carried in a child's swinging hand. Make sure the markers and stamping ink are nontoxic.

Safety Checklist

A safety checklist is one of the most effective methods for establishing and maintaining safe learning centers. It will help you to set up the classroom initially with safety in mind and will assist you in checking daily on the condition of the classroom. The Learning Center Safety Checklist in Figure 1.2 serves this purpose. Have a different child every day serve as an assistant safety inspector to go around with you to check each center. This kind of hands-on approach teaches children safety in a most immediate and effective manner.

General Room Conditions

Check the heating system in your room. Exposed pipes should not be allowed unless they are thoroughly protected with nonasbestos insulation. Radiators and space heaters should be sectioned off to prevent children's direct contact. Portable electric or kerosene heaters are generally prohibited by fire codes or insurance regulations. Be sure that safety equipment such as smoke detectors and fire extinguishers are in working order and that staff members know what to do and how to use them in the event of a fire.

Electric cords and wires should not be accessible to children. Avoid using extension cords whenever possible. Place aquariums, incubators, and other classroom electrical equipment near electric outlets that are inaccessible to little hands. Exposed electric outlets should be covered with safety plugs.

Check your walls, furniture, and cupboards for peeling paint. Children love to pick off the pieces and put them in their mouths. Be sure the surfaces are sanded and refinished with nonlead paint. Remove broken toys and furniture and have them repaired. Don't wait until someone gets hurt. Check wooden equipment and room dividers for splintery surfaces and have them refinished. What about the corners of the room dividers? Will children be hurt if they stumble against the edges? You may need to tape padding onto edges that are sharp.

Be sure your rugs and carpeting lie flat. Wrinkles in carpets cause tripping. Area rugs should have nonskid backing. Use carpets where children will be sitting and

Art Center

_____ Scissors are supervised

_____ Toxic materials removed

_____ Water spills cleaned up

_____ Goggles used with modeling sand, glitter

Block Center

_____ Free-standing shelves low & sturdy

_____ Building heights within limits

_____ Block accessories free of broken parts

_____ Riding trucks kept out of center

Book Center

_____ Appropriate carpeting

_____ Heat vents not accidentally covered

_____ Rocking chairs away from children on floor

_____ Bookshelves low and sturdy

Computer Center

_____ Computer monitor at child eye-level

_____ Electric cords in surge protector out of child's reach

_____ Water and liquids kept out of center

Cooking Center

_____ Appliances in compliance with safety codes

_____ Sharp implement use supervised

_____ Electric appliances controlled by adult

Dramatic Play Center

_____ Dolls, toys with no removable parts

_____ Earrings large, bead strings unbroken

_____ Plastic dishes, cutlery unbroken

_____ Clothes hooks above eye level

Writing Center

_____ Desks against wall

_____ Lamps plugged into wall sockets

_____ No extension cords

_____ Sharp pencils kept in center

_____ Nontoxic markers and ink used

Large Motor Center

_____ Climbing equipment cushioned

_____ Safety rules for riding vehicles

_____ Loft at adult eye-level

_____ Railing slots close together

_____ Balls made of soft material

Manipulative/Math Center

_____ Tiny beads or counters removed

_____ Materials with broken parts, peeling paint discarded

_____ Sharp or pointed objects eliminated

Music/Listening Center

_____ Electric cords out of reach

_____ Mercury battery equipment eliminated

_____ Volume on headsets, players controlled

Water/Sand/Sensory Table

_____ Water and sand at low levels

_____ Spills cleaned up promptly

_____ Broken, rusty or glass implements removed

_____ Safety goggles used with sand

Science/Discovery Center

_____ Children's collections covered with clear, plastic wrap

_____ Aquarium, incubator wires out of reach

_____ Live plants nonpoisonous

_____ Pets, handled gently, cages clean

Woodworking Center

_____ Small adult-sized tools used, supervised

_____ Safety goggles used

_____ Safety rules enforced

General Room Condition

_____ Floor covering smooth, unbroken

_____ Heating pipes covered, sectioned off

_____ Smoke detectors, fire extinguishers okay

_____ Sharp corners of dividers padded

Figure 1.2   Learning Center Safety Checklist

Source: Adapted from *Safety in Preschool Programs* (p. 39) by Janice J. Beaty, 2004, Upper Saddle River, NJ: Pearson Education, Inc. Reprinted with permission.

playing on the floor. Loop pile carpeting is especially good because it retains its appearance and is easily accessible for wheelchairs. In eating and art areas where spills are likely, washable floor coverings are more practical (Fye & Mumpower, 2001, p. 18).

Inclusion

Check the physical environment of your classroom to see if you need to modify it for children with special needs. You may need shelves or water containers at special heights for children with disabilities. As Wellhousen and Crowther (2004) also note, "Children in wheelchairs or walkers should be able to move in and out of spaces easily." Place colorful footprint cutouts or wide colored tape on the floors to identify routes to different areas of the classroom (p. 26).

Bathroom

Slippery floors may be the most common cause of injuries. Make it a practice to check bathroom floors from time to time during the day, and clean them whenever there are spills. Sinks and toilets should be cleaned and disinfected and floors mopped daily. If the sink is not child size, use a sturdy nonskid stool for children to reach it. Water temperature should not exceed 110 degrees. Mark the faucets with hot and cold symbols in red and blue.

Always store bathroom cleaning and disinfecting materials in cabinets out of the reach of children, and be sure that cabinets containing caustic or poisonous materials are locked. If first-aid kits or materials are stored in the bathroom, keep them out of reach of the children but accessible to adults.

Stairs/Exits

What about stairs leading into or out of the building? Can children reach the railings? Are steps sturdy and unbroken? If covered with carpet, is the carpeting smooth and in good condition? As a teacher of young children, you are accountable for all aspects of children's safety in the building. Although others may be responsible for repairs and replacements, it is up to you to ensure safety by reporting problems and making sure they are corrected. Cutout footprints mounted as a trail can guide children to exits. The standard for exits in child-care facilities is as follows: "Each building or structure, new or old, shall be provided with a minimum of two exits, at different sides of the building or home, leading to an open space at ground level. If the basement in a small family child care home is being used, one exit must lead directly to the outside. Exits shall be unobstructed, allowing occupants to escape to an outside door or stair enclosure in case of fire or other emergency" (American Academy of Pediatrics and American Public Health Association, 2002, p. 194). The checklist in Figure 1.3 should be followed.

Figure 1.3 Bathroom, Stairs, and Exits Safety Checklist

Bathroom

_____ Sinks clean, toilet flushed

_____ Stable step stools available

_____ Slippery floors cleaned up

_____ Cleaning and disinfecting materials locked up

_____ First-aid kit out of children's reach

_____ Liquid soap, paper towels accessible

Stairs/Exits

_____ Exits clearly labeled

_____ Two exits in every classroom

_____ Stair steps smooth, unbroken, nonskid material

_____ Carpeting, mats smooth, untorn, not slippery

_____ Stairs well lighted

_____ Railings within children's easy reach

Outdoor Playground

Select outdoor play equipment with care, making sure it is developmentally appropriate for preschool children in size, usage, and location. Belt or tire swings are preferable to swings with hard seats, because the latter cause many injuries. The U.S. Consumer Product Safety Commission recommends a minimum 8-foot safety zone around each play unit, such as swings or slides, as well as a resilient safety surface under and around each unit. A cushioning of sand, wood chips, shredded bark, or special mats may be used, but grass, dirt, concrete, or blacktop are not acceptable.

Use child-size equipment with railings and platforms on the slides. Swings should not be attached to climbing structures as in backyard sets. Climbing, sliding, and swinging equipment should be securely anchored in the ground with buried concrete footers. Eliminate dangerous equipment such as merry-go-rounds, trampolines, and teeter-totters (seesaws). The teeter-totter is a dangerous piece of playground equipment for preschoolers. A young child can be thrown off even a small teeter-totter when the child at the lower end jumps off unexpectedly. The safe use of a teeter-totter is too complex a concept for most 3- and 4-year-olds to learn; most teachers prefer not to have them.

Merry-go-rounds are also too difficult for most preschool children to use safely. Getting on and getting off when merry-go-rounds are moving can throw children to the ground; trying to stay on when they are spinning fast is beyond the capabilities of most preschoolers. Even supervising adults have difficulty preventing spills when merry-go-rounds are going.

Is the equipment on your playground in safe condition? Check to make sure there are no loose parts, sharp edges, or slivers. There also should be no spaces or protrusions where children's heads or body parts can become entrapped or their clothing entangled. Safety product guidelines are available from the U.S. Consumer Product Safety Commission by calling 1-800-638-2772.

You as teacher, teaching assistant, or student teacher are an especially important safety feature on the playground. You must accompany children whenever they go outside, preceding them to the playground and making sure conditions are safe for them to follow. Should there be a strange animal or person on the grounds, you will then be able to address the situation, sending the children back inside if necessary. While the children play you should be an alert observer, not spending time visiting with another adult, but watching for possible dangerous situations among children on the climbing, swinging, or sliding equipment.

Finally, the playground should be properly fenced off from roads, driveways, or parking lots. Each time you use the playground, make sure to check it first for broken glass or other dangerous debris. Your children deserve a fun-to-use, hazard-free playground. A child can serve as an assistant playground inspector to help you survey the playground daily using the checklist in Figure 1.4.

Using trikes, scooters, and other riding equipment can be an exciting experience if done safely. Child-size bike helmets should be used when riding and removed as soon as the child gets off equipment to prevent getting snagged in other equipment. Some states such as Florida provide free safety education programs and materials, with helmet fitting and distribution to children in need (Page, 2006, p. 18).

Inclusion

Use your ingenuity to find ways to include children with limited physical abilities in playground activities. Did you think a child with impaired vision would not be able

Figure 1.4   Outdoor Playground Checklist

Source: From Janice J. Beaty, *Skills for Preschool Teachers,* Ninth Edition. Copyright © 2012 by Pearson Education, Inc. All rights reserved.

_____ Playground enclosed with fence

_____ Debris, broken glass removed

_____ Mushrooms, poisonous plants, berries removed

_____ Tripping hazards such as rocks, holes corrected

_____ Cushioning under climbers, slides appropriate

_____ Large equipment anchored properly with buried footers

_____ Swings of safe material (belts, tires)

_____ Slides and other metal equipment not rusty

_____ Wooden equipment not splintery

_____ Railings around high platforms with slats close together

_____ Sharp edges, missing or loose parts corrected

_____ Sand boxes covered when not in use

_____ Young child-size equipment, riding toys used

_____ Adequate supervision when in use

to ride a trike? Flynn and Kieff (2002) tell us that a beeper can be placed on the back of the tricycle of another child, and the child who is blind can play "follow the leader" to the sounds he or she hears. They both need to go very slowly with you beside them as a safety supervisor (p. 21).

Books as Lead-Ins to Playground Safety Activities

Children can begin to understand safety if you introduce safety precautions on the playground by reading an appropriate book to a small group at a time.

> In the animal story *Chicken Chickens* (Gorbachev, 2001) Mother hen takes her two little chickens to the playground, but they are afraid to try the play equipment until Beaver helps them slide down the slide on his tail. Have your children look closely at the pictures to decide if this playground is really a safe place. Can they point out things that are safe and unsafe? Does anyone notice that the adults are sitting and talking—not paying attention to their children? Have them build their own playground in the block center.

Bike and playground books as lead-ins to activities include

Duck on a Bike (Shannon, 2002)

Mike and the Bike (Ward, 2005) [Includes CD]

Queen of the Scene (Latifah, 2006)

Sally Jean, the Bicycle Queen (Best, 2006)

PLANS AND IMPLEMENTS NECESSARY EMERGENCY PROCEDURES

As you plan for the safety needs of the children in your care, be sure to consider unexpected emergencies that may arise. These may include illnesses or injuries when prompt emergency action is necessary; weather emergencies when prompt precautions must be taken; and fires, floods, explosions, or earthquakes when emergency exiting is required.

Emergency Illnesses or Injuries

Know your children well. Do any of them have chronic illnesses such as asthma or diabetes? Heart problems? Breathing problems? Seizure disorders? Allergic reactions? Bleeding problems? A health record for each child should be on hand in the classroom for quick reference. Plans for children with emergency health needs should be made at the beginning of the year with the advice of parents and the program health professional. Be sure to have emergency access to someone who speaks the language of every

Figure 1.5 Emergency Management Conditions

Source: From *Caring for Our Children, National Health and Safety Performance Standards: Guidelines for Out-of-Home Child Care Programs* (p. 23) by the American Academy of Pediatrics and the American Public Health Association, 2002. Reprinted with permission.

Bleeding	Sprains, fractures
Burns	Dental emergencies
Poisoning	Head injuries
Choking	Allergic reactions
Injuries, including insect, animal, and human bites	Eye injuries
	Loss of consciousness
Shock	Electric shock
Convulsions or nonconvulsive seizures	Drowning

non-English-speaking child in the program. Have phone numbers for them at hand. Be alert to symptoms and learn to recognize signs that may signal an emergency. Know the location of the nearest emergency room and how long it takes to get there. Have transportation available at all times. Use the 911 emergency number when necessary.

Preparing for Accidents

Post near your telephone the emergency numbers for police, sheriff, fire department, doctor, ambulance, hospital, and poison control center. All adults in the classroom should be familiar with the location of these numbers. Also, post near telephones simple directions for handling emergencies, written in two languages if your program is bilingual. A list of children's home telephone numbers, parents' cell phone numbers, and the names and numbers of persons to contact if no one is home should be available near your telephone and carried in your first-aid kit as well.

All staff involved in direct care of children should be certified in pediatric first aid that includes rescue breathing and first aid for choking as developed by one of the following organizations: the American Red Cross, American Heart Association, or National Safety Council. Such a course should include emergency management of the conditions listed in Figure 1.5.

Make plans with the staff about each person's duties during an emergency. Practice together to see how you can respond best as a team. Your program also should devote a staff meeting to emergency procedures and first aid. Keep two well-stocked first-aid kits available at all times, one for the classroom and one to take on field trips. Make sure each staff member knows how to use all the items in it. Figure 1.6 lists the contents of a first-aid kit as approved by the American Academy of Pediatrics and the American Public Health Association.

In addition, be sure to have on hand near the telephone or first-aid kit an easy-to-use, easy-to-read first-aid emergency handbook. Two excellent spiral-bound handbooks with illustrated, step-by-step first-aid procedures for common medical and health emergencies are *A to Z Health and Safety in the Child Care Setting* (Stoll, 2000) and *Childhood Emergencies: What to Do* (Marin Child Care Council, 2000) also in Spanish.

Figure 1.6   First-Aid Kit

Source: From *Caring for Our Children, National Health and Safety Performance Standards: Guidelines for Out-of-Home Child Care Programs* (p. 226) by the American Academy of Pediatrics and the American Public Health Association. 2002. Reprinted with permission.

Disposable nonporous gloves	Cold pack
Sealed packages of alcohol wipes or antiseptic	Standard first-aid text
	Coins for use in pay phone
Scissors	Insect sting preparation
Tweezers	Poison control center phone number
Thermometer	Water
Bandage tape	Small plastic or metal splints
Sterile gauze pads	Soap
Flexible roller gauze	Safety pins
Triangular bandages	Nonglass thermometer
Eye dressing	Syrup of ipecac (use only if recommended by poison control center)
Plastic bags (for materials used in handling blood)	
Pen/pencil and notepad	

Injury Safety Activities

Children can also become aware of situations requiring first aid by hearing stories about helping someone who has been injured or by playing doctor or nurse in the dramatic play area. You can read them a story such as *Love Can Build a Bridge* (Judd, 1999) about pairs of multiethnic children helping one another. One boy helps another who has been hurt on a slide, a boy helps a girl who has fallen while in-line skating, and another boy helps a girl who has injured her arm while jump-roping. Have them choose to be one of the characters and tell what they would do in the same situation.

If a real injury should occur, make a note of what happened and when, the child's reaction, and your response. Pass such information on to parents and emergency personnel on your center's accident report form, and also keep a copy for your own program.

Weather Emergencies

Violent weather can cause emergencies in which teachers and child-care workers must help protect children. When warnings for tornadoes, hurricanes, typhoons, thunderstorms, flash floods, tidal waves, windstorms, and dust storms are issued or sirens are sounded, emergency procedures must be followed immediately. Different rules are necessary for different types of storms. Learn the rules that apply to your area, and practice them with the children under your care until they can respond quickly and without panic. Safety drills such as "Duck-and-Cover" need to be practiced when appropriate, as well as emergency exiting where necessary.

Books as Lead-Ins to Emergency Weather Activities

Tornados are a frequently occurring weather emergency in certain states. Children need to learn what to do when warning sirens sound. If children enjoy hearing the story of Aunt Minnie and the twister, have them talk about how the life of these farm children is different from their own lives. What would they do if they lived with Aunt Minnie today and a twister occurred? Although earthquakes are not caused by weather, they nevertheless require safety actions, usually the emergency exiting of a building.

> A book that may help children understand about tornados is the old-time story *Aunt Minnie and the Twister* (Prigger, 2002) about Aunt Minnie and her nine nieces and nephews who live together on a farm in Kansas. They respond quickly when she rings her big bell, and all hide in the root cellar until the storm is past. Have your children practice duck-and-cover drills or whatever is appropriate for children in school when tornados occur.

Other storm books as lead-ins to activities:

Earthquack (Palatini, 2002)

Storm Is Coming! (Tekavec, 2002)

The Big Storm (Tafuri, 2009)

Emergency Exiting

Certain situations demand rules and order. Emergency exiting from the building is one of them. Fire drills, earthquake drills, chemical spills, bombs, civil disturbances, or other street emergencies call for buildings to be cleared as quickly as possible. Children should practice this procedure repeatedly so that everyone understands how to do it without panic. Do not wait for a fire inspector to make this happen. It is your responsibility to yourself, the children, and their families to see that emergency evacuations are accomplished with ease. Figure 1.7 lists rules for emergency exiting of a building.

Figure 1.7 Emergency Exiting of a Building

Source: Adapted from *Safety in Preschool Programs* (p. 88) by Janice J. Beaty, 2004, Upper Saddle River, NJ: Pearson Education, Inc. Reprinted with permission.

1. Line up children quickly but calmly
2. Teacher at head of line, staff member at rear
3. Carry emergency duffel bag and daily attendance sheet
4. Follow quickest safe route to outside
5. Assemble at evacuation site outside building
6. Count to make sure all children are there

Inclusion

Children with physical disabilities may need special help during an emergency exit. Be sure your center is in compliance with ramps, railings, and handholds in place. Classroom staff members should be assigned to children with special needs to help them move quickly but safely out of the building. Emergency exit signs and directions should be posted in several languages if your program is multilingual. Designate a safe spot outside the building where children should always go whenever there is emergency exiting.

Books as Lead-ins to Firefighting Activities

Before emergency drills take place, talk with your children and read them stories in preparation.

> *Miss Mingo and the Fire Drill* (Harper, 2009) is a light-hearted story of how Miss Mingo's class (of animals) learns what to do in case there's a fire. They practice exiting with hilarious results until they finally get it right. How could your children help Miss Mingo? Have your class hold its own practice drills.

Other firefighting book lead-ins:

Even Firefighters Hug Their Moms (Maclean, 2002)

Stop Drop and Roll (Cuyler, 2001)

This Is the Firefighter (Godwin, 2009)

Emergency Evacuation Plans

It is important to plan for emergency evacuations ahead of time with staff, parents, children, and evacuation personnel. The school or center director needs to arrange for primary and secondary evacuation sites. Sometimes buses or other transportation may be needed. Parents should be informed of these plans when they enroll their children and whenever plans are changed. An emergency duffel bag should be prepared and be on hand at all times. One of the staff should be responsible for carrying it. Figure 1.8 lists the contents of an emergency duffel bag.

 ## PROVIDES A SAFE CLASSROOM ATMOSPHERE THROUGH TEACHER BEHAVIOR

Teacher's Behavior

The key to helping children respond quickly and sensibly to safety emergencies is the teacher's behavior. Teachers and other classroom staff must keep their own poise, remaining calm, unstressed, and in control. No matter how uneasy you may feel, it must

Figure 1.8   Contents of Emergency Duffel Bag

Source: Adapted from *Safety in Preschool Programs* (p. 80) by Janice J. Beaty, 2004, Upper Saddle River, NJ: Pearson Education, Inc. Reprinted with permission.

- Bottled water
- Paper cups
- Snacks (crackers, dried fruits)
- Battery-operated radio and extra batteries
- Blanket
- First-aid kit and handbook
- Emergency contact information for each child and staff member
- Photos of each child
- Cell phone
- Cards with games and songs

not show in your face, your voice, or your actions. Concentrate instead on the children and how you can help them come through the situation without becoming panicked or hysterical yourself. Figure 1.9 offers some suggestions of what you can do.

Dissipate Fear

In today's world unexpected things happen. Teachers and staff members should be as prepared as they can be for all kinds of disasters: common and uncommon, expected and unexpected, minor and serious. One factor common to all of these situations is fear. Fear is a crippling emotion that can cause panic and chaos among those experiencing it. If you recognize this fact, you can help to dissipate fear among the children through your own behavior as already mentioned. You can also talk with the children about the fears they may have and how to handle such fears. Fears such as the fear their mother or father will not come for them, fear of the dark, fear of loud noises, and fear of animals are some of the fears they or you might talk about, in addition to the emergency situations previously mentioned.

Figure 1.9   Teacher Behavior in Emergency Situations

- Be quiet: Help children to become quiet; become quiet yourself; whisper
- Use body language: Smile; nod; make eye contact with each child
- Come close: Touch children; hug them; hold their hands; put arm around them
- Use verbal cues: Use calming words; use compliments
- Laugh quietly together: Whisper a silly word or verse; make a silly face
- Hold hands: Everyone hold hands close together in a circle (Standing or seated)

When teachers show children unconditional love, they help to dissipate children's fears during times of crisis and confusion. The six examples of teacher behavior during emergency situations in Figure 1.9 are demonstrations of love toward children. This love in turn fosters reciprocal feelings of love and security within the children, helping to dissipate fear.

Supervising Classroom Areas

Early childhood programs are fortunate to have more than one staff member present at all times. A teacher, an assistant, and sometimes a third staff member, student teacher, or Foster Grandparent volunteer can contribute to children's safety by supervising activities and areas where safety precautions are necessary. Plan during staff meetings what the role of each staff member will be. Include volunteers in your plans and give them a role where appropriate. Help them to model calm and unruffled behavior during times of crisis and accidents, and how to handle emergencies.

Overall responsibility for safety belongs to the teacher, who can survey the entire classroom as other staff members work with children in particular learning centers. Be sure that room dividers are not so high that they prevent you from seeing all of the children. If your program uses more than one room at a time, be sure a staff member remains in each room.

Learning centers that need safety supervision include large-motor, computer, woodworking, and cooking. The bathroom, the playground, and the stairs are other safety supervision areas. Keep an eye on the children in all of these areas, but do not stand over them. The more unobtrusive that staff members can be in their supervision, the more freely children will explore activities or learning centers independently.

Anticipating Unsafe Behavior

Unsafe child behavior can take many forms. It may consist of running in the classroom or halls, pushing other children, climbing too high, playing too rough, or using materials in unsafe ways. You may be able to eliminate much unsafe behavior by anticipating it ahead of time. Arrange the physical environment so that children do not have room for uncontrolled running. Have children walk with partners in the halls or on city streets. Carefully supervise potentially unsafe situations.

Children love to play with water. If they squirt it on the floor in the classroom or in the bathroom, they have created a slippery condition for others. You need to stop them firmly, not harshly, and redirect them by involving them in helping you to clean up the water. Make the task interesting, not a punishment.

Redirecting Unsafe Behavior

Telling a child to stop climbing so high or to stop building such a tall block building will not resolve the safety problem. Commands like these only encourage young children to climb higher and build taller. A sensitive teacher knows that one of the best

You can anticipate unsafe behavior by observing how children use playground equipment.

ways to deal with such situations often requires redirecting unwanted behavior, not by referring to it, but by calling the child's attention to something else.

For instance, go to the child personally (don't shout across a room) and ask the child to show you how he or she can climb horizontally or swing hand over hand, or to show you how a very wide building would look. Giving a child another challenge will often redirect potentially unsafe behavior into something more constructive.

Modeling Safe Behavior

You and the staff members are the models of safe behavior for your children. When they see you taking precautions with saws, hammers, knives, or electrical equipment, they will imitate you. Your behavior is much more effective than your trying to tell or "teach" children the proper rules. As you practice normal adult safety behavior, describe it verbally to the children. "See how I cut the pumpkin? I move the knife away from me so that I don't get cut. Now you try it." You also should not practice any unsafe behavior such as consuming hot liquids or setting a hot cup of coffee down in the classroom area.

You and your staff, including volunteers, should discuss safety practices in the classroom so that all of you agree on the limits you will set for children. This agreement will thus help you to enforce the limits consistently. Young children do not necessarily understand rules by being told. Most often they learn by doing, by being involved in the situation. For instance, you can demonstrate at the workbench how to hold the saw and make it work, or you can have a parent come in and demonstrate. Then let each child try it. When a child has learned to use the saw, let him or her show the next child how to use it. If one child can show another child how to perform the task, then that child has really learned it.

Involving Children in Safety Rules

Let the children be involved in helping to decide on the safety rules for each classroom area. All of you should agree on the rules. How many children should be allowed in the woodworking area at one time? How high can a block building be built and still be safe? Should a child be allowed to stand on a chair to make the building higher than he or she can reach from the floor? The children need to know the answers to these questions. If they help make the rules, they will be more willing to follow them.

Do not overburden the children with rules. Make simple ones that everyone understands and that you can easily enforce. Children should be concerned with the safety basics such as not hurting themselves or others. We adults are sometimes overly concerned about rules and regulations. If there are too many rules, young children simply will not respond. Keep rules simple, basic, and few in number.

Car and School Bus Safety

Most states have enacted legislation governing car safety for young children. The laws state that children younger than age 4 must sit in state-approved car seats when riding in private cars. As a teacher, you can encourage children to follow this practice through classroom play activities. Bring in a car seat and let them practice using it themselves or with dolls during dramatic play. Or fasten a seat belt to a chair and let children pretend to be riding in a car.

Talk to the children about bus safety (see Figure 1.10). If any of the children are transported to the center or school by bus, have the bus driver come in at the beginning of the year to talk about bus safety. How should they sit in a moving vehicle? What should their behavior be like? Then they should go outside and practice "bus manners" in an empty parked bus. Some teachers prefer to read a book as a lead-in to school bus manners.

Books as Lead-Ins to School Bus Safety Activities

After reading this book, line up chairs in the dramatic play center like seats in a bus and have children choose the characters' props you have put out: driver's cap,

Figure 1.10 School
Bus Manners

- Sit, don't stand when bus is moving
- Keep arms and hands out of windows
- Keep bus aisles clear
- Keep noise down so driver can hear
- Follow driver's directions promptly
- Walk single file when getting on and off
- Stay 10 feet away from parked bus
- Never go behind a parked bus

backpacks, toy hamster and cage, lunch box, Game Boy, comb and brush, magazine, lunch box, notebook and pencil, trading cards, books, an iPod and headset. Children can reenact the story as you reread it.

The book *Bus Stop Bus Go* (Kirk, 2001) is a fine story for looking carefully at the illustrations, listening closely to what the children are saying as they ride the bus to school, and then deciding what they are doing that is safe and what is not safe during this trip. Have your small group of listeners give suggestions on every page of what can be done to bring the bus back to its proper safety standards. Which bus manners do the children follow or fail to follow? Have them decide the best way to learn these manners.

Other school bus books as lead-ins to activities:

The Bridge Is Up (Bell, 2004)

I'm Your Bus (Singer, 2009)

The Little School Bus (Roth, 2002)

We All Go Traveling By (Roberts, 2003) [CD included]

The Wheels on the School Bus (Moore, 2006) [song]

Field Trip Safety

Field trips require special preparations. Teachers need to familiarize themselves with the field trip site to prepare the children. Are there special safety hazards that need to be addressed? On a visit to a farm, for example, how close should children get to the animals? What about riding on a tractor? On a visit to a fire station, will the children be allowed to climb onto a fire truck? Are any special precautions necessary for a visit to a zoo?

In addition, children may need to learn how to walk in pairs, how to cross busy thoroughfares, and how to wait for the teacher before they go forward. The adults as well as the children need to understand such procedures ahead of time. Parents or volunteers should be assigned to several children or a single child who may need

Figure 1.11   Field Trip
Manners

> - When walking, hold buddy's hand
> - Stay with the group; don't run ahead
> - Sit next to your buddy in the bus
> - Keep track of your buddy at the site
> - Listen to the teacher or the parent volunteer
> - If you become frightened, go to the teacher or volunteer
> - If you become separated, go to someone at the site and tell him or her

special help. Talk with these adults ahead of time discussing what their roles will be, what they can expect, and how they should respond in case of an emergency. They also need to know the limits on child behavior, and how to remind children to practice the field trip manners they have learned (see Figure 1.11).

If children are transported in cars, buses, or subways, they and the drivers or parent helpers must be aware of safe and unsafe child behavior in a vehicle. One of the adults should also be certified in pediatric first aid and should take along a first-aid kit. To anticipate the safety problems inherent in any field trip, make a preliminary visit to the site, if possible using the same mode of transportation the children will use. Then you can make notes about safety situations for preparing the staff and the children. Talk to the people at the site in case they have safety rules or advice you will need to know ahead of time. As you look at the field trip site, try to anticipate the kinds of exploring your active children will attempt to do. Would any of these things be dangerous? What about children becoming separated from the group or going off by themselves? One of your staff members can be assigned to check on this problem.

Before taking a field trip, walk through the trip with the children discussing where they are going, how they will get there, what they will do and see when they get there, and any special instructions you may have. You will be assigning each child to a buddy they should stay close to. Have them practice walking around the classroom with their buddy.

Preparing Children for Personal Safety

The personal safety of the children in your care includes protecting them from harm or victimization by predatory adults. Sexual abuse of children by adults is one of the primary dangers involved. Although this is a very real threat to certain young children, many professionals feel that the child-care community has overreacted to the threat in ways that are potentially harmful to children.

Through films, diagrams, games, and exhortations, teachers have alerted young children to "stranger-danger" in centers. In addition, teachers have made children feel that it is their responsibility to protect themselves from such adults. However, we delude ourselves if we believe that 3-, 4-, and 5-year-old children can successfully ward off the advances of abusive adults. In addition, if children have been taught what to do, but then find they can't prevent the abuse, their own guilt feelings may add to the psychological damage, and they may come to believe that the abuse is their own fault.

As a result of this kind of overreaction to the situation on our part, we find many children in child-care centers who are afraid of the other adults in the building, who run from friendly college students, who will not let health professionals examine them, or who may even show fear when a parent undresses them for bed or a bath. In addition, some child-care professionals themselves worry that entering the bathroom area with the children in their care or helping children clean themselves after accidents may cause children to overreact and report to their parents that they were touched. Male child-care workers are especially vulnerable to such charges, and as a result, many of the much-needed male role models for young children have been driven out of the child-care profession.

We need to step back and think about the effects of instilling this kind of fear in young children. This kind of fear not only inhibits learning but also makes children all the more vulnerable to victimization. We also need to realize that most child sexual abuse occurs in the home, and that 85 percent of such abuse is perpetrated by someone the child knows (Hull, 1986, p. 18).

What, then, should be our role in protecting the children in our charge? We should use our common sense in helping children learn not to go with strangers or accept rides from people they do not know. However, scare tactics and "stranger-danger" films and lessons are out of place.

We as teachers are the ones who really need to be educated in this matter. We should look carefully at the message we want to get across to children. It should not be that there is danger in every stranger. It should not be one of "good touches" and "bad touches." How is a preschooler to distinguish between the two? With such messages, we may be producing a generation of paranoid children who will keep their distance from one another as adults. Do we want to live in a society where caring, touching, and loving are perceived as threatening acts? Instead, we should encourage children to do the following:

1. *Children should talk to a trusted adult when they feel uncomfortable.*
2. *They should go only with a trusted adult on the street or in a car.*
3. *They should ask a trusted adult when they are unsure of what to do.*

The child-care staff and parents need to be involved in sensitive discussions of this issue and how it is to be handled in the center and at home. You may want to invite psychologists or health professionals to contribute their expertise. A positive approach, in which children learn to feel good about themselves and the people around them, should be your goal.

You and your staff also should take special precautions in not allowing a child to leave the center with any person other than the designated parent or caregiver. If someone you do not know demands to take the child home, do not comply. Call the parent or social worker for advice on what to do. Otherwise, keep the child in your care until the proper adult caregiver responds.

Bullying

Riley and Boyce (2007) define *bullying* as "intentionally hurtful behavior inflicted upon a victim or victims" (p. 4). These behaviors may include teasing, taunting, threatening, hitting, and stealing. They are often directed toward one individual and are repeated until someone stops them, Bullies experience the feeling of power over those they can threaten or hurt. Their victims often feel powerless and isolated.

Does bullying occur among preschool children? Unfortunately, it does. We do not hear so much about bullying in the early years because young children are not so verbal. They are often too scared of the bully to report it to a parent or teacher. Although bullies have been traditionally thought of as boys, girls can be bullies as well. Boys tend to use physical aggression in their bullying, while girls mainly use relational aggression (i.e., gossip and exclusion). That may be changing. Riley and Boyce report: "Recent research has found evidence that physically aggressive bullying is common with male and female bullies, and the number of girls who exhibit physically aggressive behavior continues to rise" (p. 8). Bullying is an important safety issue.

Whether or not bullying has been noticed around your children, you need to take steps to create a safe learning environment that will prevent bullying from happening. First of all, children need to be made aware of bullying so that it will not be kept secret. Teachers need to talk openly about what bullying is, and how children should report it to a trusted adult if they should see it or experience it. Reading a positive book about bullying is a good start.

Books as Lead-ins to Talking About Bullying

Read the story to two or three children at a time having them sit close enough to see the pictures. Do they like what Freckleface did? How would they respond if they were scared of Patrick? Does anyone mention reporting him to the teacher if he doesn't stop? Bullies often lack the social skills of finding friends, so they intimidate others. Riley and Boyce suggest working with parents, teachers, and children to create an atmosphere that promotes "buddying, not bullying" (p. 5). It means helping each of the children find a buddy.

Freckleface Strawberry and the Dodgeball Bully (Moore, 2009) shows a bright, active little girl being scared of Windy Pants Patrick in the gymnasium because he throws the ball too hard in dodgeball to get every child out. When she is the last one left she scrunches up in fear, but when the ball doesn't hurt, she becomes a big scary monster who hops on one foot roaring at Patrick. He is the one to be scared, and they end up being friends.

Some children bully others on the playground by throwing a ball at them.

A teacher could talk quietly with a ball-thrower about how the other child feels; how he or she feels; and what the ball-thrower could do to make the other child feel better.

Another book about a bully, this time a girl, is *Bootsie Barker Bites* (Botner, 1992) about the biting Bootsie Barker who terrorizes the little girl narrator of the story when she visits her home, pretending to be a girl-eating dinosaur. The scared girl tells her mother, but her mother only says: Tell Bootsie not to play that game any more. The girl finally invents a new game, and when Bootsie next comes into a darkened play-room, the girl stands tall, waving a leg bone, proclaiming in a terrible voice: "I am a paleontologist who digs up dinosaur bones!" Bootsie runs for her life.

This is a great book for a story reenactment with children playing the roles of Bootsie, the little girl, and her mother as you read the story. Use real props and see how your children solve the problem. Afterwards talk about feelings—both the bully's and the victim's. Your positive response to any frightening situation helps make your classroom safe and welcoming.

SUMMARY

Information from this chapter will help you to set up and maintain a safe classroom environment and to reduce and prevent injuries. You should be able to assess the curriculum areas in the room for possible safety hazards such as electrical cords, exposed heating pipes or vents, slippery floors, rugs that do not lie flat and could cause tripping, and rough edges and sharp corners on room dividers. You should understand how to promote safety in each area with illustrated signs, simple basic rules, supervision where necessary, anticipation and redirection of unsafe child behavior, and role playing and demonstration of safe behavior.

Through games, book readings, dramatic play, and other developmentally appropriate activities, children can learn the safety rules and precautions they must practice on stairs and exits, in the bathroom, in the school bus, on field trips, and in cars. You yourself should be aware of the importance of planning for children's emergency illnesses and injuries and of being prepared to give first aid if an accident occurs. You should also be aware of procedures to follow during fires, earthquakes, weather emergencies, or emergency exiting of the building during drills or real situations. Remaining calm yourself and helping to dissipate children's fears through positive, loving behaviors will help children remain calm in times of crisis. As a role model for safe behavior in the classroom, you will be taking the first step to assure children and their families that your program is making a serious commitment to each child's safety and well-being.

Ethical Dilemma

A child who is emotionally disturbed has been enrolled in your classroom. The child's behavior disrupts the class's activities and takes a great deal of the teacher's and other children's time. Because of the child's hitting, kicking, and throwing of heavy materials, a safety issue for the other children is also involved. The parents have refused services in a more appropriate setting. How can you and your program balance the requirements of this child with special needs with the needs of the other children in the classroom?

LEARNING ACTIVITIES

1. Read one or more of the Suggested Readings or view a Web site cited in this chapter. Begin a card file with 10 file cards that describe in detail ideas you have gained for promoting safety in your classroom. Include the reference source on the back of each card

2. Assess the safety of your classroom, bathroom, and playground by using the Safety Checklists in Figures 1.2, 1.3, and 1.4. What changes can you suggest?

3. Have one of your staff members hold a fire drill or emergency exiting drill. Observe and record what happens. Report on the results and make recommendations for improvement.

4. Help a small group of children learn a particular safety concept using ideas and techniques from this chapter. If you are not in a classroom write up a lesson plan you would use to teach a safety concept.

5. List the contents of your classroom first-aid kit and describe a use for each item.

6. Describe how you have rearranged your classroom or made other arrangements for children with special needs so they can participate with the others.

SUGGESTED READINGS

Bales, D., Walinga, C., & Coleman, M. (2006). Health and safety in the early childhood classroom: Guidelines for curriculum development. *Childhood Education, 82*(3), 132–138.

Berson, I. R., & Baggerly, J. (2009). Building resilience to trauma: Creating a safe and supportive early childhood classroom. *Childhood Education, 85*(6), 375–379.

Bullard, Julie. (2010). *Creating environments for learning; Birth to age eight.* Upper Saddle River, NJ: Merrill.

Engley, E. A., King, N. M., & Hilber, C. B. (2006). Bullying behavior in early childhood: How does it begin? *Dimensions of Early Childhood, 34*(3), 21–27.

Hansen, C. (2006). Bullying is a big deal. *Dimensions of Early Childhood, 34*(3), 16–20.

Israel, M. S. (2004). Ethical dilemmas for early childhood educators: The ethics of being accountable. *Young Children, 59*(6), 24–32.

Mercurio, M. L., & McNamee, A. (2008). Monsters that eat people—Oh my! Selecting children's literature to ease children's fears. *Dimensions of Early Childhood, 36*(2), 29–37.

WEB SITES

American Academy of Pediatrics
http://www.aap.org

Child Care Safety Checklist for Parents and Child Care Providers
www.cpsc.gov/cpscpub/pubs/childcare.html

Consumer Product Safety Commission
http://www.cpsc.gov

National Association for the Education of Young Children
http://www.naeyc.org

National Fire Protection Association
http://www.nfpa.org

National Safe Kids Campaign
http://www.safekids.org

CHILDREN'S BOOKS

Bell, B. (2004). *The bridge is up!* New York: HarperCollins.

Best, C. (2006). *Sally Jean, the bicycle queen.* New York: Farrar, Straus and Giroux.

Bottner, B. (1992). *Bootsie Barker bites.* New York: Putnam.

Cuyler, M. (2001). *Stop drop and roll.* New York: Simon & Schuster.

Godwin, L. (2009). *This is the firefighter.* New York: Hyperion.

Gorbachev, V. (2001). *Chicken chickens.* New York: North-South Books.

Harper, J. (2009). *Miss Mingo and the fire drill.* Somerville, MA: Candlewick.

*Judd, N. (1999). *Love can build a bridge.* New York: HarperCollins.

*Kirk, D. (2001). *Bus stop bus go.* New York: G. P. Putnam's Sons.

*Latifah. (2006). *Queen of the scene.* New York: HarperCollins.

Maclean, C. K. (2002). *Even firefighters hug their moms.* New York: Dutton Children's Books.

Moore, J. (2009). *Freckleface Strawberry and the dodgeball bully.* New York: Bloomsbury.

*Moore, M-A. (2006). *The wheels on the school bus.* New York: HarperCollins.

Palatini, M. (2002). *Earthquack.* New York: Simon & Schuster.

Prigger, M. S. (2002). *Aunt Minnie and the twister.* New York: Clarion Books.

Roberts, S. (2003). *We all go traveling by.* Cambridge, MA: Barefoot Books.

Roth, C. (2002). *The little school bus.* New York: North-South Books.

Shannon, D. (2002). *Duck on a bike.* New York: The Blue Sky Press.

Singer, M. (2009). *I'm your bus.* New York: Scholastic Press.

Tafuri, N. (2009). *The big storm.* New York: Simon and Schuster.

Tekavec, H. (2002). *Storm is coming!* New York: Dial.

Ward, M. (2005). *Mike and the bike.* Salt Lake City, UT: Cookie Jar Publishing.

*Multicultural

CHAPTER 2

Maintaining a Healthy Classroom

☐ General Objective

To be able to set up and maintain a healthy classroom that promotes good child health and nutrition and is free from factors contributing to illness

☑ Specific Objectives

_____ Encourages children to follow common health and nutrition practices

_____ Promotes and uses materials to ensure children's health and cleanliness

_____ Recognizes unusual behavior or symptoms of children who may be ill and provides for them

HEALTH practices, like those of safety, are best taught to young children through behavior modeling on the part of classroom adults, as well as through lighthearted games, stories, and activities involving the children. Nutrition facts, for example, become meaningful for young children, not by memorizing the basic food groups, but through fun classroom experiences with real food. Children learn to wash their hands before meals, not because they know it kills germs, but because they see the teacher doing it.

ENCOURAGES CHILDREN TO FOLLOW COMMON HEALTH AND NUTRITION PRACTICES

Physical Fitness

In the eyes of many adults, young children are always on the go. Why should the preschool provide more exercising activities than children already engage in naturally, you may wonder. Children's energy is deceiving. It may be evident to everyone, but the opportunities to express it are vanishing in most children's everyday life. No longer can youngsters run and play freely when streets are unsafe. Young children who formerly walked with their parents to school in the morning more often ride or are bused nowadays. And instead of vigorous sidewalk games, most children spend more time watching television after school. It has become a sedentary society for children as well as adults.

Preschool programs are thus called on to help fill this important need—that is, the need to help children develop healthy bodies through exercise. Every preschool must provide large-motor equipment for both the classroom and the outside playground, and this equipment must be made available daily. You should also plan time daily for strenuous running and movement in a gymnasium or outdoor playground. If neither is available, instead take the children for a follow-the-leader run around the building.

Physical Fitness Guidelines

Health-related physical fitness for young children incorporates "cardiovascular endurance, muscular strength, muscular endurance, flexibility, and body composition" (Pica, 2006, p. 13). Specific guidelines have been developed. One states that young children should not be sedentary for more than 60 minutes at a time except when sleeping, and that preschoolers should accumulate at least 30 to 60 minutes of daily structured physical activity (pp. 15–16). The American Heart Association recommends "10-to-15 minute 'bouts' of at least moderate-intensity physical activity, adding up to 30 [or 60] minutes, on most or all days of the week" (p. 15).

Pica also recommends that "playing tag, marching, riding a tricycle, dancing to moderate-to-fast-paced music, and jumping rope are other forms of moderate-to-vigorous-intensity exercise for children" (p. 13). The best strength training uses children's own weight in physical activities they enjoy, such as jumping, playing tug-of-war, and pumping their legs to go higher on a swing (p. 14). It is important that these activities be scheduled daily both inside and outside the classroom.

Physical Fitness Activities

For programs that do not have an indoor or outdoor space large enough for running, have children run in place to a chant. Start out slowly and increase the speed with every verse.

Step, step, step,
Make your feet trep, trep
Make your legs hep, hep,
As you keep in step.

Trot, trot, trot
Make your toes dot, dot,
Make your heels hot, hot,
As you trot, trot, trot.

Faster, faster, faster,
Make your feet go faster, faster,
Make your legs go even faster,
STOP!

Children enjoy such body action chants and want them repeated over and over. But you need to control the action and take a "breather" from time to time. As noted by Werner, Timms, and Almond (1996), "Young children have small bodies and lack muscular endurance. They tire easily and quickly, yet they also recover quickly. Activities should be designed with this in mind. Exercise should be in short bouts with time-outs for rest and recovery. Then, it's off again for more activity" (p. 50).

If you want to keep children interested in such daily movement exercises, ask them to help make up some of their own running chants. They love to be included in planning activities, and they love variety in their activities even more. "Everybody get ready to run in place like Alex's gerbil! Can you do it holding hands? Let's see how fast you can go."

Books as Lead-Ins to Classroom Physical Activities

Children simply love some of the humorous new books featuring animals engaged in wild movements. First read the book, then have a small group at a time act out the movements as you reread it.

Inclusion

Help children who cannot stand and run to sit and make movements with their feet or arms, to play catch with a beanbag, or provide some other activity that encourages them to move. For example, have children who use wheelchairs touch their toes, knees, shoulders, and heads to a different chant while seated. Everyone can enjoy this kind of body action chanting if they are all seated. Make up your own chants with the children's help, and you may be surprised at the creative rhyming words they invent.

In *Stretch* (Cronin, 2009) a cartoon dog stretches high for snacks in trees, stretches wide for a ride on the breeze. Up to the ceiling, down to the floor, with a whisper, then a roar. He takes in breath to stretch his lungs, then stretches with a partner. Have your children make up their own zany movements (and then fall over laughing!).

Children love to strrretch.

Read a book about a child who is physically challenged when this is appropriate. *Susan Laughs* (Willis, 1999) is a simple story with an illustration of a lively little red-haired girl laughing, singing, flying, swinging; or dancing, riding, swimming, and hiding just like any of your children. Are they surprised to see Susan on the last page sitting in a wheelchair?

Other books as lead-ins to physical activities:

Bounce (Cronin, 2007)

Wiggle (Cronin, 2005)

Move! (Jenkins, 2006)

Resting

Healthy young children seem to be perpetual motion machines, never stopping to take a breath. Yet they do need to practice a balance of active and quiet activities. The classroom staff should make sure a rest time is also part of the daily program.

This does not mean the teacher should make the children put their heads down on the table for 15 minutes every morning at 10 o'clock whether or not they need a rest. Rest time should come as a natural follow-up to exertion, rather than as a formal period at a certain time of day. If there has been no strenuous activity during the morning, a group rest time is unnecessary. If you schedule one anyway, you will probably spend most of the time trying to keep the children quiet.

When children are truly tired, they welcome a nap. In fact, such a rest is necessary for healthy bodies. As Desjean-Perrotta (2008) notes: "If children are expected to remain awake when they really need to nap, everything from their motor skills and coordination to critical thinking and creativity suffers" (p. 3).

Some programs have a quiet period just before lunch, when the children put mats on the floor and pursue quiet activities by themselves. Playing soft music is conducive to calming children down and encouraging quiet activities. Solitary activity is a refreshing change of pace if children have been with a large and active group all morning or have just come in from the playground.

Inclusion

Children with physical disabilities or health impairments may tire more quickly than others. You and your staff should recognize the situation, provide a quiet place for such children, and make sure they stop to rest when they need it.

If yours is an all-day program, provide a formal nap period in the afternoon. Use cots or mats wherever you have spare space. If you are using the regular classroom space, section off an area for children who no longer take afternoon naps. Dim the lights in the room, but after the nappers have fallen asleep, you can whisper to the nonsleepers that they may go to this special area and play quietly. Individual mats marked with the children's names help make this a quiet time for nonsleepers as well.

Books as Lead-Ins to Resting/Napping

Books featuring dinosaurs are at the top of the list for many children. They see these ancient creatures not as monsters but as gentle giants they can love and control.

How Do Dinosaurs Say Good Night? (Yolen, 2000) treats its 10 dinosaurs first as naughty children who don't want to go to bed, and then as loving (but huge) and obedient children who give hugs and kisses. Read it to a small group at a time so they can see the wonderful illustrations, and then have them lie down for their naps as you read it to the next group.

Another fine napping lead-in book:

I Am Not Sleepy and I Will Not Go to Bed (Child, 2001)

Nutrition

Most children love to eat. This makes your role in helping to shape their eating habits an enjoyable one. Preschool programs are usually responsible for providing lunch and snacks, although some also provide breakfast for early arrivals. You will want to include a wide variety of foods. No one food provides all the nutrients necessary for healthy bodies. Moreover, the earlier children learn to like a new food, the longer such learning will stay with them.

Nutrition for young children is somewhat different from nutrition for older children and adults, because preschool children have not yet completed their principal physical growth. For instance, low-fat diets are not suitable for young children. As Appleton, McCrea, and Patterson (2001) note, "The guidelines on fat for healthy adults are not appropriate for infants and young children. Because of high nutrient requirements during childhood, the energy and nutrient content of children's diets must be higher than for adults. Fat is an essential part of the diet and provides a concentrated form of energy for growth and development" (p. 117).

Eating itself for young children is also different from adults' eating because their stomachs are smaller. They need to eat smaller meals more often to maintain energy for their active lives. Thus portions at mealtimes should be smaller with seconds available for those still hungry. Nutritious snacks should be served at midmorning and midafternoon.

Figure 2.1   Food Groups

Grains: bread, crackers, muffins, cereal, rice, pasta, tortillas, dumplings

Vegetables: beans, beets, broccoli, carrots, celery, corn, onions, peas, potatoes, spinach, sprouts, squash, tomatoes, yams

Fruits: apples, apricots, cantaloupes, cherries, grapes, grapefruit, oranges, papayas, peaches, pears, plums, pineapples, prunes, strawberries

Dairy: milk, cheese, butter, yogurt, cottage cheese, ice cream, custard

Meats and alternatives: beef, lamb, pork, venison, chicken, fish, eggs, dry beans, nuts

Fats and sweets: dairy fats, eggs, oils, meats, fruit desserts, dates, cookies

If yours is an all-day program, the children should be getting half of their daily food requirements from the foods you serve in lunch and snacks. The other half should come from the foods they eat at home. Foods can be chosen from these examples or others from the six food groups listed in Figure 2.1.

Nutrients

Nutrients are chemicals present in foods that are necessary for the proper functioning of the body. They include the energy nutrients of fats, proteins, and carbohydrates (sugar and starch), and the helper nutrients of vitamins, minerals, and water. Young children need to eat and drink a balance of food containing these nutrients every day. For example, carbohydrates are the first source of energy the body uses. They are found in milk, grains, cereals, and pasta, as well as in fruits, vegetables, and beans. Carbohydrates provide the energy necessary for using the fats and proteins to run the body, work the muscles, and help the body grow (Robertson, 2003, p. 172).

Fats are the body's second source of energy. Fatty acids are critical for promoting brain development and the proper growth of children. Fats are found in red meats, fish, poultry, eggs, and milk products, as well as in corn, soybean, safflower, canola, and coconut oil. Protein is the third source of energy and the major building block of the body. It is found in milk, meats, fish, eggs, grains, and legumes. The helper nutrients of vitamins, minerals, and water assist the energy nutrients to perform their proper functions. Figure 2.2 shows how vitamins, minerals, and water help young children stay healthy.

Analyzing Food Choices

How nutritious is the food you are serving your children? To find out, write down each food and drink you serve for one day under one of the six food groups (Figure 2.1).

Figure 2.2   Nutrient
Categories

Vitamin A: good vision, healthy skin and bones (in yellow and orange vegetables and fruit, green leafy vegetables, fish, milk, eggs, liver)

Vitamin C: heals wounds, healthy blood vessels, prevents infections (in citrus fruits and juices, cabbage, broccoli, turnip greens)

Vitamin D: helps calcium make strong bones and teeth (in sunshine, fish, liver, eggs and butter; added to milk)

Calcium: strong bones and teeth (in milk and dairy products, dark green leafy vegetables)

Iron: forms red blood cells that carry oxygen (in liver, green leafy vegetables, whole grains, meats, fish, poultry, dried beans, peas, dried fruits)

Sodium: balances fluids in body (in salt, celery, milk, eggs, meats, poultry, fish, and canned foods)

Potassium: metabolizes protein and carbohydrates; keeps water balance; maintains heartbeat (in vegetables, fruit juice, bananas, tomatoes, meats, and cereals)

Water: protects organs, regulates body temperature; carries nutrients, and oxygen; helps eliminate wastes (in natural state and in most foods, especially fruits and fruit juices)

Were all six categories included in your daily menu? Was any group missing? Was any more prominent than the others? Do the same for your food menus for an entire week. Tally the number of times each food was served (Figure 2.3). Was this balance better than the daily one?

Figure 2.3   Analyzing
Food Choices

1. List each food and drink for 1 day under a food group
    • Look for a daily balance
2. List each food and drink for 1 week under a food group
    • Tally number of times each food has been served
    • Look for a weekly balance
3. List each food and drink for 1 week under one or more nutrient categories
    • Look for a weekly nutrient balance

Finally, write down the nutrient categories (Figure 2.2), and list each of the foods served under one or more of the categories. Be sure to include foods served at birthdays or special occasions. Were any of the categories lacking? What about water? If children don't like the taste of chlorinated water, put a filter on your water tap or use bottled water. Pure water is more healthful for young children than sugar-loaded fruit-flavored drinks. How balanced have your choices been? What changes should you make?

A Head Start Program's menu for one week is shown in Figure 2.4. Apply the same kind of food analysis to the foods served in this program. What kind of balance do you find? How does it compare with the foods you serve?

	BREAKFAST	LUNCH	SNACK
Monday	Crispy Rice Cereal Bananas Milk	Macaroni with Ham Tomato Slices Fruit Cocktail Rolls Milk	Banana Bread Squares Milk

Tuesday	Pat's Egg and Biscuit
	  Casserole
	Orange Juice
	Milk
		Tater Tot and Hamburger
		  Casserole
		Peas
		Sliced Apples
		Rolls
		Milk
			Frozen Yogurt
			
			Grapes
			Water

Wednesday	Oatmeal with Brown Sugar Raisins Grape Juice Milk	Homemade Chicken and Vegetable Pot Pie Apricots Milk	Applesauce Hermits Milk
Thursday	Waffles Fresh/Frozen Blueberries Apple Juice Milk	Homemade Burrito or Burrito Casserole (with lettuce and tomatoes) Fruit and Gelatin Salad Tortilla Chips with Salsa Milk	Animal Crackers Milk

Friday	Bagels with Cream Cheese
	Orange Wedges
	Milk
		Swedish Meatballs on
		  Egg Noodles
		Steamed Broccoli
		Peaches
		Milk
			Ants on a Log
			  (Peanut Butter,
			  Raisins, Celery)
			Water

Figure 2.4   Head Start Weekly Menu

Source: From Columbia, Missouri Head Start Program.

Food in the Classroom

Children learn very quickly what foods we consider important, not by what we say, but by observing the kinds of food we serve in the classroom. Do you serve cookies and milk for a snack? Do you serve cake, cupcakes, or candy for birthdays? Sugar found in such foods has been linked to the formation of dental cavities and to obesity. If you want children to become acquainted instead with delicious fruits and interesting vegetables, plan some exciting food activities with these foods as well. Talk to parents about sending in something besides cake or cupcakes for birthdays or about coming in to help the children prepare their own treats.

How about a "Banana Surprise" or a "Smoothie" or a "Hairy Harry" for a birthday celebration? The children can have the fun of making their own party refreshments as well as eating them. "Banana Surprise" uses bananas, graham cracker crumbs, and peanut butter and gives children practice with the small-motor skills of peeling the banana, spreading it with peanut butter, and rolling it in cracker crumbs. If you substitute raisins for the cracker crumbs, you will be making "Ants on a Log."

For children who come without breakfast, be sure to provide it.

"Smoothies" blend together orange and lemon juice, mashed bananas, honey, and milk. Children also enjoy making "Hairy Harrys" out of apple slices spread with peanut butter and topped with alfalfa sprouts and raisins. To make their own peanut butter, have them grind up peanuts. Be sure, of course, that none of the children has a peanut allergy.

In addition to parties, let the children also make their own daily snacks, such as stuffed celery. In addition to scrubbing and cutting the celery, they can make fillings from cream cheese or peanut butter. Other nutritious snacks include low-fat yogurt or cottage cheese that can be spread on crackers or used as a dip for carrots, celery, broccoli, or strawberries (American Cancer Society, 2000). The Cancer Society's *Kids' First Cookbook* with its luscious color photos will keep your children busy creating everything from French Toast Fingers to No-Bake Boulders.

Do the children in your care eat breakfast? It is important for young children to start the day with a nutritious meal. If they skip breakfast, they may become cranky and inattentive. Research shows that children who eat breakfast are more alert and may even learn more during late morning hours. Consider providing a breakfast for your children. Fruit or juice, milk, and cereal can be varied with nontraditional breakfast foods such as melted cheese on toast or a peanut butter sandwich on whole-grain bread. Don't forget to serve as a model by eating breakfast with the children. If you don't serve breakfast, be sure to check for children who come without breakfast, so you can provide it.

Once children have had some experiences with healthy foods, teachers can introduce other fun nutrition activities. Food puppets can visit the class to talk about their favorite foods. How about a "junk food puppet" who thinks everyone should eat nothing but candy bars, potato chips, and soda? How will your children respond?

Snacks

Some programs make snacking an individual affair offered at a learning center during activity periods. They provide individual portions of a variety of foods for children to eat when they are hungry. The snacks represent an equal number from each of four food groups: fruits, vegetables, grains, and dairy. As Bernath and Masi (2006, p. 22) describe, "The snack center consists of a table and chairs set up for four to six children. Food is easily accessible, presented either pre-portioned in cups or in small store-bought packaging. Children learn the healthy snacking routine of serving themselves and eating one portion of each food item that appeals to them. They consider whether they need another helping before cleaning up and moving on to another choice of activities."

Cultural Food

Most early childhood programs serve children of many cultures these days. The languages spoken, books read, and activities pursued reflect these cultures. Food should also include a variety of cultural meals, snacks, and cooking activities. Potluck suppers for families can be a helpful resource for new cultural food ideas. Children's books are another resource. Children enjoy hearing them read as lead-ins to food activities they will be pursuing.

Books as Lead-Ins to Cultural Food Activities

For example, tortilla chips with salsa along with homemade burritos are served for lunch on Thursday from the menu in Figure 2.4. If you have Hispanic children, can they tell you about tortillas being served at home? You can also read *The Runaway Tortilla* (Kimmel, 2000) about Tia Lupe who makes the best enchiladas, burritos, tacos, and fajitas in all of Texas in her little restaurant. Her cowboy customers warn her if she makes tortillas any lighter, some day one will up and run away. And that's what happens—just like with the gingerbread boy.

Inviting family members to the class to help children and teachers make their favorite foods is yet another way to introduce cultural foods. Can anyone's grandma make pumpkin tarts?

> *The Empanadas That Abuela Made* (Bertrand, 2003) is a bilingual cumulative story about three children, their grandfather, their family, their cousins, and their dog who come running together in a hilarious rolling pin adventure to make pumpkin tarts. Choose a child to represent each character and have them say their simple line every time their turn comes up. Have Spanish speakers say the lines, too.

Other books as lead-ins to cultural food activities:

Bee-bim Bop! (Park, 2005), Korean [recipe]

Dim Sum for Everyone! (Lin, 2001), Chinese

Mud Tacos! (Lopez, 2009), Hispanic

Obesity

Obesity in early childhood is becoming an increasingly alarming problem. Huetting and colleagues (2004) state in no uncertain terms: "[T]he epidemic of childhood obesity in the United States is *the* critical health issue of this decade. The National Health and Nutrition Examination Survey shows the prevalence of being overweight or obese is 20.6% in children ages two to five, increasing the chances that these children will suffer health risks commonly seen in obese adults: high blood pressure, insulin resistance, glucose intolerance, and type two diabetes, among others. Perhaps the most significant impact of obesity on the children may be the damage to their self-esteem because of teasing about their body size" (pp. 50–51).

Childhood obesity is caused by an energy imbalance. If more energy (from food) is taken in than is put out, the excess is stored as fat. As noted by Aronson (2002), "Obesity is a complex problem with multiple causes. Some combination of overeating, poor food choices, inactivity, social or emotional factors, and genetics is usually responsible. Helping children learn healthy eating and exercising habits is the key to preventing obesity" (p. 57).

Giving children portions that are too large and requiring them to clean their plates may also be a contributing factor. Not all children want or need the same amount of food. Having children serve themselves may help, but in case they take too much, do not force them to eat all of it. Fruit juices from natural fruits, fruit jellies without sugar, non-sugar-coated cereals, and low-fat or skim milk should be served. You can also promote the drinking of water rather than sodas. Then keep the children on their feet afterward, cleaning off the tables, putting away the food containers, and moving around the classroom in preparation for the next activity.

Each of the learning centers in the classroom needs to build a "movement segment" into its activities. Standing rather than sitting at the cutting table is one. Marching around the art table three times before sitting down to work is another simple exercise. As Winter (2009) suggests, "A move-to-learn curriculum approach can

Figure 2.5   Obesity
Prevention

- Respect children's food choices
- Have children serve themselves small portions
- Do not force children to clean their plates
- Serve natural unsweetened fruits, juices, and jams/preserves
- Promote drinking water, not sodas
- Lead children in vigorous exercises
- Substitue nutrient-rich homemade food treats for birthday cakes and cookies
- Allow time in the schedule for outdoor play

significantly increase physical activity of children" (p. 287). She suggests that adding music and movement into all academic activities can add extra minutes of physical action to a child's play. Figure 2.5 summarizes these suggestions.

Picky Eaters

Because of the rise of obesity, it is important to establish healthful eating habits early. The diets of many preschool children are often high in fat, sodium, and sugar, causing them to gain too much weight. Yet to get them to change and try new foods is often difficult. As Bellows and Anderson (2006) tell us, "Preschool children go through a normal developmental phase called *neophobia*, or fear of new things—in this case, new foods. Many adults refer to this stage as 'picky eating'" (p. 37). Preschool programs can help by consistently offering a variety of foods. When picky eaters see other children eating the new foods, the majority of them will eventually accept them. This program found that 8 to 12 experiences are necessary for a child to try and then accept a new food.

Books as Lead-Ins to Helping Picky Eaters

Children love to hear Child's wacky adventures of big brother Charlie and little sister Lola, who wants to have her own way, no matter what.

In *I Will Never Not Ever Eat a Tomato* (Child, 2000), Charlie finds a clever way to entice his fussy-eating little sister Lola to eat all the vegetables and fruits she hates by calling carrots orange twiglets from Jupiter, mashed potatoes cloud fluff from Mount Fuji, and other exotic names. Imagine his surprise when she asks him to pass the dish of moonsquirters (some people call them tomatoes)! Have your children rename their food hates too. You can write down the names.

And what child can resist Yolen's naughty dinosaurs, this time in *How Do Dinosaurs Eat Their Food?* (2005). Do they burp, belch, make noises quite rude, or spit out broccoli partially chewed? No, they suddenly shape up and try at least one bite of every new thing. After reading this book, hang dinosaur pictures on yarn necklaces around the necks of all your eaters and see how they handle their food. Make eating fun!

PROMOTES AND USES MATERIALS TO ENSURE CHILDREN'S HEALTH AND CLEANLINESS

Keeping the Classroom Clean

The classroom must be clean and sanitary. Even when a janitorial staff does the cleaning, it is your responsibility to make sure they have done it properly and that it remains in good condition throughout the day. Floors, tabletops, and food serving areas should be kept clean. Food should be stored properly and garbage disposed of promptly. Keeping your classroom clean and sanitized can prevent the spread of infectious diseases. Children can be a part of this cleanliness effort, too. Help them remember to dispose of paper towels, napkins, and tissues they use.

To disinfect toys and surfaces the children have touched, wash or wipe them with a solution of $1/4$ cup bleach to 1 gallon water, prepared fresh each day. Whenever children have been exposed to a communicable disease, such as chicken pox, be sure to notify parents. Use the Classroom Cleanliness Checklist each day to make sure your center is clean and sanitary (see Figure 2.6).

Light, heat, and ventilation should be kept at healthy levels. Children and their parents need to be informed about the type of clothing children should wear at the center. If an extra sweater is necessary, be ready to provide it if the family does not. Keep a supply of clean extra clothing items on hand in case children have spills or accidents or lose clothing items such as mittens. Be sure to launder the clothing after use.

Your outside playground should also be kept clean and free of debris. If you have a sandbox, keep it covered so that animals cannot get in it. If you have tire swings, have holes punched in them so that water does not collect and provide a breeding place for germ-carrying mosquitoes.

Your classroom also needs a basic supply of tissues, paper towels, paper cups, and liquid soap. If you use sheets or blankets for napping, these must be individually labeled and washed periodically. To prevent the spread of germs, be sure children use only their own labeled sheets and blankets for naps. Also make sure eating utensils are washed appropriately at temperatures hot enough to kill bacteria, and then stored properly.

Personal Hygiene

Hand washing can do more to prevent the spread of infectious diseases than almost any other health practice. Children must learn to wash their hands upon arrival, before meals, after using the bathroom, and after handling pets. Do you serve as their

Figure 2.6   Classroom Cleanliness Checklist

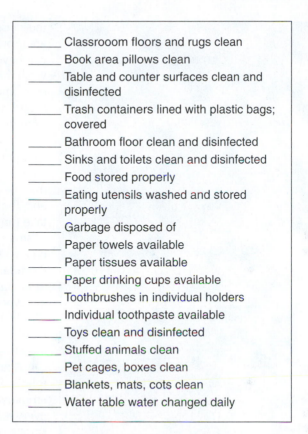

_____ Classrooom floors and rugs clean

_____ Book area pillows clean

_____ Table and counter surfaces clean and disinfected

_____ Trash containers lined with plastic bags; covered

_____ Bathroom floor clean and disinfected

_____ Sinks and toilets clean and disinfected

_____ Food stored properly

_____ Eating utensils washed and stored properly

_____ Garbage disposed of

_____ Paper towels available

_____ Paper tissues available

_____ Paper drinking cups available

_____ Toothbrushes in individual holders

_____ Individual toothpaste available

_____ Toys clean and disinfected

_____ Stuffed animals clean

_____ Pet cages, boxes clean

_____ Blankets, mats, cots clean

_____ Water table water changed daily

model? They will do it because you ask them to and because it is an interesting sort of task, but you must model the same behavior. They should see you washing your hands too. Demonstrate with liquid soap how a person should wash the front and back of the hands, between the fingers, and under the fingernails. Then rinse, dry your hands with a paper towel, wipe off the faucet, and dispose of the towel in the trash container.

Be sure you wash your own hands when you arrive, before preparing food, before eating, after helping a child use the toilet, and especially after wiping a child's nose. All of the classroom staff should do the same to prevent the spread of germs.

Discuss with the children how germs cause diseases, and then have the youngsters practice their own hand-washing skills to get rid of pretend germs that you will put on their hands. Sprinkle cinnamon on their hands and let each one try to wash it off. Did they get rid of every "germ"?

It is essential to have a sink in the classroom as well as in the bathroom. If you do not, set up a hand-washing stand with plastic basins for washing and rinsing, and devise a method for disposing of the water after use.

You can promote the practice of cleanliness through washing in other ways. For example, have the children bathe the dolls in the dramatic play area once a week. If

Hand washing prevents the spread of infectious diseases.

the classroom does not have a toy sink in the area, bring in a plastic tub. Both boys and girls can have an enjoyable time with water. Let them wash the dolls' clothes as well. This activity presents another good opportunity to talk about cleanliness and how it keeps us healthy and free from disease.

Children especially love to play with water, so approach these activities with a sense of pleasure rather than drudgery. Hand washing may be a daily routine, but it can be fun if you and the children make it so. Have each child take turns bathing one of the plastic dinosaurs in a small basin, for instance. (Don't forget to change the water every time.) Then read them the hilarious book *How to Get a Gorilla out of Your Bathtub* (Hall, 2006), a story about a little girl who can't take a bath because there's a gorilla in her bathtub. Ask the children what they would do. Put out a toy gorilla in the water table after this one.

Again, you are the model for the children to follow. Be sure your own health practices are exemplary. If you want children to eat some of every food on their plates, set the example. If you smoke, do it in a private place away from the children. If you want children to stop biting their fingernails, be sure you don't bite yours.

Be sure that children have separate combs and hair brushes. Do not use the same comb or brush for more than one child. If head lice are detected, all parents should be notified, and parents of that child should be informed of procedures. The child may remain until the end of the day and return when the problem is cleared up.

Precautions also need to be taken whenever anyone is exposed to blood or body fluids containing blood discharged from injuries. Use disposable gloves when cleaning up bloody areas, and then use an antiseptic on the area.

Teeth

Brushing teeth after meals is an important habit for your children to learn. Each child needs his or her own individual brush, marked with a name or symbol that the child can recognize. Also, put the child's mark on the place where children store their brushes. You might use an inverted egg carton, or a parent could make a wooden toothbrush holder.

Using only one tube of toothpaste increases the possibility of passing germs from one child to the next. Have small marked individual tubes for each child. Some centers instead turn small paper cups upside down and place a blob of toothpaste on each cup bottom. The child then swipes the paste off the bottom of the cup and onto his or her toothbrush. After brushing, the child can rinse with the cup and then throw it away. However you prefer to do it, make sure children brush hygienically after each meal.

Books as Lead-Ins to Toothbrushing

Using books as lead-ins to activities accomplishes several learning objectives for young children. It brings children together with good books. It helps children focus on the topic at hand. Every time they hear the story they are reminded of what the activity taught them.

If you do not have one of the books described in this text, make up your own story. Have the children help you make it up. In the following case, a humorous story about a crocodile who has so many teeth to brush, she never gets out to play with her friends, you can make up your own story without the book. Have one hand be the crocodile's jaw that opens and closes and the other hand, the imaginary toothbrush. Try it.

Other books as lead-ins to tooth activities:

My Wobbly Tooth Must Not Ever Never Fall Out (Child, 2006)

Tabitha's Terrifically Tough Tooth (Middleton, 2001)

Sun Protection

Although we do not ordinarily think of skin cancer as a threat to young children, Fulmore and colleagues (2009) tell us: "Exposure accumulates over a lifetime. Consequently, primary prevention must begin during early childhood to reduce excessive exposure to UV radiation" (p. 293).

Skin damage is likely to occur with as little as 30 minutes of unprotected sun exposure when the UV (ultraviolet) index reading is between 6.0 and 7.0. Levels of UV radiation are highest near noon. Teachers can limit the amount of sun exposure by limiting playground time, by having children wear protective clothing, and by applying sunscreen lotion (SPF 15) to children prior to their going outside (p. 294).

Teachers can help protect children's skin with sunscreen lotion.

In *Clarabella's Teeth* (Vrombaut, 2003), all of Clarabella the crocodile's friends quickly brush their teeth when they get up. And
Clarabella? She brushes, and brushes, and brushes. When she
finally finishes brushing, it is time to get ready for bed! The friends
finally give Clarabella a gift: a toothbrush the size of a piano keyboard! Then they can all play together. Have your children repeat
the lines "she brushes." Bring in a toy crocodile or alligator and an
appropriate-size toothbrush. (Maybe a hairbrush?).

RECOGNIZES UNUSUAL BEHAVIOR OR SYMPTOMS OF CHILDREN WHO MAY BE ILL AND PROVIDES FOR THEM

Sickness

Sick days for the children in your program are inevitable, and you need to be prepared. Can you recognize when children are ill? Does your center have the space
and staff to provide for them? If not, have you arranged with parents for alternate
caregivers?

Policies about caring for sick children must be discussed with the staff and
communicated to the parents so that everyone is familiar with the procedures. First,
you must make sure that all of the children are immunized against diphtheria-
tetanus-whooping cough, measles-mumps-rubella, polio, hepatitis, and influenza
type B.

You must also check on children when they arrive each day. Any of the symptoms in Figure 2.7 may indicate the child is ill and needs attention (see Figure 2.7).

NAEYC Criteria for Health Standard
Describe how your teachers meet the following standard:
5.A.05 Staff and teachers provide information to families verbally
and in writing about any unusual level or type of communicable
disease to which their child was exposed.

How sick is too sick? Child caregivers need to know general information about
the seriousness of children's illnesses. For instance, children with a runny nose, slight
cough, slight headache, or slight stomachache may remain in the classroom if this is
your policy. But children with a fever, vomiting, an earache, a congested cough, a severe headache, or a sore throat should be sent home or to the alternate caregiver.

Unusual paleness	Unusual tiredness	Fever, chills
Skin rash	Abdominal pain	Sore throat
Red, watery eyes	Nausea, vomiting	Earache
Swollen neck glands	Diarrhea	Bruise marks
Stomachache	Headache	Burns

Figure 2.7 Symptoms of Illness

Until the child leaves, the child needs to be isolated from the others, with someone on hand to offer help and comfort. These arrangements should be set up ahead of time by the program and the family.

You should also be familiar with children's health needs. Are any of the children on medication? Do any of them have asthma or allergies? What about physical limitations? Some children become fatigued more easily than others do. Whether or not you are responsible for keeping the children's health records, familiarize yourself with them, talk with parents, and be prepared to respond to individual needs.

Allergies

Allergies are sensitivities to particular substances that most people find harmless. They are the most common health impairment of young children and account for a third of all chronic health conditions of preschool children. Plant pollen, dust, and animal dander may give allergic children the coldlike symptoms of red and puffy eyes, dark circles under eyes, frequent runny nose, sneezing (four or five times in a row), a dry hacking cough, mouth breathing, frequent nosebleeds, skin irritations, or rashes. If children exhibit such symptoms, especially related to weather or the allergy season, contact the families to learn whether the children have known allergies or should be tested for them (Deiner, 1993, p. 225).

You may need to have the classroom scrubbed and vacuumed frequently, and not merely dusted. Air conditioner and heating system filters should be cleaned or replaced often. The classroom animal pets may need to be exchanged for pets without fur or feathers.

Foods are another source of potential allergies. The most common foods to cause allergies for children are milk, eggs, peanuts, soybeans, tree nuts (pecans, walnuts), wheat, fish, and shellfish. Other foods some children are allergic to include oranges, chocolate, legumes, rice, and meats. Allergic reactions can include itching, swelling of lips, runny nose, difficulty breathing, nausea, vomiting, abdominal cramping, and diarrhea (Holland, 2004, p. 43). If a child exhibits an allergic reaction after eating, contact the parents or the health specialist.

Insect bites pose serious problems for certain allergic children and can even be fatal. Swelling or hotness around the face and neck followed by difficulty in breathing must be responded to immediately. Field trips to sites where wild plants grow and bees or mosquitoes live can cause problems for allergic children. Be sure to find out what reaction such a child is likely to have, what you should do, and what the side effects of any medication may be (Deiner, 1993). Children sometimes pick up fuzzy caterpillars like the woolly bear. These caterpillars frequently cause skin reactions such as itching or rashes. Wash the affected areas thoroughly.

Asthma

Asthma affects about 9 percent of the population and often develops in early child-hood (Lim et al., 2009, p. 307), with boys having the condition twice as often as girls. Asthma is caused by an obstruction of the small bronchial tubes and results in short-ness of breath, coughing, wheezing, and choking. Allergies are the most common cause, although excitement or exertion can also trigger an attack. Asthma attacks come more frequently in the early morning and may occur without warning, thus frightening the child and others around him or her.

The factors (triggers) that cause asthma vary greatly from child to child. Exercise is a common asthma trigger. Children with asthma often experience coughing, wheezing, and chest tightness when they engage in physical activity. Emotions such as fear are another trigger (Lim et al., 2009, p. 310). Dramatic play can help children who have allergies or asthma work out their fears, just as it does for children who are afraid of doctors and shots. Some classrooms set up their dramatic play areas as an emergency room with pretend examining tables, X-ray machines, and a breathing ap-paratus. Children wear personalized face masks "so we don't catch germs from each other," says one pretend player (Goldberg, 1994).

Teachers need to know ahead of time how to help the child with asthma to use the prescribed medication, emergency inhaler, or nebulizer, and how the child should sit (not lie down) during an attack (Deiner, 1993). An emergency treatment plan is also necessary.

Chicken Pox

Chicken pox is a highly contagious viral infection that most children contracted be-fore a vaccine became available in the mid-1990s. Be sure to check with parents and your health specialist to make sure all of your children are immunized. Some may not be. Because chicken pox is contagious for 2 days before the rash appears, it is possible for unvaccinated children to become infected if they come into contact with a child who has the virus but no sign of the rash or blisters.

Although chicken pox is not serious for most children, it can cause extreme itch-iness from the pox sores, which break open easily and form a crust on top. Children should be kept home from school until the rash has completely scabbed over and no new pox has appeared in 24 hours. Try to keep children from scratching by having their fingernails cut short or even putting socks on their hands as Goldie Locks does in the story that follows. Doctors may also prescribe an antihistamine ointment to re-lieve itching (Woolf, Kenna, & Shane, 2001, p. 499).

Book as Lead-In to Chicken Pox Theme

> In *Goldie Locks Has Chicken Pox* (Dealey, 2002), Goldie Locks and her brother not only have chicken pox but also visit all the familiar nursery rhyme characters (Three Bears, Henny Penny, Jack-Be-Nimble, Little Bo Peep, Little Red Riding Hood) to see if they have them too. The little brother makes fun of the entire situation until the last page, when his face shows all the signs in red polka-dot designs. Your children can reenact this story taking the parts of all the characters.

Colds/Flu

These common upper respiratory viral infections in young children are bound to be present in the classroom on and off throughout the year. You may see more colds in winter when children are indoors and germs can circulate more easily. With colds children may suffer from a congested or runny nose, sneezing, coughing, a sore throat, and red, watery eyes. With the flu, children may have the same but more severe symptoms. In addition, flu causes aching muscles, fever and chills, headaches, diarrhea or vomiting, and fatigue or weakness.

Cold and flu germs are spread from person to person through sneezing, coughing, touching an infected person's hands, or from contaminated objects such as toys, books, phones, drinking cups, and tabletops (Woolf et al., 2001, p. 507). To cut down on the spread of germs, have children cover their mouth and nose when coughing and sneezing, use tissues and discard them promptly, and wash their hands frequently.

Books as Lead-Ins to Using Tissues

> In *Tissue, Please!* (Kopelke, 2004), Frog and his friends do everything together, even sniffling and snuffling when they have runny noses. When Frog's mother provides him with a box of tissues, he and his friends all use one, eventually creating "The Dance of the Tissue Box Fairies." Have your own box of tissues ready after reading this one—and a waste basket for disposing of used tissues.

In *The Flea's Sneeze* (Downey, 2000), all the animals in the barn are sleeping peacefully, when suddenly a flea who lives on the mouse makes a loud sneeze, waking everyone. The mouse finally gives the flea a tissue and they all go back to sleep again—except for the hog, whose nose tickles and he has to sneeze. Every two lines ends in a rhyme that the children love to repeat. Can they also figure out where the hog's sneeze came from?

Ear Infections

Ear infections are the second most frequent illness among young children; only the common cold occurs more often. It is important for teachers and child caregivers to recognize this illness, because children with ear infections have fluid in their middle ear that may cause mild to moderate hearing loss for weeks and sometimes months. When such a hearing loss is experienced over long periods of time, children can have difficulty in learning language or paying attention (Watt, Roberts, & Zeisel, 1993, p. 65).

Teachers can help reduce the incidence of ear infections by trying to prevent the spread of colds in the classroom because colds often lead to ear infections. Help children with colds to cover their noses and mouths with an arm when they cough and sneeze, and be sure that you, they, and everyone practices frequent and careful hand washing after using tissues. Also, clean and disinfect any toys, faucets, or equipment handled by the children. If any child exhibits a hearing loss, contact the family and suggest they have the child's hearing tested. Ear infections are generally treated with antibiotics, but in persistent infections, the child's ears may also be drained with tubes.

Your classroom environment can also facilitate children's hearing if you make speaking easier to hear. Rugs on floors, curtains at windows, hangings on walls, and acoustical tiles on ceilings help absorb background noise. Have children use headsets when they are listening to music rather than adding music to the background commotion in the room. Work with children in small activity groups rather than the entire class. Sit or stand close to children when speaking and make eye contact with them so they can see your lips moving. Children with other types of hearing impairment will also benefit from an environment where speaking is easier to hear.

Special Conditions

Attention Deficit/Hyperactivity Disorder (ADHD)

ADHD is not an illness but a developmental disorder of self-control, with symptoms of inattention, hyperactivity, and impulsive behaviors affecting 6 percent of children in the United States (Reimers & Brunder, 2006, p. 7). These behaviors often begin in children between the ages of 3 and 5 years, the same ages children are in preschool. This is also the time many children are naturally more active and impulsive, making it difficult to diagnose ADHD. Boys are more likely to exhibit these behaviors than girls. If these behaviors occur to such an extreme that the child is out of control much of the time, he may be exhibiting the beginning of ADHD.

Children who are easily distracted, have difficulty listening, cannot sit still, run around excessively, talk at inappropriate times, or have trouble following directions may have the disorder. But not all children with these behaviors have ADHD. The condition needs to be diagnosed by a professional. Although it is not known what causes ADHD, research has determined what *does not cause it:*

- Sugar and chemical food additives
- Yeast

- Bad parenting
- Fluorescent lighting
- Inner ear problems (p. 10)

Teachers can help by establishing clear rules so the child understands what is or is not acceptable behavior; keeping the child near enough to maintain eye contact; using gestures to emphasize directions; helping the child focus attention when you speak to him or her; providing a quiet area for the child when he or she feels overloaded; using immediate rewards and praise for positive behavior; and communicating often with the parents about how the child is doing in school and at home (Robertson, p. 426).

Autism Spectrum Disorder (ASD)

ASD affects one-and-a-half million people in the United States with boys four times as likely as girls to have a form of this neurological disorder. There are five recognized types of autism with severe symptoms at one end and mild behaviors at the other. This medical condition needs to be diagnosed by a pediatrician or team of specialists (Willis, 2009, p. 81).

Some symptoms exhibited by children with autism include poor social interaction, no eye contact, little emotional expression, delay in communication, repeated movements (finger popping, hand flapping), and obsessive preoccupation with objects (turning lights on and off). They may respond to sensory stimuli by screaming or reacting strongly to light, sound, or motion.

Children with autism in regular early childhood classrooms are usually those with Asperger's Syndrome, in the midrange of the spectrum. Although they behave much like children with other types of autism, as they grow or age they learn how to socialize, communicate, and behave in a socially acceptable manner. They have normal or above normal intelligence and may learn new skills more quickly than their peers (Willis, 2009, p. 82).

Because 40 percent of children with autism are nonverbal, teachers can help them learn to communicate with sign language, pictures, or cue cards. Routines are important. Be sure you use the same simple words and phrases every time. One of the many commercial tools for children with communication difficulties is the Picture Exchange Communication System (PECS, Frost & Bondy, 1994). Children use representative pictures to initiate interactions. Or you can make your own picture cue cards. Be sure to make a set of cue cards for the child to take home, as well. It is especially important for you to communicate frequently with parents about how their children are doing at home and in school.

Medical Exams

Although a classroom teacher is not usually responsible for setting up medical tests and examinations for children, you can clearly support the health specialist who does. You, parents, and the specialist need to work together to plan and carry out classroom activities to acquaint children with these examinations to make them less threatening.

Before an eye test, for instance, let the children practice holding a card over one eye and responding to letters on an eye chart. Later they can give a similar "test" of their own to the dolls in the dramatic play center. Before an ear test, have the health specialist demonstrate or talk to the children about what will occur. The nurse in one Head Start program pasted together a three-dimensional model of an ear inside a shoe box. Through a hole in one end of the box, the children could shine a pen flashlight to see the inner parts of the "ear," just as the doctor does. Be honest with children about what will happen. If their fingers will be pricked to draw blood, arrange for a demonstration with a nurse.

Invite a dental hygienist to demonstrate a dental checkup. According to Texas Child Care (1994), "After offering these experiences as a foundation, set up a pretend medical office or hospital in the dramatic play center. If children have had frightening experiences, role-playing will help them work through their fears and hurts. If they've never been to the dentist or eye doctor, dramatic play will help them prepare for the first visit and feel secure" (pp. 22–26).

It is important for young children to act out their feelings about doctors, nurses, having shots, and going to the hospital. Thus medical role playing in the dramatic play area of the classroom serves a therapeutic as well as an educational role for the youngsters. Some children can pretend to be the doctor or nurse giving shots to other children or dolls, and others can pretend to be the patients who roll up their sleeves for shots. This is scary business for youngsters. Working out their fears of doctors and shots in this nonthreatening manner helps children to prepare for the real thing.

Books as Lead-Ins to Doctor and Dentist Visits

In *Harry and the Dinosaurs say "Raahh!"* (Whybrow, 2001), Harry takes his bucket of plastic dinosaurs to the dentist with him. He rides up and down in the dentist's chair as all of them open their mouths wide for their exams, then have the fun of rinsing and spitting. The dentist is afraid they will bite him, but they only bite drills, says Harry. How would your children examine the teeth of the classroom's plastic dinosaurs? Set up a dentist office in your dramatic play area and let the children make up their own dentist dramas.

Other books as lead-ins to medical exams:

Froggy Goes to the Doctor (London, 2002)

How Do Dinosaurs Get Well Soon? (Yolen, 2003)

Open Wide! (Barber, 2004)

SUMMARY

Set up and maintain a healthy classroom that promotes good health and nutrition and is free from factors contributing to illness. You will be providing daily opportunities for your children to exercise both indoors and outdoors whether or not a large space is available. The balance of active and quiet activities you set up will include rest periods as a natural follow-up to exertion, although you will accommodate individual needs for children who no longer nap during the day. Washing hands and brushing teeth will be an important part of the program, with care taken to prevent transfer of germs during toothbrushing. Nutritional needs for the children under your care will be met through snacks and meals. In addition, they will learn good food habits through their own fun experiences with nutritional foods.

You will use the Classroom Cleanliness Checklist in Figure 2.1 as a reminder of specific areas that need special attention or cleaning. Your children will be prepared to take medical tests and examinations through preliminary classroom activities set up by you or a health specialist. You will be able to recognize symptoms of illness in children and know how to deal with them. You will include children with special needs in all activities.

Ethical Dilemma

When one of the children developed chicken pox, the teacher checked to make sure all of the others had been vaccinated. She found that one boy had not had any immunizations. For him to remain in the program he would need to be vaccinated. His parents refused on religious and health grounds. Furthermore, they said they would sue if their boy was put out of the program. What should this teacher do?

LEARNING ACTIVITIES

1. Read one or more of the Suggested Readings or view the Web sites listed. Make 10 file cards with specific ideas for promoting health and nutrition in your classroom. Include the reference source on each card.

2. List all of the food you use for a week according to Figure 2.3, "Analyzing Food Choices." How balanced have your choices been? What changes should you make?

3. Use the Classroom Cleanliness Checklist in Figure 2.1 for a week, making any corrections necessary to keep the room clean and sanitary.

4. Make a card for each child in your class on which you can record information about general health, energy level, napping habits, eating habits, any special health concerns, and, when necessary, suggestions for health improvement.

5. Use ideas from this chapter to help a small group of children learn a particular health or nutrition practice.

6. Celebrate a child's birthday with one of the nutritious food ideas described in this chapter.

7. Choose one of the illnesses or disorders discussed in this chapter and learn all you can about it: how to prevent it, how to help a child in the classroom who has acquired it, and what agencies in the community can be called on for help. Use one of the Web sites to gather information.

SUGGESTED READINGS

Colker, L. J. (2005). *The cooking book: Fostering young children's learning and delight.* Washington, DC: NAEYC.

Cotugna, N., & Vickery, C. (2007). Educating early childhood teachers about nutrition. *Childhood Education, 83*(4), 194–198.

Desjean-Perrotta, B. (2008). Five essential reasons to keep naptime in the early childhood curriculum. *Dimensions of Early Childhood, 36*(3), 3–11.

Joneja, J. V. (2007). *Dealing with food allergies in babies and children.* Boulder, CO: Bull Publishing.

Kalich, K. A., Bauer, D., & McPartlin, . (2009). "Early sprouts:" Establishing healthy food choices for young children. *Young Children, 64*(4), 49–55.

Rodriguez, D. (2009). Culturally and linguistically diverse students with autism. *Childhood Education, 86*(5), 313–317.

Stregelin, D. A. (2008). Children, teachers, and families working together to prevent childhood obesity: Intervention strategies. *Dimensions of Early Childhood, 36*(1), 8–15.

Wolfberg, P. J. (2009). *Play and imagination in children with autism.* New York: Teachers College Press.

WEB SITES

Action for Healthy Kids
http://www.actionforhealthykids.org

American Academy of Allergy Asthma and Immunology
http://www.aaaai.org

American Academy of Pediatrics
http://www.aap.org

American Dental Association
http://www.ada.org

American Dietetic Association
http://www.eatright.org

Asthma and Allergy Foundation of America
http://www.aafa.org

Centers for Disease Control and Prevention
http://www.cdc.gov

Healthy Choices for Kids
http://www.healthychoices.org

KidsHealth
http://www.kidshealth.org

My Pyramid
http://www.mypyramid.gov

CHILDREN'S BOOKS

*Barber, T. (2004). *Open wide!* London, England: Chrysalis Children's Books.

*Bertrand, D. G. (2003). *The empanadas that abuela made.* Houston, TX: Pinata Books.

Child, L. (2000). *I will never not ever eat a tomato.* Cambridge, MA: Candlewick.

Child, L. (2001). *I am not sleepy and I will not go to bed.* Cambridge, MA: Candlewick.

Child, L. (2006). *My wobbly tooth must not ever never come out.* New York: Grosset & Dunlap.

Cronin, D. (2005). *Wiggle.* New York: Atheneum.

Cronin, D. (2007). *Bounce.* New York: Atheneum.

Cronin, C. (2009). *Stretch.* New York: Atheneum.

Dealey, E. (2002). *Goldie Locks has chicken pox.* New York: Atheneum.

Downey, L. (2000). *The flea's sneeze.* New York: Henry Holt.

Hall, J. (2006). *How to get a gorilla out of your bathtub.* Lakeland, FL: White Stone Books.

Jenkins, S. (2006). *Move!* Boston: Houghton Mifflin.

*Kimmel, E. A. (2000). *The runaway tortilla.* Delray Beach, FL: Winslow Press.

Kopelke, L. (2004). *Tissue, please!* New York: Simon & Schuster.

*Lin, G. (2001). *Dim sum for everyone!* New York: Dell Dragonfly Books.

* London, J. (2002). *Froggy goes to the doctor.* New York: Viking.

*Lopez, M., & Wong, M. L. (2009). *Mud tacos!* New York: Celebra Children's Books.

Middleton, C. (2001). *Tabitha's terrifically tough tooth.* New York: Phyllis Fogelman Books.

Park, L. S. (2005). *Bee-bim bop!* New York: Clarion Books.

Vrombaut, A. (2003). *Clarabella's teeth.* New York: Clarion.

Whybrow, I. (2001). *Harry and the dinosaurs say "Raahh!"* New York: Random House.

Willis, J. (1999). *Susan laughs.* New York: Holt.

*Yolen, J. (2000). *How do dinosaurs say good night?* New York: Blue Sky Press.

*Yolen, J. (2003). *How do dinosaurs get well soon?* New York: Blue Sky Press.

*Yolen, J. (2005). *How do dinosaurs eat their food?* New York: Blue Sky Press.

*Multicultural

CHAPTER 3

Establishing a Learning Environment

☐ General Objective

To be able to set up and arrange an early childhood classroom with stimulating activities that motivate children to become involved

☑ Specific Objectives

_____ Sets up stimulating learning centers in appropriate spaces

_____ Provides appropriate materials for children's self-directed play and learning

_____ Provides a high-activity, low-stress environment where children can learn happily together

Colors as Stimulators

To be stimulating for children and staff, the learning environment in an early childhood center should, first of all, appeal to the eye. As you enter your classroom, look around you. What catches your eye? Is it the loft at the end of the room with its giant blue and yellow floor pillows to lounge on? Or the round blue circle-time carpet with red, purple, and green squares for children to sit on? Or could it be the science center with its tropical fish aquarium in the center of a sea green rug? Or what about the book center with purple shelves on one side, a puppet tree on the other, and yellow beanbag chairs on the floor?

Wherever you look there is color: bright, primary colors set against muted pastel walls and white ceilings. A visitor's eyes will be drawn to these colors, and so will the children's. They will gravitate to the brightest colors first. What Taylor (2002) says is true: "Because color can be the single most powerful visual cue in attracting the attention of young children, it should be chosen with special care" (p. 369).

Repainting a dull room is not necessary. Rooms can be brightened and made appealing to the eye with fabrics, flowers, and vinyl coverings. Bright-colored fabric bags, for instance, can be fastened to cupboards and room dividers to hold dolls and stuffed animals. Althouse, Johnson, and Mitchell (2003) suggest adding color to the plain brown shelves of a science/discovery center by placing red, blue, and yellow vases on the windowsill of the area (p. 14). A reproduction of van Gogh's *Sunflowers* can be mounted next to the real sunflower a child brings in.

Look at your learning centers to see how you can make them more eye-appealing by adding not only color, but also interesting objects such as mirrors, paper lanterns, balloons, or green glass fishnet floats. A puppet theater or a butterfly habitat can add even more excitement. If you are adding color to specific areas, note that Taylor also says, "Color has been found to influence academic achievement. For example, red is a good choice for areas planned for gross motor activities and concept development activities; yellow is good for music and art activities; and green, blue, and purple are effective in reading areas" (2002, p. 369).

Colors can also help you create a balance between the activities in the classroom: large and small groups, noisy and quiet games, or fast and slow movements. Warm colors such as red, yellow, and orange, for instance, call for action. Cool colors such as blue, violet, and green are more restful and calming.

The manner in which other colorful materials are displayed can also stimulate learning. Frame children's art and mount it on colored paper backing. Bring in Native American pottery, baskets, or woven rugs to grace walls and countertops. Other cultures can be featured from time to time as well. Drapes can be chosen to match or harmonize with the colors of the carpeting or furniture. Textured fabrics, patterned area rugs, and wall hangings can contribute their own beauty. To assess the eye-appealing qualities of your classroom, use Figure 3.1, "Classroom Eye-Appealing Qualities Checklist."

Figure 3.1 Classroom Eye-Appealing Qualities Checklist

_____ Bright primary colors on pillows, rugs, and chairs

_____ Colorful fabrics, flowers, vinyl coverings

_____ Interesting objects: mirrors, puppet theater, balloons

_____ Activities, spaces, and colors balanced

_____ Red, yellow, and orange in active areas

_____ Blue, green, and violet in quiet areas

_____ Children's art in frames or backing

_____ Fabrics, wall hangings, pottery, paintings of various cultures displayed

We like to give children exciting, magical things to interact with.

As Friedman (2005) tells us, "Children deserve beauty and so do adults. We like to give children beautiful, magical things to interact with" (p. 48). Children will flock to your classroom, eager to participate and learn, if you make it exciting, magical, and beautiful with color.

Noise Levels

Many early childhood classrooms are just too noisy to be comfortable for either children or adults. In addition, children with hearing impairments may not understand anything the teacher says. Speaking louder on the part of the teacher does not resolve the noise-level problem but only makes it worse. Instead, many programs have learned to install acoustical ceilings, carpeting, area rugs, wall coverings, partitions, or draperies.

Curtains or drapes at windows absorb more noise than blinds or shutters. Some classrooms also use corkboards for bulletin boards or cork panels in learning centers because cork absorbs sound so well. Other classrooms feature colored burlap fastened to backs of room dividers, on bulletin boards, and for wall hangings. Fabric-wrapped fiberboard can, in fact, be used to cover an entire wall. Placing fluffy area rugs here and there on the carpeting also provides sound absorption.

Use your ingenuity to cut down on noise. For instance, large cardboard cartons or delivery cases can be cut apart, covered with colorful cloth, and used for learning center dividers. Young children at work or play are always noisy. Is it really this important to reduce classroom noise levels without having to shush children constantly? Yes. Noise creates stress, and constant noise creates a chaotic rather than an exciting learning atmosphere.

Room Arrangement

The learning environment in early childhood classrooms is based partially on the physical arrangement of equipment and materials. This arrangement is one way of conveying to children what kinds of activities are available for them and what they can and cannot do with the materials. Wide-open spaces may encourage them to run and shout. Small closed-in spaces indicate quiet and limited access for only a few children at a time. Carpeted areas tempt children to sit on the floor; pillows near bookshelves invite them to relax and look at a book.

Water tables filled to the brim are asking to be spilled. Several inches of water in the bottom give children the freedom to move it around without spilling. Tall shelves stuffed with art materials say to most children, "This is not for you to touch." To the adventurous ones they say, "See if you can reach us!" One puzzle on the table with four chairs bids four children to sit down, but it also invites a squabble. Thus how you arrange your classroom helps decide what will take place in it.

What do you want to happen? The primary goals of many early childhood programs are to promote children's positive self-images, their self-direction, and their joy of learning. If these are your goals, you will want to arrange your classroom in a way that will help children feel good about themselves as people, motivate them to become involved in the activities, and help them to become self-directed in their learning. The physical arrangement of the classroom can do this if you keep the children in mind when you arrange the learning centers.

SETS UP STIMULATING LEARNING CENTERS IN APPROPRIATE SPACES

Learning Centers as Brain Stimulators

Learning centers are the areas in your classroom devoted to particular curriculum activities such as block-building, art, books, writing, dramatic play, math, science, music, and large-motor activities. It is these centers, in fact, and not a written plan, that primarily determine the curriculum of early childhood programs. Why have learning centers? When set up appropriately, learning centers help children to choose and focus on particular activities, giving them the freedom to pursue these activities on their own.

When children are actively involved in their own learning, they tend to find such hands-on experiences meaningful and relevant in their own lives. As Rushton (2001) notes, "Research on the brain discloses that neurons change during such experiences. As a child experiences an event for the first time, for example, new dendrites form on nerve cells. The belief is that the greater number of dendrites and connections of dendrites to each other, the greater the speed of recall and memory. The classroom environment determines, to some degree, the functioning ability of children's brains" (p. 79).

Determining Learning Centers

The numbers and kinds of learning centers in your classroom depend on your program goals, space available, and number of children. Although state and federal regulations may vary, an early childhood program serving children 3 to 5 years of age should plan on having 40 to 60 square feet of space per child. Where there is a high density of children and little room for necessary activities, there is often a marked increase of negative and idle behavior (Taylor, 2002, p. 367).

Room Layout

To determine where in the room you should place each learning center, first look at the room layout as a whole and locate the permanent features:

Doors (entrance, exit, and bathroom doors)

Openings (halls or between rooms)

Sink

Windows

Closet

Walls

The space leading to doors and openings must be reserved for people to pass in and out. You may need to section off nearby learning centers so that walkers will not interfere with the children's activities. Close to the entrance door locate the youngsters' cubby area, where outside clothing is hung and personal items stored. In some centers, cubbies are outside the classroom; but if your cubbies are inside, be sure they are near the entrance so that children need not walk across the room for coats or sweaters.

Location of the sink helps determine where to place wet activities. For example, the art center should be as close as possible to the sink because children will be getting and returning water, rinsing brushes, and washing hands. A water table can be farther away because the teachers will fill it. Although cooking also uses water, it is often a temporary activity that can be set up on a counter near the sink whenever necessary.

Windows also help determine where to place learning centers. A bay window with a window seat, for instance, makes the ideal location for the book or library area. The science area can be set up in front of a regular window to provide sun for plant-growing experiments. Windows are also essential as a source of natural lighting: daylight. Its importance in a classroom is pointed out by Caples, an award-winning school-facilities architect (1996): "We strongly believe that daylight is a necessity in each classroom, especially for full-day programs. Not only does sunlight destroy mold and bacteria and provide a needed source of vitamin D, it also contributes to a sense of optimism and offers connection with the natural world" (p. 16).

What use do you make of a classroom closet? Is it for the usual storage area or teachers' coats? Why not convert the closet to a learning center extension? A closet with its door removed makes a unique extra room for the dramatic play area. Children need to be in sight at all times, so be sure to remove the closet door. A classroom closet can also become an extension of the large-motor area if you outfit it as a jumping room with inflated floor cushions and wall bars, handholds, or a rope climber. Ask the children what use of the closet they would like to make. Change it from time to time.

Separating Activities

In addition to taking advantage of permanent classroom features such as doors, windows, and closets, teachers need to separate the various learning centers from one another so that children can clearly see what activities are available and can make independent choices without confusion. A book center, science center, and manipulative center all in a row along one side of the room may be understandable to teachers but bewildering for children unless each area is clearly sectioned off.

Bullard (2010) describes a learning center as a "self-contained area with a variety of hands-on materials organized around a curriculum area or topic. Well-designed learning centers respect children's learning styles and interests, and allow them choices, thereby fostering their self-esteem and decision-making abilities" (p. 85).

Most classrooms use shelves, cubbies, or dividers to separate the learning centers from one another. Use your ingenuity to section off your own areas. Instead of placing bookshelves against the wall, for instance, use them as dividers between the book area and another learning center. Use block shelves the same way. The play stove, sink, and refrigerator can serve as dividers in a dramatic play area, rather than standing against a classroom wall. As Caples notes, "The furniture used to create the dividers should be selected for merchandising appeal, allowing children to see and select items, whether they be blocks arranged by shape, books with their covers facing out, or musical instruments on pegboards" (1996, p. 15).

Dividers should not be so high that they conceal children from one another or the teacher. The room itself should be open and cheerful, with spaces used effectively. In lieu of room dividers, place large furniture to section off areas. Easy chairs or couches with colored corrugated cardboard fastened to their backs can serve as dividers for particular areas.

Some classrooms install a loft to give it interesting extra spaces not only for large-motor climbing activities but also for learning center extensions on top and underneath. Music activities with players and headsets, for example, work especially well under a loft. The entire loft, both above and below, can also be part of a dramatic play area.

Use room walls as the backs of learning centers, with dividers forming the sides. Mount photos, posters, pictures, and hangings appropriate to the area on the walls as well. Pictures of buildings, bridges, and towers at children's eye level serve as great motivators for building in the block area, for example. After a field trip, mount photos from the trip or cut out appropriate pictures from magazines.

Be careful not to enclose each area so completely that it is totally cut off from the other learning centers. Young children like to see what is happening in other centers and need to move easily from one to another. A completely enclosed area with only a small opening also causes group-entry problems. The children inside may decide

Figure 3.2 Learning Center Location Checklist

Source: From Janice J. Beaty, *Skills for Preschool Teachers,* Ninth Edition. Copyright © 2012 by Pearson Education, Inc. All rights reserved.

Permission is granted by publisher to reproduce this checklist for evaluation and record keeping.

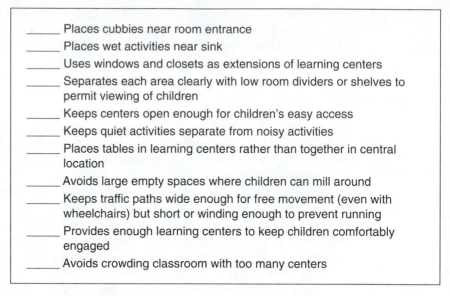

_____ Places cubbies near room entrance

_____ Places wet activities near sink

_____ Uses windows and closets as extensions of learning centers

_____ Separates each area clearly with low room dividers or shelves to permit viewing of children

_____ Keeps centers open enough for children's easy access

_____ Keeps quiet activities separate from noisy activities

_____ Places tables in learning centers rather than together in central location

_____ Avoids large empty spaces where children can mill around

_____ Keeps traffic paths wide enough for free movement (even with wheelchairs) but short or winding enough to prevent running

_____ Provides enough learning centers to keep children comfortably engaged

_____ Avoids crowding classroom with too many centers

that the center is their private space and try to prevent others from entering. You need to anticipate potential behavior problems like this as you organize the centers.

Before you begin rearranging the classroom, step back and watch how children use it as it is now. Do they crowd together in one area? Do they mill around in the room center without much direction? Do they have to walk through the block center to get to the bathroom? Are certain centers more popular than others? What seems to make the difference?

To rearrange learning centers so that children can choose them freely and use them with ease, spend time to determine how the room works in its present arrangement. Use Figure 3.2 to assess your current room arrangement.

Floor Planning

Next, make a simple floor plan of the present arrangement and record directly on it as you observe children during the free-choice period for 15 minutes on three different days. Use symbols such as x's and o's for girls and boys. Record directly on the plan where individual children are located for the 15 minutes of your observation. Use arrows to show how children move from one center to another. This exercise will help you to step back and evaluate the children's use of the classroom objectively.

Discuss your findings with members of your team. If movement, work, and play are not orderly or not even taking place in certain centers, you may want to make some changes. As Wien and her team (2005) say, "We sat down and thought about how every minute of the day should be in terms of children's comfort, and how efficiently it should work."

What will the changes be? The answer depends on how much empty space you have. Large areas of empty space encourage children to run around wildly or aimlessly. Would your program be better served if you sectioned off some of that space into learning centers? You may feel that you need the space for circle time, creative movement, or other whole-group activities. Instead, consider using the block area for large-group activities when the blocks are on the shelves. Whole-group activities do not require exclusive space when little is available or when such space will reduce the number of necessary learning centers. For circle time and whole-group activities the class in Floor Plan A (see Figure 3.3)used their music center. They also used the music center for expanded dramatic play activities when necessary.

Even though some teachers place all tables together in the center of the room, try to determine if this is necessary in your classroom. Wouldn't the room be more interesting if the large central space was sectioned off and the tables moved into appropriate learning centers? The size and shape of the room help to determine this arrangement, as well as the children's use of the space.

Is there an activity area that few children use? Why does this happen? Some classroom book centers consist only of a bookshelf against the wall with one chair nearby. Few children may use this area because it is not sectioned off for privacy, because it is too close to a noisy area, or because it is just not inviting. Pull the bookshelf away from the wall and use it as a divider. Bring in some bright pillows, stuffed animals, or puppets that go with the books. Put a fluffy area rug on the floor. Be sure that your books are in good condition and appropriate for the age and interests of the youngsters (a developmentally appropriate practice). Mount colorful book posters on the walls of the area at the children's eye level. When a learning center like this becomes attractive, it will soon fill up with youngsters.

How do the children get from one area to another? Do you have children with physical challenges? Can they move freely? They should not have to squeeze between tables and room dividers or move around someone's block structure. But you need to avoid one long traffic lane that encourages running from one end of the room to the other. Simply arrange a shelf or divider to redirect the traffic and prevent uncontrolled movement. See Floor Plan B in Figure 3.4.

Self-Regulating Methods

Do your observations indicate problems with too many children in any one area? Children can regulate their own numbers if you make it interesting for them. For example, you can mount pictures of four fish on the wall by the water table, six construction workers in the block center, or four books in the book center, with a hook under each picture. Then children who want to play in the particular area can hang their name tags on chosen hooks. When the hooks are full, newcomers must either trade a place or play elsewhere.

Wearing colored tags is another method for helping children choose a learning center. The tags can be kept on a Velcro board in front of the room for the children to choose from, or color-coded Velcro signs can be mounted in each learning center. Other classrooms use necklaces hanging in each learning center for youngsters to wear when they are playing in the center of their choice.

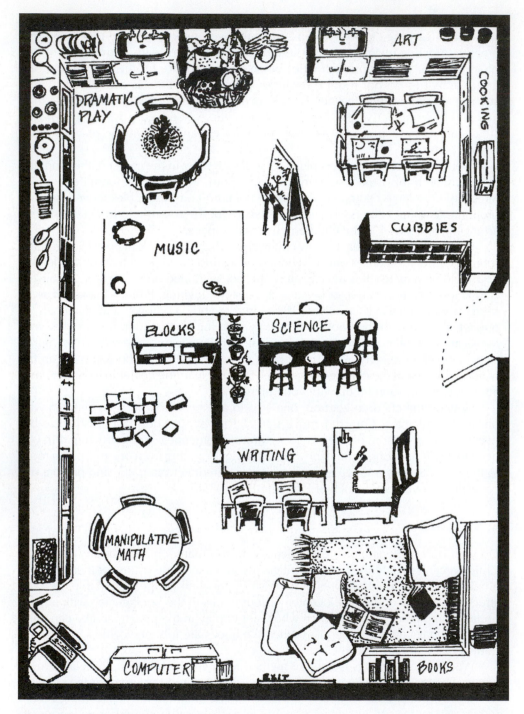

Figure 3.3   Floor Plan A

Source: Reprinted with permission of artist Xellaine Beith.

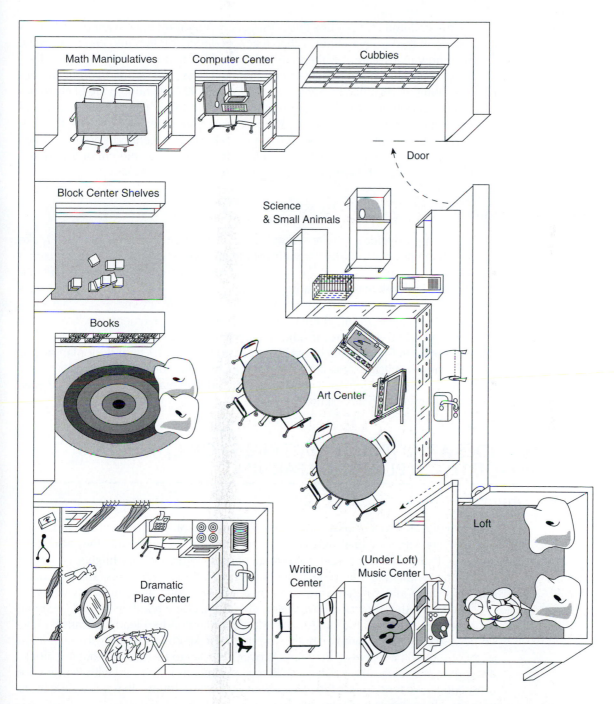

Math Manipulatives

Computer Center

Cubbies

Door

Block Center Shelves

Science & Small Animals

Books

Art Center

Dramatic Play Center

Writing Center

(Under Loft) Music Center

Loft

Figure 3.4   Floor Plan B

Giving children choices like this is especially important if we want them to gain confidence in their own abilities. When teachers direct children into certain centers, tell them how many can play there, or tell them what materials they must use, they make the youngsters more dependent on them and less sure of their own newly developing abilities. As noted by Shepherd and Eaton (1997), "Children are likely to become more self-directed rather than teacher-directed if they can make choices and decisions about materials to use. . . . When children are given real choices, they are more likely to remain at an experience or a task for an extended period of time" (p. 45). We need to remember that the classroom belongs to the children too and should be arranged for them to use on their own as much as possible.

Follow-Up Planning

When you have decided how to rearrange the room, try it out on paper first. Make another floor plan that you discuss with your team and the children. Don't forget that it is their room as well as yours. You may want to change only one area at a time to see how the children respond. Many youngsters prefer the stability of keeping things the same; thus a total rearrangement can be disorienting for them.

After you have rearranged the room, check to see if movement, work, and play are more orderly than before. If other changes are necessary, repeat the space assessment process to determine what else needs to be done. A final floor plan on paper can show what the new arrangement will look like before you begin moving furniture. Let everyone join in. If children are included in making room arrangements, they are more likely to accept them.

PROVIDES APPROPRIATE MATERIALS FOR CHILDREN'S SELF-DIRECTED PLAY AND LEARNING

Play as Learning

Children of ages 3 to 5 years spend a great deal of time playing. We understand about their playing with toys; that's what toys are for. But then we notice that they also seem to play with materials that are not toys (e.g., pens, paintbrushes, flashlights, computer keyboards). Such materials, in fact, become toys for these youngsters, and they often play with them in ways that were never meant to be. Don't they know any better?

The fact is that they do know better. This is exactly what they should be doing because play is the natural process by which young children learn. Because adults do not use play in the same manner, we often mistake children's play for recreation or inconsequential activity. "Play time is over," we say to them. "Let's put the blocks away now and learn about numbers." Because play has little to do with learning for most adults, we tend to feel the same about play for children—that it has little to do with their learning. We are wrong.

Preschool children do not learn numbers by sitting down, being quiet, and listening to the teacher. They do not really learn how to use the computer by following adult directions. Instead, they accomplish most of their learning by the hands-on method of playing with materials and equipment to find out how they work. Every object becomes a toy that they manipulate playfully until they learn what it does. We call this the *self-discovery method of learning,* and it is very effective.

Most early childhood researchers understand that play is the foundation of early learning for children. Jones and Cooper (2006) describe what being competent in play means: "being self-directed, able to find something to do, to get absorbed in it, to discover things in the process and go on to more elaborated play or to self-defined work" (p. 24).

The wise preschool teacher thus sets up the entire classroom so that children can spend the majority of their time teaching themselves through play. Maxim (1989) points out the importance of play: "Play is a need of every child. . . . And when we observe children at play, we often see enjoyment and delight. Because of this fun aspect, adults sometimes think of play as a form of amusement or fun only, not as something to be taken seriously. However, play is an important childhood activity that helps children master all developmental needs" (p. 261).

Equipping Learning Centers

The preschool teaching staff must equip each of the learning centers with developmentally appropriate materials that children can choose and use in a self-directed manner. The Learning Center Checklist in Figure 3.5 assists teachers in seeing at a glance the necessary ingredients and arrangement they must consider.

Use the checklist as a guide to setting up a new classroom or as an assessment tool to evaluate your present arrangement. Then you must consider how to arrange the materials so that children can use them for learning in a self-directed manner. Following this checklist are suggestions on how to set up each of the 13 learning centers so that children can use them most effectively.

However, do not be too rigid about the use of materials. As Curtis and Carter (2005) remind us, "Far too often teachers become rigid in the way they think about and control the use of space in a classroom. Standardization and rules begin to take over. 'Remember, those dishes belong in the dress-up area.' 'Climbing is for outdoors.' 'Let's keep our books in the book area.' Teachers need to reexamine and modify their classroom rules to meet the learning needs of individual children" (p. 36).

Block-Building Center

Block-Building

_____ Blocks lengthwise on shelves

_____ Enough blocks for building large structures

_____ Small figures, trucks, and other accessories

_____ Shelves marked with symbols of blocks and accessories

Observer _____ Classroom _____ Date _____

Block-Building

_____ Blocks lengthwise on shelves

_____ Enough blocks for large structures

_____ Small figures, trucks, and other accessories

_____ Shelves marked with symbols of blocks and accessories

Books

_____ Books on low shelves, covers visible

_____ Books in good condition

_____ Multiethnic books

_____ Puppets and dolls for book extension activities

_____ Pillows, cushions, and comfortable chairs

Dramatic Play

_____ Appropriate equipment, furniture, and accessories

_____ Adult dress-up clothes and prop boxes

_____ Clothes arranged for easy selection

_____ Full-length mirror

_____ Dolls of different skin colors

_____ Language props such as cell phones

Manipulative/Math

_____ Tables, floor space near materials

_____ Puzzles, blocks, and games

_____ Shape, color, counting, and number games

_____ Cash register, abacus, number beads, and rods

_____ Necessary parts and pieces not missing

Art

_____ Easels and tables set up for daily use

_____ Paper, paints, brushes, crayons, scissors, and collage materials on nearby tables

_____ Clay, play dough, fabrics, and squeeze bottles available

_____ Children's art products displayed beautifully

Large Motor

_____ Climbing equipment (bars, ladder, climber loft)

_____ Balancing equipment (balance beam, blocks)

_____ Jumping equipment (inflated mat)

_____ Children's basketball net and balls

_____ Lifting materials (large hollow blocks)

_____ Wooden riding vehicles and scooter boards

Music

_____ Sound- and rhythm-producing materials

_____ Tape recorders, CD players, and headsets

_____ Electronic keyboard

_____ Strumming instruments

_____ Percussion instruments (drums, xylophone)

Science/Discovery

_____ Magnifying glasses, scale, and magnets

_____ Animal, fish, or insect pets

_____ Plants and seed-growing experiments

_____ Children's collections, and displays

_____ Books about science activities in progress

Writing Center

_____ Desk, storage space, and mailboxes

_____ Pens, pencils, markers, and chalk

_____ Paper, pads, notebooks, and envelopes

_____ Rubber stamps, peel-off stickers, and stamps

_____ Computer

Computer Center

_____ Computer on low table with two chairs

_____ Printer and paper

_____ Several appropriate software programs

_____ Games, puzzles, and materials to extend each program

Figure 3.5   Learning Center Checklist

Sensory Center

_____ Squeeze bottles, basters, and eggbeaters

_____ Children's water play aprons, and safety goggles

_____ Sand toys, shovels, and sifters

_____ Cleanup tools for children's use

Woodworking

_____ Pounding and sawing tools, and safety goggles

_____ Marked tool storage shelves or pegboard

_____ Woodworking table or tree stump; vise

_____ Wood scraps, ceiling tiles, and nails

Cooking Center

_____ Knives, spoons, beaters, and food mill

_____ Measuring cups, and mixing spoons

_____ Microwave or toaster oven, blender, and frying pan

Figure 3.5   _continued_

Source: From Janice J. Beaty, _Skills for Preschool Teachers,_ Eighth Edition. Copyright © 2008 by Pearson Education, Inc. All rights reserved.

Wooden unit blocks have played an important role in early childhood programs since their introduction during the early years of the century by American early childhood educator Carolyn Pratt. Her units, half units, double units, quadruples, arches, and ramps stimulate children's imaginations and creativity in building structures of all sizes and shapes. The blocks help develop children's perceptual skills, such as eye-hand coordination, as they match sizes or balance one block on another in building towers and bridges. Block-building also promotes counting and categorizing skills as children learn to sort shapes and sizes during pickup. Concepts gained on field trips can be reinforced when children use them to reconstruct, for example, the fire station or farm they have just visited.

Many prepackaged nursery school sets of unit blocks contain too few blocks for children to construct even a small number of moderate-size buildings at one time. Try out a set and see what your children do with it. If you note that they don't have enough blocks for several children to build large buildings, then order more. You can't have enough unit blocks, most teachers agree.

Store blocks lengthwise on low shelves so that children can see their sizes and shapes and decide easily what they need for building. A cutout or outline of the block at the back of the shelf enables children to return the blocks to the proper shelves during pickup and helps them learn to match the block with its outline. Careful arrangements like this allow children to become independent and self-directed in their play.

It is also important to store building accessories in the same area with the unit blocks so that children will know they are available and can use them with the blocks. Small figures of people and animals, especially dinosaurs, are popular if you want to encourage dramatic play in the block area. Be sure to include multicultural people characters. Sometimes children prefer to play only with blocks, but often they want to pretend that people and animals are doing things in the block structures. Although small vehicles are appropriate accessories, large wooden riding vehicles belong in the large-motor area, not here where they can knock down the carefully constructed buildings. If you want children to return the toys to their places, don't forget to mount cutouts of accessories on the shelves where they belong.

Book Center

Books

_____ Books on shelves at children's height, covers visible

_____ Books in good condition

_____ Multiethnic books

_____ Puppets and dolls for book extension activities

_____ Pillows, cushions, and comfortable chairs

Early childhood specialists tell parents that reading to their preschool children is one of the most important things they can do to improve their children's literacy development. Preschool programs must go even further. You should not only read to the children but also provide opportunities for children to use books on their own. To succeed in school and develop essential verbal skills, young children need to find their way to books early on.

The book center itself should be one of the most comfortable and inviting areas in your classroom. A soft throw rug, bright puffy pillows, and a beanbag or upholstered child-size chair may be the items you choose. Children enjoy participating in furnishing the book corner. Dust jackets from colorful picture books can be clipped to a clothesline against the back of the center, for example. Bring in square rug samples and have the youngsters help carpet the floor with them. In one classroom the children decided to put in a little plastic wading pool filled with "coral" (colored beanbags) and soft pillows to relax on and read. They called it their "Reading Pool" (Friedman, 2005, p. 52).

Because the book center needs to be quiet, it should be separated from noisy areas by room dividers or placed next to other quiet activities such as writing or manipulatives. Display books in the most inviting way possible. The covers should always be facing out so that children are attracted to particular books by their covers and can make easy choices. If book covers are torn or missing, repair them or replace the books. Torn books are not inviting to children. Torn books imply that teachers are not concerned about keeping books in good condition and, therefore, that books are not important. Or children may decide that it must be all right to tear a book because someone already has.

If you have a large book collection, consider displaying only part of it and changing the books from time to time. Putting out too many books at once tends to confuse young children. Be sure the books are displayed at children's eye level. Bookshelves made for older children should be scaled down to the children's height. Making the book area as easy to use as possible promotes children's self-directed learning.

Where do the books come from? A bookmobile? A library? A catalog? A resource room? Private donations? No matter what their source, you should be the one to

Children can extend book experiences if you provide character dolls and puppets.

choose the books for your classroom. Preschool children do not yet know how to select the best books. With the large number of children's books presently being published, you must become familiar not only with the best books but also with selection techniques. (See Chapter 6.)

Some books should feature multiethnic characters. Whether or not you have African American, Hispanic, Native American, or Asian American children in your classroom, choose books that portray the multiethnicity of American life. Excellent picture books are available today showing children of almost every race or culture (see Beaty and Pratt, *Early Literacy in Preschool and Kindergarten: A Multicultural Perspective,* 2011).

Children enjoy extending their experiences with favorite books if you also stock the book area with character dolls, puppets, and stuffed animals to go with the books. Children's book departments and school supply companies such as Constructive Playthings (1-800-832-0572) and Lakeshore Learning Materials (1-800-778-4456) offer both multiethnic dolls and puppets that can serve as book characters. Call for catalogs. Cooking supply stores also stock hot pad gloves in the shapes of animals that make excellent hand puppets; or you and the children can make your own hand puppets from mittens, small paper bags, and socks. A book center should also contain a player with headphones and book CDs to accompany some of the books on the shelves. (For more information on children's books, see Chapter 6.)

Dramatic Play Center

Dramatic Play

_____ Appropriate equipment, furniture, and accessories

_____ Adult dress-up clothes and prop boxes

_____ Clothes arranged for easy selection

_____ Full-length mirror

_____ Dolls of different skin colors

_____ Language props such as cell phone

Young children live in a world of pretending. To adults who often view fantasy with misgivings, this may seem unhealthy, but it is quite the contrary. Through pretending, young children are not trying to escape from reality; they are, in fact, trying to understand it. They are doing their best to deal with people and circumstances that sometimes confuse them. Dramatic play helps to bring some sense, order, and control into their world.

To assist them in their pretending, we provide a classroom learning center that encourages imaginative play. Some programs call it the "housekeeping center," "home center," or "dress-up area." Others prefer to call it the "family life area." This center often contains child-size kitchen furnishings such as a stove, refrigerator, sink, cupboards, and table. Some programs set up a store with shelves of empty food packages. Some have a bedroom with a mirror, dresser, and doll beds, or a restaurant with tables and chairs.

All these arrangements are familiar to children and encourage them to dress up and play a variety of roles without teacher involvement. These roles include that of mother, father, uncle, aunt, grandmother, grandfather, sister, brother, baby, doctor, nurse, storekeeper, and waitress. Playing these roles helps children experience life from another point of view. It helps them to understand these roles and, in many instances, helps them to work out fears and frustrations in their own lives. Fears of going to the doctor and getting a shot, for example, can be directly faced in such pretending. Self-directed dramatic play experiences like this help a child gain a healthy and positive self-concept.

You need to provide both men's and women's clothing, hats, shoes, belts, wallets, and purses. Teenagers' clothes are just as appropriate and fit the children even better than adult sizes. Don't forget filmy scarves for princesses, a wand, a walking stick, and hats of every variety. Hang the clothes on separate hooks or hangers for the children's easy selection and return. Clothing crammed into a box or drawer makes it difficult for youngsters to see what is available.

Prop boxes, however, are the exception. Each box should contain the clothes and props needed for a special role, for instance, a firefighter. Such a prop box might contain a firefighter's hat, boots, and raincoat. After each field trip, fill a cardboard prop box with appropriate items to help children recreate the trip. Mark the boxes with illustrated signs and place them on shelves in the dramatic play area.

Children learn much about themselves through dramatic play. They quickly learn how other children respond to them in the frank give-and-take of peer play. They should also be able to look at themselves in the full-length mirror that is part of every good dramatic play area. Then children can see what they look like dressed up as someone else. Such pretend roles give children an entirely different perspective of themselves.

Have a large selection of baby dolls in this area. They should be of different skin colors, whether or not your children are, to introduce children as early as possible to the fascinating variety of people in America. Attitudes that last a lifetime develop in the early years. Also include at least two toy telephones (or several cell phones) to encourage children's language development as they play out their pretend roles.

Keep the area neat if you want youngsters to use it. When play is finished, children can help pick up and clean up by putting clothes back on the dolls, props in the boxes, dress-up clothes on hooks, or a baby doll asleep in the crib, and by getting the table set for its next role players. (For more information on dramatic play, see Chapter 9.)

Manipulative/Math Center

Manipulative/Math

_____ Tables, floor space near materials
_____ Puzzles, blocks, and games
_____ Shape, color, counting, and number games
_____ Cash register, abacus, number beads, and rods
_____ Necessary parts and pieces not missing

Manipulative skill is the ability to use one's hands and fingers with dexterity. It is important for young children to develop such skills so that they learn not only to button and zip clothes, tie shoes, and hold a pencil with ease, but also to learn to read without difficulty later on. Eye–hand coordination is important for developing the visual perception necessary to read from left to right.

Math is a manipulative skill that preschoolers can practice. Children need experiences with concrete three-dimensional materials in sorting, classifying, and counting before they can progress to more abstract work with number symbols. Many commercial manipulative materials are currently available to fill your shelves: knob puzzles, wooden puzzles, magnetic shapes, interlocking blocks, stacking toys, snapping blocks, stringing beads, threading spools, lacing shapes, stick pegboards, button boards, parquetry blocks, dominoes, counting frames, sorting trays, interlocking cubes, and more.

Nevertheless, you will want to add teacher-made games to the area. You can not only save money with homemade materials but also provide directly for the children's particular needs. Homemade picture puzzles showing each child's face, for instance, promote positive self-concepts as well as their motor skills for putting them together.

These puzzles, sets, and games can be stored on shelves backed by cutout symbols for children to match when they return the items. As with books, do not put out all the manipulative materials at once, for too large a selection can be overwhelming. Check periodically to make sure the puzzle pieces and game parts are not missing. If pieces are missing, either replace them or discard the item. Some classrooms use plastic containers with an outline of a part traced on the cover for children to locate particular materials and to return the pieces to the container where they belong during pickup. Opening and closing these containers give children additional practice in small-motor coordination.

The manipulative center should be large enough to contain at least one table as well as floor space near the shelves of materials. Although teachers often put out puzzles on the table before children arrive, let the youngsters make their own choices too. If the materials are arranged simply and attractively on nearby shelves, children should have no trouble finding what they want. If the puzzle they select first is too difficult, they can take another.

Art Center

Most early childhood programs use art activities almost every day. Unfortunately, adults seem to control art projects more often than almost any other activity. Teachers or aides often get out the art supplies, pass out the paper, give instructions, and then remain in the area to make sure their instructions are carried out.

If we truly want children to become self-directed in their learning, we should allow them to be as independent in art as in dramatic play or block building. Freedom to explore and experiment encourages creativity. Although directions are surely appropriate in certain crafts projects, we must also give children the opportunity to try out paints and brushes of their own choosing with paper they select.

This independence is possible when child-level shelves hold the art materials near the tables or easels where they will be used, when materials are arranged in order for easy selection and return by the children, and when children are allowed and encouraged to participate in setting up and cleaning up art activities. When children become independent in art, they will happily choose this activity on their own during the daily free-choice period.

Teachers may want to have easels set up with paints and brushes ready for children daily. But children can also learn to choose their own paper from the shelf and put it up with the teacher's help. On days when prepared play dough will be used, children can help get it out of storage. Other times, they can help mix it.

If you have a water source in the room, the art center should be nearby. With minimum direction, children can become entirely independent in setup and cleanup when the materials are nearby.

It is important that you take the next step with children and their art: display their products the most creative and beautiful way you can. As Seefeldt (2002) tells us, "Displaying children's work dignifies and recognizes the value of children's expression of their thoughts, ideas, and imaginations. Displays, along with labels describing children's work, give children the idea that meaning can be shared and gained through pictures and print" (pp. 12, 14). One method is by having children make frames for their pictures. They can cut strips of colored paper for frames and cover them with glitter and peel-off designs. Or they can paint or color tongue depressors and fasten them around their pictures. (For more information on art activities, see Chapter 7.)

Large-Motor Center

Large Motor
_____ Climbing equipment (bars, ladder, climber, loft)
_____ Balancing equipment (balance beam, blocks)
_____ Jumping equipment (inflated mat)
_____ Children's basketball net and balls
_____ Lifting materials (large hollow blocks)
_____ Wooden riding vehicles and scooter boards

If your program has a well-equipped outside playground, you may wonder why you should provide a large-motor area inside. It is essential during the preschool years for children to practice large-motor skills as often as possible every day, whether or not they go outside, as mentioned in Chapter 2. An indoor wooden climber is perhaps the best single piece of equipment if you have room for only one piece. Molded plastic climbing and sliding equipment is popular in some programs; others use giant plastic waffle blocks with tunnels and slides that snap together. A homemade substitute can be a packing crate and a ladder or a loft with a ladder and slide. Cardboard cartons with low doors cut in both ends make fine tunnels to promote crawling skills. Commercial foam or cloth tunnels are also popular.

Ordinary chairs and tables can serve as climbing, jumping, and crawling stations in an obstacle course when nothing else is available. Creative teachers find that almost anything is possible with masking tape and a little imagination. Children, too, enjoy making their own balance beams from unit blocks placed together in a long or winding road.

In classrooms with little or no space for a permanent large-motor area, you can use a corner to fasten climbing bars or a climbing rope with a mat cushion underneath; or you could consider converting a closet into a large-motor jumping room as described earlier in this chapter. Free-standing or mounted basketball rims can also be used in an out-of-the-way corner, with foam balls that will not bounce into other areas. Ask the children what other climbing and jumping activities they want to try in the room.

Use your own judgment about wooden riding vehicles. If you include them in the classroom, be sure there is space enough for children to ride them without running into things. They can help you mark out roads and make traffic signals if necessary. (For more information on motor activities, see Chapter 4.)

Music Center

> **Music**
> _____ Sound- and rhythm-producing materials
> _____ Tape recorders, CD players, and headsets
> _____ Electronic keyboard
> _____ Strumming instruments
> _____ Percussion instruments (drums, xylophones)

Music is important in the early childhood classroom. Young children are at a stage in their growth and development when they want to express themselves freely in all sorts of ways. Music is one of those ways. It is up to you to provide an atmosphere where music is as much a natural part of the day as conversation. Chanting, singing, moving to rhythm, listening to tapes or CDs, and playing instruments should be a part of every day's activities for both children and adults.

Store rhythm instruments separately on shelves or attached to pegboards in the music area so that children can see what is available and make independent choices. Mount a tracing of each instrument on its shelf or board space to give children yet another opportunity to match shapes and return materials to their proper places. Every classroom music center needs a tape recorder or CD player with headsets for children's private listening. Records, CDs, and tapes, however, should not be the extent of your classroom music. Children also need opportunities to make their own music, for example, singing, humming, whistling, or playing a drum or keyboard. (For more information on music, see Chapter 7.)

Science/Discovery Center

> **Science/Discovery**
> _____ Magnifying glasses, balance scale, and magnets
> _____ Animal, fish, or insect pets
> _____ Plants and seed-growing experiments
> _____ Children's collections and displays
> _____ Books about science activities in progress

In some programs, science activities are relegated to a side cupboard or window ledge. But teachers and assistants who realize that such an area can be the most exciting spot in the classroom often reserve much more space: a cozy corner with a table for the daily "science object," shelves for children's collections, and space for the tools of science. The tools of science include a stand-up magnifying glass and several small magnifying glasses, a giant magnet, an assortment of small magnets, tweezers, prisms, a tape measure or windup ruler, a balance scale, a fish net, binoculars, and several see-through plastic jars.

Is there space in your classroom for a terrarium full of ferns, moss, and wintergreen gathered on a trip to the woods? You might also include an aquarium for goldfish or tropical fish, with a book nearby for identifying them. An ant farm, insect habitat, or butterfly bower can display the latest occupants. A cage on the counter may have a gerbil or guinea pig in residence. Shelves closest to the window can contain bean sprouts in paper cups.

An exciting activity of some kind happens daily in such a classroom. It may be an egg carton full of a bean-seed mixture that encourages children to sort and classify or to weigh the items with the balance scale. A chart to record how many inches each child's beans have grown invites all kinds of measuring with the windup ruler. A sealed box in the middle of the table with a sign, "Guess what's inside! Tell your guess to the tape recorder," has the curious ones trying to find out what the sign says, shaking the box vigorously, and cautiously recording their guesses. Another sign, "Bring something green tomorrow," sets off a babble of ideas.

Children in such a classroom expect to be challenged to find out something independently. They know they must use their five senses plus the available science tools to discover "how much" or "what kind" or "how many." What's more, these youngsters can learn to do it on their own because of the careful arrangement of the materials and the stimulating manner in which science objects are displayed.

Writing Center

> Desk, storage space, and mailboxes
> Pens, pencils, markers and chalk
> Paper, pads, notebooks, and envelopes
> Rubber stamps, peel-off stickers, and stamps
> Computer

The news about preschool children and writing is good indeed. Child development specialists and teachers around the world are discovering a growing number of young children who have taught themselves to write (and even to read) naturally. Some preschool youngsters have always had this ability to advance from scribbles into writing on their own, but it was seldom recognized and therefore not encouraged. Instead, children had to wait until elementary school where writing would be taught formally. Now we know better. Today both preschools and kindergartens are setting up a writing area for children to experience this natural emergence into writing through play with writing implements just as they play with painting implements.

Early childhood teachers can facilitate this natural process by encouraging children to experiment with writing but not teaching them formally how to make letters or words. As noted by Schickedanz and Casbergue (2009), "Using marks to create pictures comes fairly naturally to children. Using marks to create print develops alongside the development of children's picture-making skills, between 3 and 5 years of age. Beginning during the preschool years and continuing through kindergarten, children very gradually build an understanding of how print actually works. Little by little, marks that children put on a page begin to stand on their own" (p. 6).

Because writing is more often done at a desk, it makes sense to set up a classroom writing area around a desk. A child's home desk with drawers is ideal, or you can develop a little "office area" with a small file cabinet and shelves to store the materials. A table can serve for scribbling space. The classroom computer can be located here if you choose not to set up a separate computer area. Keep the computer on a separate table, however, with two chairs for two children to use at the same time.

Children relish the opportunity to try out all kinds of writing implements. Stock the area with pencils and pens of all sizes and shapes. Some children prefer gripping the thick primary pencils, but a few like to use regular adult pencils. The all-time favorites seem to be felt-tip markers of every color. With young children's stubby fingers, they make marks easier than pens or pencils. Be sure your markers and ballpoint pens are water-soluble.

The types of writing, printing, and stamping materials you supply will influence the kinds of scribbles, mock writing, and print the children produce. Put out only a few kinds of writing implements, paper, and tablets at first to get them started. Then from time to time add other materials, such as blank postcards, greeting cards, stationery, and envelopes.

Children especially enjoy receiving and sending letters even when their writing is still in the scribble stage. Be sure to include mailboxes in the writing area to motivate letter writing. Shoe boxes decorated by the children and labeled with their names and pictures make good mailboxes when stacked together on a shelf in the writing center. Add a bulletin board for children to display their own writing products. (For more information on writing, see Chapter 6.)

Computer Center

> **Computer Center**
> _____ Computer on low table with two chairs
> _____ Printer and paper
> _____ Several appropriate software programs
> _____ Games, puzzles, materials to extend programs

Adults who are unfamiliar with the computer may be surprised that preschools and kindergartens are encouraged to set up such a learning center or that young children are invited to use it on their own. To an adult, a computer seems to be an expensive, complicated, high-tech piece of equipment that only older children could learn to use.

As it turns out, appropriate computer programs are no more complicated to operate for children 3 to 5 years of age than are television programs. With the proper software and a minimum of instruction, young children can teach themselves to operate the programs by themselves. Computers, in fact, are set up to teach in the same manner that young children are set up to learn: through playing around with the keys, by trial and error, and through playful self-discovery.

Appropriate computer programs are not difficult for young children to use.

Software programs for preschool children in the form of simple games can involve the youngsters in learning about themselves, their families, the environment, animals, vehicles, letters, numbers, shapes, and colors. But be sure your center is set up for two children to use at once. Children can then teach each other how to operate the program. They also learn turn-taking, cooperation, and problem solving as they try to work the programs through trial and error.

Because computers are an expensive item for most preschools and kindergartens, teachers and directors should ask for help from parents or businesses in acquiring them. Often an older, less powerful model of a computer can be donated that easily accommodates the early childhood software you will be using. Choose the computer on the basis of the software programs available.

To choose the software, it is important to understand how children will use it. Familiarize yourself with popular programs for young children through a hands-on approach. Visit a public school computer resource center or a library software collection and borrow sample programs for trial use by you and the children.

The number of software programs you purchase will depend on the particular curriculum areas of the classroom in which you plan to integrate computer software, as well as the developmental levels of the programs. Some teachers start by purchasing one or two programs each for shapes, colors, opposites, numbers, letters, drawing, painting, and constructing. They introduce the programs one by one, leaving them in the area for the children to try out for a week or so at a time before introducing a new program.

Meanwhile, teachers should include concrete activities related to each program in other learning centers. For example, when an alphabet program is in use on the computer, a magnetic letters game can be put out. In this way, computer programs are translated into three-dimensional hands-on classroom activities so necessary for young children's learning. (For more about computers, see Chapter 5.)

Sensory Play Center

Sensory Table (Sand/Water)

_____ Squeeze bottles, basters, and eggbeaters

_____ Children's water play aprons and safety goggles

_____ Sand toys, shovels, and sifters

_____ Cleanup tools for children's use

Water has an irresistible appeal for youngsters. Watch them wash their hands or get a drink. The splashing and squirting that often occur are not so much misbehavior as they are a part of the playful discovery process that children use to learn about new things. Yet it is more than that. Water seems to have a mesmerizing effect on children. They revel in its smooth or bubbly feel, its gushing and gurgling sound, and the way they can squirt it, spray it, or pour it. Even children with short attention spans can play with it for hours. The hyperactive or unruly child often quiets down remarkably during water play. Its calming effect makes it an excellent quiet activity, a wonderful change of pace after a hectic morning.

The physical arrangement of the water play area, just as with the rest of your classroom, determines whether children can enjoy playing in water on their own or whether there will always be squabbling and the need for close adult supervision. If you have a water table, put only a few inches of water in it. Children can have fun with this much water and still keep themselves and the floor fairly dry. Have equipment for use in the water table on nearby shelves or hanging from a pegboard rack in the area. To avoid arguments, be sure to have more than one of the favorite toys. Most children especially enjoy large plastic basters and eggbeaters. A supply of empty plastic squeeze bottles of various sizes, as well as plastic pitchers, plastic bottles, plastic hoses, and eye droppers, should be standard equipment. Plastic or wooden boats and figures of people are also popular.

To keep children's clothes dry, have aprons available, either hanging on hooks or folded on shelves nearby, so that the children can get the aprons by themselves. A water table can usually accommodate a maximum of four children. Place the number 4 or four stick figures of children in the center, and let the children regulate themselves.

If you don't have a water table, use four plastic dishpans on a regular classroom table. The sink in the housekeeping area also makes a good, if small, water play area for doing the dolls' dishes or laundering doll clothes. Put a squirt of liquid detergent in the water at times and let children play with bubbles. Another day, let them use food coloring and droppers to mix colors.

Water tables can easily be converted to sand tables for another activity children really enjoy. The same directions apply. Generally, 2 or 3 inches of sand are plenty. Keep sand accessories and cleanup equipment in the area. Help children understand a few simple rules, for example, that they must keep the sand in the table and that only four children are allowed in the play area at a time. Then enforce the rules with quiet, consistent firmness. If sand is spilled, children can help sweep it up.

Small containers, sifters, hoppers, scoops, shovels, small dump trucks, and figures of people are popular sand toys. Be sure to have enough for four to play without squabbles. Have the children wear safety goggles to keep sand out of their eyes.

Woodworking Center

> **Woodworking**
> _____ Pounding tools and safety goggles
> _____ Marked tool storage shelves or pegboard
> _____ Woodworking table or tree stump, vise
> _____ Wood scraps, ceiling tiles, and nails

Wood is another medium especially attractive to children. You can see this by the way they handle wooden blocks. The fact that wood can be pounded and turned into something other than itself makes it as creative a medium as paint. Both boys and girls love to pound. Thus woodworking is an excellent channel for the acceptable venting of frustration. Children can pound wood and let off steam harmlessly.

Not every early childhood program can afford a workbench. Tree stumps make an excellent substitute and are even more effective for pounding on. Just for the fun of pounding, let children nail things onto the tops of tree stumps. A box of nails of many sizes and another of pine wood scraps are enough to keep your woodworking area going for many days. Children should wear safety goggles for this activity. Putting on goggles for an activity like this makes children feel really grown up.

Some teachers substitute ceiling tiles for wood because with this softer substance children have better control over hammers and nails. Children with limited muscular strength appreciate this. Building supply dealers will sometimes donate extra tiles. Children can also pound nails more easily through plastic foam boards than through wood. Small adult tools are more effective than children's toolbox toys. They can be stored on shelves or hung from pegboards, with outlines traced so children can match shapes and return the tools easily.

Cooking Center

> **Cooking Center**
> _____ Knives, spoons, beaters, and food mill
> _____ Measuring cups and mixing spoons
> _____ Microwave or toaster oven, blender, frying pan

Adults sometimes misunderstand the idea of cooking in the preschool classroom. Teaching a child to cook is not the purpose. Cooking is instead an exceptional vehicle for promoting learning experiences such as eye–hand coordination, small muscle strength, cause and effect, prereading skills, sequencing, measurement, nutrition, and sensory exploration. For example, peeling shells from hard-boiled eggs offers unparalleled practice in small-motor skills. Scraping carrots, dicing potatoes, mixing batter, and turning the handle of an eggbeater strengthens hand and arm muscles.

Children's intense interest in food and food preparation provides the motivation for learning, and your ingenuity supplies the activities. There are no limits to the learning possibilities of a cooking center. Cooking is especially fascinating to children because it is a real activity, not a pretend one, and they can eat the results!

A cooking center need not be a permanent fixture. Cooking can take place in the classroom at a table set up for it, on a counter near an electrical outlet, or in the center kitchen. A microwave oven, a toaster oven, or an electric frying pan can supply the heat if your safety and insurance regulations permit hot cooking.

Child's Private Area

A child's private area is not a curriculum area as such, but it should be provided on a permanent basis if your goal is to promote a child's positive self-image. It is a place where a child can get away by himself or herself when the need arises. If yours is an all-day program, such a location is a necessity. Three- and 4-year-olds, especially, find large groups of children overpowering if they must be with them for any length of time.

An overstuffed chair in a comfortable corner away from noisy activities may be all that is needed. Some classrooms use a large cardboard carton with a cutout door and window for a hut or playhouse. This can serve as the private area when dramatic play is finished. A packing crate serves the same purpose. So does a card table covered with a blanket for the child to crawl under. A colorfully painted claw-footed bathtub lined with pillows makes a wonderful retreat. Some centers have a loft that can be used for a child's private space. The book area of some classrooms makes a cozy retreat as well. Bunnett and Davis (1997) explain, "We discovered that children need more than one 'cozy nest,' and designed several soft and quiet places. Over the years, we have used mattresses, bean chairs, hammocks, and rag pillows, to name a few. We found that with additional quiet spaces children can do their work with fewer disruptions, feel less fatigued, and can retreat to a quiet place without negative connotations" (p. 44).

It is important that the private area be located in the classroom and not totally isolated in another room. Children need to be by themselves, but at the same time, they like to know what others are doing. Being isolated in a different room is too much like punishment.

Inclusion

Children having special needs such as hearing or vision impairments and physical or mental disabilities may need special accommodations in the classroom. Simplifying the environment may be all that is necessary. This means that learning centers are clearly designated. Areas are kept uncluttered with only the materials in use kept on open shelves. All curriculum materials have cutout illustrations marking their spaces on the shelves. Walls are painted in soothing pastel colors and kept uncluttered. Children's art and writing are displayed in one location rather than spread around the room. Noise is kept at minimum levels through the use of floor carpeting, wall curtains, and acoustical ceiling tiles. Pathways through the room are wide enough for a wheelchair. Other accommodations can be arranged depending on the need. Talk with parents and health specialists about including children with special needs without calling attention to disabilities.

NAEYC Criteria for Physical Environment Standard

Describe how your program meets the following standard:

9.A.12 Indoor space is designed and arranged to provide children with disabilities full access (making adaptations as necessary) to the curriculum and activities.

Russian psychologist Lev Vygotsky believed that children with special needs learn in the same way as typically developing children, through social interactions between peers and adults. Althouse et al. (2003) had this important insight to add: "In many respects, Vygotsky was a forerunner of inclusion. Through use of his concept of the Zone of Proximal Development, teachers and parents can look not only at the weaknesses of children with special needs, but also at their strengths; their abilities are as important to consider as their disabilities. He felt that they learned best in an environment in which they had more freedom to move and explore than in highly structured environments" (p. 7). Your classroom learning environment should fit this description.

Developmentally Appropriate Materials

Children of different ages have distinct preferences for the toys and materials they want to play with. Toddlers, for instance, often prefer push toys that make sounds as they roll across the floor. Preschoolers disdain such toys but may flock to shelves containing trucks, cars, and figures of people and animals. Likewise, children at different developmental levels may use the same materials in different ways. Some 3-year-olds, for instance, fill containers with building blocks and then dump them out. Others build roads, towers, and even bridges with the same blocks.

Some materials are obviously more appropriate than others for children of different ages and stages of development. Yet for preschool programs to satisfy all of their youngsters' widely divergent interests and needs, teachers must also understand children's development as they progress from one level to another.

Exploratory Play Levels

Observers of young children have noted that most children begin to explore a new object in the same way. They play around with it, exploring it with their senses. With a toy telescope, for instance, they may first use it as a hammer, a horn, or a tower, or they may look through the wrong end and laugh before figuring out its real use. With a paintbrush, they may swish paint around on a paper, change hands and slap on another color of paint, change hands again and cover the paper with still another color. We call this beginning exploration of a new material *manipulation*. Young children everywhere seem to try out new objects in the same manipulating manner.

Once children have accomplished this beginning exploration and learned how to work the material, they go on to a second level of use: *mastery*. Here they repeat the correct use of the object or material over and over. With a toy telescope, they may push it together to close it, open it, look through it, and close it again—over and over. Or they may grip a paintbrush in the right hand while they fill their paper with lines and take another sheet and fill that with lines—again and again. It is almost as though they are practicing the skill they have just taught themselves.

Finally, many—but not all—preschool children evolve into a third level of exploration: *meaning*. Here children put the same object or material to some new and different use, giving it their own meaning. For example, with a telescope, they might use it in their large block "spaceship" as a control lever. With a paintbrush, they may begin painting suns and people.

These three developmental learning levels that most children work through spontaneously with no outside help can be referred to as the *3 M's: manipulation, mastery,* and *meaning.* For teachers and assistants in early childhood programs, it is important to recognize these levels as they witness children playing with materials. It helps to know, for example, that Sarah, who is filling page after page of paper with lines of scribbles, must be at the mastery level in spontaneous writing. Don't try to stop her. She is engaged in her own play practice and will progress beyond her repetitive actions when she has mastered line scribbling. Nor should you try to redirect Zack's efforts at the easel as he slaps paint every which way on his paper, first with one hand and then the other. He is still manipulating the medium.

Over the years, observers of children have determined the sequences most children follow as they interact on their own with particular objects and materials. For example, children begin manipulating unit blocks by filling containers with blocks and then dumping them out. They eventually progress to the mastery level by stacking blocks in horizontal lines (roads) or vertical lines (towers). Finally, they emerge into inventive construction of buildings and bridges, giving meaning to their work. It is fascinating for adult observers to watch this progression of levels develop in a child and to note that every child seems to follow the same progression and in almost the same manner.

Teachers, teaching assistants, student teachers, and volunteers should be aware of these developmental levels as they make their plans for individuals and the total group. By carefully observing and recording how children interact with materials, teachers can determine whether each child is in the manipulation, mastery, or meaning stage. After this determination is made, teachers can add appropriate materials to each of the learning centers to support children's own progression through their levels of exploration. For example, provide new and challenging puzzles in the manipulative center when children have completed the old ones over and over. For children who are still filling and dumping table blocks rather than building with them, let them continue this beginning exploration before adding new materials, but support their current efforts by giving them new containers to use. (For more information about observing children and the Learning Center Involvement Checklist, see Chapter 12.)

Changing Materials

Look around your classroom and what do you see? Some classrooms appear to be the same all year round. The same books are on the shelves of the library area; the same paint colors fill the jars at the easel; the same science project occupies the shelf by the window. These materials may have appealed to the children at first, but after continued use over long periods of time, they eventually lose their attraction. It is time for a change, but not a complete change.

Young children need new stimulation, but within the comfortable learning centers they are used to. This means you should add new materials to each of the classroom centers from time to time. Put away a few items for the time being and add something new to each area at least once a month. Researchers Petrakos and Howe (1996) note, "There is evidence to support the notion that the physical arrangement of the play setting may directly influence the types of children's play. Although the housekeeping corner is designed to encourage dramatic play, it can be limited and static in terms of the arrangement of space, equipment, and theme" (p. 66).

If yours is a center where the toy refrigerator, stove, and sink remain in the same position for an entire year, consider bringing in something different: perhaps a large cardboard refrigerator box and letting the children invent their own setting. With your help they can cut out doors and windows and then paint their new "house," "ticket booth," or "castle."

One program enclosed its housekeeping center with walls containing Plexiglas windows that went up and down, a doorbell, a mailbox, and a small lamp on a dresser table inside (Bunnett & Davis, 1997). Another program brought in a steamer trunk with drawers and compartments containing fancy dress-up clothes, costume jewelry, and accessories. Children suddenly became motivated to dress up as actors and put on plays for each other.

Evaluating Room Arrangement

Your children's behavior in the classroom will tell you whether you have planned and arranged well for them. Large groups of children milling around aimlessly may mean there is too much open space or not enough learning centers. A great deal of running may mean that open areas need to be sectioned off with room dividers.

On the other hand, your room could be too cluttered, so that children, especially 3-year-olds, have difficulty making choices and settling down. Perhaps they are suffering from "sensory overload." Simplify the environment by putting away some of the materials and taking unnecessary pictures off the walls. When most of the children become involved in the areas and engrossed in the activities, you will know that your arrangement is working as it should.

During the year, you will want to rearrange the room for variety or for new challenges. It is best to change only one or two areas at once, because young children are easily upset by abrupt changes. It helps to let them participate in the planning and rearranging, because it is their room as much as yours.

PROVIDES A HIGH-ACTIVITY, LOW-STRESS ENVIRONMENT WHERE CHILDREN CAN LEARN HAPPILY TOGETHER

Brain Research and Stress

The results of brain research of the past decade can help teachers of young children to understand why creating a high-activity, low-stress, brain-compatible learning environment is essential if young children are to grow and learn. As Rushton (2001) points out: "A nonthreatening environment is crucial if students are to feel safe in encountering and exploring stimulating new ideas" (p. 76).

Research findings on how the brain functions show that high levels of stress can inhibit learning. When a teacher yells at a child or calls out his name across the room to stop him from doing something, the child and those around him often become afraid. This fear causes the brain to release the hormone cortisol, which stops the child from thinking clearly. Lasting high stress or threat can reduce the brain's capacity for understanding and can interfere with high-order thinking (Rushton, 2001, p. 78).

Teachers who belittle, ridicule, or criticize the children create situations that can hinder learning. Teachers who allow children to be teased or bullied by other children or kept out of group activities also add to their stress. Classrooms that are too crowded or too empty create children's discomfort. Environments that are sterile and nonstimulating do the same.

In contrast, low-stress, high-activity environments treat all children as worthy individuals; provide a wide range of exciting activities for children to choose from; use colors, lamps, and music to create warm and comfortable settings; help all children to experience success; have a balance of quiet and active learning times, of total-group, small-group, and individual activities; and have teachers and staff who use humor, love, and affection to interact with children while modeling positive interpersonal behaviors.

Floor Time

Young children love to be in classrooms where smiling teachers get down on the floor and have fun with them; where laughter rings out all day long and teachers

Children love to have teachers get down on the floor and play with them.

know how to pretend just as children do to engage their attention. Are you excited to see the children come in every day? You need to show it. You need to tell children how happy you are to see them. You need to begin with one activity at the beginning of the day that gets them laughing and feeling happy. As Rushton (2001) further notes, "Emotions are biological functions of the nervous system, and they strongly influence attention and memory. Children engaged in interesting activities at the beginning of the day will have a more positive disposition toward the day's activities as a whole" (p. 77).

Kordt-Thomas and Lee (2006) explain that the concept of *floor time* itself is "a play-based approach to helping children develop relationships, language, and thinking, originated by Stanley Greenspan" (p. 86). Although Greenspan used it with infants, toddlers, and preschool children with a range of special needs, it can also be used for children who are developing normally. As Greenspan and Lewis (2000) describe it, the caregiver gets down on the floor with the child, where he feels most comfortable and where his toys and play things are located. Greenspan says, "When you are playing eye-to-eye with your child, you generate a sense of equality that encourages him to engage with you, take initiative, and act more assertively" (p. 331).

When you get down on the floor, it is a signal to the children in your program that you are giving up your role as teacher and joining them in their fun. It creates an entirely different atmosphere in the classroom when children can lead an adult into fun activities. Your tone of voice, your facial expressions, and the words you use let children know you love the way they play and want to participate in it—if only for a short time. When teachers and staff engage in floor time with the children, it lessens stress and promotes children's intellectual, emotional, and physical development by simply following their lead and joining in.

Using Humor

Using humor also helps to lessen stress. Observe what is happening in each of the learning centers every day and see how you can add something humorous to the children's activities. You might decide to have a surprise "drop-in-and-laugh" time in each of the learning centers from time to time, where you come in with a funny story to read to the small group or a fun activity to add to what they are already doing. Put on a dress-up hat or colorful scarf or cape to signal your new role.

Or perhaps you can hang a pacifier around your neck and drop into the dramatic play center where a small group is playing with the new baby doll, to read *Oonga Boonga* (Wishinsky, 1998), the story of baby Louise who wouldn't stop crying until her brother Daniel came home and said "oonga boonga" to her. Children love funny words like this as you will soon find out when you hear them whispering "oonga boonga" to one another and dissolving into gales of laughter.

What does this have to do with the environment of the classroom? Everything! It is the way you and the children put the environment to use every day that will make the difference in your program. Use your imagination, tap into the children's creativity, and the environment will blossom in ways you never expected.

SUMMARY

This chapter provides ideas for setting up and arranging an early childhood classroom so that children will become self-directed in their learning. You will need to articulate your own program's goals to decide what curriculum areas to include in your classroom. Using the Learning Center Checklist in Figure 3.5 should help you understand how each activity area can promote your program's goals for young children.

Because the physical arrangement of a preschool classroom is the structure for an open and flexible curriculum, you will want to arrange your room carefully, using aids such as the Learning Center Location Checklist in Figure 3.2. This checklist can help you learn to separate one area from another by pulling shelves away from the walls and using them as dividers to make the areas obvious to the children. Self-regulating devices such as hooks and tags or charts and necklaces can also help children become independent in using their environment.

You will begin to understand how children's play serves as their vehicle for learning and how they go through developmental levels of manipulation, mastery, and meaning as they explore the curriculum materials you provide. You will also learn to know the importance of changing the learning centers and adding new materials to support different curriculum topics. Then you will understand how stress prevents children from learning and how floor time and humor can keep them playing and learning together all day long. The chapters that follow extend the discussion of each learning center and describe how teachers can promote young children's natural growth and development in these areas.

Ethical Dilemma

One of the parents disagrees with your use of the woodworking center, especially allowing children to use adult hammers, because she feels it is unsafe. You feel that this center contributes greatly to children's eye–hand coordination, small-muscle development, and self-image. The parent threatens to report your program to the community child protection agency if you do not remove the adult hammers. What should you do?

LEARNING ACTIVITIES

1. Read one or more of the Suggested Readings or Web sites. Add 10 cards to your file with specific ideas for setting up the classroom. Include the reference source on each card.

2. Use the Learning Center Checklist in Figure 3.5 to assess your present room arrangement. Set up a new learning center or rearrange an old one based on the checklist results and ideas presented in this chapter. Or visit another classroom and assess it.

3. Visit another early childhood classroom and make a floor plan showing the areas children were using during your visit. Record on file cards at least three new ideas for classroom arrangement gained from this visit.

4. Set up and implement a children's self-regulating method for choosing learning centers in your classroom. Report on how this works.

5. Make outlines of the materials and equipment in each area and mount them on their particular shelves and hook boards. Observe how children access and return the materials afterward.

6. Bring in new games, books, pictures, or props that illustrate a field trip you have taken and add them to one or more learning centers. Observe how children use them.

7. Bring in three humorous picture books and read them to the children, afterward using book extension activities in several of the learning centers.

SUGGESTED READINGS

Bottini, M., & Grossman, S. (2005). Center-based teaching and children's learning: The effects of learning centers on young children's growth and development. *Childhood Education, 81*(5), 274–277.

Bullard, J. (2010). *Creating environments for learning: Birth to age eight.* Upper Saddle River, NJ: Merrill.

Cowles, M. (2006). Creating emotionally safe and supportive environments for children. *Dimensions of Early Childhood, 34*(3), 36–38.

Curtis, D., & Carter, M. (2003). *Designs for living and learning.* St. Paul, MN: Redleaf Press.

Greenman, J. (2005). *Caring spaces, learning places.* Redman, WA: Exchange Press.

Readdick, C. A. (2006). Managing noise in early childhood settings. *Dimensions of Early Childhood, 34*(1), 17–22.

Reifel, S., & Sutterby, J. A. (2009). Play theory and practice in contemporary classrooms. In S. Feeney, A. Galper, & C. Seefeldt, (Eds.), *Continuing issues in early childhood education* (3rd ed., pp. 238–257). Upper Saddle River, NJ: Merrill.

Wellhousen, K., & Crowther, I. (2004). *Creating effective learning environments.* Clifton Falls, NY: Thomson/Delmar/Cengage.

WEB SITES

**Bright Horizons Family Solutions Resource Room—
Environment and Design**
http://www.brighthorizons.com

Child Care Information Exchange
http://www.childcareexchange.com

**National Association for the Education of Young
Children**
http://www.naeyc.org

**The National Child Care Information and Technical
Assistance Center**
http://www.nccic.org

CHILDREN'S BOOKS

*Wishinsky, F. (1998). *Oonga boonga*. New York:
Dutton.

*Multicultural

Advancing Physical Skills

☐ **General Objective**

To promote children's physical development by determining their needs and providing appropriate materials and activities

☑ **Specific Objectives**

_____ Assesses children's large-motor skills and provides appropriate equipment and activities

_____ Assesses children's small-motor skills and provides appropriate materials and activities

_____ Provides opportunities for children to engage in creative movement

THE *PHYSICAL* growth and development of young children during their preschool years is such an obvious occurrence that we sometimes take it for granted. Children will, of course, grow bigger, stronger, more agile, and more coordinated in their movements without outside help. It is part of their natural development. But at times, we are suddenly surprised by the 4-year-old who cannot run without stumbling, who has trouble holding a paintbrush, or who cannot walk up and down stairs easily.

We realize that individual differences in development account for many such lags. Some children are slower than others in developing coordination. Others may have neurological problems. But for many children it is the lack of opportunity to run, jump, climb, and throw freely. The streets may be dangerous and parks too far away. Unfortunately for many young children, television and video games have replaced active play. As Pica (2006) tells us, "Children today lead much more sedentary lifestyles than their predecessors, and society places less and less value on movement and recreation. Consider that 40% of 5- to 8-year-olds show at least one heart disease risk factor" (p. 12). Those risks include obesity (as discussed in Chapter 2) and high blood pressure.

Gellens (2005) adds another important factor: "Movement is good for the brain. By adding movement and eliminating long sedentary periods, the curriculum can boost brain power" (p. 14). She goes on to describe how the amount and type of physical movement affects children's healthy brain development. "Physical activity helps the blood flow to the brain and helps move information from temporary memory to permanent memory." As an example she cites the simple action of clapping out a telephone number, which helps children to memorize this number (p. 14). When we realize that young children's brains are still being developed, we must include all kinds of movement activities in the daily curriculum.

Physical activity also helps children develop strong and healthy bodies, builds bones and muscles, improves muscular strength and endurance, helps control weight, decreases blood pressure, and reduces the risk of heart disease, diabetes, and certain kinds of cancer (Staley & Portman, 2000, p. 68). We also know through brain research that "the time to lay the foundation for motor control circuitry in the brain is between the prenatal period and age five" (Miller, 1999, p. 58). In other words, physical activity in early childhood programs is a necessity if we want children to develop normally.

Classroom workers in early childhood programs can and must help young children improve both large- and small-motor coordination by providing activities, materials, and equipment that will give them practice with basic movements. Such activities do not have to be added outside of the regular curriculum. This chapter provides examples of how movement activities can be included and integrated into the learning centers.

ASSESSES CHILDREN'S LARGE-MOTOR SKILLS AND PROVIDES APPROPRIATE EQUIPMENT AND ACTIVITIES

All children pass through the same sequence of stages in their physical growth, but some do it more quickly or evenly than others. Because individual children in a single classroom will be at many different levels of physical development, the teacher should determine at the outset each child's physical capacities to provide appropriate activities to promote this growth.

NAEYC Criteria for Curriculum Standard

Describe how your program meets the following standard:

2.C.04 Children engage in experiences that enable those with varying abilities to have large-motor experiences similar to those of their peers.

Figure 4.1   Large-Motor Checklist

Source: Adapted from Janice J. Beaty, *Skills for Preschool Teachers,* Ninth Edition. Copyright © 2012 by Pearson Education, Inc. All rights reserved.

Permission is granted by publisher to reproduce this checklist for evaluation or record keeping.

Child's Name _____ **Date** _____

_____ Walks up and down stairs

_____ Walks across a balance beam

_____ Balances on one foot

_____ Hops, jumps with both feet over a low object

_____ Runs, gallops, and skips without falling

_____ Climbs up and down a piece of climbing equipment

_____ Crawls, creeps, or scoots across the floor

_____ Picks up and carries a large object

_____ Throws a beanbag/ball

_____ Catches a beanbag/ball

_____ Rides wheeled equipment

To provide relevant help for the children in your care, you need to determine which large-motor skills they already possess, as well as the skills they need to strengthen. It is best to avoid a formal evaluation in which each child attempts the activities as you watch and record. This type of assessment tends to create a win-or-lose situation that makes children self-conscious and less free in their movements.

Instead, make an informal assessment while the children play in the large-motor area, on the playground, or in the block-building area. Observe the children as they go up the steps and into the building. You will soon learn which children move with confidence and which have difficulty. Take a beanbag out on the playground and toss it back and forth to individuals. Put out tricycles for children to ride. You will soon have a comprehensive survey of each child's large-muscle development.

The checklist in Figure 4.1 includes the large-motor skills you will want your children to perform. Copy it onto a 5-by-7-inch card for each individual and check off items as they are accomplished in the natural environment of the classroom and playground. Add the date after each skill to keep a record of the children's accomplishments.

The activities you plan as a result of this assessment should not necessarily be singled out for a particular individual. There is no need to focus attention on an awkward child. All the children can benefit from practice with large-body movements. But you will want to be sure to involve children who need special help in particular activities.

Inclusion

Children with special needs should be included in all of the movement activities. Observe them to see if special accommodations need to be made or if they can handle the activities on their own. For example, children with visual impairments may be helped with bright colors, musical cues, or partners. Children with physical challenges may be helped with larger-than-usual manipulative materials, sitting instead of standing, or touching before participating.

As Sanders (2002) reminds us, "Research and experience confirm that young children do not necessarily develop physical skills simply through play. Thus creating opportunities for children to participate in planned movement experiences is critical to physical skill development" (p. 10).

Walking

Although most preschool children seem to walk with no trouble, uncoordinated children may not walk smoothly. They need as much practice as you can give them. By playing walking games with small groups of children, you can make this practice fun for all. Play "Follow the Leader" with different kinds of walking: tramping, striding, tiptoeing, strolling, shuffling, marching, and waddling. You need to say aloud the kind of steps you are making as you walk. Then have the children also say what they are doing. For example, "Tramp, tramp, tramp, shuffle, shuffle, shuffle," and so forth. Do this both inside and outside of the classroom.

If a child always walks on tiptoe, Pica (2008a) suggests playing a game in which everyone walks on heels only; or stick bottle caps to the heels of their sneakers and have children make noise as they walk. If a child doesn't swing his or her arms when walking or running, tie a streamer to each wrist and challenge the child to make the streamers move back and forth (p. 49).

Books as Lead-Ins to Walking Activities

This text also uses books to lead children into learning activities as noted previously. Every book you have can lead the children into such activities if you use your imagination.

In *Rap a Tap Tap Here's Bojangles—Think of That!* (Dillon & Dillon, 2002), the famous African American tap dancer Bojangles dances along city streets to one-line rhymes at the bottom of each page. Read it to a small group and show them the pictures of his movements. As you reread it, have them put on hats and walk with yardstick canes. Or have a pair of children at a time do the walking, tapping, and hat tipping while the rest clap out the rhythm of the rhyme.

Other books as lead-ins to walking activities:

Do Princesses Wear Hiking Boots? (Coyle, 2003)

How Do You Wokka-Wokka? (Bluemle, 2009)

Children also love to copy the movements of animals. Are they familiar with mammoths from TV and the movies? In the book *Mammoths on the Move* (Wheeler, 2006), these huge lumbering beasts go on their annual migration. You can have a small group at a time move around in a circle while you read the story slowly. Children can swing their tusks (arms) slowly as they clear the tundra of snow, and then step, stomp, march, and tromp across the frozen ground and swim across rivers. Even allow a couple of bulls to spar, butt, and clash if they can do it in a friendly manner.

Dinosaurs are also all the rage with youngsters these days. One of the best picture books for dinosaur movements is *Saturday Night at the Dinosaur Stomp* (Shields, 1997). Each of several species of the beasts tramples, tromps, plods, or flies in for the big bash. After rereading it several times, have the children choose a yarn necklace with the name or sticker showing the dinosaur they want to be. Then as you read it, they can do their stomping one by one in a dino parade. Play an appropriate tape or CD, or use a drum to beat out the rhythm. Body action chants give children another way to participate. Make up your own chant with the children's help, or use the following one. Be sure they say the chant as they move, to activate the brain as well. For children unable to move, have them move your plastic dinos as they chant:

Dinosaurs, dinosaurs,	Pterodactyl fly, fly, fly;	Dinosaurs, dinosaurs.
See them clump;	Here comes the huge	Fade away;
Dinosaurs, dinosaurs,	Tyrannosaurus rex;	Flop right down
Thump, thump, thump;	See him trample,	Till another day.
Allosaurus leap so high;	Stretch, stretch, stretch;	

Another walking activity involves cutting out and mounting a trail of contact paper stepping-stones on the floor and having the children step from one to another. Some teachers prefer to use stepping-stones of floor tile squares or carpeting instead. Walking up and down stairs calls for coordination and balance. Children can also make their own stairs with large hollow blocks pushed together. If you don't have music, use a drum, tom-tom, or tambourine to beat out the rhythm as the children walk. Can the children clap as they walk to a beat? Then have them trot, tiptoe, or stamp to the beat.

Balancing

To make any kind of movement with confidence and stability, children must be able to balance themselves. They must maintain body stability while being stationary as well as during movement. To promote stationary balance, play a different "Follow the Leader" in the classroom. You be the leader, demonstrating how to stand on one foot, then shift to the opposite foot. If you have large hollow blocks, have children balance on a horizontal block and finally very carefully on top of a vertically placed block. Can anyone do it?

Another stationary balancing activity involves pretending to be animal and bird statues. Large pictures of animals placed around the room at the children's eye level will help them choose which animal to mimic. They might choose to be a bird dog pointing, a heron standing on one leg in a frozen position, or a frog getting ready to hop. Let someone count out loud to find out how long they can hold their poses. Or have one child pretend to be one of the pictures and let the others guess which one.

Activities to promote balance while moving involve the traditional balance beam. This can be purchased from a school equipment company or made by placing blocks in a row. Children can practice walking across the wide side of the beam and then the narrow edge. Children should walk on the balls of their feet and not their heels. Have them balance on the beam walking forward and then try sideways or backward.

For another walking balance activity, the teacher can cut out vinyl adhesive footprints and handprints and fasten them on the classroom floor in a series of "baby steps," "giant steps," "frog hops" (i.e., both hand and footprints), and "tiptoes" for the youngsters to follow during "Follow the Leader."

Inclusion

Also include "crutch marks," "cane marks," and "wheelchair tracks" for everyone to follow while using this equipment. Don't limit this activity to children with disabilities. Everyone should try it. Children like to invent their own balancing challenges. "Ice skating" with feet on wooden unit blocks or "skiing" down a gentle block ramp they have built can give them wonderful practice with arms out to the side for balance. Children too unstable to accomplish skating and skiing on their own can do it with a partner who holds on.

Hopping/Jumping/Leaping

Once children have learned to balance on one foot, they can try hopping. The hopping movement is done on one leg. At first have youngsters practice hopping in place on one leg and then on the other. Then they can try moving forward with their hops. Make a hopping trail across the room just as you did for balancing. Place several single right footprint cutouts in a row on the right side of the trail. Then place single left footprints in a row on the other side. When children come to these, they will have to hop first on the right foot and then on the left foot, again on the balls of their feet rolling down to their heels.

Children do jumping with both feet together.

Jumping is the same as hopping, only with both feet together. Children can try to jump in place, to move forward, to get over something, or to get down from a height. Then have them try to jump over the "river" you create on the classroom floor with two strips of masking tape for the "riverbanks." Keep the banks close together at first, but widen them as the children improve their jumping skills. Encourage them to jump with both feet together and not to leap across with one foot. Once children develop the skill of jumping over lines, let them try jumping over a unit block with both feet together.

Children also enjoy jumping down from a height. You may want to use a mat for a landing pad. Jumping off a low chair is high enough for 3- and 4-year-olds. One teacher found that her children liked to measure and record their jumps. She planned a "jumping jack period" once a week in which each child from a small group jumped off a low wooden box; another child marked the landing spot; and together they measured the length of the jump. This was recorded on a "jumping jack chart." The children tried to better their own previous record, rather than seeing who could jump the farthest. Avoid competition in physical skills with young children because it discourages those who have trouble accomplishing activities.

Pica (2006) tells us, "When children jump like rabbits and kangaroos, they develop muscular strength and endurance, and depending on how continuously they jump, cardiovascular endurance" (p. 16). At the same time they are learning concepts such as high/low, up/down, slow/fast. Brain research has shown that children learn best by experiencing such concepts physically.

Leaping is easier than jumping for most children. It is done from one foot and can carry the child farther than a jump. Children can pretend to be deer leaping through a forest or runners leaping over hurdles.

Running/Galloping/Skipping

Because most preschool children seem to do a great deal of running, we sometimes take this form of locomotion for granted. Pica (2008b) points out: "When the child begins to run, he won't automatically achieve a mature form simply because he's able to walk well. Because running is a much more demanding skill, gravity will once again prove to be a challenge, as will posture and coordination" (p. 45). You will need to give everyone many opportunities for running. Keep track on your accomplishment cards of who runs well and who does not run much at all.

Although children who can run well spend a great deal of time doing so, uncoordinated children need special practice. But when you plan running games, be sure all the children are included and encouraged to run. Games on the playground or in the gymnasium can include "Follow the Leader" and relay races. Avoid traditional games where certain children have to wait to be chosen and often are the last to be picked. Avoid emphasizing competition with its winners and losers. Instead, praise the efforts of each child. If someone is declared the "winner," it may very well discourage a slower child, who will not want to participate in an activity for fear of being a sure "loser." Yet this is the child who needs the most practice.

Galloping is a combination of a walk and a leap. The child takes a step with one foot, then brings the other foot behind it and leads off with the first foot again. In other words, one foot always leads. Children enjoy pretending to be horses and galloping around the room to music or tambourine beats.

Skipping is a much more complex skill. It is a combination of a step and a hop. Although most children do not master this skill much before age 5 or 6, some 4-year-olds will want to try it. You can have them hop on one foot, then the other, and do it over and over. If they don't catch on, tell them to try it later when their hopping gets better.

Books as Lead-Ins to Leg and Feet Actions

In *Ready, Set, Skip!* (O'Connor, 2007) a little girl who can perform all kinds of skills feels sad because she cannot skip like the other kids. Simple colorful illustrations show all the things she can do: leap, creep, twirl, and skate. Her mother shows her how to hop on one foot, then the other. That is skipping, says her mother. She tries it and it works! (For age 4 and up.)

Other books with leg/feet actions:

Oh, Look! (Polacco, 2004)

Snip Snap! What's That? (Bergman, 2005)

Climbing

Climbing can be done with legs or arms or both. To ensure the safety of the children because of the height involved, purchase commercial materials from reliable firms. Any homemade climbing equipment (including lofts) needs to be tested carefully before children use it.

Wooden indoor climbers include wooden jungle gyms, rung ladders, and the climbing house. Metal indoor climbers include nesting climbers of different heights that can stand alone or be used to support a walking board, a horizontal crossing ladder with wooden sliding boards. Indoor climbers are usually movable, rather than anchored to the ground like those on outdoor playgrounds. For safety's sake, classroom workers need to stand nearby when children are using them. Thick pads or mats should be placed underneath in case of falls.

Outdoor climbing equipment includes metal dome climbers, satellite climbers, jungle gyms, molded plastic climbers, giant snap blocks, rung ladders, rope ladders, link chain ladders, and cargo nets, to mention a few. The equipment the children use outside should not include large-size playground pieces. Not only is large equipment dangerous for 3-, 4-, and 5-year-olds, but the skills required for use are beyond the capacity of most young children. Outside climbing equipment should be anchored firmly to the ground and cushioned underneath with either wood chips, bark, sand, or other soft materials.

Books as Lead-Ins to Climbing Activities

A popular fingerplay may serve for classrooms without climbing equipment. "Itsy Bitsy Spider," an all-time favorite nursery school fingerplay, is in picture book form as *Itsy Bitsy Spider* (Toms, 2009). It can easily be converted to a whole-body action chant rather than a fingerplay. Better still, bring in a small ladder or a kitchen stepstool and have the children climb up and down, one at a time, while you hold the ladder and everyone else says or sings the verses.

Giant snap blocks promote creeping and climbing indoors and out.

Crawling/Creeping/Scooting

The crawling movement is made with the body flat out on the floor, with arms pulling and legs pushing. Children can pretend they are worms, snakes, lizards, beetles, caterpillars, or alligators. They can crawl to spooky music from a tape or record player or to tambourine or drumbeats that the teacher makes. They can also pretend to be swimmers who are swimming across a river or lake (the room). You can read or tell the class a story about some creature and ask the children to move like the creature. You might play music while they are moving.

Creeping, in contrast, is done on hands and knees, with the body raised above the floor. Some children have difficulty creeping in a cross pattern (i.e., moving the opposite arm and leg in unison). If this is the case with any of your children, give them many opportunities to practice. Have them creep across the floor of the block-building area with a few blocks on their backs. Can they make it without losing the blocks? Put a few more blocks on the backs of any children who want to join in this unusual block pickup game. Have a child or two stationed at the block shelves to unload the creepers as they arrive. If the blocks on the floor are already close to the shelves, have the block carriers crawl around in a circle before they give up their loads.

Children can also pretend to be any one of a number of animals as they creep: cat, mouse, possum, tiger, lion, dinosaur. They can creep to music or drumbeats.

They can creep through tunnels made from cardboard boxes, card tables, or two chairs tipped forward with their backs together. Commercial creeping equipment includes plastic barrels and fabric or foam tunnels. You can create an obstacle course around the room for creeping only, with the path marked by masking tape. Children can pretend to be an animal or a mountain climber as they creep through the course.

Scooting is done by sitting, kneeling, or standing on a movable piece of equipment and pushing it along with one or both feet. Children can also sit on a piece of cardboard and push themselves backward across a polished floor with their feet. Commercial scooter boards are for children to sit on and push with their feet or hands to move the caster wheels on the bottom. Skateboards are actually scooters. But young children do better by sitting and pushing rather than standing on skateboards. Small scooter vehicles with two wheels at each end are appropriate for preschool children who can learn to balance and steer. Some trikes are moved by children's feet on the floor rather than by pedals. Children also like to push themselves around on large wooden vehicles. It is excellent exercise for leg muscles.

Picking Up/Carrying

Use hollow blocks or something similar for the children to pick up and carry one by one. When all the blocks have been moved in one direction, reverse the course. This exercise helps children develop arm and back strength as well as stamina. Children can also carry large pillows, plastic basins, empty cartons, chairs, mats, and large toys. Make up a story about it. Have them build a castle or a fort.

Throwing/Catching

Adults who believe children will naturally develop physical skills on their own should observe to see how many can throw and catch. They may be surprised at how few children are able to accomplish these basic skills. A great deal of practice is necessary for young children to become skilled at the arm and hand movements of throwing and catching. Catching is the more difficult of the two. For children to experience success in your classroom, start with something large and lightweight, for example, a beanbag, a foam ball, or a beach ball. Young children usually catch with both hands and their bodies. To develop catching skills, you can throw children objects like yarn balls, Nerf balls, beach balls, and beanbags at first. Later use smaller rubber balls.

Children can throw to one another, to the teacher, up in the air, or at a target such as a carton or a preschool-size basketball basket. Children can perfect their underhand throwing skills with other objects, such as rings and ring-toss targets. Beanbags can also be thrown into a wastebasket or at a cardboard carton with a clown's open mouth on it.

A giant ball like the heavy-duty tumble ball can be used inside or out for children to roll, bounce, or carry. "Who can carry this giant ball across the playground?" was one teacher's challenge. Another class liked best to somersault over the ball—with the teacher's help. They were soon lined up to take a turn.

Books as Lead-Ins to Playing Basketball/Baseball

Small preschool-size basketball baskets make it possible for young children to learn to shoot "hoops" these days. Although boys may dominate a basket out on the playground, give the girls a chance at your indoor basket as well.

> The book *Hoops with Swoops* (Kuklin, 2001) shows simple cutout action photos against a white background of the African American woman's basketball star Sheryl Swoops: jumping, catching, stepping, shooting, and making a basket. Have each of the children try copying her moves with a small basketball. Use a digital camera as each one performs an action, and soon you will have your own book of "hoops."

For children younger than 5 years old, games with rules are often beyond their abilities. But with so many little leagues and community teams for younger and younger children, even preschoolers want to get involved. Books that encourage such youngsters to prepare for the time they will be old enough to play baseball include Luke Goes to Bat (Isadora, 2005), about Luke, the little African American boy who wants to play stickball with the neighborhood kids during the 1950s but strikes out when he is finally given the chance. He retreats to his rooftop overlooking Ebbets Field at night and imagines his hero, Jackie Robinson, hitting a home run. Then he actually finds a ball on the roof and knows it is the home-run ball Jackie hit.

Other books as lead-ins to playing baseball include:

Hit the Ball Duck (Alborough, 2006)

Just Like Josh Gibson (Johnson, 2004)

Rainy Day! (Lakin, 2007)

Riding Wheeled Equipment

Tricycles and wheeled equipment help young children learn the skills of pedaling and steering at the same time, a coordination skill. Some centers have halls that can be used for riding activities. Others have sidewalks outside. Keep track not only of children who accomplish pedaling a trike easily, but also those who never try it. Use the color of their clothes as a cue to involving them in trike riding without embarrassing them (e.g., "Now is the special trike time for all the children wearing blue shirts"). Give anyone who is having trouble a hand in getting started and making the trike go. (See Chapter 1 for bike-riding children's books.)

Making Plans for Individuals

Once your assessment of a child is complete, begin planning for his or her continued physical development. As previously mentioned, do not single out a child who has a

Figure 4.2   Duane's
Large-Motor Checklist

Child's Name _____ *Duane L.* _____   **Date** _____ *4/15* _____

___✓___ Walks up and down stairs

___✓___ Walks across a balance beam

___✓___ Balances on one foot

___✓___ Hops, jumps with both feet over a low object

___✓___ Runs, gallops, and skips without falling

_____ Climbs up and down a piece of climbing equipment

_____ Crawls, creeps, or scoots across the floor

_____ Picks up and carries a large object

_____ Throws a beanbag/ball

_____ Catches a beanbag/ball

___✓___ Rides wheeled equipment

---

particular need, but instead plan a small-group activity that will address the particular need and include that child. Focus on a skill the child already possesses. Whenever possible, begin with the strengths of a child to help develop an area of need. For example, see 5-year-old Duane's Large-Motor Checklist, shown in Figure 4.2, which was prepared by his teacher on a 5-by-7-inch card.

The teacher was surprised at the throwing/catching results, because Duane's running and jumping skills were better than average and he was such an active boy. He seemed to love balls and would try hard to throw and catch, but without much success. It seemed strange that his arms were not as strong or coordinated as the rest of his body. A conference with his parents revealed that Duane's right arm had been injured in a car accident, and although it had healed, he did not use it as well as he should be able to. It embarrassed him not to be able to keep up with his friends in ball games.

The teacher decided to find a physical activity that would help to strengthen Duane's arm. She discussed the problem with a physical education teacher, who suggested playing with a preschool-child-size tetherball. It worked very well, because Duane enjoyed any kind of ball game. This particular activity was so new to the whole class that no one was any better at it than anyone else. As the teacher noted on the back of Duane's card, he spent a great deal of time playing tetherball, and his arm became much stronger.

ASSESSES CHILDREN'S SMALL-MOTOR SKILLS AND PROVIDES APPROPRIATE MATERIALS AND ACTIVITIES

Small-motor coordination involves using the fingers with dexterity to manipulate objects. This is also known as eye–hand, visual–manual, fine-motor, or perceptual-motor coordination. It is an important skill for young children to develop as a prerequisite for learning to read and write from left to right and to use a writing tool effectively. Children who experience difficulty in these checklist areas sometimes

Figure 4.3 Small-Motor Checklist

Child's Name _____   **Date** _____

_____ Inserts a puzzle piece

_____ Zips a zipper

_____ Twists, turns implements

_____ Pours a liquid without spilling

_____ Strings beads

_____ Cuts with scissors

_____ Cuts with a knife

_____ Pounds nails with a hammer

_____ Traces objects with crayon, felt-tip pen

_____ Writes with an implement

_____ Paints with a brush

exhibit a lack of small-motor coordination. Young boys frequently show less dexterity with their fingers than do girls of the same age. As with girls and large-motor skills, the lag may result from inherent genetic differences, but encouragement and practice in small-motor activities nevertheless benefits both boys and girls.

Small-Motor Assessment

Children's small-motor abilities can be assessed using a checklist, as were large-motor skills. Copy the Small-Motor Checklist (see Figure 4.3) onto a card for each child. Observe and use the checklist to assess the children's small-motor skills as they play naturally during classroom activities. Be sure to provide the necessary small-motor activities for children who need help in a particular skill and for other children as well. Do not make a fuss about developmental lags certain children may exhibit. Everyone has his or her own timetable for development. Individual differences in young children are to be expected.

Inserting

Small-motor activities help establish handedness in young children. Most of the children will already have exhibited a preference for either right- or left-handedness by the time they enter a preschool program. Note which hand a child uses more frequently and help the child strengthen handedness through manipulative games. Do not try to change a left-handed child. You can best help the child by providing opportunities to become proficient with the left hand. Talk with parents about this, especially if parents are trying to change the left-handedness.

Picking up small objects with the preferred hand helps children develop and strengthen their handedness. This activity also promotes eye–hand coordination, allowing children to manipulate the object they are viewing. It further helps strengthen finger muscles that will eventually be needed for grasping a writing implement.

Teacher-made sorting games are especially helpful in this area. In addition to promoting manual skills, sorting games help children develop cognitive concepts such as sorting and matching according to size, shape, or color. Use pasta shapes, buttons, poker chips, golf tees, or nuts. Shoe boxes and plastic margarine containers are handy accessories for these games. Each shoe box can contain a separate game. Label each empty margarine container with the picture and name of the item it should contain. Then cut a hole in the top large enough to permit the item to be dropped in. Have one extra container to hold the entire assortment of items. Label the outside of the shoe box with an illustration of the items so that children can identify separate games.

To begin, the children pour out the collection into the top of the shoe box for ease in sorting. Once they have finished the fun task of dropping the items through the holes in the proper container tops, they should remove the tops to see how accurate they were in their sorting. If the game has captured their interest, they can pour the items back into the top of the shoe box and sort them over and over. You will recall that repeating a task again and again means the youngsters are at the mastery level of exploratory play.

Many commercial games also promote finger dexterity: wooden puzzles with knobs on each piece, Legos, pegboards, lacing boards, stringing beads, bristle blocks, slotted wheels, Montessori cylinder blocks, and shape inlays. Puzzles require the same finger skill: picking up and inserting an item into a space. The first puzzles for young children are the large wooden ones with only a few pieces to be inserted into a cutout wooden frame. Children who have never assembled a puzzle are more successful when each puzzle piece represents a whole item rather than a part of an item in the picture. Check your puzzles carefully. You will need a wide selection because of the children's range of abilities.

It is important at the beginning of the year to have puzzles that new children can complete successfully. If they have had no previous experience with puzzles, you may need to sit with them for encouragement or for actual help until they complete the puzzle. They may have no clue about how to do it. Take turns with them at first, finding a piece and inserting it yourself. Then tell them to find a piece and encourage them to try it out until they discover where it fits.

A wide range of commercial puzzles is available, but you can also make your own. Enlarged photographs of each child can be glued or laminated to vinyl poster board and then cut into puzzle pieces with a modeler's knife. Store the pieces in separate manila envelopes with a picture label on the front. Do not put out the puzzles for use until pictures of everyone are available. It is too distressing for children to find that they have been left out.

Zipping

You can observe and record how children zip their own clothing, or you can make or purchase a zipper board. Cut the zipper and plenty of cloth around it from an old skirt or jacket. Then fasten the two sides to a board. Don't forget to sand the wood so that there are no sharp edges.

Twisting/Turning

Different small muscles are developed to accomplish the skills of twisting or turning something with the hands. You can help by giving children opportunities to use tools like eggbeaters, food mills, or can openers in their cooking activities or water play. Start collecting small plastic bottles with screw-on tops. When you have several, wash them out and put tops and bottles in a shoe box for the children to try to put together. They must practice the additional skill of matching sizes before they can screw on the tops successfully.

You can also make or purchase a board with bolts of different sizes protruding through the surface, with a container of nuts the children can screw onto the bolts. Squeezing oranges for orange juice is another activity that promotes the twisting and turning skill—if children use a hand-operated juicer. Have children make their own orange juice for a snack.

Pouring

Children need the practice of pouring liquids. Do not deprive them of it by doing all the pouring yourself. Use small pitchers for snacks or lunches, and the children will be able to pour their own juice and milk. Even programs using pint or half-pint milk cartons should empty these into small pitchers for the children to use on their own. Be sure to have plastic bottles and pitchers in the water table as well. You may also want children to experience pouring something other than a liquid. Let them pour rice from a pitcher to a bowl and back again. Salt and sand are other pouring possibilities.

Stringing Beads

These days stringing beads can be more than an exercise in small-motor development or eye–hand coordination. It can become a surprising multicultural enterprise that can bring children closer to Native Americans, Egyptians, Africans, Italians, and people all over the world who make and string their own beads.

Books as Lead-Ins to Bead-Stringing Activities

Start by reading the children *A String of Beads* (Reid, 1997), the story of a little girl and her grandma who spend the story sorting out store-bought beads, making their own, learning where different beads come from, and finally stringing them into marvelous necklaces for everyone to wear. The book illustrations are as dazzling as the beads themselves.

The youngest children should continue to string mainly the easy-to-handle large wooden beads on thick shoelace-type strings. Older preschoolers can sort out and identify flat store beads that Grandma calls "disks," ball beads she calls "spheres," long round beads she calls "cylinders," and long tube beads she calls "bugles."

The youngsters may want to sort and string them by size or shape or even by color. Some beads are large seeds from Amazon jungles, and others are seashells from tropical waters. Native Americans carve animal-shape beads called "fetishes." Bead stores and hobby shops display a wide variety these days. Your children can make their own colorful beads by dyeing pasta of various shapes with food coloring and then stringing them on yarn for bracelets, anklets, or ponytail holders. Or they can squeeze and twist polymer clay of different colors into long rolls that they cut and roll into beads with holes made by a toothpick.

Another book as a lead-in to bead stringing activities:

White Bead Ceremony: Mary Greyfeather Gets Her Native American Name (Watkins, 1994)

Cutting with Scissors

There are several ways to help children who have not yet learned to cut. Show them how to hold the scissors with their favored hand. If they are left-handed, provide left-handed scissors. Then hold a narrow strip of paper stretched taut between your two hands for the child to practice cutting in two. Once the child can do so without difficulty, have another child hold the paper and let her take turns holding and cutting.

On another day, show the child how to hold the paper in her own hand and cut with the other hand. Let her practice on different kinds and sizes of paper, including construction paper, typing paper, and pages from old magazines. Finally, draw a line

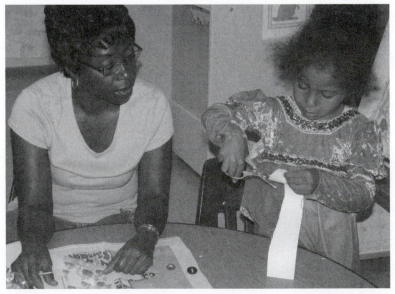

Show the child how to hold scissors in one hand and paper in the other.

on a sheet of paper and let the child practice cutting along a line. For fun as well as practice, have children cut up colored ribbon into small pieces for confetti.

Later, have a cutting day at the emptied sensory table after you place paper scraps and old magazine pages in it. Tie several pairs of scissors with lengths of yarn to the table and turn interested children loose during the free-choice period to "cut up a storm."

Cutting with a Knife

Young children can also learn to handle knives safely. Not only does cutting with a knife provide excellent small-motor coordination practice, but it is also a highly satisfying adult-type skill for young children to accomplish. You can start with table knives and soft items. Children can learn to hold the knife in one hand with the sharp edge of the blade down while holding a peeled hard-boiled egg, cooked potato or carrot, or peach or pear with the other hand. They may have to make a sawing motion to get started. After they have learned to control a table knife, they can begin learning to use a sharp paring knife for cutting the same kind of soft items. Eventually they should be able to help prepare food for a snack such as raw carrots, apples, or celery.

Using a vegetable scraper is another satisfying skill for children to learn. Carrots are best to begin with, but children will eventually be able to peel potatoes successfully. These are real experiences rather than games or simulations, and children understand the value of such skills because they have seen grown-ups do them. It gives children great satisfaction to realize that they too can take part in the adult world. Their teachers can feel satisfaction as well, knowing that cooking experiences provide excellent opportunity for children to develop small-motor control.

Other cooking tools such as shredders, graters, grinders, and melon ballers are also valuable for small-motor development. Have children make their own melon ball fruit cups for snacks from different kinds of melons.

Holding and Hammering

To pound a nail with a hammer takes well-developed eye–hand coordination even for an adult. Let children practice at the woodworking table with soft materials at first, such as plasterboard or ceiling tiles and large-headed nails. They can pound pieces of tile or wood together, or they can pound objects such as plastic foam onto a board. Small adult hammers are more effective than children's toy box tools.

Be sure to bring in several slices of tree stumps and have children pound nails into them for the fun of pounding and the practice of eye–hand coordination. Put out two cross sections of tree stumps along with hammers and nails on a classroom table to create a favorite pounding center for both girls and boys. Nails go into tree stumps easier than into boards. Put towels under the stumps to cut down on noise. When the top of a stump is covered with nails, you can have it sliced off with a chain saw, thus getting it ready for the next pounders. Once children learn the knack of holding and hammering, they can make designs or even pound their initials on the stumps. As Leithead (1996) points out, "Hammering nails is an excellent perceptual motor exercise, an effective way for young children to build eye-hand coordination. As soon as children are old enough to grasp a hammer, few can resist the urge to pound nails" (p. 12).

Too many teachers fail to see the need for providing a woodworking center like this, perhaps because they have little interest in hammering themselves. Instead, we need to put aside our adult considerations and plug into children's own strong interests, whenever we are fortunate enough to discover them, to support children in their own development.

Books as Lead-Ins to Hammering

In *I Love Tools!* (Sturges, 2006), a boy and girl help their father and mother build a bluebird house. A line of rhyming text on each page describes what they do as they hold each tool. An outline of each tool appears on the end pages. Have your children make their own outlines after using particular tools by tracing around each one and telling how they used it. You can collect their outlines and make a tool book for everyone to look at.

Other books as lead-ins to hammering:

Henry Builds a Cabin (Johnson, 2002)

Thump, Quack, Moo: A Whacky Adventure (Cronin, 2008)

Printing and Tracing

A writing area offers children a chance to experiment with holding all kinds of writing and marking tools: pencils, pens, crayons, chalk, and markers. They can make scribbles, mock writing, print, and make signs. Be sure to have paper, pads, tablets, notebooks, file cards, and envelopes on hand. Mount alphabet letters, signs, and symbols in the area. Have geometric shapes for youngsters to trace around.

Then let them practice their scribble writing and printing of letters. Some children may want to try printing their names. Others will want to trace around various objects. This is excellent practice for strengthening finger muscles and developing control of the writing tool. (For more information on emergent writing, see Chapter 6).

Planning for Individuals

Once the small-motor assessment has been completed, you and your classroom team will have a better idea of the activities you should provide. Although you will be planning for individuals, be sure not to single them out as being deficient in these skills. Because a classroom of children exhibits such a wide range of motor abilities, all the children should be accepted as they are. If one child's development seems to lag behind another's, simply involve that youngster in activities that will strengthen that particular skill. As with large-motor activities, all the children can benefit from the small-motor activities you provide for certain children.

Inclusion

Youngsters with physical impairments should be encouraged to accomplish as many large- and small-motor activities as they can. Once you have assessed what they are able to do, you will be ready to make appropriate individual plans to challenge them, just as you do for all the children.

 ## PROVIDES OPPORTUNITIES FOR CHILDREN TO ENGAGE IN CREATIVE MOVEMENT

Movement, Music, and Brain Research

Whether or not you are a dancer yourself, it is imperative that you provide opportunities for young children to move to music, to engage in creative movement, the structured or free-flowing movement activity done to music and percussion beats. As Davies (2000) reports, "Music synchronizes the right and left hemispheres of the brain. Researchers report that the left hemisphere analyzes the structure of music, while the right hemisphere focuses on the melody. The hemispheres work together when emotions are stimulated, attention focused, and motivation heightened. Rhythm acts as a hook for capturing attention and stimulating interest. Once a person is motivated and actively involved, learning is optimized."

Where does creative movement come in? We learn that researcher Howard Gardner (1993) recognizes multiple intelligences: verbal-linguistic, logical-mathematical, musical-rhythmic, visual-spatial, bodily-kinesthetic, interpersonal, intrapersonal, and naturalistic. He theorizes that people learn through combinations of these intelligences. Furthermore, Hap Palmer (2001), the well-known composer of animated songs for young children, suggests that "music and movement, with its rich combination of rhythm, melody, lyric, motion, and group interactions, touches each of these areas" (p. 14).

Observe how your children move when you play particular tapes or CDs, or beat out a rhythm on a drum or tom-tom. Do some of them let loose and run around wildly? Do some make up their own steps? Do some look to you to provide the directions on how to move? Do others pull back and refuse to join in? The Creative Movement Checklist in Figure 4.4 lists some of the movements children may engage in during a creative movement activity. Copy the checklist on file cards for individual children so you can observe where their strengths lie and what areas need strengthening.

Palmer noted when he first began teaching that young children's attention span was so short and their squirminess so ceaseless, that he decided to write songs for them combining music and movement. One was "Alphabet in Motion" from his recording *Can a Jumbo Jet Sing the Alphabet?* (1998). As the children sing or listen to the bouncy tune, they must also "do your moves one by one." A, arch, B, bend, C, clap, D, droop, and so on. He explains that "as the children shift from shape to shape, they develop balance, coordination, strength, and endurance; learn the elements of movement; and gain a sense of mastery of their bodies and spatial relationships. They

Figure 4.4 Creative Movement Checklist

Child's Name _____   **Date** _____

_____ Engages in structured movement activities led by teacher
_____ Makes body movements while standing in one place
_____ Makes creative movements while moving across the floor
_____ Participates in group movement activities
_____ Moves creatively on own or with another child
_____ Moves to imitate particular animal, person, or object
_____ Uses prop (ribbon, scarf, hoop, balloon) to do creative movement
_____ Engages in unstructured movement activities
_____ Moves freely to music or drumbeats
_____ Has favorite song(s) for doing creative movement
_____ Uses arm, hand, leg, feet, body movements to express feelings
_____ Makes up own movements

develop confidence and self-esteem because their ideas and creative expressions are valued" (pp. 13–14).

Rather than calling these activities "creative movement," a new movement variant known as "movement-based learning" has become popular in many preschool programs across the country. It is based on the concept that, as Sanders (2002) tells us, "Movement experiences are a primary source for learning by young children. For example, as children participate in locomotor activities of walking, galloping, and skipping, they also have opportunities to express their emotions, participate socially with others, and think about and gain an understanding of how movement takes them in a variety of different directions and pathways in space" (p. 9).

To help children become involved in such movement, you can start with having them stand in one place while moving their bodies. Play CDs with words that tell children what to do, or you can sing out a movement word to any instrumental music. Accept any movement children make, whether or not it illustrates the movement word. They may not have any idea what a word like "arch" means, or how a person should make an arch movement with their bodies. If you are modeling the word "arch," children may copy your movement or they may not. The purpose of the activity should be enjoyment of moving to music, not the accuracy of the movements. Once children get the idea, have them move across the floor doing movements to the words they hear. Basic movement words include *walk, run, jump, hop, gallop, leap, roll, crawl, clap, bend, wiggle, swing, shake, turn, twist, tiptoe, freeze.*

When children are familiar with the basic movement words, Palmer suggests adding some colorful variations such as "bounce, bubble, crinkle, crouch, dangle, dart, fling, glide, lunge, melt, ooze, plunge, quiver, rise, scamper, scatter, wobble, and zoom" (p. 14). Children love fun words like this and should soon be making up silly motions to go with them. You and they can also make up motion words to familiar tunes and then act them out while singing (e.g., to "Row, Row, Row Your Boat"). Or wake up children's bodies after a nap, says Dow (2010), by moving their tongues, twisting their heads, shrugging their shoulders, until every body part is moving.

Have children move to music in any way they want.

Books as Lead-Ins to Movement Activities

Reading the right book may help to get the children started making motions that illustrate words.

In *Chicken Dance* (Sauer, 2009) two chickens, Marge and Lola, try to win the barnyard talent contest for tickets to see singer Elvis Poultry. A flock of heckling ducks try to stop them. But Elvis Poultry makes them part of his act and the cows take care of the ducks. Have your children reenact this goofy story with all its wacky moves.

Other books as lead-ins to dancing include:

The Jellybeans and the Big Dance (Numeroff & Evans, 2008)

Twist with a Burger, Jitter with a Bug (Lowery, 1995)

Once they understand the concept of moving to music, children can begin on their own with something familiar to imitate in their own way. Let them move like familiar animals. Put up pictures of dogs, cats, birds, rabbits, mice, guinea pigs, snakes, beetles, and spiders around the room at the children's eye level. Let them try to move like one of the animals. Do it to appropriate music such as Palmer's *Sally the Swinging Snake* or *Walter the Waltzing Worm* CDs from Constructive Playthings (phone: 1-800-832-0572) or *Kids in Motion Creative Movement* or *Shake Rattle and Rock* CDs from Lakeshore (phone: 1-800-778-4456). Encourage the children to watch how classroom pets move. But be sure you accept whatever movements they make as their own interpretations of animal motions.

One or two children may want to demonstrate their own movements while the rest clap a rhythm. You may want to tap on a tambourine or drum as children move like animals. Follow the rhythm established by the children rather than making your beats faster or slower. Young children have difficulty following an outside beat at first and usually move to their own inner rhythm.

For children who are still uncomfortable with creative movement, read them *Giraffes Can't Dance* (Andreae, 1999), about Gerald Giraffe with his crooked knees and long skinny legs whom the other animals make fun of at the Jungle Dance because he is so awkward—until he finds he can twirl and swirl and dance to the moon music all by himself. Or as he tells the others, "We all can dance, when we find the music that we love." Have your children bring in some of their own music.

Movement Props

Awkward or shy children can often be enticed to engage in movement activities if they have an object to hide behind as they make their motions. Ribbons, scarves, paper streamers, hula hoops, or balloons can be used. Then the focus is on the object, not the child. Put out movement props like these for everyone to choose from. Have them move around the room slowly at first and then faster to music or tambourine beats.

Some children may feel free enough in the beginning to move like trees in the wind, like ocean waves, or like lightning in a thunderstorm, but others need to try more structured movements before they feel free enough to let go and move creatively. Have them try to move across the room silently, then heavily, then slowly, and then rapidly. Can they be a plane moving down the runway, an eagle soaring through the sky, or a skier going downhill? Eventually they may be able to express emotions such as happiness, sadness, anger, and surprise in their movements.

Sometimes the music itself creates the mood for movement. Play nature music and see what happens. Some of the CDs available include Palmer's *Quiet Places* from Constructive Playthings or *Sea Gulls Music* from Lakeshore. Do not force children who are not ready to join the group. The activity should always be fun for individuals, not embarrassing. The children who do not participate can observe and may later try out their own movements. Hold the hand of a nonparticipant and swing it back and forth while watching the others move to music. Leave animal pictures and movement props in the music corner along with music CDs and a tambourine to encourage children to try out body movements on their own.

Inclusion

Clements and Schneider (2006) give many suggestions for including children with special needs in movement activities. They say, "The combination of using imitative and movement exploration permits more children to succeed through their natural ability to copy, imitate, and follow the teacher" (p. 23). Children with visual impairments may be able to follow brightly colored props and floor markings or to move with a partner who can assist them when necessary. Children with hearing impairments should have the teacher in front of them with cue cards, hand signals, or facial expressions. Children with physical disabilities may need more space for wheelchairs and more time for using braces, crutches, or prosthetics (pp. 23–24).

SUMMARY

To promote children's physical development, determine their needs at the outset and then provide appropriate materials and activities. The use of checklists of large- and small-motor skills and creative movement for informal observation of children helps the classroom worker to assess more clearly each child's motor ability. Then the teacher can make individual plans based on the child's needs by using the child's strengths as a starting place.

A child with a particular developmental need should not be singled out for special help but should be included in small-group activities designed for that child but worthwhile for others as well. Getting children involved in creative movement activities is also described, with special focus on starting with movement words. Ideas for imitating animals, using books to motivate movement, using props, moving to music, and making up their own movements help children develop physically and creatively.

Ethical Dilemma

Some of the parents were upset when a child with cerebral palsy was admitted to the program. They felt too much of the staff's time would be focused on that child, to the detriment of their own children. What should you do?

LEARNING ACTIVITIES

1. Read one or more of the Suggested Readings or view Web sites. Then add 10 cards to your file with specific ideas for helping children develop large- and small-motor skills. Include the reference source on each card.

2. Assess each child's large-motor skills using the checklist in Figure 4.1.

3. On the basis of your results, construct a game, bring in materials, or conduct an activity to promote the large-motor skills of children who need help as suggested in the text.

4. Assess each child's small-motor skills using the checklist in Figure 4.3.

5. On the basis of your results, construct a game, bring in materials, or conduct an activity to promote the small-motor skills of children who need help as suggested in the text.

6. Help a child who has not been involved in creative movement by standing in place and moving to a "movement word."

7. Read a book to the children that will lead them into a creative movement activity as described in the text.

8. Reread the suggestions under "Inclusion" for helping children with special needs. Use one of the movement ideas with such a child and record the results.

SUGGESTED READINGS

Bernath, C., & Masi, W. (2005). Movin' and groovin': Integrating movement throughout the curriculum. *Dimensions of Early Childhood, 33*(3), 22–26.

Dow, G. B. (2010). Young children and movement: The power of creative dance. *Young Children, 65*(2), 30–35.

Gellens, S. (2005). Integrate movement to enhance children's brain development. *Dimensions of Early Childhood, 33*(3), 14–21.

Pica, R. (2009). Can movement promote creativity? *Young Children, 64*(4), 60–61.

Pica, R. (2006). *Moving and learning across the curriculum.* Clifton Park, NY: Delmar/Thomson/ Cengage.

Sanders, S. W. (2006). Physically active for life: Eight essential motor skills for all children. *Dimensions of Early Childhood, 34*(1), 3–10.

WEB SITES

American Alliance for Health, Physical Education, Recreation, and Dance
http://www.aahperd.org

Body, Mind and Child Radio
http://www.bodymindandchild.com

Early Childhood Music and Movement Association
http://www.ecmma.org

Human Kinetics
http://www.HumanKinetics.com

National Association for Sport and Physical Education
http://www.aahperd.org/NASPE

PE Central
http://www.pecentral.com

President's Council on Fitness, Sports & Nutrition
http://www.fitness.gov

CHILDREN'S BOOKS

Alborough, J. (2006). *Hit the ball Duck.* La Jolla, CA: Kane/Miller.

Andreae, G. (1999). *Giraffes can't dance.* New York: Orchard.

Bergman, M. (2005). *Snip snap! What's that?* New York: Greenwillow.

*Bluemle, E. (2009). *How do you wokka-wokka?* Somerville, MA: Candlewick Press.

Coyle, C. L. (2003). *Do princesses wear hiking boots?* Flagstaff, AZ: Rising Moon.

Cronin, D. (2008). *Thump, quack, moo.* New York: Atheneum.

*Dillon, L., & Dillon, D. (2002). *Rap a tap tap: Here's Bojangles—think of that!* New York: Blue Sky Press.

*Isadora, R. (2005). *Luke goes to bat.* New York: G. P. Putnam's Sons.

Jenkins, S. (2006). *Move!* Boston: Houghton Mifflin.

*Johnson, A. (2004). *Just like Josh Gibson.* New York: Simon & Schuster.

Johnson, D. B. (2002). *Henry builds a cabin.* Boston: Houghton Mifflin.

*Kuklin, S. (2001). *Hoops with Swoops.* New York: Hyperion.

Lakin, P. (2007). *Rainy day!* New York: Dial Books for Young Readers.

*Lowery, L. (1995). *Twist with a burger, jitter with a bug.* Boston: Houghton Mifflin.

Numeroff, L., & Evans, N. (2008). *The Jellybeans and the big dance.* New York: Abrams.

O'Connor, J. (2007). *Ready, set, skip!* New York: Viking.

Polacco, P. (2004). *Oh, look!* New York: Philomel Books.

*Reid, M. S. (1997). *A string of beads.* New York: Dutton.

Sauer, T. (2009). *Chicken dance.* New York: Sterling Publishing.

Shields, C. D. (1997). *Saturday night at the dinosaur stomp.* Somerville, MA: Candlewick.

Sturges, P. (2006). *I love tools!* New York: HarperCollins.

Toms, K. (2009). *Itsy bitsy spider.* Hertfordshire, England: Make Believe Ideas.

*Watkins, S. (1994). *White bead ceremony.* Tulsa, OK: Council Oak Books.

Wheeler, L. (2006). *Mammoths on the move.* Orlando, FL: Harcourt.

*Multicultural

CHAPTER 5

Advancing Cognitive Skills

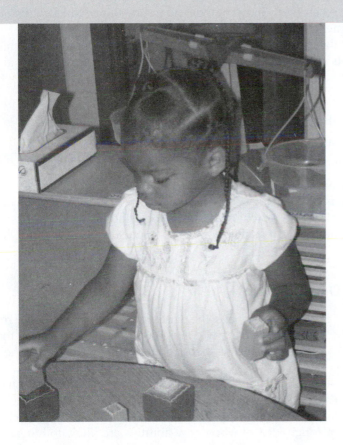

To promote children's cognitive development by involving them in exploring their world

☑ **Specific Objectives**

____ Helps children develop curiosity about their world through sensory exploration

____ Helps children develop basic concepts about their world by classifying, comparing, and counting objects in it

____ Helps children apply basic concepts about their world through high-level thinking and problem solving

C*OGNITIVE Skills* are thinking skills that grow out of children's need to know. In the past, many preschool programs downplayed this important area of child development. Somehow we believed we should not teach children to learn until they entered elementary school at age 5 or 6. The preschool, we declared, should be concerned principally with children's play.

We were right about children's play, but we were very wrong about their learning. Now we know better. Now we realize that young children learn through play. Unlike play for adults, young children's play is not only for their recreation but also for their learning: for their trying out and finding out what makes things tick. It is essential that preschool teachers understand this about children's cognitive abilities: that children develop cognition through their hands-on, playful exploration of materials, animals, plants, fish, birds, and insects, both inside and outside of the classroom. Children need to have the freedom to explore these materials. Plus, they need to do this exploration on their own. Showing them how something works undercuts their cognitive development.

To understand what they are discovering in their sensory exploration, young children form basic concepts about their world. These cognitive concepts help them answer questions such as:

How big is it? (size)

What does it look like? (shape, color)

What kind is it? (classification)

How many are there? (number)

Once they can answer these questions, they are able to apply this information to the world around them, finally making sense of their discoveries. Thus, to promote children's cognitive development, teachers must provide children with all sorts of materials and opportunities, as well as the motivation to pursue this sort of playful exploration.

Pioneers in Children's Cognitive Development

Swiss psychologist Jean Piaget was perhaps the most important of the early researchers to influence the development of early childhood curriculum models in the United States. Figure 5.1 shows the stages he theorized that children follow in their cognitive development.

A great deal of research about young children's cognitive development has taken place since Piaget's day, some of it contradicting his findings. Not all modern researchers agree with his stage theory. As McDevitt and Ormrod (2007) note, "Piaget's stages provide a rough idea of when new abilities are likely to emerge" (p. 158).

This chapter, in fact, proposes that young children can "hypothesize" and "think about thinking" much earlier than age 11. One of his important findings, however, is the fact that children's thinking is not the same as that of adults. Figure 5.1 shows how children younger than age 7 think mostly in concrete terms. For readers unfamiliar with his research, one of his most unexpected findings was that children actively construct their own knowledge. Current brain research confirms this finding.

Whereas Piaget's theories are a description of children's mental development, rather than a model for working with young children, the theories of the pioneer

Sensorimotor Stage (Birth to age 2)

Thinks in visual patterns

Uses senses to explore objects

Learns to recall physical features of object

Does not use objects to symbolize

Develops object permanence (realizes object is there even when out of sight)

Preoperational Stage (Age 2–7)

Acquires symbolic thought (mental images represent actions and events)

Uses objects to symbolize things (e.g., pretends a block is a car)

Is deceived by appearances

Cannot reverse his thinking

Concrete-Operational Stage (Age 7–11)

Can deal with changes of things

Is able to reverse thinking

Understands how things relate to one Another

Formal-Operational Stage (Age 11+)

Can think about thinking

Can think in abstract terms without needing concrete objects

Can hypothesize about things

Figure 5.1 Piaget's Stages of Cognitive Development

Source: Based on Wadsworth, 1989; Beaty, 2006.

Russian psychologist Lev Vygotsky speak directly to the adults who work with young children. According to Vygotsky (1981), cognitive development is caused by an individual's social interactions within his or her environment. Higher mental functions such as logical memory, selective attention, decision making, and comprehension of language are products of psychological tools, or what he calls "signs," such as inner speech (Dixon-Krauss, 1996, p. 11).

Vygotsky agreed with Piaget that children construct their own knowledge. But he believed that cognitive development cannot be separated from its social context. People play an important role by creating the environment and interacting with children. He developed the concept of the *zone of proximal development,* or ZPD, which he defined as the area between where the child is at the moment in mental development and where he might go with assistance from an adult or more mature child. Vygotsky calls the help the child receives in order to progress *scaffolding* (Bodrova & Leong, 2007, p. 8). But for Piaget, a child's cognitive development occurs primarily in interactions with physical objects.

Brain Research

Current research on brain development using brain-imaging technologies has allowed neuroscientists to study how the brain actually develops over the first 6 years. Such research has provided us with increased understanding of developmental periods of dramatic brain growth, as well as how outside influences affect children's brain development.

We now know that *neurons* (brain cells) are the basic material of the brain and responsible for communicating messages within the brain and from the brain to the body (Gallagher, 2005, p. 13). Most neurons are in place before a child is born. The output fiber of a neuron is called an *axon.* The axon sends out information from one neuron to another. Neurons receive this information through input fibers called *dendrites.* The space between the sending axon and receiving dendrite is called a *synapse.* The synapse is thus the communication point between two neurons. The production of synapses and the pruning or cutting back of unused synapses causes the brain to grow and develop (Sprenger, 2008, pp. 10–14.)

After birth, these *synapses* develop rapidly, allowing messages to travel in the brain and information to be processed (Bloom, Nelson, & Lazerson, 2001). Many more synapses are produced than the child will need in order to be ready for use when the child interacts with the environment. When neurons are not used, their synapse connections decrease.

Newberger (1997) tells us: "Positive interactions with caring adults stimulate a child's brain profoundly, causing synapses to grow and existing connections to be strengthened. Those synapses in a child's brain that are used tend to become permanent fixtures; those that are not used tend to be eliminated. Neural plasticity, the brain's ability to adapt with experience, confirms that early stimulation sets the stage for how children will continue to learn and interact with others throughout life" (p. 5).

Positive interactions with caring adults stimulate a child's brain profoundly.

Cognitive Development in Preschool

According to Rike, Izumi-Taylor, and Moberly (2008), it is the richness of a child's experiences that directly affects the development of the brain. They say: "[R]ecent brain and educational research clearly shows these neural pathways can be made richer and stronger through appropriate early care and challenging experiences that take place in carefully designed, nourishing environments" (p. 23). The learning centers you arranged according to ideas in Chapter 3 have set the stage. The activities you and the children carry out can provide the experiences.

All of the activities you offer support children's cognitive development, but science and math are especially important. How do you feel about science and math? Some teachers and staff feel reluctance because they feel unprepared in these fields. Now is the time to overcome such reluctance. You must be able to interact in exciting ways with children's playful exploration of everything around them. Science for preschool children is simply *a process for finding out*. Math provides *the basic concepts to be used in this process*. Together they equip young explorers with the necessary tools for making sense of their world. An exciting prospect, isn't it?

HELPS CHILDREN DEVELOP CURIOSITY ABOUT THEIR WORLD THROUGH SENSORY EXPLORATION

Sensory Exploration

Preschool children are born explorers. Even as infants, they come with all the necessary equipment to be great discoverers: inquisitive eyes, nose, mouth, tongue, lips, ears, fingers, and toes. In addition to such an array of sensory apparatus, each child also starts out with a strong natural drive or curiosity to put this equipment to good use. They want to find out about everything. Young children are forever trying to poke, pry, bite, chew, lick, rub, pinch, sniff, stare at, listen to, or examine playfully in great detail any object or situation they come into contact with. As noted in Chapter 3, we call this initial investigation of new things *manipulation*.

This is how youngsters learn about themselves and their world. They have to touch and test and pull things apart. They may also throw or drop breakable objects, not to be naughty, but to find out what happens when objects hit the floor. Young children are true scientific explorers of their environment. Children between the ages of birth and 6 years explore and take in knowledge best through their senses. "They gain better understanding when they involve themselves in activities that bring them into *direct* contact with the natural world" (Humphryes, 2000, p. 16).

Yet some 3-, 4- and 5-year-olds seem to make no use of their sensory equipment in exploring the world around them. They don't seem to notice anything new or different in the classroom. In fact, they show little interest in their surroundings. Because we know they were born with a great natural curiosity, we can only surmise that somewhere along the way they lost it.

Child's Name_____ **Date**_____

_____ Notices new materials

_____ Investigates new objects

_____ Asks "what," "where," "when," and "how" questions

_____ Wants to know "why" about things that happen

_____ Uses senses (sight, hearing, smelling, touching, tasting) to explore things

_____ Likes to do experiments

_____ Can compare one object with another

_____ Uses science tools (magnets, magnifying glasses, binoculars)

_____ Uses math tools (balance, tape measure, abacus, timers, counters)

_____ Plays matching, counting games

_____ Makes collections, charts, records

_____ Is involved with classroom pets, aquarium, plants, insects

_____ Chooses books about science, counting, animals, plants, ecology

---

Figure 5.2   Children's Curiosity Checklist

Source: From Janice J. Beaty, *Skills for Preschool Teachers,* Ninth Edition. Copyright © 2012 by Pearson Education, Inc. All rights reserved.

Permission is granted by publisher to reproduce this checklist for evaluation and record keeping.

Perhaps their curiosity was mistaken for mischief by the adults in their lives, and they were punished for it. Perhaps adults never took the time to answer their questions or to support their exploratory activities. Whatever the reason, it is now up to you, the teachers, assistants, and student teachers in preschool classrooms, to reawaken children's curiosity and sense of wonder if they have lost it or to direct it toward exploring their environment if they have not.

Assessing Children's Curiosity

What about the children in your classroom? Do they still retain their natural sense of wonder? Do they make comments or ask questions about new materials? Take a moment to observe their actions when they first enter their new environment. Listen also to the questions they ask. The "Children's Curiosity Checklist," Figure 5.2, will help you to observe and assess the curiosity displayed by each of your children. Then you can begin planning activities to promote this important characteristic.

You should soon be able to identify those children with a drive to explore and those who seem to have little interest in the new things around them. It is up to you to provide new and intriguing materials and activities. Then you need to find ways to motivate uninterested children in as many of these activities as possible.

You might begin by bringing in several pieces of tree bark you have found: a piece of sycamore bark (this tree sheds its bark periodically), a piece of maple bark, a piece of shagbark hickory bark, or any one of a number of other tree barks (e.g., white birch, willow, cottonwood, or pine). Do not peel the bark from a tree to cause damage, but instead look for pieces of bark shed naturally or from a broken branch. Place each of three different barks on a piece of colored backing paper on top of the room divider or other flat surfaces in different parts of the room. Then wait to see what happens.

Does anyone notice one of the bark pieces? More than one? If someone points out one, ask them if they can find any others. Be sure to keep track on your checklist of each child who notices these new items, asks questions about them, or handles them. When several children have shown this interest, gather these youngsters into a small group in your science discovery center along with one or two other children who have shown little interest. Then try to extend everyone's curiosity with a few *sensory* questions.

Sensory Questions

Sensory questions ask what things look like, feel like, smell like, taste like, and sound like. They are not questions with a right or wrong answer. Instead, they should engage children in using their senses to explore new things.

Show them one of the bark pieces and ask, "What does this look like to you?" (sight). Accept any answers they give, but keep on asking questions. "What does it feel like to you?" (touch). Pass the bark around. "What does it smell like?" (smell). "What does it sound like when you tap it?" (sound).

Repeat the answers the children give. You might even want to write down what each child says on newsprint or a chalkboard. "Tracy says it looks like a piece of wood. How can you tell, Tracy? . . . She says wood is brown like that and sort of rumply on top. . . . Yes. Ben says it's a scrap of wood. . . . How can you tell, Ben? . . . Oh, your mom collects scraps of wood and leaves for her garden. Okay. . . . Ramon says it feels like wood and smells like wood, but it's really tree bark. Is tree bark wood? . . . How can you tell, Ramon? . . . You're right, Ramon, we do have wood with bark on it right over in our woodworking center. . . . Yes, our tree stumps. Good for all of you for using your eyes, and fingers, and even your noses to find out what it was."

Questions and responses like this start the cognitive thinking processes in yourself and your children. If you do not hear children asking such sensory questions about the new objects you bring into the classroom, start asking them yourself. Your job is to reawaken children's natural curiosity and encourage them to find out things for themselves. But you may need to serve as a behavior model of curiosity to get them started.

Reawakening Your Own Curiosity

Have you retained your own childlike sense of curiosity? If not, you must first reawaken this sense of wonder in yourself. Look around the room when the children are not present and try to see the classroom from their perspective. Get down on your knees for a better view. What is one thing you notice that might attract the attention of a 4-year-old?

Assume that one of the things you notice is wood shavings and curls under the woodworking table. Now pretend you are a new child visiting the room for the first time. What would you want to know about such things if you had never seen them before?

What are they?   Where did they come from?
What do they feel like?   What are they for?

If you are a curious child, you would probably go over and pick up some of the shavings. You might crush one in your hand to see what it feels like or maybe put some on your head for curls and look at yourself in the dramatic play area mirror.

Have any of your children tried doing this? What happens to the wood shavings on the floor? Are they usually swept up and thrown away? Ask your children what they could be used for in the classroom. If the children are learning about recycling things (and they should be), they will be able to suggest some creative uses for such scraps. Does anyone make any of these suggestions?

Put them in the collage basket for art.

Put them in our terrarium.

Put them in the guinea pig's cage for floor covering.

Questions and responses like these start the cognitive thinking processes in yourself and your children. If you do not hear such questions in the classroom, then ask them yourself. What other kinds of questions are the children asking? Get into the habit of writing them down on the "Children's Curiosity Checklist" you are recording for each child.

For example, Ramon asks, "Why do we always have to have orange juice for snack time?" Later he wants to know, "Where is Mrs. Appleton? Isn't she coming to our room anymore?" And still later, "Is this a piece of bark too? I found it under the woodworking table. But it doesn't look like the other bark."

From this record of Ramon's questions and checklist responses, you begin to realize that he is a curious boy who remembers things, notices changes as well as new materials, and wants to find out about them. He is even able to make comparisons about new objects with something he has seen previously. You will want to provide Ramon with further opportunities to explore, or you may want to team him as a model with another child who has not shown this curiosity.

Shelley, however, asks only, "Can I play with the baby buggy now?" a permission question, not a sensory question. She does not seem to notice the tree bark displayed on the science table as Ramon did, nor does she comment on the new arrangement of the dramatic play area.

The questions children ask tell us many things about them. First of all, they tell us if the children are curious. Children who are not curious ask few *how, why,* or *where* questions, or they may not ask any questions at all. If their questions contain few sensory terms, we realize they are probably not engaged in sensory exploration. Then it is up to us to reawaken their curiosity by helping them start thinking in terms of sensory questions. We may need to start the questioning process for such children. Children closely imitate the adult models around them. If we are successful in our own questioning, many of the children may soon copy us.

Open-Ended Sensory Questions

Open-ended sensory questions are the most valuable. They require children to think and imagine and explore with their senses to come up with an answer. The answers to open-ended questions are never right or wrong; they are merely possibilities. They ask a child to look at an ordinary situation from a new perspective—from the point of view of a scientist trying out and testing the object or idea. You do not need to know the answers to these questions at the outset. Instead, you should become familiar with the method scientists use to find out answers. Then together you and the children can be scientists searching for answers to questions about the fascinating objects and ideas in the world around you.

Scientific Inquiry: The Guessing-Game Method (A High-Level Thinking Process)

How do you find out the answers to the questions you and the children have posed? Scientists also begin their explorations of new things or ideas with questions. Then they follow a particular sequence of problem-solving steps to find out the answers. Sprung, Froschl, and Campbell (1985) suggest the following steps:

1. State a question or problem.
2. Predict the answer (a hypothesis).
3. Conduct experiments.
4. Observe results.
5. Make conclusions.
6. Document final results.

You and the children in your care can have an exciting time following this same sequence. Conducting a scientific inquiry is like going on a treasure hunt. Maybe you'll find something, but maybe you will not. Whatever happens, it is the hunt itself that makes the project worthwhile. In other words, it is the *process* of questioning and trying to find out that is most important, and not the *product* or answer. Translated into early childhood terms, the scientific inquiry includes the following steps:

1. Ask the question you want answered.
2. Guess what the answer may be.
3. Decide how to find out and try it.
4. Watch what happens.
5. Talk about what happened and whether your answer turned out right or wrong.
6. Record what you did and what happened.

What scientific inquiry can turn out to be for young children is a wonderful guessing game, just the type of fun activity that they would invent for themselves if

The teacher talks with her class about items the children have brought in.

scientists had not already done so. This is another reason why you as a teacher of young children need to be alert to children's curiosity about things. It could lead you all on a discovery trip you would not want to miss.

One day Jessica asked her teacher, "Why is our aquarium getting all dirty on the inside of the glass?" The teacher could have responded with, "Oh, I guess it needs to be cleaned." But she realized that this was an excellent opportunity for all of them to learn something new through sensory exploration. Although the teacher knew how to take care of an aquarium, she was not sure what was making the glass dirty. Finding out could be a scientific adventure for all of them.

The teacher talked with the children about Jessica's question. Most of them said they thought that the fish were making the aquarium dirty. They all agreed that they would like to find out. The teacher then asked, "What would happen if we took a glassful of water out of the aquarium and let it sit on the shelf? Would the glass get dirty like the inside of the aquarium?"

Some children thought that maybe it would. She asked them why they thought this, but they did not know. Other children, however, were very insistent that the water glass would not get dirty because there would not be any fish in it. The teacher was excited to hear this comment because it told her that these children were really thinking. Whether right or wrong, they had a reason for their answer involving cause and effect, a new concept for many preschoolers.

The teacher wrote down the steps for finding out on a large sheet of newsprint. She left space under each step to record what the children said and did. Although these were preliterate children who did not yet read or write, they were fascinated to see the teacher writing down what they said and then reading it back to them.

1. *Our question:* Why is our aquarium getting dirty on the glass inside?

2. *Our guess about the answer:* The fish are making it dirty.

3. *How can we find out?* Put some aquarium water in a glass without any fish.

4. *Watch what happens. Use your senses.* The glass began to get dirty in seven days. The "dirt" spread over the glass. Jessica says the dirt felt greasy when she touched it. She says it smelled bad too. Ramon says the magnifying glass made the dirt look green.

5. *Talk about what happened. Did we guess correctly?* The glass got dirty without any fish in the water. The fish didn't make the glass get dirty. We didn't answer the question on why it got dirty.

6. *Record what we did and what happened.* Listen to our tape: "Aquarium Water Experiment."

After the experiment was finished, the teacher put a blank tape in the cassette player and had every child who wanted to speak into the microphone and tell what they did and what happened. Then she recorded the date and time, and afterward she labeled the tape "Aquarium Water Experiment."

The children may not have been able to read the words the teacher had written, but they understood what had happened. They were excited to contribute to the tape recording, and afterward they listened to the tape every chance they got.

"What did we learn from our experiment?" the teacher asked. Children made these comments:

The glass got dirty anyway.

The fish didn't make the glass get dirty.

The water smelled bad.

The aquarium is still dirty.

We still don't know why it got dirty.

We need to clean the aquarium.

Don't be too concerned if you do not find out all of the answers. At this stage of their development, children are more interested in the *process* of finding out rather than the results. Finally, Ramon asked, "Why is the dirt so green and slimy? I think the water is polluted." Four-year-old Ramon, with his inquisitive nature and remarkable vocabulary ("green and slimy" and "water is polluted"), was leading them all on a further science adventure. What should they do next?

The teacher brought in a book that might help them find out more: *Pet Care Guides for Kids: FISH* (Evans, 1993). Brightly illustrated with color photographs of fish as well as children setting up various types of aquariums, the book was an instant hit. Although the children could not read it, they could follow the illustrated steps for aquarium care quite easily. The teacher read the words aloud.

Because their classroom tropical aquarium had been started the previous year, these particular children had not participated in the setup process and selection of the fish. No wonder they had shown little interest in the fish tank until Jessica asked her question about the tank getting dirty. Children must have hands-on experiences like this one from the beginning if they are to learn.

Where will their further explorations take them? The sensitive teacher will follow the lead of the children, listening carefully to what they are saying and asking, and then guiding them to find their own answers by using the "guessing-game method" of scientific inquiry. With children like this, such inquiry will surely take them in the direction of learning about topics like these:

How water gets polluted

What makes algae "pollute" the water

How to keep a "balanced" aquarium

How many fish to have

How much food to feed the fish

How snails and algae-eating fish keep the aquarium clean

The list of topics is almost endless when we allow and encourage curious children to take the lead with hands-on exploration of things they can see, smell, hear, taste, and touch.

Equipment and Materials in the Classroom

To arouse children's curiosity, they need something to be curious about. Children will often bring in an interesting item from home or something they have picked up on the way to the center. This can be the beginning of their exploration, especially if you display it attractively as a center of attention.

At the outset, however, it is often up to the adult classroom worker to bring in new materials to stimulate children's curiosity. Set up a special table or counter-top to feature a new or unusual item that you or the children bring and label it the "Discovery Center." Feature a new item every week, placing it on an attractive backing as you did the bark. Add science tools for children to use in exploring the new item: several magnifying glasses, a balance for weighing, a magnet, a measuring tape.

Once you have captured the children's interest in a new object, be sure you are prepared to help children follow up their exploration. For instance, if other children are as intrigued as Ramon was by the bark you brought, you can take them outside to explore living trees by touch. Then they may enjoy doing a bark rubbing by taping light paper against the tree and rubbing the side of the crayon over it.

Before they do the rubbing, ask them a guessing-game-method question. Ask them to guess (predict) what the rubbing will look like. Does anyone guess that it will look like the bark underneath? Because everything in their world is new to them, many are not really sure what will happen when they do something. After their rubbings are finished, have them check to see whether or not they guessed correctly. Prediction questions are excellent stimulators for young children's high-level thinking.

The bark-rubbing activity may start a flurry of art rubbings back in the classroom. If you have set up your art area for children's free access to materials as suggested in Chapter 3, then be prepared to have rubbings made of all sorts of classroom objects, even shoes. The bottoms of sneakers make wonderful rubbings.

Field Trips Around the Building

The immediate environment of the center offers unlimited opportunities for children to explore and discover. Take the children on an outside walk around the building. Give them each a paper bag for collecting anything that strikes their fancy. Take a tape recorder with you to record the sounds of the environment and any questions or comments the children make. Take a digital camera to record the scenes.

Humphryes (2000) suggests, "Observation excursions are fun with all ages of children. While out in a natural setting like your backyard or playground, ask the children to observe one selected item, such as a stream, a one-square-foot microcosm (use a string to mark this), or a cloud, for five minutes. Then ask them: Is it alive? How do you know? What does it feel like? Does it move? What does it do? If you kept it, what would happen? If you stepped on it, what would happen?" (p. 17).

What will you find out? Once again you will learn who are the curious children. You will also find out whether you yourself are tuned in to children and their interests. Was it a child who pointed out the dandelion growing from the crack in the sidewalk, or was it you? Once again you may have to get down on your knees to look at the world from the perspective of a 3-year-old before you can become a behavior model for exploring.

Field trips need not be elaborate, all-day, long-distance affairs. Brief ventures out or around the building are best because this is the environment the children are most directly involved with and want to find out about. Their own personal environment is always more meaningful to children than a visit to a remote and distant site they may never see again.

What else can you do on a field trip? If the children have not already begun to do so, you can start by asking exploratory questions involving the senses: "Close your eyes and what do you hear?" "Does anyone smell anything different?" or "Put your hand on this. What does it feel like to you?" Take photos. Make rubbings. Make a tape recording of the sounds. Take something back with you to the classroom to help children remember, and clarify, and try to understand what they have seen and done.

Have children empty their collecting bags when they get back. Have them talk about what they collected. Perhaps they would like to display the objects by making a collage of them or dictating a story about them. If a new interest emerges out of the experience, plan to follow it further with the children using the guessing-game method.

Inclusion

Don't forget to include all the children in your science investigations. Those who cannot stand or walk can sit inside or out at a "lab" table to record, count, or draw what others bring them.

Books as Lead-Ins to Outside Sensory Exploration

> In *The Looking Book* (Hallinan, 2009) a mother turns off the TV and sends her two boys out to play. She gives each a pair of glasses without lenses that she calls *lookers*. With great excitement they put them on and start looking. Kenny sits down and finds all kinds of twig-things and rock-things and little black bug-things. Mikey finds a stick with a ladybug on it. Bring in some old glasses for your children and see what they can find.

Books as follow-ups to the ladybug experience:

The Beetle Alphabet Book (Pallotta, 2004)

Beetle Bop (Fleming, 2007)

Ladybug Girl and Bumblebee Boy (Soman, 2009)

Face-to-Face with the Ladybug (Tracqui, 2002)

Are You a Ladybug? (Allen, 2000)

The Grouchy Ladybug (Carle, 1996)

One group actually found a ladybug and brought it inside in a collecting jar, to look at more closely with a magnifying glass and then let go. All kinds of questions tumbled out:

What does it eat?	Where does it live?	Is it a good bug?
Where does it go at night?	Will it sting you?	

The children and teacher found answers in the books listed above. But when they read the story *Ladybug Girl and Bumblebee Boy,* they wanted to make their own bug and bee costumes and act out their own stories, which they dictated to the teacher. Someone brought in a ladybug puppet and used it to tell more ladybug stories. Then they wanted to find out about bumblebees. And so it went. Books always lead to exciting follow-up experiences if teachers listen to children's comments and questions. Every learning center in this classroom became involved in the ladybug experience before it was over. The children learned, just like Kenny and Mikey, that you don't even have to wear "lookers." You can see things without them!

HELPS CHILDREN DEVELOP BASIC CONCEPTS ABOUT THEIR WORLD BY CLASSIFYING, COMPARING, AND COUNTING OBJECTS IN IT

As young children begin to explore the world around them, they need to establish some sort of order out of all this incoming data. To make sense of the new information, they need to develop basic concepts about their discoveries. How do they do this? Lind (1996) tells us, "Concepts are acquired through children's active involvement

Child's Name_____ Date_____

_____ Sorts out from a collection the objects that are alike

_____ Matches unit blocks on the floor with block outlines on shelves

_____ Identifies the biggest and the smallest from a collection of toy
        dinosaurs, trucks, animals, or people figures

_____ Identifies the following shapes by finding examples in the
        classroom: circles, squares, rectangles, triangles

_____ Identifies the following colors by pointing out clothing the
        children are wearing in red, yellow, blue, green, orange, brown

_____ Counts to 10 or to 20 accurately

_____ Counts the number of children present accurately

_____ Counts out accurately different numbers of items according to written numerals

Figure 5.3   Cognitive Concepts Checklist

Source: From Janice J. Beaty, *Skills for Preschool Teachers,* Ninth Edition. Copyright © 2012 by Pearson Education, Inc. All rights reserved.

Permission is granted by publisher to reproduce this checklist for evaluation and record keeping.

with the environment. As they explore their surroundings, they actively construct their own knowledge" (p. 17).

As they learn to sort the things they find into categories, compare them with one another, and count them, children develop the basic cognitive concepts that make the world around them meaningful. To keep track of each child's development of basic concepts, use the checklist in Figure 5.3, "Cognitive Concepts Checklist."

Sorting and Classifying Objects That Are Alike

Adults often take for granted that preschool children know intuitively how things are alike and what makes them different. This is not usually the case. Young children see objects in general before they notice specific details. You can help them develop perceptual and thinking skills through activities that encourage them to find the objects in a group that are the same. They will be looking at the items in general and not for specific details at first. You may need to help them determine what makes the objects alike.

You may also need to provide many concrete three-dimensional games and materials (never workbooks or ditto sheets) in the manipulative/math center that call on children to sort out the items that are alike. Plastic sorting chips, disks, cubes, beads, dinosaurs, bears, or fruits are a few of the collections available. Or bring in your own sorting collections of buttons, seashells, or nuts, along with a basket to hold the collection and several plastic bowls for sorting.

Look around the classroom for items children can sort for likeness. What about the figures of people in the block center? How will they sort these? Maybe by families? Science collections of seashells, leaves, bark, or rocks can also be sorted. Have children sort small items that are alike into egg carton sections and cover the cartons with clear wrap for display. Leaves that are alike can be pressed between sheets of clear contact paper. Bark pieces that are similar can be placed in a pocket wall chart or fastened to a bulletin board.

By now you should be talking with the children in terms of the categories for sorting, not merely "sorting for likeness." "Josh, can you sort out all the *arches* on the block shelves?" or "Juanita, can you bring me a basket of plastic *fruit* from the house area food cupboard?"

Sorting should eventually lead into matching for your youngsters. From the start they should be able to match the unit blocks on the floor with the ones on the shelves or by the block outlines you have mounted on each shelf. Many programs keep their manipulative areas stocked with commercial matching games all year round. But you may want to wait before putting out matching boards or lotto games until everyone has learned to sort by likeness.

NAEYC Criteria for Curriculum Standard

Describe how your class meets the following standard:

2.F.03 Children are provided varied opportunities and materials to categorize by one or two attributes such as shape, size, and color.

Comparing Objects by Size, Shape, Color, and Number

Size

Children's brains seem to pay special attention to the relationships between things. The concept of size is one of those relationships. Learning to understand the property of size helps children make sense out of the new things they are discovering. There are various orders of size, usually thought of in terms of opposites: big-little, large-small, tall-short, long-short, wide-narrow, thick-thin, fat-thin, or deep-shallow. Direct comparison of objects based on these aspects seems one of the best ways for youngsters to learn size.

Most young children can relate to only one aspect of an object at a time when they are comparing. First they must learn a single concept, say the concept of big, through many games and concrete activities—never with worksheets. Next they can contrast that concept with the concept of little. But don't confuse them by bringing in the concepts of thick-thin or short-tall all at the same time. Give them plenty of time to learn the concept of big as contrasted with the concept of little through all sorts of real three-dimensional materials before moving on to another pair of opposites.

It makes sense to start with objects in the classroom environment that children can compare and contrast in size. Children need to handle the objects, play with them, and use them in different situations. For instance, can they compare the plastic animals from the accessory shelves in the block center?

Because children seem especially attracted to dinosaurs, why not start with them? Does your collection of plastic dinosaurs show differences in size? Sets of "museum dinosaurs" make this differentiation. Read a dinosaur story to a small group while they hold some of the plastic dinosaurs. Can they tell which is the biggest animal? The smallest?

Books as Lead-Ins to Comparing Objects

> In the brilliantly illustrated *Dinosaur Roar!* (Stickland & Stickland, 1994), each double page shows two dinosaurs portraying opposite characteristics against a white background. One roars, but the other squeaks. A little one is fierce, but a big one is meek. Your child "dinosaurs" can act out these new words and concepts to make them meaningful.

Other follow-up dinosaur books as lead-ins to size activities:

Dino Pets (Plourde, 2007)

The Dinosaur (Milbourne, 2004)

Dinothesaurus (Florian, 2009)

Some teachers may feel that bringing dinosaurs into the classroom can create an out-of-control situation of wild running around and pretend attacks. But children need to learn that only certain dinosaurs were fierce. Others were meek and mild. We as teachers need to plug into children's strong interests like this to help them learn appropriate classroom behavior as well as new concepts.

Shape

Research shows that children develop concepts in a certain sequence. The concept of shape is one of the earliest to be formed. Young children begin to discriminate objects on the basis of their shape quite early. Be sure to focus on this one concept alone when you first present the idea of shape. Then give children plenty of time and opportunity to make the concept a part of their thinking process before going on to the next concept. In every instance, activities should involve familiar concrete objects at first, not drawings on ditto sheets or in workbooks.

Young children learn through exploring with their senses, but the way they do it is far different from adult scrutiny of a new object. As we have noted, children learn through play. They try out a new object or new concept in a playful way to see what it will do or what they can do with it. Be sure your shape activities provide children with all kinds of hands-on play opportunities for this learning. For children to learn about circles, squares, rectangles, and triangles (the basic shapes), they will, for example, need to play circle games, sing square songs, make triangle hats, and have shape-hunting contests, lotto games, and puzzles. They can pick up unit blocks on the basis of their shapes, or mold clay circles and squares, or saw wood into different shapes.

Present one shape at a time, for instance, the circle, by filling the classroom with circles. Put paper circles of different sizes, but all the same color, as well as circular cookie cutters and play dough in the art area. In the manipulative area, put out games, puzzles, table blocks, stringing beads, and plastic wheels and gears featuring circles. At the writing table, supply circular forms to be traced, circle peel-offs for decorating envelopes, and the magnetic alphabet letters that are mainly circular in form. Place hula hoops in the large motor area for children to dance in. Place large vinyl adhesive circles on the floor of the block area to see if they will motivate building in circles. Can children find the round cylinder blocks that have circles on their ends?

Simple shape-finding field trips with a small group of children can also support the classroom shape activities. One program took its children down a city street to search for circles. They took photos of stoplights and street signs. Then the children wanted to go into a used car lot. Although such a site held little interest for the adults, it was a new world for the youngsters to explore. The teachers were surprised to find these youngsters more interested in the car wheels than the cars. This should not have been surprising because young children tend to focus on things at their own eye level. Back in the classroom, the youngsters found circle blocks to use for the snap-block cars they built.

Color

Although young children seem to talk about colors first, research shows that they develop the color concept shortly after that of shape. Children also name the colors before truly understanding what they mean. You can help them to clarify color concepts just as you did with shapes by starting with one color at a time and providing them with all kinds of games and activities relating to that color. One color at a time, start with the primary colors of red, yellow, and blue because young children seem to recognize these colors most easily. Then, one at a time, introduce the secondary colors of green, then orange when Halloween comes, and pink for Valentine's Day.

To introduce colors successfully, you can relate each color to the children personally in terms of their clothing, shoes, socks, or hats. As you feature each color, check to see which children are wearing that color. Ask if anyone can wear that color tomorrow. Have them all make paper hats from colored construction paper in the color of the day. Have a color-finding search throughout the classroom, looking for that particular color among the block people, animal figures, dinosaurs, dolls, and dress-up clothes. Bring in different color stickers for the children with that color to wear and to attach to the dolls and toys displaying that color. Once they know the primary colors, they can play sorting games based on color. Some are also based on size and shape.

Books as Lead-Ins to Color Activities

My Crayons Talk (Hubbard, 1996) is just the sort of book young children like to laugh over. Its child-size crayons and funny girl narrator have a purple crayon shouting yum, bubble gum, and a brown crayon wanting to play mud pie day. Children can choose a crayon of their own and draw or scribble an appropriate colored picture.

Children can play sorting games based on color and size.

Other books as lead-ins to color activities:

Red Sings from Treetops: A Year in Colors (Sidman, 2009)
Beautiful Blackbird (Bryan, 2003)
De Colores, Bright with Colors (Diaz, 2008)

Inclusion

Children with disabilities can learn color concepts along with the other children. Set up the activities as you do everything in your classroom so that children with physical and mental impairments can participate. A child in a wheelchair, for instance, may not be able to do a color dance on her feet, but she can listen to you read the book *Color Dance* (Jonas, 1989) and afterward do her own "color dance" on the wall or ceiling by shining a flashlight covered with colored cellophane to the music you play for the other children who dance on their feet.

Mixing Colors

What about mixing colors? Children often learn by accident that mixing two colors together makes a new color. You can set up your easel with only two jars of different primary colors for children to experience this surprising occurrence. On another day, put out muffin tins with water and two food colors. Later put two finger-painting colors at the same table, or two different crayons with paper. What colors will they be? Red and yellow mixed together make orange, red and blue make purple, and blue and yellow make green, the most dramatic change of all.

Light from flashlights covered with colored cellophane (red, yellow, and blue) can also be mixed together by shining their colored lights on the wall. Have the children predict (guess) what the new color will turn out to be before they start color mixing. The youngest children may not know the names of the secondary colors, but they can guess something.

Number

Children encounter the spoken form of numbers long before they understand their meaning. Many can count accurately to 10 or even 20 without having the slightest idea of what 6 or 13 means. They are counting by rote, in other words, repeating a memorized series of number words in a given sequence. This is how learning to count begins. Nursery rhymes such as "One, Two, Buckle My Shoe" encourage this skill.

Is counting really so important for young children? Yes. As Unglaub (1997) puts it, "Why is the ability to count rationally so important? If unable to count rationally, the child is not ready to start more formal activities that lead to mathematical concepts" (p. 48)—in other words, high-level thinking and problem solving.

Hirsh-Pasek and Golinkoff (2003) report that Gelman found that most young children by the age of 3 have extracted and use the following important counting principles entirely on their own (pp. 48–51):

1. The one-to-one principle (that one item gets only one number)
2. The stable order principle (that numbers occur in a fixed order)
3. The cardinal principle (that the number of items is the same as the last named number)
4. The abstract principle (that anything can be counted)
5. The order-irrelevance principle (that it doesn't matter where you start counting)

How did children do it? According to Hirsh-Pasek and Golinkoff, "This knowledge is based on things that children like to do on their own, unsupervised, with whatever objects they can lay their hands on. In other words, children come to these principles through that magical activity we call *play*" (p. 48). Sounds a lot like the natural way children emerge into literacy, doesn't it? Thus these findings remind us not to make counting or learning numbers a chore, but a game: interesting, exciting, and fun.

There is nothing wrong with counting by rote. Have children count from 1 to 10 again and again. Sing it; clap it; dance it; march it; wave it; twirl it around until everyone gets dizzy and falls down! Then get up and do it again. That is how young children learn: by participating in physical concept games and repeating them over and over. If they make a mistake in the name or number order, never mind. They will soon refine their counting skills when they hear you and the others doing it correctly.

Once children have learned the number names and number order from 1 to 10, they are ready to count things. It may still not be clear to them that 3 means three

Children love to play board games where they can count each move.

objects and 7 means seven things. They need to learn the concept of *one-to-one correspondence*—that is, that each number represents one thing. They can start by counting their fingers. How many are there? Don't assume young children know the answer is "5" on one hand or "10" on both (and it may not be for every child). Then they can count the small group of children in each curriculum area. From there they can practice counting dolls, toys, or any other three-dimensional object that is meaningful to them. Be sure they touch each object they count. Children also love to play board games. Bring in simple ones where a player must make an object move a certain number of spaces.

Soon children will go beyond 10 to 20 in their counting. Have the children help you take attendance every day by touching each child in the morning circle as they count. At this point give the youngsters all sorts of counting opportunities. This is not a chore for them; they love it. They may want to count their science collections, for example. How many nuts, shells, leaves, or stones do they have?

One class became so engrossed in counting things that they insisted on counting the ants in the class's ant farm! How could they possibly keep track of all the busy little creatures as they scurried around? Every time children started a count, they lost track of either the ants or the numbers. The teacher suggested that they "tally" each ant that was visible by making a mark. Soon children were going around with pencils and file cards recording a mark for each ant and then counting up the marks.

If your children like to tally, give them each a file card and a paper punch. They can punch one hole for every car or truck or bicycle that goes by the window. Another day, paste a picture of the kind of vehicle on each card and take the children out for a vehicle-tallying field trip. Don't forget to have them count up their final tally.

This may be the time for you to change the signs in the activity areas that regulate the number of children allowed in each. Put number symbols beside the stick figures you may be using. Later, remove the stick figures altogether and use only numerals. Can the correct number of children go to each of the centers? Try it and see. Have someone count how many children are in each center and see if this number agrees with the number sign in the center. As you can see, learning to count is important for children.

Once children have learned to count and you have introduced true number symbols, be sure to give them many opportunities to play with numbers using concrete materials and three-dimensional numbers. Toy cash registers, toy money, stepping-stone numerals, plastic numbers, and computer number games are appropriate activities.

Books as Lead-Ins to Number Activities

Children themselves can also be each number and perform the actions read by the teacher about climbing to the top of the apple tree. What can they climb up? A step stool? You can also purchase the tree set from Lakeshore Learning Materials (1-800-778-4456). Remember, if you don't have this book as a lead-in, make up your own game and story:

Chicka Chicka, 1, 2, 3 (Martin & Sampson, 2004) is a follow-up to Martin and Archambault's much-loved alphabet book *Chicka Chicka Boom Boom.* Like the alphabet letters, the numbers in this book climb up a tree and then fall down. Some classrooms make a free-standing tree wrapped in burlap that Velcro-backed numbers can climb. The tree can also be mounted on a wall with construction paper that number stickers can climb, or on a refrigerator door with magnetic numbers.

Other books as lead-in's to counting activities:

1 2 3 Pop! (Isadora, 2000), superheroes

Click, Clack, Splish, Splash (Cronin, 2006)

Max Counts His Chickens (Wells, 2007)

HELPS CHILDREN APPLY BASIC CONCEPTS ABOUT THEIR WORLD THROUGH HIGH-LEVEL THINKING AND PROBLEM SOLVING

As young children develop their cognitive abilities through scientific inquiry, they need to learn to apply these concepts to the natural world around them. Preschool is the right time and proper place to awaken young children's awareness of Earth's precious gifts: the air they breathe, the water they drink, the food they eat, the plants and animals they depend on, and the beauty around them. They also need to learn that the world around them deserves proper use and protection from abuse.

Holt (1992) notes, "We should emphasize the environment and the role humans play in consuming, or protecting Earth's riches. Each child's interactions with the world affect not only the child but the world. . . . Concepts of balance, harmony, cooperation, and interdependence can be found in any nature study. Teachers should make certain that these ideas are emphasized: These are ways in which all forms of life coexist and support each other naturally. It is an emphasis long overdue" (pp. 132–133).

Following a Broad But Simple Concept

In making year-long science plans for preschool children, teachers should start with a broad but simple concept that can last much of the year and take the class in a variety of directions depending on their interests. This concept should involve one of the gifts that the earth gives us, so that children can in turn look for ways to protect that gift and to show their appreciation. For example, some programs focus on this broad but simple concept: *We use water.*

To get them started with their science planning, one teacher started out by asking her co-teachers and the children to think of all the uses we make of water. "We drink water" was the first use. Sometimes children's long drink of water is also for looking and for listening to the splash. "We wash our hands in water." But we know that children are doing more than just getting their hands clean. They are fascinated by water. They love its sound and its feel. Wise teachers use children's intense interests to provoke further thinking.

Another teacher started her science activities for the year by bringing in a container of bottled water from the supermarket for her Discovery Center. This in turn stimulated the children to wonder and talk about other kinds of water. They filled a glass of water from the tap and visually compared the bottled water with the glass of water. They looked the same. The teacher then asked a small group who had gathered around the display table, "How else can we tell if there is any difference between bottled water and tap water?"

After one child suggested smelling the two types of water, everyone wanted a turn. All decided there was a difference that was hard to put into words, but they agreed that the tap water smelled stronger. Next, of course, everyone had to taste the two. Most of the children liked the bottled water better. The teacher recorded the results on newsprint after each child's name.

When the teacher asked what other kinds of water are around us, someone mentioned pond water in the nearby park, which eventually led to a picnic and field trip to the park. While at the pond, the children became excited when they saw mallard ducks swimming around. They wanted to feed the ducks with their sandwiches. But a park attendant told them that too many people feeding too much bread to the ducks was creating algae that made the pond polluted. He said that ducks were healthier when they fed on underwater plants as they were supposed to.

Underwater plants? Could they find any? This got the children wondering about what else grew in the water. As they walked around the pond, Anthony found some tadpoles and collected them in a jar of greenish pond water. Tracy saw some underwater plants near shore, and the teacher let her pick a few stems and leaves. But other children found discarded paper cups and plastic trash on the shore and put them in their collecting bags. They talked to a man fishing from the shore, but he told them that he didn't catch much anymore because the pond was so polluted.

Back in the classroom the children decided to make a collage out of the trash they had collected by gluing it to a poster board and then displaying it on the wall for all to see. The collage said *LITTER IS NOT BEAUTIFUL* and *PLEASE DO NOT LITTER IN THE PARK*. Tracy put her stems into Anthony's jar of pond water for the tadpoles to rest on and to see if they would grow.

Next, the children wanted to know what else uses water. Jordon told them that Whiskers, the classroom guinea pig, drinks a lot of water. He was the guinea pig attendant for the week. They wanted to know how much water. So Jordon used his number-concept learning by recording with a paper punch and file card each time he filled its drinking bottle. Then children began talking about how much water their pets drank at home. The teacher set up a chart for recording their pets' names and how much water they drank every day. Everyone was surprised when Jasmine announced that her pet was a plant, a geranium, and that it too drank water.

"How can you tell?" they asked. "That's a good question," replied the teacher. "How can we tell if a plant drinks water?" she asked. "Give it a glass of water!" laughed one of the children. The next day the teacher brought in a white flower (a carnation) and a stalk of celery. The children helped her set up a water-drinking plant experiment by pouring about an inch of water into two glasses and mixing it with red ink. The teacher then trimmed the stems of the flower and celery and stood each one in a glass of the red liquid. "What do you think will happen?" she asked. The children tried to guess (hypothesize), but they really were not sure.

They watched the two plants closely all morning, but nothing happened. Then Jasmine noticed a change. The liquid was going up into the flower and celery! They were turning red! By the end of the day, both had turned a definite pinkish red color. "Do plants drink water?" the teacher asked them. "Yes!" was the loud reply. "And what if the water is polluted with red ink?" she wanted to know. A vigorous discussion followed. Preschool children like this can begin to think seriously about what is happening to water, one of the Earth's priceless gifts. But the children were not finished with their inquiry into using water. As the days and weeks went by, they asked and tried to answer other questions:

How does water get polluted?

How can we stop pollution from getting into water?

How can we get pollution out of water?

They learned that the green in the pond water was actually tiny plants called algae. Although algae was not pollution, too much algae was a sign of pollution in the water, perhaps from lawn fertilizer or from bread thrown to the ducks. They also learned that too much algae could make fish die. They remembered the algae that grew on the inside of their aquarium and how they found ways to get rid of it.

From the book *My First Green Book: A Life-Size Guide to Caring for Our Environment* (Wilkes, 1991), they used ideas about making a natural filter in a flower pot with blotting paper, sand, and gravel to make Anthony's green pond water clean. Some of the green came out. They also tried using an aquarium pump and filter to clean the water, and finally they added one of their aquarium snails to help clean their pond water.

Inclusion

Be sure that everyone in the class gets to go on field trips, even brief ones outside the building. Children with special needs can be accompanied by a volunteer or family member when necessary.

Problem Solving, Divergent Thinking, and Metacognition

In this chapter children have used high-level thinking to solve the problems they have faced. They used creative thinking, often called *divergent thinking* because it diverges from conventional thought that looks for the right answer and follows rules invented by someone else. Divergent thinking, in contrast, invites children to brainstorm solutions. What are all the possible ways of doing anything, of solving any problem (Jones & Cooper, 2006, p. 12)? Divergent thinking creates new ideas or uses materials in new ways. As children use this type of thinking they will be using many of the concepts they have developed previously, especially classification and number. According to Jensen (1998), "The single best way to grow a better brain is through challenging problem solving" (p. 35).

Part of such problem solving also involves what is known as *metacognition,* that is, thinking about thinking. Adults seem to do this automatically. They pose questions in their minds like these: What will happen next? What if I do this? How do I know this? Why should I do this and not that? Do children also reflect on their own thinking? They need to stop and think before they answer a question or start in a new direction. You can help engage them in metacognition by asking some of the questions just posed.

In the carnation experiment the teacher asked the children, not what will happen, but "What do you *think* will happen?" when she stood the white flower in a glass of red liquid. The children hypothesized (guessed) a number of possibilities, which the teacher wrote down. The teacher then asked them why they thought so. Most had based their answers on their own knowledge or experience. They were not just shouting out an answer but were thinking about different possibilities. Picture books can also help children think about thinking if teachers choose appropriate books and pose thought-provoking questions.

Books as Lead-Ins to Thinking Activities

Magic Thinks Big (Cooper, 2004) tells about a very large cat, Magic, who sits in front of an open door in his home on a lake in Maine. He thinks about his next move. Should he go out or stay in? He goes over all the reasons for each move in his mind, illustrated by pictures in the book. As you read it, ask the children what they think Magic will do and why.

If You Give a Cat a Cupcake (Numeroff, 2008) is another in this author's well-loved series about what will happen, "If you. . . ." Have your children hypothesize what will happen next in each hilarious episode. If you give a cat a cupcake, she'll want sprinkles to go on it. Then what? Children will need to think about their sorting skills. What goes on a cupcake? Sprinkles. If you give her sprinkles, what will happen? After the reading, have the children make their own book about things that happen in the classroom. "If you put one more block on your block tower. . . ."

Problem Solving with Computer Programs

How do you feel about computers in the preschool classroom? Some feel that computer programs are too abstract for preschool children, who learn best from concrete materials. Others feel that they take children away from more appropriate learning activities or that children cannot understand computer software before they reach Piaget's concrete operational stage (see Figure 5.1).

Regardless of these concerns, most classrooms today do contain computers. They can be important learning tools if used properly and with appropriate software that leads to concrete classroom activities. The strength of the computer is its ability to bridge concrete and abstract thinking and learning, say Fischer and Gillespie (2003, p. 88). In fact, Clements and Sarama (2003) also note, "Research indicates that computers can facilitate both social and cognitive interactions—each to the benefit of the other. Good software encourages children to talk about their work as well as engage in more advanced cognitive types of play than they do in other centers" (p. 35).

The key to successful computer use with young children is in the software you select. CD-ROM programs that feature activities to strengthen cognitive skills such as sorting, classifying, sequencing, patterning, counting, and one-to-one correspondence for problem solving are best. Choosing programs based on your popular picture books quickly ties them to classroom activities. How will you know which ones to choose?

One method is to log on to a Web site that evaluates current programs for young children. For example, *http://www.amazon.com* is a good children's software site to evaluate and order programs. Several of the recommended CD-ROMs to support children's cognitive development that are also tied to children's books include these titles:

Arthur's Computer Adventure Ages 3–7

Curious George Preschool Learning Games

Disney's Ready for Reading and Math with Pooh

Dora the Explorer Adventure 3 Pack

Dr. Seuss: Pre-School–1st Grade

Because these titles change frequently, you need to search the Web personally when you are ready. Other sources of software programs are computer, appliance,

Figure 5.4 Choosing
Computer Software

- Tried out by teacher ahead of time
- Based on children's books being used
- Attractive to young children
- Easily used and understood by children
- Teaches appropriate skills
- Tied to learning center activities

and office supply stores. Besides choosing programs with high ratings as already suggested, you need to be aware of other criteria as shown in Figure 5.4.

Most young children love to use the computer. Some have used it at home. Others can't wait to try out this adult-type machine. You can introduce a new program to two children at a time who are seated in front of the computer. Cooperative learning like this is the best way to begin. They will learn to take turns, to talk with each other, and to teach each other how the program works.

Be sure to install the program ahead of time and have it ready for use. Use only one program at a time until all the children are thoroughly familiar with it. Most software contains several games and activities at increasing levels of difficulty. You need to try it yourself to see which game they should start with. Some children may need

Children can teach each other how the program works.

to watch how you do it at first. Then let them try it. Turn off the program and let them start it up over and over.

At first everyone will want a turn. Have a sign-up sheet for them to sign or scribble their names. After the novelty wears off, two children at a time can use the computer during the free-choice period by wearing the two computer necklaces you have provided. Be sure to have on hand the extension activities that each computer program supports: books, blocks, counting games, or manipulative materials appropriate for cognitive learning.

SUMMARY

This chapter looks at ways to promote children's questioning, exploring, and problem-solving skills to develop their thinking skills. Early childhood classroom workers need to be aware of how children use their senses to explore the world around them and need to set up classroom activities to promote such exploration. Using children's natural curiosity, or reawakening it if they seem to have lost it, should be the classroom workers' goals in the cognitive development of young children. Bring in new materials, pose questions about them, take children on nearby field trips, and make photo, taped, and written records of happenings. Be sure to record the questions that children are asking so that you will know what direction to take next in planning cognitive activities.

Help children develop cognitive concepts such as that of size, shape, color, and number, using them to classify and compare objects in the classroom. Children can then apply these concepts to the exploration they are already doing as

they collect, compare, and record interesting materials in their environment. Interact with the children yourself to stimulate their curiosity and encourage them to think and solve problems. Help them to become "guessing-game scientists." Become one yourself.

Ask open-ended sensory questions and listen to the way the children answer them. This should give you clues as to what direction you should take next with individuals and the group in providing them with new cognitive activities or extending the present ones. Read books and provide computer games for children to play to reinforce the concepts they are learning. Get children involved in problem solving by using divergent thinking (brainstorming) and metacognition. As they search for answers, help children to appreciate the beauty of nature around them and to understand the earth's rich gifts of air, water, food, plants, and animals, as well as how they can protect and preserve these treasures.

Ethical Dilemma

A volunteer who is a retired kindergarten teacher is insistent that the teachers and children follow her way of doing things. She brings in tracing pictures for the children to color, "ditto sheets" for them to choose the right answer, and scolds the children when they are not quiet enough or polite enough for her. The staff has tried different strategies to get her to change, but nothing seems to work. What would you do?

LEARNING ACTIVITIES

1. Read one or more of the Suggested Readings cited or a Web site listed and add 10 cards to your file with specific ideas for helping children develop cognitive skills. Include the reference source on each card.

2. Observe and record several of your children's actions using the "Children's Curiosity Checklist." Bring in a new material or find another way to improve their curiosity. Record what you did and the results.

3. Take a small group of your children on a brief field trip to a nearby area after reading a book as a lead-in. Follow up with a classroom activity to clarify concepts or support learning. Record the results.

4. Help the children learn a new concept using ideas from this chapter. Write down questions they ask and how they learned the answers.

Record how you know what concepts children learned from this activity.

5. Help children investigate a science interest using the guessing-game method of scientific inquiry. Record what happens.

6. Support children in their investigation of an environmental issue concerning plants, animals, insects, fish, birds, butterflies, water, or air. Record what you did and what happens.

7. Read a picture book that will lead the children into a cognitive skills activity that you have set up. Record the results.

8. Describe several of the differences between Piaget's and Vygotsky's theories of children's cognitive development. Tell how you would apply one to the classroom and children.

SUGGESTED READINGS

Blake, S. (2009). Engage, investigate, and report: Enhancing the curriculum with scientific inquiry. *Young Children, 64*(6), 49–53.

Charlesworth, R., & Lind, K. K. (2007). *Math & science for young children,* 5th ed. Clifton Park, NY: Thomson/Delmar/Cengage.

Eisenhauer, M. J., & Feikes, D. (2009). Dolls, blocks, and puzzles: Playing with mathematical understandings. *Young Children, 64*(3), 18–24.

Galizio, C., Stoll, J., & Hutchins, P. (2009). Exploring the possibilities for learning in natural spaces. *Young Children, 64*(4), 42–48.

Helm, J. H. (2009, January–February). Best brains in science under five: Helping children develop intentionality. *Exchange,* 50–52.

Worth, K., & Grollman, S. (2003). *Worms, shadows, and whirlpools: Science in the early childhood classroom.* Portsmouth, NH: Heinemann.

WEB SITES

AAA Math
http://aaamath.com

Better Brains for Babies
http://www.fcs.uga.edu/ext/bbb

Building Blocks
http://www.gse.buffalo.edu/org/buildingblocks

Figure This!
http://www.figurethis.org

FunBrain
http://www.funbrain.com/numbers.html

Ladybug
http://www.ladybugmagkids.com

Mother Goose Programs
http://www.mothergooseprograms.org

Zero to Three/Brain Wonders
http://www.zerotothree.org/brainwonders

CHILDREN'S BOOKS

Allen, J. (2000). *Are you a ladybug?* Boston: Houghton Mifflin.

Bryan, A. (2003). *Beautiful blackbird.* New York: Atheneum.

Carle, E. (1996). *The grouchy ladybug.* New York: HarperCollins.

Cooper, E. (2004). *Magic thinks big.* New York: Greenwillow.

Cronin, D. (2006). *Click, clack, splish, splash.* New York: Atheneum.

*Diaz, D. (2008). *De colores, bright with colors.* Tarrytown, NY: Marshall Cavendish.

Fleming, D. (2007). *Beetle bop.* Orlando, FL: Harcourt.

Florian, D. (2009). *Dinothesaurus, prehistoric poems and paintings.* New York: Atheneum.

Hallinan, P. K. (2009). *The looking book.* Nashville, TN: Ideals Children's Books.

Hubbard, P. (1996). *My crayons talk.* New York: Henry Holt.

*Isadora, R. (2000). *1 2 3 Pop!* New York: Viking.

*Jonas, A. (1989). *Color dance.* New York: Greenwillow.

Martin, B., & Sampson, M. (2004). *Chicka, chicka, 1, 2, 3.* New York: Simon & Schuster.

Milbourne, A. (2004). *The dinosaur.* London, England: Usborne Publishing.

Numeroff, L. (2008). *If you give a cat a cupcake.* New York: HarperCollins Children's Books.

Pallotta, J. (2004). *The beetle alphabet book.* Watertown, MA: Charlesbridge.

Plourde, L. (2007). *Dino pets.* New York: Dutton.

Sidman, J. (2009). *Red sings from treetops: A year in colors.* Boston: Houghton Mifflin.

Soman, D. (2009). *Ladybug girl and bumblebee boy.* New York: Dial Books for Young Readers.

Stickland, P., & Stickland, H. (1994). *Dinosaur roar!* New York: Dutton.

Tracqui, V. (2002). *Face-to-face with the ladybug.* Watertown, MA: Charlesbridge.

Wells, R. (2007). *Max counts his chickens.* New York: Viking.

*Multicultural

CHAPTER 6

Advancing Communication Skills

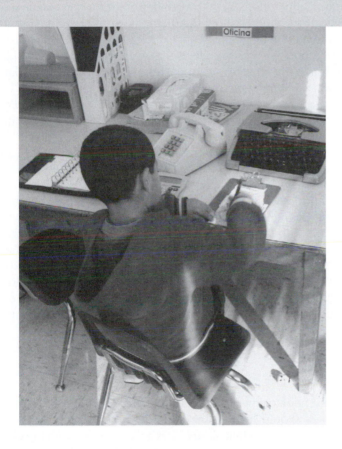

☐ **General Objective**
To promote children's communication skills through listening, speaking, emergent reading, and emergent writing

☑ **Specific Objectives**
____ Talks with individual children, including dual language learners, to encourage listening and speaking

____ Uses books and stories to motivate listening, speaking, and emergent reading

____ Provides materials and activities to support emergent writing

*C*OMMUNICATION *Skills*, the ability to listen, speak, read, and write, are a most important aspect of young children's development in the preschool classroom. We understand that the drive to communicate is inherent from birth in all human beings. We also know that children strive endlessly to accomplish this goal of communication with the others in their environment, unless they are impaired, neglected, or somehow thwarted. And we know that poor development of communication skills during the early years can affect children's thinking and learning abilities throughout life. As Kalmar (2008) points out: "Language production at age 3 predicts reading comprehension scores at age 9 to 10" (p. 88).

Brain Research

Brain research shows us the importance of early child–adult interactions from birth on. A baby's early communication efforts help to wire her brain for the spoken and written language to follow. These studies show that humans are preprogrammed to learn language, even more than one language at once. Interacting with the linguistic environment around them, especially with people, is the way they acquire language. Infants, toddlers, and preschoolers emerge into speaking naturally by hearing language spoken around them and trying it out themselves.

Language is a function of the left hemisphere of the brain, and brain research shows that babies are already using the left side of their brains for babbling and other language sounds at 5 to 7 months. As Hirsh-Pasek and Golinkoff (2003) report, "Babies are primed to analyze the language stream coming at them, just as they are primed to walk. Nature has given them the tools to absorb the jumble of language and find a way to break apart its never-ending flow" (p. 69).

By 20 months of age, children may have a sizable vocabulary—that is, if their caregivers talk to them, cuddle them, and interact with them. Research shows that youngsters whose mothers talk to them frequently average 131 more words than children whose mothers are less verbal. If children do not develop strong oral language skills even before they start school, they will begin to fall behind. Roskos, Tabors, and Lenhart (2009) emphasize, "From age 3 onward, they should build a vocabulary store of at least 2,500 words per year. They should encounter and explore at least 2 new words each day. They need to learn how to attend and listen on purpose" (p. 1).

Talk-Rich Environment

This does not mean that preschool teachers should sit children down and teach them new words. Instead, teachers should involve the children in stimulating activities with exciting materials that children can talk about. They talk, talk, talk with the children, and then listen closely to their responses. As Kalmar (2008) describes it, a *talk-rich environment* "is an accepting place where teachers encourage young children to talk, and they model the use of stress, pitch, and dialect to help children refine their language skills" (p. 89). When teachers talk with individuals the children begin to understand sentence structure and multiple meanings of some words.

Language modeling behavior by the adults around them is the key factor in children's learning to communicate. Youngsters from highly verbal homes often speak early and well, whereas children from homes where nonverbal communication is the norm are often delayed in learning to speak fluently. In other words, all young children need to hear language spoken around them to learn to speak it themselves.

*When teachers talk with individual children, the children begin to
understand sentence structure and word meanings.*

It is your role, then, as a teacher, assistant, volunteer, or student teacher in a
preschool program, to promote children's communication skills in some of the following ways.

TALKS WITH INDIVIDUAL CHILDREN, INCLUDING
DUAL LANGUAGE LEARNERS, TO ENCOURAGE
LISTENING AND SPEAKING

For children to learn to speak they need to learn to listen to the speaking going on around
them. How do they learn to listen? Their teachers must make it a point to model and
teach active listening themselves. Are you a good listening model for your children?

Listening with Intent

Listening with intent takes more than merely stopping your own talking while another
person speaks. It requires you to listen with intent to hear and understand what is spoken in order to reply. It requires you to take some sort of action. Figure 6.1, "Listening with Intent," gives you some points to consider:

You may believe you are already a good listener, but Jalongo (1995) found that
according to some studies, "American adults listen at only 25% efficiency; most adult
listeners are preoccupied, distracted and forgetful nearly 75% of the time" (p. 13). If

Figure 6.1 Listening With Intent

1. Quiet your mind's flow of thoughts.
2. Receive and process the incoming speaking.
3. Concentrate on the key points of what is being said. Make and hold eye contact.
4. Get involved emotionally with what you hear. Nod or shake your head.
5. Do not respond by speaking until you know the speaker is finished.

we expect children to listen to us, then we must make a concerted effort to model good listening behavior ourselves.

To practice good listening, first face the person who is speaking, and then make and keep eye contact. If a child is speaking to you, squat down or sit down next to her rather than leaning over her. Then really listen to what is being said. Let her finish; don't interrupt. When you reply, *try to repeat something she said.* This lets the child know you have heard her. Besides serving as a model for a child to emulate, your listening to a child like this helps him or her to feel valued as a person.

Your response should also encourage the child to continue talking. You might suggest, "Tell me more about that funny puppy you saw on the way to the center this morning." If your concentrated listening and sincere response show that you are genuinely interested in children's communications, they will be motivated to continue speaking and listen more carefully themselves.

Do you listen with intent? To check your own listening and speaking skills, do a self-analysis using the Teacher Listening and Speaking Checklist in Figure 6.2.

Figure 6.2 Teacher Listening and Speaking Checklist

Source: From Janice J. Beaty, *Skills for Preschool Teachers,* Ninth Edition. Copyright © 2012 by Pearson Education, Inc. All rights reserved.

Permission granted by the publisher to reproduce this checklist for evaluation & record keeping.

_____ Makes eye contact with child at child's level
_____ Listens by quieting the mind's flow of thoughts
_____ Concentrates on key points of what is being said
_____ Gets emotionally involved in what is being said
_____ Repeats something that the child has said
_____ Listens attentively to the child's reply
_____ Listens to an audiotape a child has made and makes comments
_____ Greets each child individually when child arrives
_____ Converses with individuals in learning centers
_____ Talks to individuals on pretend telephone
_____ Converses with individuals at lunch table
_____ Says good-bye to each child at end of day
_____ Speaks slowly and clearly
_____ Uses simple sentences, good grammar
_____ Uses more comments than questions

Helping Children Listen with Intent

If children pay little attention to what you are saying to them or do not seem to hear what you say, they may need to be screened for hearing impairments or attention deficits. Do not wait until they enter elementary school. The earlier such deficits can be identified, the sooner they can be modified. Be sure children and their parents are referred to appropriate professional assistance without delay.

Many teachers spend more time talking to groups than to individuals. Yet to involve children in learning to listen with intent to hear something, you need to spend time talking individually with each child every day. Make listening and speaking to individuals an important part of your daily routine. Keep a list of children's names handy and check it off each time you speak with an individual. Did you miss anyone? Be sure to catch up with them the next day. What kinds of adult speaking can individual children expect to hear in your classroom?

- Greeting each child when he or she arrives
- Talking to a child in a learning center
- Talking on a pretend telephone to a child
- Reading a book to a child
- Helping a child start or complete a project
- Conversing with individual children at the lunch table
- Giving verbal support to a child who needs it
- Having a private conversation with a child
- Saying good-bye to each child at the end of the day

Remember that children 3 to 5 years old are at the beginning of their language development and may not understand everything you say. Kratcoski and Katz (1998, p. 31) suggest the following teacher communication behaviors to help facilitate child language understanding:

- Use simple sentences.
- Speak slowly and clearly.
- Vary your expression by emphasizing key words.
- Pause between sentences.
- Use a concrete vocabulary.
- Use comments rather than questions.

Soundproofing the Room

Children need to hear words and how they are used to use the words themselves. Make sure your classroom is full of talking, but not loud talking. Listen for it. If you hear only noisy sounds or shouting, it may be a sign that your room needs soundproofing. Youngsters should be able to hear one another without raising their voices.

If they cannot, you should improve the room's sound absorption. Install carpeting on the floor and sound-absorbent tiles on the ceiling. Hang floor-length drapes at the windows and colorful picture rugs or cloth hangings on the walls.

If you do not have the authority to install carpeting or ceiling tiles, you can still help to soundproof the room. Use area rugs on the floor and draperies on the walls. Cloth absorbs sound better than cardboard or wood. Think of ways you can include cloth rather than cardboard in different parts of the room. For example, use colored cloth backing for the signs that label each curriculum area. Cover your bulletin board with colored burlap. Make your jobs chart out of cloth with pockets for each child's job card. Fasten cloth curtains to the backs of room dividers. Bring in several bright pillows for the book and housekeeping centers. Now your children should be able to hear clearly and speak without shouting. But as Selman (2001) points out, "Talking involves communication—speaking with and to someone, getting feedback, and composing language in response to that feedback. Talking with someone implies a continuous exchange—a dialogue" (p. 15).

Helping Children Become Speakers

For verbal communication to occur with preschool children, two factors seem to operate. First, there must be a stress-free environment that allows but does not force them to communicate. Children need to feel support from those around them to express themselves in their very personal but still imperfect mode of communication. Second, there must be a necessity for language. Children must have the need to communicate in the classroom.

Stress-Free Environment

For many children, verbalizing is a new and untried skill outside their homes. They need not only opportunities to become proficient in speaking but also encouragement to continue. Children usually respond well to anything closely associated with themselves. Try playing name concept games to put them at ease.

"I'm thinking about someone with white-and-blue sneakers and a black T-shirt with a tiger on it. Guess who I'm thinking about? Robbie, right! Now you tell me who you are thinking about, Robbie, and see if I can guess."

Give children positive feedback for their verbal skills just as you would for their block buildings or paintings. "I like the way you said my name, Breanna. Breanna is such a nice-sounding name too."

A stress-free environment also means that you accept the children as they are, which means you accept their language no matter how poorly pronounced or how ungrammatical. Language is a very personal thing. It reflects not only the child's early stage of development but also his or her family. Therefore, be especially careful not to correct children's language in a way that shows a lack of respect for them or their parents. Try to avoid telling them they are saying a word incorrectly. You may wonder, then, how they are going to learn the correct pronunciation. They will learn it by hearing you use words correctly and by imitating and practicing new words in the many interesting language activities you provide.

A stress-free environment also means that your classroom is free from stressful situations for young children. They should not be forced to perform verbally, creatively, or in any other way. Offer them interesting opportunities and warm encouragement, but do not force a shy or unsure child to speak.

Finally, in a stress-free language environment, you talk to children with *responsive language* that conveys respect for them, rather than with *restrictive language* that conveys disrespect and teacher control. Researchers who observe teachers and caregivers of young children have noted that the manner in which they talk to youngsters tells a great deal about the way they treat children in general. As Stone (1993) notes, "Responsive language is language that conveys a positive regard for children and a respect for and acceptance of their individual ideas and feelings" (p. 13).

Teachers who use responsive language in the classroom give reasons for the statements they make. For example, they may say, "It's too wet to go out now. We'll wait till the grass dries," rather than, "We're not going out now. Why? Because I said so." They encourage children's independence and choice making rather than teacher control. For instance, they may say, "Everyone can choose the learning center he or she wants to play in. Just take one of the area necklaces," instead of the restrictive, "Jamal, you and Carlos work at the art table now."

When rules and limits are verbalized, teachers who use restrictive language may say, "No yelling in the room" instead of the responsive "Let's speak softly." They may comment on children's beginning art products with the restrictive "You didn't try very hard, Ethan. That's just a scribble," instead of "You really enjoyed using all those colors, Ethan."

How do you talk to children? Do you treat them as full-fledged human beings to be respected or as inferior little beings who are too young to know much? Your feelings and attitudes toward the children are expressed more clearly than you may realize in the language you use around the youngsters. Think twice before beginning your sentences with words and phrases such as *don't, stop, no,* or *not that way.* Think of ways you can convey the same meaning respectfully.

Your use of restrictive language, whether directed toward one child or to all of them, makes the classroom a stressful environment for everyone. Listen to yourself talk to the children. Is your language responsive or restrictive? Turn on the tape recorder and make a tape of your speaking mode to find out. If you decide to change your method of speaking to a more responsive style, note the children's reactions. Are they also more responsive, positive, and happy? Nonverbal children are much more likely to begin their own tentative classroom speaking when they hear how sensitively the teacher speaks to them.

Books as a Lead-Ins to Responsive Language Activities

No, David! (Shannon, 1998) shows a little boy getting into trouble at home on every page, and his mother responding by saying "no!" Have your individual listener sit close to see the pictures and tell how he or she would respond. Finally, on the last page the mother relents and says yes, that she loves him. Ask your listener what the mother could say on the other pages rather than "no."

Confidence

The so-called nonverbal child is frequently one who lacks confidence to speak out-side the confines of the home. At home he may be a regular chatterbox. To assure yourself of the child's verbal ability, you may want to talk with the parents to learn how much their child communicates verbally at home. It is not necessary to tell parents that their child is not speaking in school. The pressure they might put on the child to speak in school could well have adverse effects.

Your principal task with shy or uncommunicative children is to help them feel comfortable in the classroom. All classroom workers need to be aware that overt ef-forts to get such children to speak before they are at ease in the classroom may well be counterproductive. Instead, the staff should direct their efforts toward accepting the children as they are, using smiles, nods, and words of acceptance for their posi-tive accomplishments when appropriate and leaving the child alone when necessary.

It takes a great deal of patience and forbearance on the part of an early childhood classroom staff to allow shy children to become at ease in their own good time, but this is often the only successful method. Weeks and even months are sometimes nec-essary for the extremely sensitive child to respond. If you have persisted in your support-without-pressure approach, you will be rewarded one day by a smile and even a whispered sentence. Do not make a fuss when shy children say their first words. Accept their speaking matter-of-factly, just as you have always accepted them.

Books as a Lead-Ins to Children Gaining Confidence

Sometimes young children do not speak right up because their family members have always jumped in to speak for them. Such is the case for Oliver.

In *Oliver Has Something to Say* (Edwards, 2007) little Oliver never gets a chance to say anything because his mom, dad, or sister always answer for him without waiting for him to speak. Finally, when he goes to pre-school his teacher asks him a question and actually waits for him to reply. The words in his mouth come tumbling out, and still haven't stopped. What would your chil-dren say for each of the questions his family asked?

Necessity

Do children have the need to communicate in your classroom? You can provide op-portunities for communication to take place. Remember, you are the role model. You need to communicate verbally yourself whenever possible. Set aside a time of day when you greet the children and they greet one another.

Have a small group or a circle time in which the children have a chance to tell about something. A shy child might talk through a hand puppet at first. You can demonstrate how, but don't force the issue if the child does not want to use the puppet. Give the children a chance to pretend in the dramatic play area or with blocks or water. Ask one child to help another with a new tool or piece of equipment. Give children oral messages to carry to someone else in the room. Have them ask someone a question and return to you with the answer. Sit with the children at snack or lunchtime and start a conversation about something of interest to them.

Conversations

If children feel confident, they will probably converse with others. However, if they feel more comfortable talking with adults than with other children, as many preschoolers do, their lack of peer conversation may be one of socialization rather than language. Be sure to eat with children at lunchtime or snack time, especially with shy or nonverbal children. This will give you an informal assessment of which children converse spontaneously and which ones do not. Try engaging each child at your table in conversation but without pressure. Then give them something to talk about with one another.

As Morrison (2004) tells us, "In conversations, adults and children share information in a personal give and take. Conversations may be about feelings, ideas or events in their personal lives. Conversations that are honest and sincere, rather than didactic and contrived, help children build trusting relationships with adults. They also foster language and literature development." (p. 27).

Because oral language is the basis for all other learning, teachers must provide opportunities for one-on-one conversations with every child every day. Toy telephones help promote conversational language in a very direct way. Children notice that most adults have a cell phone in their hand much of the time. They can feel more adult-like if they have one too. Even shy children will pretend with a cell phone. Ask parents to donate old cell phones, take out the battery, and watch how children use them. Be sure to have at least two phones, one for the caller and one for the receiver. For children who need special practice in speaking, put in a pretend call yourself and talk with them every day if necessary. Other children will see you doing this and soon begin calling on their own.

Listen to their conversations. If one child speaks in extended sentences and the other in one-word replies, you can scaffold the latter's speaking skills by pretend-calling him yourself

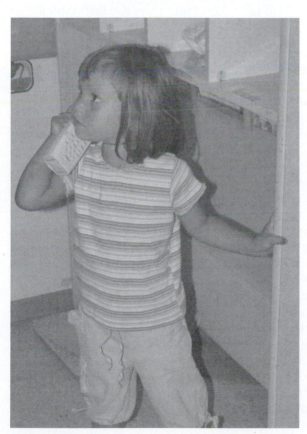
Even shy children may speak with a toy cell phone.

and asking him to describe something: where he is, what he wants to play with next, or what his favorite toys are. For example,

TEACHER: Hi, Roberto. Is that you I am talking to?

ROBERTO: Yes.

T: Oh, I'm so glad to hear your voice, Roberto. Tell me, are you wearing your new sneakers today?

R: Yes.

T: Tell me what they look like. I can't quite remember.

R: Black.

T: Oh, yes, black. But wasn't there something special about them?

R: White. White arrows.

T: Really? Oh, that sounds super.

R: Red lights that flashed.

T: I don't remember seeing those lights.

R: They flash when I walk. They flash fast when I run. I can run fast! Watch me run!

And so it goes. You need to keep track of children with single-word replies to involve them in longer conversations about things they like. This teacher might ask Roberto to call Dominic and tell him about the sneakers. Maybe they could turn the lights off in the room to watch Roberto's sneakers flash.

An important but frequently overlooked element in stimulating children's conversations in early childhood classrooms is the mix of children. Is your classroom composed of a single age group, such as all 3-year-olds or all 4-year-olds? Or are these two age groups combined? Because children learn so much of their language through imitation of others, it is helpful for them to be around children a bit more advanced than themselves. The language of 3-year-olds will develop much faster with 4-year-olds in the same classroom.

To promote spontaneous conversation between yourself and the children, you need to be an active communicator with responsive, not restrictive, speaking habits. This means you are a person the children are able and willing to approach. You may have to take the initiative with shy children. They may lack the confidence to approach you on their own. Try stationing yourself in a particular learning center near these children to create opportunities for conversation. If the children do not respond, you may need to talk on your own awhile, describing what is going on in the area and wondering what else is going to happen. In most cases, they will eventually join in the conversation.

Observers of teacher behavior note that teachers usually respond mainly to the children who talk the most. Quiet or inarticulate children—those who truly need conversational practice—are frequently ignored. You must therefore make a special effort to ensure that you do not unintentionally overlook such children. Remember, patience, not pressure, should govern your approach.

Books as Lead-Ins to Children's Conversations

Charlie and Lola books (see Chapter 3) are all conversations between Charlie and his sister Lola.

In *I Am Too Absolutely Small for School* (Child, 2004) Lola is determined not to go to school. Charlie tells her each good thing that will happen but she has negative replies to everything. Counting to 100? Counting to 10 is enough—even if 11 elephants want a treat. Child listeners love to follow the pictures and are soon contributing to the conversation. Have them choose character roles and reenact the story next time. Or you can be Charlie and have several child-Lolas to answer each of your reasons with imaginary replies of their own.

Other Charlie and Lola books as lead-ins to conversations:

I Will Be Especially Very Careful (Child, 2009)
I Completely Know About Guinea Pigs (Child, 2008)

Dual Language Learners

Young children who are learning to speak English in your program while still learning to speak a different language at home are called "dual language learners" (DLLs). More and more children are entering preschool these days not speaking English. Macarina and colleagues (2009) report that in 2004 19 percent of the school-age population spoke a language other than English. By 2030 dual language learners are expected to comprise 40 percent of the school-age population (p. 27).

In Head Start (a national program for low-income children ages 3 to 5) today, 85 percent of the grantees serve children and families whose primary language is not English, according to Espinosa (2010). She lists the following languages in order of frequency:

Spanish (84 percent)	Pacific Island
East and South Asian	African
Middle Eastern	Caribbean
European	Native North American and Alaskan (p.12)
Native Central and South American	

How can you help these children in your classroom? Morrow (2009) tells us: "Preschool and kindergarten children will acquire the language [English] when immersed in language-rich classrooms where there are good models of English and sensitive teachers. This is mostly true with children whose native language is well-developed and not necessarily so with children whose language is not well developed" (p. 74).

This means DLL children need to hear their home language spoken in the classroom in addition to English. Nemeth (2009) points out: "All children everywhere deserve to have conversations every day—in their own languages" (p. 36). If you or one of the staff does not speak a child's home language, try to arrange for a speaker to visit the class as often as possible. If no one is available, can you arrange for someone in the home to tape-record questions and answers in their language? When you meet with children's parents, will they let you tape record a few phrases in their language for you to say to their children? (Phrases like *Hello, How are you? What is your name? Come and play, Your mother is coming soon, See you tomorrow*).

Dual language learners are fortunate to attend a preschool program that recognizes their native language as well as English because they will have the opportunity to become fluent in both languages during their period of natural language acquisition (i.e., birth to age 6). At no other time in their lives will they be able to acquire another language so easily. To learn a second language, they must hear and practice it, and you must provide opportunities for them do so. These should not be formal teaching lessons.

NAEYC Criteria for Teaching Standard

Describe how you would meet the following standard:

3.F.04 Teaching staff help children understand new spoken language by using pictures, familiar objects, body language, and physical cues.

Young children acquire native and second languages in a most informal and spontaneous way—by hearing it spoken around them, by trial and error in speaking it themselves, and by subconsciously extracting the rules of the language—not through formal grammar teaching. As Morrow and colleagues (2009) tell us, "Preschoolers are likely to acquire English simply through immersion in an English-speaking classroom, something that older children cannot do. But it is important that they hear their own language as well" (p. 8).

If most of the children speak English as a first language, but a few speak, say, Spanish, you or one of your coworkers should also speak both languages. Most of the day you will be speaking mainly English, but spend an hour a day, or a half-hour in a half-day program, speaking nothing but simple Spanish. Those children who speak Spanish will respond naturally. Those children whose native language is English will pick up a great deal of Spanish, not by being taught formally, but by hearing it spoken around them.

Read children's books in Spanish, sing songs in Spanish, do painting or build with blocks making comments in Spanish, and have a wonderful time during your "Spanish hour" every day. To include music call Lakeshore (1-800-778-4456) for their Spanish/English learning song CDs.

By the end of the year, you may have many so-called Anglo children responding in Spanish as fluently as your native Spanish speakers. A second language is a true gift. Everyone will feel good about receiving it: the Hispanic children whose language you have recognized by using it in school and the non-Hispanic children who have learned to say and understand simple phrases in a new language.

Instead of having an instructor or a parent with a second language come in and "teach" the children to say *hello, good-bye, how are you?* and how to count to 10, ask this person to come into your classroom and spend time with the children speaking nothing but the second language. Don't use a translator. The children will be able to pick up enough nonverbal cues to understand—perhaps better than you do! Eventually, they will be able to reply in the second language. You may want to start by reading bilingual picture books with the children. Try to find bilingual books using both English and Spanish. Books with clear illustrations of the words are best.

Books as Lead-ins for Dual Language Activities

In *What Can You Do with a Rebozo?* (Tafolla, 2008) the girl narrator asks and then answers the question with a dozen wonderfully illustrated ideas for using her mother's red Mexican shawl. Her mother spreads it like a butterfly over her dress or carries baby brother in it on her back. Tio uses it to wipe up a spill, and Daddy washes it afterwards. Children cover their eyes with it when trying to hit the birthday piñata. Or it is used for a superhero's cape on Halloween. Have your children be thinking of their own ideas for how they would use it as you read this bilingual book in English and then Spanish. How silly can they get?

Be sure to have a real shawl available after reading this book. Would the children like to make up their own rebozo book with their ideas? Have your digital camera ready.

Other bilingual books as lead-ins to dual language activities:

Bebe Goes Shopping (Elya, 2006)

Carlos and the Squash Plant (Stevens, 1993)

Drum, Chavi, Drum (Dole, 2003)

I Love Saturdays y domingos (Ada, 2002)

Oh, Crumps! ¡Ay, Caramba! (Bock, 2003)

Books in Spanish and English can be obtained through Lectorum (1-877-532-8676). Another book you might find very useful is *10 Languages You'll Need Most in the Classroom: A Guide to Communicating with English Language Learners and their Families* (Sundem, Krieger, & Pikiewicz, 2008). It includes a picture dictionary, useful phrases, and little stories in 11 languages (Spanish, Vietnamese, Hmong, Chinese [Cantonese], Korean, Haitian, Creole, Arabic, Russian, Tagalog [Filipino], and Navajo).

Activities Using a Second Language

Besides the many English-language activities you provide for your children, also plan specific activities using the second language, such as name chants and songs. The children can speak daily on the toy telephone with another second-language speaker. A bilingual puppet can be part of your daily activities, talking to individuals and groups in both languages. Children can also learn to greet one another and say goodbye in the second language.

Dramatic play is one of the best vehicles for children's language development because natural conversation occurs. Be sure you allow enough time in your daily schedule for bilingual children to become involved in pretend play using a second language. If they seem shy, help them take on a role yourself by playing alongside these children until they feel comfortable with the other youngsters. (See Chapter 7.)

USES BOOKS AND STORIES TO MOTIVATE LISTENING, SPEAKING, AND EMERGENT READING

Emergent Reading

During the 1980s and 1990s, educators realized that more and more preschool children were entering elementary school already able to read. What was happening? Were more parents teaching their children to read? Were children learning from television? Educational researchers found something quite different. They learned that when conditions were right, some young children were actually teaching themselves to read just as they taught themselves to talk.

This process is now called *emergent literacy*. Some children seem to "emerge" naturally into reading and writing by interacting playfully with the "print" in their environment, subconsciously extracting the rules about reading and writing and then trying out reading and writing through trial and error until they get it to work for them. Educators also realized that learning to communicate is a holistic process encompassing listening, speaking, reading, and writing together, not separately. They also realized that this process starts for children at birth.

Learning to read is different from learning to speak because its words are in *print* rather than *sounds*. With speaking, children learn by imitating the sounds of words they hear around them. With reading, children must first learn how to decode the print of words before they can say them. Some children do teach themselves what the print says. Others need the help of the adults around them to scaffold this learning through games, songs, chants, books, puppets, flannel boards, story reading, storytelling, computer programs, and playing with alphabet letters.

If children's environment is a "print-rich environment," filled with print materials such as books, newspapers, magazines, television, computer programs, fast-food restaurant signs, and labels on cereal boxes, toys, and T-shirts, many children try to figure out what this print says. If people around them tell them what some signs say, and if the adults in their lives are readers themselves who read to the youngsters, then some of these children will manage to extract the rules for reading on their own before they enter school.

To support all children in acquiring these skills, a new philosophy, *emergent literacy*, for teaching reading and writing in preschool and kindergarten has thus emerged. Children learn from children's literature like the books discussed here. Classrooms are encouraged to develop a "print-rich environment" in which written communication is evident everywhere: recipe charts, posters, letters, curriculum area signs, words to songs, rules charts, labels for objects, children's name tags, alphabet games, computer software, sign-up sheets, magazines, newspapers, and books.

Figure 6.3   Young Children's Reading Behaviors

- Holds book right side up
- Starts with first page
- Turns pages right-to-left without skipping
- Does pretend reading
- Labels objects in pictures
- Treats each page as a separate unit
- Retells story by naming the pictures
- Retells story through memorization
- Recognizes that the print tells the story
- Does finger-point reading of some words
- Can read simple sentences

Preschool teachers need to become aware of their children's emergent literacy because it is happening whether or not they notice. Emergent reading in preschool, however, *does not involve the formal teaching of reading and writing.* Instead, it encourages teachers to set up a print-rich environment with activities for children to accomplish on their own. And it involves *reading to children.* The most important experience a preschool child can have, in fact, is a happy adventure with storybooks. As Roskos et al. (2009) tell us, "Adults need to show children how to think with print in order to make it meaningful. That is why reading to and with children is so powerful—because it shows them how to do what they need to do to comprehend the print code" (p. 15).

For teachers to know where children stand in their emergent literacy, "Young Children's Reading Behaviors" in Figure 6.3 lists some of the steps most children go through as they emerge. Surprising at it may seem, some children do not know how a book works at first. Perhaps they have never held a picture book in their hands before. They learn by watching others and through scaffolding by the teacher.

Another surprise is that many young children at first believe it is the pictures in a picture book that tell the story, not the print. Print awareness is something they learn on their own through the many literacy activities and much book reading you provide. As Neuman and Roskos (1993) remind us, "This sense of story comes about by hearing stories, and by being read to on a regular basis. Perhaps no other finding in research is as well documented as the simple fact that reading regularly to young children significantly influences their understanding of what reading is all about as well as their later proficiency in reading" (p. 37). Where do your children stand in their natural emergence?

If preschoolers are to meet with success and enjoyment in learning to read, they need to have a pleasant encounter with books at the outset. It is hoped that a child's acquaintance with books will begin in the home long before the child enters a classroom. The books and activities you provide will be a follow-up and extension of the story reading that occurs at home. But for some children, the experience in your classroom will be their initiation into the exciting world of books and reading. You will want to make it a joyful one.

When children see their teachers and parents reading, they begin to internalize the idea that reading is something important that the adults around them like to do.

It is something they themselves will want to learn as soon as they can. Adults who read to a preschool child are saying something else important: "I like you enough to take time out of a busy day to share something nice with you." It creates a good feeling for all concerned.

Books to Motivate Listening

To acquire speaking skills, young children need to be able to listen and to hear, as previously discussed. One of the best ways to promote good listening skills in young children is to read them books that attract their attention. What kinds of books are these? They are picture books, of course, but to attract children's initial attention, these books should have enticing pictures on the cover and inside.

Preschool listeners also like book action that is exciting, fast paced, and fun, with only brief text on each page. Books with longer texts are for older children. Three- and 4-year-old listeners want you to get on with the story and keep turning the pages. If you stop on a page for too long, they often lose interest. For their exciting pictures and text, try these with your children.

Captain Cheech (Marin, 2008), boat race with a school bus

Charlie Hits It Big (Blumenthal, 2007), pet guinea pig goes to Hollywood

Friday My Radio Flyer Flew (Pullen, 2008), boy's little red wagon flies

Hot Rod Hamster (Lord, 2010), hamster builds his own hot rod and wins

Word Play

The words themselves also attract preschool story listeners. They like words with distinctive sounds to laugh about and say over and over. Remember that children's first level of learning on their own is *manipulation* (see Chapter 3). Is children's wordplay actually manipulation? Yes. Just as they play with blocks, toys, and each other, children also play with words. Youngsters make up nonsense words, repeat word sounds, mix up words, say things backward, make up chants, and repeat rhyming words. Most people pay little attention to this activity because it seems so inconsequential. What we have not seemed to realize is that through this playful activity, children are once again at work creating their own knowledge. This time the content is language rather than cognitive concepts, and this time the child is manipulating the medium (words) with his voice rather than his hands. Preschool teachers should feel a great deal of relief when they realize that it is playful activities like this that help children emerge into literacy.

Flip Flop Bop (Novak, 2005) appeals to young children immediately with its yellow cover showing off three cartoon children dancing in flip flops. In the story they go clippety clop down to the Flip Flop Shop, shedding their socks and shoes to don flip flops of all colors. Parents, children, even grandparents are flip flop bopping all over the place. When it rains and the ground turns to mud, they go glippy, gloppy, slippy, sloppy—soon even the words get out of control—wonderful words for children to play with. Children can see the words easily in the cartoon balloons and will soon be repeating them.

In the hilarious book *Don't Be Silly, Mrs. Millie!* (Cox, 2005), it is the teacher who plays with words and the children who catch all her mistakes. She tells them to hang up their goats (instead of coats); not to step into a poodle (instead of puddle); to wash their hands with soap and walrus (instead of water); and to sit on the bug for story reading (instead of rug), among other things. The pictures illustrate her words, making the book one that children will want to sit close to so they can see, hear, and laugh.

As you read these books to children, note how attentively they are listening—waiting for their favorite word. Then they often go into spasms of laughter or repeat the word over and over. This *repetition* is the next stage in children's interaction with new things, you remember. When children ask you to "Read it again, teacher," be sure that you comply.

Children's level of language learning requires that words and stories be repeated again and again for real learning to take place. They will soon know their favorite stories so well that you won't dare skip a word when reading. Does this really matter? Jalongo and Ribblett (1997) have this to say about it: "Educators now know, based on emergent literacy research, that an important breakthrough in the literacy process occurs when a child knows a few books so well that she can tell if any portion of the text has been skipped or altered" (p. 15).

In some books the important words are printed in large-font, boldface print. Have children sit close so they can see them as you read. Run your finger under the words as you read them. Soon you may have children who want to try reading those words by themselves. They may begin to understand that it is the words, not the pictures that tell the story. Books about vehicles often emphasize such words:

Roadwork (Sutton, 2008), construction sound words

Tip Tip Dig Dig (Garcia, 2008), vehicle action words

Toot Toot Beep Beep (Garcia, 2008), car noises

Words in large-font print help children become readers.

Figure 6.4   Book
Selection Checklist

Source: From Janice J. Beaty,
Skills for Preschool Teachers,
Ninth Edition. Copyright ©
2012 by Pearson Education,
Inc. All rights reserved.

Permission granted by the
publisher to reproduce this
checklist for evaluation &
record keeping.

_____ Title intriguing

_____ Illustrations attention getting

_____ Characters exciting

_____ Action fast paced, fun

_____ Text brief (a sentence or two per page)

_____ Words that rhyme and/or are funny

_____ Words or phrases repeated

As you choose books for preschool children, keep in mind the criteria listed in Figure 6.4 to help in your selection.

Predictable Books

Research has found that the best books to promote emergent reading in young children are *predictable books,* that is, picture books that "contain selections with repetitive structures which enable children to anticipate the next word, line, or episode" (Bridge, 1986, p. 82). This makes sense when we remember how important repetition is in the early childhood learning process.

For preschoolers, these books also need to be simple, fast paced, and fun. Some may have episodes that are repeated in a cumulative fashion as new episodes are added. Other helpful books have rhyming words that children can remember. Still other helpful features are pictures that clearly illustrate words or sentences. Then when children hear these stories read aloud again and again, they remember what is coming next—what word, what line, or what episode. They want to chime in and say it. Eventually they will be able to connect that written word, line, or episode in the book with the spoken word, line, or episode. Finally, they will be able to look at the written word, line, or episode in the book and say it themselves.

Are we saying, then, that you should begin "teaching" your preschool children to read? No. We are saying that you should read predictable books to them over and over and provide them with such books to explore for themselves. The children themselves will take it from there.

To select predictable books from the wide array of children's books available, consider the criteria in Figure 6.5, "Predictable Books for Preschoolers." Children's finger plays, chants, and songs also make excellent predictable books because children already know the rhyming, repetitive words and are accustomed to saying or singing them. More of these fine chanting books are being published each year. Be on the lookout for them. The purpose of such books is not to teach children the chants, but to show them what their already familiar chant or song looks like when it is written in words and illustrated in pictures.

Figure 6.5   Predictable
Books for Preschoolers

- Text has repetitive or rhyming words, lines, episodes.
- Text has rhythmic cadences.
- Text has cumulative episodes.
- Text has sequential patterns.
- Text may be words to familiar song, fingerplay.
- Text is brief, fast-paced, fun.
- Pictures clearly illustrate the words.

Some popular books in each of these categories include the following:

Repetitive or rhyming words, lines episodes

Dinosaur Roar!	*Bee-bim Bop!*	*Tip Tip Dig Dig*
Flip Flop Bop	*Itsy Bitsy Spider*	*Toot Toot Beep Beep*

Rhythmic Cadences

Chicka Chicka Boom Boom	*Twist with a Burger, Jitter with a Bug*
Miss Mary Mack	*Do You Do a Didgeridoo?*

Cumulative Episodes

Drat that Fat Cat!	*The Empanadas That Abuela Made*
The Bridge Is Up	*Bein' with You This Way*

Sequential Patterns

We All Went on Safari	*We're Sailing to Galapagos*
Feast for 10	*Warthogs in the Kitchen*

Miss Mary Mack (Hoberman, 1998) makes a fine predictable book because the last word on every line rhymes and is repeated three times: Miss Mary Mack, Mack, Mack; All dressed in black, black, black. This traditional jump-rope rhyme about the elephant who jumps so high he reaches the sky and doesn't come back until the Fourth of July can be chanted or even sung by the children to the tune on the end page.

Inclusion

Audiocassettes are available for some predictable books. Use them to give children an opportunity for exploring books on their own. Children with hearing impairments will especially find them useful, because they can turn up the volume. Youngsters can use a headset to listen to the tape as they turn the pages of the book. Some tapes include page-turn signals to help them know when to continue. You may need to help individuals get started using tapes or CDs like this. Book tapes should not, however, replace your own reading to children. Youngsters need your personal touch and encouraging comments or questions.

Reading Books to Children

Until recently, picture books in preschool programs were seriously *underused* by teachers. All too often the books were relegated to bookshelves for children to look at on their own. Instead of reading books, teachers used cassettes, videotapes, or CD-ROMs of books.

Teachers need to know that these abstract representations are not the same as an actual teacher reading a real book to a live child. *Reading books to the children in your program may be the single most important activity that you engage in.* Plan your daily schedule to allow children to choose and look at books on their own sometime during the day. But you or one of your coworkers should be responsible for reading at least once a day to the individuals.

You may choose to read to an individual child or a small group at a time while the rest of the children engage in another interesting activity. Be sure the others also have their turn to hear the story later on. Children need to sit near the reader to see the pictures, to become personally involved in the story, and to enjoy the sense of closeness that develops with the teacher and other children while the story is being read. A small group makes it easier to accomplish this closeness. Make story reading a personal experience for your children by reading to both individuals and small groups.

Although individual children will readily come to you with books to be read, you should also approach particular children with a book you have picked out especially for them. A dual language learner or a child you have previously identified as needing help in speaking can benefit by having stories read individually. To be a successful story reader, keep these hints in mind (see Figure 6.6).

Know Your Book Well

If you have chosen your book on the basis of the information in the "Book Selection Checklist" (see Figure 6.4), then you are already well acquainted with it. If not, read through the pages and note these features:

1. Sound words for which you can make the sound rather than reading the word
2. Places where you might substitute the listener's name for the name used in the book

Figure 6.6   Reading to Children

- Know your book well
- Start with an attention-getting device
- Make your voice as interesting as possible
- Help children get involved through participation

3. Picture details you might ask a listener to look for

4. Places in the story where you might want to pause and ask your listeners, "Guess what comes next?"

5. Places in the story to stop and ask the listener for the next word

Start with an Attention-Getting Device

Your story reading will not be successful unless you have your listeners' attention. You will not want to stop to reprimand disruptive children. It is better if they are all ready and eager for you to begin. You can help them become ready by beginning with an attention-getting device. The simplest and most effective device is to ask the children something about the cover illustration.

Make Your Voice as Interesting as Possible

Do you enjoy reading aloud to children? Your voice often reflects your feelings. If you are enthusiastic about story reading, the children will know it by the tone of your voice. They love to have the teacher dramatize the story by making her voice scary or whispery or deep. Can you do that? Most of us don't know until we try. Even then, we're not sure how we come across. Turn on the tape recorder during story reading time and record your voice. Then play it for yourself later when you're alone. Do you like the way you read the story? Practice alone with a tape recorder until you have developed the voice you think enhances the story the most.

Help Children Get Involved Through Participation

Young children enjoy stories better if they are a part of them. You, the story reader, can get children directly involved in a number of ways. For instance, you might ask your listener to say the next word. Be careful, however, with a large group. Child participation often disrupts the group, because everyone wants a turn to say the answer. Avoiding that problem is another advantage for reading to small groups and individuals. With a small group you can keep control of what happens by calling on a particular child by name, instead of opening it to everyone.

For groups that are not used to sitting still and listening to a story, you may not want to interrupt the flow of the story with individual involvement at first. You must decide whether your priority for the children is to complete a story without interruptions or to get the children involved by offering them opportunities to participate. After you finish reading, don't put the book away. Look for follow-up book activities to bring children back to these books.

Follow-Up Book Activities

Look for books with a character on the cover who speaks as the story progresses. If the children enjoy the book and want you to read it again, you can involve them in speaking for the character. Start with simple stories where a single character repeats words throughout the story. An animal character is often a good one to begin with because children are so attracted to talking-animal stories.

Use a Puppet

Try using an animal puppet or stuffed animal toy for the child to speak for the character. Hiding behind a puppet who talks is a good way to involve even the shyest children. Animal puppets can be made by you or the children from small paper bags with the bag bottom as the face. Paint or glue on eyes, nose, mouth, and animal ears. Socks also make good puppets, with peel-off circles as the eyes and nose. The puppeteer opens and closes his hand within the end of the bag or sock while he speaks for the puppet. Hot pad gloves in the form of jungle animals make excellent puppets as well. Many toy stores and children's book stores sell stuffed animal toys or puppets to accompany particular books. Educational supply companies also stock toys and puppets to accompany children's books.

An exciting approach for motivating children's speaking is to have a child put on the puppet and speak for the animal as you read the story. Ask for a volunteer to be the talking animal. You will quickly have more volunteers than you need, so start with a small group of children. If the animal doesn't speak in the story, have the child make up its words. Yes, they will want the story repeated until everyone gets a chance to be "Lloyd the llama" from *Is Your Mama a Llama?* or whomever. Children need the *repetition* to practice this "book language." Be sure to congratulate all of your animal speakers, pointing out what you liked about their speaking.

Story Reenactment (Also Called Story Drama)

Once children are used to speaking for the characters, they are ready for the next step in their development of communication skills: taking on a character's entire role through simple playacting called *story reenactment*. Look for books showing characters on the cover who seem to be speaking. Just as preschoolers enjoy taking on the spontaneous roles of mother, father, doctor, and nurse in the dramatic play area, they can also enjoy playing the roles of favorite book characters. In story reenactment, children play character roles while you read the story. They can copy the characters' actions and words just as they are in the book or make up their own.

Books as Lead-ins to Story Reenactment

For example, *Hello! Is This Grandma?* (Whybrow, 2007) shows little Logan dialing the telephone trying to get Grandma, but every time he gets a wrong number: first sheep, then duck, then cow, then cranky crocodile, all of whom have something to say. Finally, Grandma calls him and invites him and his friends to a party. If your children show strong interest in the story, this may be a book to involve them in *story reenactment*, where they each take a character's role while you read the story.

Other books as follow-ups for story reenactments:

Drat That Fat Cat (Thomson, 2003)

I'm Calling Molly (Kurtz, 1990)

Miss Brooks Loves Books (and I Don't) (Bottner, 2010)

Owl Babies (Waddell, 1992)

Snip Snap! What's That? (Bergman, 2005)

The children who do not want a role can be the audience. This informal drama is for the children themselves and not an outside audience. If all goes well, they will want to repeat the story reenactment. Ishee and Goldhaber (1990) tell us, "Many repetitions help children. For many children it is necessary to watch a play numerous times before making the first gesture of pretense within the play. For others, repetition allows an opportunity to elaborate and expand on the story as pretended" (p. 74).

PROVIDES MATERIALS AND ACTIVITIES TO SUPPORT EMERGENT WRITING

Just as preschool children can emerge into reading, they are also able to emerge into writing if the environment is conducive. This means you should set up a writing area, as suggested in Chapter 3, stocking it with all sorts of enticing writing implements. Felt-tip pens in a rainbow of colors are the favorite writing tools for preschoolers in their early scribbling efforts.

This is a *manipulation* phase for the youngsters, when they first try out things on their own. They are playing around with using writing tools and making marks on paper. Some of their scribbles may be for drawing: underneath they make writing scribbles "to tell what the picture is about." Support them with encouragement and acceptance (e.g., "Oh, Marissa, you really like to make your scribbles in different colors, don't you?"). Children may want to tell you what their scribbles say. But just as often they may ask you what they say, because you know how to read and they don't! As Schickedanz and Casbergue (2009) tell us:

> Beginning during the preschool years and continuing through kindergarten, children very gradually build an understanding of how print actually works. Little by little, marks that children put on a page begin to stand on their own to represent messages they wish to convey. In this way the graphic world becomes a bridge to the oral world, because drawings and writings capture more of the meaning a child tries to communicate. (pp. 5–7)

Have a bulletin board nearby where children can display their writing products just as they do their art. You will easily recognize children's progression to the *mastery* level of prewriting, when they fill paper after paper with repeated rows of scribbles, much like lines of writing.

Children's early writing efforts are for fun as they explore this new medium spontaneously. At some point, however, they may want to communicate something even in scribbles. Using the materials in the writing center, you can help them make

Figure 6.7   Young Children's Writing Behaviors

Source: From *50 Early Childhood Literacy Strategies* (p. 52) by Janice J. Beaty, 2005, Upper Saddle River, NJ: Merrill/Prentice Hall. Reprinted with permission.

- Scribbles in a line across a page
- Scribbles in a line under a drawing scribble or picture
- Fills pages with lines of writing-like scribbles
- Makes a few mock letters in lines of scribbles
- Makes strings of letters
- Makes printed letters here and there, some reversed
- Prints letters of first name, not in order, some reversed
- Prints letters of name in order
- Prints other words in "invented spelling"

signs for their block buildings, write a letter to someone, write their scribbled names on a sign-up sheet for the computer, or sign out for a book to take home overnight. Children who use such "mock writing" in meaningful ways are progressing to the *meaning* level of exploratory play. Their scribbles may even begin to look like real letters.

Figure 6.7, "Young Children's Writing Behaviors," lists the steps that many children follow as they emerge into literacy. Don't expect children to progress through these steps in a few weeks or a few months. It may take a child an entire year or more to complete. The list is more for teachers as an observation tool to see if they can identify where children are in their development and where they can go with teacher scaffolding.

Some children may start "writing" their own stories. You can encourage such efforts by mounting scribble stories on the wall in the writing area. Other children may tell you, "You write it. I don't know how to write." You can answer, truthfully, "I used to know how to do scribble writing, but I forgot. So you'll have to write it for me."

Not all children will reach this level, nor should you expect them to. Encourage children to use the writing area in any way they want, just as they do the art area. Yours will be a supportive and facilitating role, not a direct teaching role. That will come later in elementary school. Instead, provide the paper and writing tools for their own private efforts and congratulate them on the results.

Taking Dictation

When children tell oral stories, many teachers write them down on an easel pad as they talk. Then they can read the stories back to the children while pointing to the words they have written. Taking dictation like this is an important introduction to the purpose of writing and the function of printed language, according to Tunks and Giles (2009). They tell us, "Through dictation children learn the general purpose of writing, become aware of the speech-to-text connection, gain basic knowledge of sound-symbol relationships, and are introduced to conventions of print, including capitalization and punctuation" (p. 23).

Some teachers send home a stuffed animal for a child to play with along with a journal for adults in the family to write a story the child tells about the animal. When the animal and journal are returned, the teacher (or the child) can read this story to the class. Other in-class possibilities for dictation include children dictating what they did on a field trip, writing an invitation to a potluck supper, or making a list of steps to take for a science experiment.

Children's Writing Opportunities

In addition, provide opportunities to motivate children's own writing, just as you do their speaking, listening, and reading. Bring in some picture postcards and have interested children "write" to one another and "mail" the cards in each other's mailboxes made from shoe boxes. Another time they may want to write to children in the class next door. Children may also want to make greeting cards and write notes to their parents and grandparents. These can be scribbled or even drawn with pictures representing words.

If children know how to regulate their own turns in the classroom curriculum areas with name tags or necklaces, have them also use a sign-up sheet for a change. A small clipboard with a pencil attached can be fastened at the entrance to each area.

Children may want to write notes to their friends or family.

The number of children allowed in the area can be noted on the clipboard tablet. Other sign-up sheets can be used for taking turns with the computer, the tricycle, the cassette/CD player, and other popular items. Children can write their names under one another's however they wish—in a scribble, with printed letters, or in a symbol. Most children can identify their own scribbles quite well.

Books as Lead-Ins to Writing Activities

Read books to the children in which the characters communicate by writing. Making lists is a simple activity that many children love to do.

> Read them *Wallace's Lists* (Bottner & Kruglik, 2004) about the little mouse Wallace who keeps a list of everything: his clothes, his pets, stories he loves, exciting weather, and to-do lists. Children can make their own to-do list every day about things they want to do in the classroom. Those who cannot write words can make a list of tiny drawings. Post these lists in the writing center.

In *Giggle, Giggle, Quack* (Cronin, 2002), Farmer Brown's duck finds a pencil and begins writing notes to Brother Bob, whom the farmer puts in charge while he goes on vacation. Hilarious chaos ensues. Children love to hear these stories and look at the pictures over and over. They quickly get their own ideas about communicating by writing, and they may want to start their own note-writing campaign, making their own demands!

In *Diary of a Worm* (Cronin, 2003), *Diary of a Spider* (Cronin, 2005), and *Diary of a Fly* (Cronin, 2007), these creatures write comical diaries that show the children yet another type of writing for communication. After reading them, staple some blank pages together for each of the children to begin keeping their own journals. Even children who only scribble can try drawing pictures to illustrate activities in their daily journal.

Alphabet Letters

Besides scribbling, preschool children will soon begin trying to print alphabet letters, usually the letters of their names. Some children have already started printing their names at home. Others may know only the first initial. Should you "teach" these children the ABCs? The answer is "not exactly." They will teach themselves the letters they need to know if you provide them with developmentally appropriate materials and opportunities. As Green (1998) notes, "Knowledge of all the letter names and forms is by no means a prerequisite to writing. Many children begin writing their names when they know only a few letter forms" (p. 226).

Children, in fact, go through another developmental sequence in learning to print letters. They may sing the alphabet song, but it is not an especially good

Some children may start printing nonsense words.

letter-learning device. In fact, children hear "elemenopee" as a single rhyming word, not the five separate letters: L-M-N-O-P. They may not even know the *names* of the letters in their name when they print them or know what the separate letters sound like at first. What they lack is an understanding of the *alphabetic principle*, that letters represent sounds.

Some children even start by printing nonsense words with strings of random letters because they do not understand that speech sounds and letters are connected. Schickedanz and Casbergue (2009) tell us, "A major developmental leap occurs when children discover that spoken words are made up of sounds, and that these have some connection to letters in printed words" (p. 48). This discovery is called *phonological awareness*.

How will they learn this? Just as they learned all the other new things in their world: by playing around with them. Put out three-dimensional wood or plastic or magnetic alphabet letters in the writing center. Children can play with them to find their own name letters or to match letters that are the same. You can play letter sound games with them as well. What objects in the classroom can they find that start with the same sound as the first letter of their name? (e.g., B for Ben: books, blocks, balls, baby dolls, etc.). You can also read books full of rhyming words. Bring in letter stampers and stamp pads, letter stencils, and peel-off letters to attach to things that start with the letters.

This is also the time for alphabet books. Today's alphabet books are anything but traditional. Try to find ones that tell exciting stories about the letters. Or even one where the letters tell their own story.

Books as Lead-Ins to Alphabet Activities

> The classic book *Chicka Chicka Boom Boom* (Martin & Archambault, 1989) is a favorite. The letters talk about meeting at the top of the coconut tree, and worry if they will have enough room. It's a rhyming race to the top, and of course they all fall down. Have each child wear a yarn necklace with a letter fastened to it and talk for their letter when it is time. Or you can make or purchase a standing tree and letters. If children get caught up with being these letters, have them make up their own rhyming story about their letters.

Max's ABC (Wells, 2006) seems destined to become another classic. Max and Ruby have an alphabetical adventure when the **A**nts from Max's **A**nt farm escape and crawl up Max's pants to **B**ite his **B**irthday **C**upcake. Your children should be able to reenact the scenario with glee while pretending about the **B**athtub, the **T**oast, and the **V**acuum cleaner.

Superhero ABC (McLeod, 2006) has Astro-Man, Always Alert for An Alien Attack along with a different alphabetical superhero on each page: Bubble-Man, Captain Cloud, Goo Girl, and Multiplying Mike, to name a few. After listening to this, children should be able to invent their own alphabet of superheroes and make up adventures for each one.

Other alphabet books:

Alpha Oops! The Day Z Went First (Kontis, 2006)

The Beetle Alphabet Book (Pallotta, 2004)

N Is for Navidad (Elya & Banks, 2007)

Computer Alphabet Programs

Children can also teach themselves about alphabet letters on simple CD-ROM alphabet computer programs (see the list of Web sites at the end of the chapter):

Alphabet Express Preschool	*Disney Learning Preschool*
Bailey's Book House	*Dr. Seuss's ABC*
Blue's ABC Activities	*Jumpstart Preschool*
Chicka Chicka Boom Boom	*Reader Rabbit Great Alphabet Race*
Curious George Pre-K ABCs	

SUMMARY

This chapter discusses how brain research shows us the importance of positive early child–adult interaction in the development of a child's communication skills. It describes children's verbal and literacy skills, giving suggestions on how teachers can help youngsters develop verbal communication by becoming active listeners, soundproofing the room so that children can hear themselves speak, providing a stress-free environment to support children's confidence in speaking, giving children reasons to communicate, and supporting children's conversations. Teachers need to evaluate their own language for their use of responsive rather than restrictive speech. Suggestions and books for supporting bilingual children, especially Spanish speakers, are included.

Books and extension activities to motivate children's listening, speaking, and emergent reading are also discussed, along with a list of young children's reading behaviors. Directions on how best to read books to children, how to help them reenact stories dramatically, and how to use book puppets are given, with special emphasis on "predictable books" to encourage emergent reading. Emergent writing is discussed along with a list of young children's writing behaviors and books that lead to emergent writing activities. A discussion of the alphabetic principle and the development of children's phonological awareness concludes the chapter.

Ethical Dilemma

Several parents have approached the teacher with a petition they are about to circulate against the program for including Spanish-speaking activities in a mostly Anglo classroom. They feel that all children should learn English, even immigrant children, and that including even the smallest amount of Spanish in the classroom will hinder the children's English learning. What would you do?

LEARNING ACTIVITIES

1. Read one or more of the Suggested Readings cited or view Web sites, and add 10 file cards to your file with specific ideas for helping children develop communication skills. Include the reference source on each card.

2. Work with a shy or nonverbal child, using suggestions in this chapter to help but not pressure him or her to speak.

3. Review 10 of the children's books discussed in this chapter, making a file card for each. Read several of these books to individuals or a small group following suggestions in this chapter. Record the results.

4. Do a story reenactment with children based on a favorite book. Record the results.

5. Bring in a new predictable book for the children and read it to them, extending the experience with a puppet or other activity, and record the results.

6. Use an alphabet book and activity with the children. Observe and record the results.

7. Have several children engage in a simple writing/scribbling activity and analyze where each stands in the "Young Children's Writing Behaviors," Figure 6.7.

8. Read one of the books to a small group about making lists or keeping a diary and have the children make lists or write in a journal.

SUGGESTED READINGS

Barclay, K. H. (2010). Using song picture books to support early literacy development. *Childhood Education, 86*(3), 138–145.

Birckmayer, J., Kennedy, A., & Stonehouse, A. (2010). Sharing spoken language: Sounds, conversations, and told stories. *Young Children, 65*(1), 34–39.

Burman, L. (2009). *Are you listening? Fostering conversations that help young children learn.* St. Paul, MN: Redleaf Press.

Gafney, J. S., Ostrosky, M. M., & Hemmeter, M. L. (2008). Books as natural support for young children's literacy learning. *Young Children, 63*(4), 87–93.

McNair, J. C. (2007). Say my name, say my name: Using children's names to enhance early literacy development. *Young Children, 62*(5), 84–89.

McVicker, C. J. (2007). Young readers respond: The importance of child participation in emerging literacy. *Young Children, 62*(3), 18–22.

Shagoury, R. (2009a). Language to language: Nurturing writing development in multilingual classrooms. *Young Children, 64*(2), 52–57.

Shagoury, R. (2009b). *Raising writers: Understanding and nurturing young children's writing development.* Boston: Allyn & Bacon.

Wanerman, T. (2010). Using story drama with young preschoolers. *Young Children, 65*(2), 20–28.

Yopp, H. K., & Yopp, R. H. (2009). Phonological awareness is child's play. *Young Children, 64*(1), 12–18.

WEB SITES

Children's Software Online
http://www.childrenssoftwareonline.com

Class Source
http://www.classsource.com

Early Years
http://www.naeyc.org

Kids Click
http://www.kidsclick.com

National Association for Bilingual Education
http://www.nabe.org

PBSKids
http://pbskids.org

Reading Is Fundamental
http://www.rif.org

Reading Rockets
http://www.readingrockets.org

Read Write Think
http://www.readwritethink.org

Super Kids
http://www.superkids.com

Teaching Strategies
http://www.teachingstrategies.org

Zero to Three/Brain Wonders
http://www.zerotothree.org/brainwonders

CHILDREN'S BOOKS

*Ada, A. F. (2002). *I love Saturdays y domingos.* New York: Atheneum.

Blumenthal, D. (2007). *Charley hits it big.* New York: HarperCollins.

Bergman, M. (2005). *Snip snap! What's that?* New York: Greenwillow.

Bock, L. (2003). *Oh, crumps! ¡Ay, caramba!* Green Bay, WI: Raven Tree Press.

Bottner, B. (2010). *Miss Brooks loves books (and I don't).* New York: Knopf.

Bottner, B., & Kruglik, G. (2004). *Wallace's lists.* New York: Katherine Tegen Books.

Child, L. (2004). *I am too absolutely small for school.* Cambridge, MA: Candlewick Press.

Child, L. (2008). *I completely know about guinea pigs.* New York: Dial.

Child, L. (2009). *I will be especially very careful.* New York, Dial.

*Cox, J. (2005). *Don't be silly, Mrs. Millie!* New York: Marshall Cavendish.

Cronin, D. (2002). *Giggle, giggle, quack.* New York: Simon & Schuster.

Cronin, D. (2003). *Diary of a worm.* New York: Joanna Cotler Books.

Cronin, D. (2005). *Diary of a spider.* New York: Joanna Cotler Books.

Cronin, D. (2007). *Diary of a fly.* New York: Joanna Cotler Books.

Dole, M. L. (2003). *Drum, Chavi, drum.* San Francisco: Children's Book Press.

Edwards, P. (2007). *Oliver has something to say.* Montreal, Canada: Lobster Press.

*Elya, S. M. (2006). *Bebe goes shopping.* Orlando, FL: Harcourt.

*Elya, S. M., & Banks, M. (2007). *N is for Navidad.* San Francisco: Chronicle Books.

Garcia, E. (2008). *Tip tip dig dig.* New York: Sterling Publishing.

Garcia, E. (2008). *Toot toot beep beep.* New York: Sterling Publishing.

Guarino, D. (1989). *Is your mama a llama?* New York: Scholastic.

*Hoberman, M. A. (1998). *Miss Mary Mack.* Boston: Little, Brown.

Kontis, A. (2006). *Alpha oops! The day Z went first.* Somerville, MA: Candlewick Press.

*Kurtz, J. (1990). *I'm calling Molly.* Morton Grove, IL: Whitman.

Lord, C. (2010). *Hot rod hamster.* New York: Scholastic Press.

Marin, C. (2008). *Captain Cheech.* New York: HarperCollins.

Martin, B., & Archambault, J. (1989). *Chicka chicka boom boom.* New York: Simon & Schuster.

*McLeod, B. (2006). *Superhero ABC.* New York: HarperCollins.

*Novak, M. (2005). *Flip flop bop.* (2005). Brookfield, CT: Roaring Brook Press.

Pallotta, J. (2004). *The beetle alphabet book.* Watertown, MA: Charlesbridge.

Pullen, Z. (2008). *Friday my Radio Flyer flew.* New York: Simon & Schuster.

Shannon, D. (1998). *No, David!* New York: The Blue Sky Press.

Stevens, J. R. (1993). *Carlos and the squash plant.* Flagstaff, AZ: Rising Moon.

Sutton, S. (2008). *Roadwork.* Somerville, MA: Candlewick Press.

Tafolla, C. (2008). *What can you do with a rebozo?* Berkeley, CA: Tricycle Press.

Thomson, P. (2003). *Drat that fat cat!* New York: Arthur A. Levine Books.

Waddell, M. (1992). *Owl babies.* Cambridge, MA: Candlewick Press.

Wells, R. (2006). *Max's ABC.* New York: Viking.

Whybrow, I. (2007). *Hello! Is this Grandma?* Wilton, CT: Tiger Tales.

Advancing Creative Skills

W HEN we speak of a person with *creative skills,* we generally mean someone who has original ideas, who does things in new and different ways, and who uses imagination and inventiveness to bring about novel forms. Can young children be creative in these ways?

Not only can they be, but they are. Creativity seems to be intuitive in young children, something they are born with. From the very beginning they have the capacity to look at things, to hear, smell, taste, and touch things from an entirely original perspective—their own. After all, preschool children are new and unique beings in a strange and complex world. The only way they can make sense of things around them is to explore with their senses: to try them out, to see what makes things the way they are, to see if they can be any different.

Isenberg and Jalongo (2010) tell us that: "Imagination is defined as the ability to form rich and vivid mental images or concepts of people, places, and things, and situations that are not present. Fantasy occurs when a person uses the imagination to create particularly vivid mental images that are make-believe. Experts on creativity have long believed that for most human beings, imagination and fantasy are very active during early childhood" (p. 14).

Young children bring to any activity a spirit of wonder, great curiosity, and a spontaneous drive to explore, experiment, and manipulate in a playful and original fashion. This is creativity. It is the same impulse that actors, artists, writers, musicians, dancers, and research scientists have.

You may respond that not all children behave like this. Some show little creativity or little interest in creative activities. As we noted in the chapter on cognitive skills, some children show little interest in anything new. Some will not engage in any activities unless directed by the teacher. These are the children who need our special assistance in rediscovering the creativity they were born with.

Acceptance and Encouragement

Creativity flourishes only where it is accepted and encouraged. Infants, toddlers, and preschoolers who have been dominated by the adults around them and not allowed to do anything their own way may not show much creativity. They have already learned the sad lesson that experimentation only gets them into trouble. Children who have been the victims of neglect, lack of love, harsh discipline, or overprotection seem to lack the spark of creativity as well.

It is thus extremely important for teachers, assistants, volunteers, and student teachers in preschool programs to help rekindle that spark. It is imperative that young children be able to use the creative skills of pretending, imaginative thinking, fantasizing, and inventiveness in learning to deal with the complex world around them. Strange as it may seem, these are the skills that will help them most in problem solving, getting along with others, understanding their world, and, eventually, doing abstract thinking. Promoting creativity is, in fact, a most effective way to promote cognitive development.

Teacher Creativity

How creative are you as a teacher of young children? Do you allow yourself to be caught up in the children's pretending and sometimes take on a zany role yourself? Or do you think it is not dignified for an adult to act in a foolish or funny manner like that? Do you like to have fun with the children, telling funny stories and laughing at their jokes? Do you make fun out of ordinary things like the teacher Mrs. Millie in *Don't Be Silly, Mrs. Millie* from Chapter 6, who had the children sit down on the bug (the rug) for a story? Try being a Mrs. Millie for a day. Think of all the objects in the classroom you could convert to something silly (for example: the clock—a rock; seat—meat; table—label; light—night; drink—ink). Can you do it? Would you want to?

If children see you as being lighthearted and full of fun, they will tend to be that way too. The way you use your creativity should be to open up their own creativity in new and spontaneous ways. Isenberg and Jalongo point out, "The outcomes of creative teaching are to set children's creativity free and support the conditions for them to create, not to put on a polished performance for them" (2010, p. 28). If Mrs. Millie was acting silly just to make the children laugh, she has missed the point. We trust she was hoping to loosen up the children so they could be creative in the way they talked, acted, and thought.

Freedom

The key to setting up an environment that promotes creativity is freedom. Children must be free to explore, experiment, manipulate, invent, and pretend spontaneously. Having an adult show them how or tell them what to do defeats this purpose. Adults do not see things or use things as children do. Young children need the opportunity to work out many ideas on their own and in their own way, without adult direction or interference.

GIVES CHILDREN THE TIME, OPPORTUNITY, AND FREEDOM TO DO PRETENDING AND FANTASY ROLE PLAYING

One of the areas where children are not only encouraged but expected to do pretending and role playing is in the dramatic play center. The setup there often includes a child-size version of a kitchen with wooden table, chairs, stove, refrigerator, and cupboards. Or it may be a child-size store with shelves of boxes and a checkout counter, or a doctor's office, or a restaurant. Children are encouraged to play roles they have seen enacted by their parents, community helpers, or people from the field trip sites they have visited. They learn how it feels to be someone else as they pretend to be a mother, father, doctor, police officer, or firefighter. This type of drama is also called *enactment.* It occurs when children adopt the actions, feelings, thoughts, and behaviors of people in particular situations. (See Chapter 9 for more on dramatic play.)

Another type of dramatic play that may be even more conducive to young children's development of creativity is fantasy role play, which involves the children in pretending to be a fictitious storybook hero or to be themselves in a fantasy setting. It can start with a realistic situation and catapult the children into an adventure that may carry them to the stars and back. Isenberg and Jalongo note, "Fantasy is a subset of imaginative thinking. Fantasy occurs when a person uses the imagination to create particularly vivid mental images or concepts that are make-believe, impossible, or at least not yet possible. Fantasy is a 'what if' situation" (2010, p. 14).

A good method for involving young children in such rich pretending is to read them a picture book featuring fantastical situations and then provide props for their own role play. Look for books whose titles start with the words "If . . ." or "What if . . . ."

Books as Lead-Ins to Fantasy Role Play

> *If I Had a Dragon* (Ellery & Ellery, 2006) is a simple book with a green fire-breathing dragon sitting on top of a tiny boy on a bike on its cover. The boy is Morton, and his mother tells him to go play with his little brother. If only the brother would turn into something fun like a kite, or a bulldozer, or a *dragon!* And he does! Morton imagines what he would do if he had a dragon. He finds out it's dangerous!

What would your children do if they had a dragon? Read the book to a small group at a time and ask them each to imagine what they would do if they had a dragon. Would they like to pretend about that? Have props ready: colored paper to cut into a long scaly tail or dragon wings they can wear. Have different colored sheets—dragons don't have to be green, you know. Put out dragon paint at the easels or dragon finger paints on sheets of butcher paper. If they want, the children can tell you fanciful tales about their dragons that you can tape-record. If they would rather turn their brothers into something else, that's okay too.

When children's imaginations are turned loose, watch out! They may even end up on Mars or Jupiter. If you don't have access to this book (or any of the books mentioned), use your own imagination. Tell the story without a book about the little boy who turns his brother into a dragon, and then what happens. Ask your children to help you tell what happens when they go on a campout, or a picnic, or when they blast off to outer space.

This boy found a magic belt to help him blast off to outer space.

Other books as lead-ins to fantasy role play:

Miss Brooks Loves Books (and I Don't) (Bottner, 2010)

If Mom Had Three Arms (Orloff, 2006)

If You Give a Cat a Cupcake (Numeroff, 2008)

NAEYC Criteria for Curriculum Standard

Describe how you would meet the following standard:

2.J.01 Children are provided varied opportunities to gain an appreciation of art, music, drama, and dance in ways that reflect cultural diversity.

Multiethnic Books

Both boys and girls should be encouraged to take on fantasy roles from the books you read. In *Abuela* (Dorros, 1991), a little Hispanic girl named Rosalba and her grandmother from New York City start out for the park, but they end up flying above the city and out to the Statue of Liberty in Rosalba's vivid imagination. When they finally land back at the park, her Spanish-speaking grandmother says, "*Vamos*" ("Let's go"), and off they go to another adventure in a rowboat on the last page.

A prop box for this fantasy can contain miniature people, boats, planes, cars, and table blocks for creating a city. The block center or the sand table can make a fine city park with a hand mirror for a pond. Can any of the children say a few Spanish words after hearing this story several times? As Burton and Edwards (2006) note, "Dramatic play is especially useful for children who are English language learners. Pretend play enables them to communicate in an informal setting and gather information that will be helpful to them, even beyond the classroom" (p. 6).

In *Tar Beach* (Ringgold, 1991), an African American inner-city girl does some pretend flying of her own. Cassie accompanies her family to the black rooftop of their apartment building during hot summer nights for a picnic, with blankets and picnic food on the "tar beach." Later as she and her brother lie on their blankets looking up at the stars and the lights from nearby buildings, Cassie imagines herself flying over the city to see the sights. (Both of these older books are available in paperback.)

Character dolls accompany a number of books such as *Tar Beach* and *Abuela*. Children love to play with character dolls such as these, inventing their own adventures. Be prepared to have Cassie and Rosalba fly around your classroom and tell about the imaginary sights they have seen. If you do not have the dolls, you can cut out paper dolls from page scans from the books, for the children to pretend with.

Nonfantasy roles of multiethnic children can also be encouraged by reading nonfantasy books such as *Too Many Tamales* (Soto, 1993) in which the Hispanic girl Maria helps her mother make tamales for a Christmas party. When the mother takes off her diamond ring to knead the dough, Maria puts it on her own thumb as she continues to help. Later on she remembers about the ring and thinks it must have fallen into the dough. She enlists her cousins to eat all the tamales. Your children may want to reenact the book story or play similar roles in the dramatic play center. Put out multicultural plastic food sets as props. In one class the children invented their own tamales by using the plastic egg rolls from a Chinese food set and wrapping them with paper for the tamale corn husks. Then they hid a toy ring in the wrapping for someone to try to find, just as in the story.

Superhero Play

Children love superheroes and love to pretend to be them at home, on the playground, and in the preschool. Most teachers, however, do not love superheroes. They see them as leading the children into loud, wild, destructive types of behavior—totally out of control. Should teachers ban such play from the classroom? Before taking such a drastic decision, teachers may want to consider two things: learning why children are so attracted to superhero play and learning how superhero play can be allowed to discharge children's pent-up energy while helping them learn positive lessons.

Eddie, age 3, has this to say about superheroes: "I like to be Superman because he's a big guy, and big guys have the power. They can do lots of things, and they never die" (Hoffman, 2004, p. 4). Superhero play is definitely fantasy play. As Hoffman points out, "In superhero play, children don't just mimic adult activities, they become larger-than-life characters that help them explore their fears, hopes, and passions" (p. 5).

Most children like to pretend to be adults in their dramatic play: mom, dad, big brother, police officer, doctor, construction worker, or firefighter, for example. These are roles that make them feel big, grown up, in control, and able to do important things. In their world of being little, helpless, not in control, and unable to do important things, children see superhero roles as even better than adult roles. Superheroes are bigger than the adults they know, and they have powers to do incredible things. If only they could be a superhero! The next best thing is pretending to be one.

Books as Lead-Ins to Superhero Play

Once teachers understand the reasons for children's strong attraction to superheroes, they can support this play by leading children to imagine superheroes who do not fight, hurt people, use weapons, or act violently. What superheroes are these? They are the ones you and the children invent by reading books such as *Superhero ABC* (McLeod, 2006) as discussed in Chapter 6. This is not an ABC book for infants and toddlers. It is definitely for grown-up preschoolers who might like to pretend to be Bubble-Man who blows bubbles at bullies, Captain Cloud who calmly catches crooks, Danger Man who does daring deeds, or Goo Girl who shoots gobs of goo at gangsters. Because only one or two pages illustrate each superhero, children need to make up their adventures with their own imaginations. The only props needed are capes and masks or safety goggles. You can provide these. Talk to the children first about what makes a superhero:

They are big and strong.	They can jump over buildings.	They can see through buildings.
They are brave.	They can fly through the air.	They have X-ray vision.
They don't get afraid.	They don't hurt people.	Girls can be superheroes.
They fight the bad guys.	They don't hurt animals.	They can run fast.
They are the good guys.	They save the Earth.	They can turn invisible.

Can girls be superheroes? Lulu from the book *Ladybug Girl* (Soman & Davis, 2008) shows them how. When her big brother won't let her play with him, she dresses all in red, wearing red boots and red paper wings with black dots, and takes off as "Ladybug Girl" who helps people. Have your children make a list of all the helping things she does. This is only the beginning—an introduction to the next book.

In *Ladybug Girl and Bumblebee Boy* (Soman & Davis, 2009) Lulu goes off to the playground in the park and finds a new friend who becomes Bumblebee Boy. Together they use their powers to scare off a monster (squirrel) and defeat a giant snake (slide). But when new superheroes try to join their Bug Squad they must use real powers to turn fighting into helping.

These books can motivate your children to try their own hand at becoming superheroes who help instead of hurt others. You can even make it a science adventure if the children decide to be insect superheroes and form their own Bug Squad. Once the children have chosen what superheroes they want to be, help them make a list of their powers and decide what missions they want to go on. If they need special props, let them use rulers, blocks, magnets, sifters, ladles, and what-have-you as imaginary equipment and make their own bug hats and wings. Afterward they can tell the class what good deeds their superheroes accomplished.

Superhero play like this can sometimes get too rough, and you may need to intervene. As Hoffman explains, "There are times when superhero play can become inappropriate or dangerous despite all attempts by the teaching staff to enforce rules respectfully and turn the play into a positive experience. As part of their fantasies, children can forget that their bodies aren't designed for flying off high places or breaking bricks with their hands" (2004, p. 79). You may need to step in and redirect the play, just as you do with other dramatic play that gets out of control. When things calm down, children can try it again, or wait until another day.

Inclusion

Creative drama and pretending is for every child in the classroom. Edwards (2006) tells how creative drama improves the attitudes of non–special needs children toward children with disabilities. They see that children with disabilities can play active

Books can motivate children to be bug superheroes.

rather than passive roles. She explains that if you ask your children to pretend to be firefighters, you must provide visual cues for a child who is hearing impaired. You need to check each prop to make sure there are no sharp edges and that the props can be easily recognized by a child who is visually impaired. Children with special needs should never be forced to participate in creative drama but encouraged gently. When the drama is finished, have children talk about what happened and what their roles were so that everyone understands what was going on (pp. 209–210).

PROVIDES A VARIETY OF ART MATERIALS AND ACTIVITIES FOR CHILDREN TO EXPLORE ON THEIR OWN

When most teachers think of creativity, the art area comes to mind first of all. Unfortunately for young children, this is often the least creative area in the entire classroom because it is entirely adult directed. Nothing happens spontaneously. Adults get out the art supplies, set up activities on tables, instruct the children on how to use them, and then stay at the tables to make sure the youngsters follow directions.

This is not creative art. It is more of an exercise on following directions. Structured activities like these should not be banished from the classroom, because they are appropriate for promoting manipulative and direction-following skills. But teachers and children should not confuse them with creative art. As Isenberg and Jalongo (2010) remind us, "If it isn't original, it isn't art" (p. 126).

As mentioned previously, the key to creativity is freedom. Children need to be free to explore, experiment, invent, and pretend with art materials just as they do with blocks or dress-up clothes. Adults rarely consider it necessary to remain in the house-keeping corner to make sure the children dress up "properly" or play roles "correctly," yet this kind of supervision occurs all too frequently with art. As Fox and Diffily (2000) insist, "Easy access to a variety of art materials and people who encourage exploration of those materials is essential to the creative process. Equally important is the children's freedom to select the topics and to stay with an activity until they determine it is finished" (p. 6).

Process Versus Product

We need to step back and think about our primary purpose for having art in the class-room. Is it to have children paint a nice picture or make a lovely collage to take home to Mother? If this is true in your classroom, then you have confused the product of art with the process. Most preschool children do not yet have the skills or the develop-ment level to turn out an accomplished art product. Our goal should instead be to as-sist children in becoming involved in the creative process, because it is this process that is most important in young children's development.

We should not be faulted for making the mistake of focusing on the product. It is much easier to see a picture than a process. Moreover, no one ever told us this was not the proper way to "teach" art. After all, isn't everyone more concerned with the picture than the painting of it? Not everyone.

Take a look at the children in your classroom who are involved in painting. The only thing that seems to matter to them is the experience, that is, the process. They focus on their product only after adults have made a fuss about it, or after they have learned that this is what pleases adults. Before that, they seem more interested in things like smearing the paint around, slapping one color on another, moving the brush back and forth, and covering everything they have painted with a new color. This is the process of art—and this type of experimentation is how creativity is born.

Easel Activities

How can you set up your art activities to promote children's freedom to create? First of all, have one or two easels that are kept out and ready for use every day. Large sheets of easel paper should be nearby for extended use. Children can choose to easel paint during the free-choice period by selecting an "easel necklace" or easel apron, for instance. No teacher direction or assistance should be needed. Children can learn to handle the brush and control the paint alone.

Observe beginners and you'll see how they manage. New painters spend a great deal of time trying out which hand to use, the best way to hold the brush, how to get paint from jar to paper, how to move paint around on the paper, and how to control the drips. In other words, they are "manipulating the medium" rather than painting a picture.

To help children manage this new medium, be sure to have short "chubby brushes" or beginner's brushes for easel painting. Some easel brushes are the right thickness for pudgy fingers but too long for preschoolers to manipulate easily. You might want to put out only one or two colors of paint until children are ready to handle more.

Art Supplies

Store commonly used art materials within children's reach. Have paper, paints, brushes, crayons, felt-tip markers, paste, scissors, and construction paper available for free use when the children arrive. Keep art supplies on low shelves next to the children's tables or work space to make it easier for children to see and select from what is available and later to return items to their shelf space when they are finished. Be sure to mount cutouts or tracings of the art items on nearby shelves for children's easy return to the proper space.

You will want colored construction paper, white drawing paper, brown paper bags, paste, glue, scissors, crayons, felt-tip pens, colored chalk, finger paints, yarn pieces, Popsicle sticks, pipe cleaners, and a basket of collage scraps. Let children know they are free to select from the materials to use at the art tables, as they wish.

At other times, you may want to set up the art activity before the children arrive and let them "play" with it creatively during free-choice periods. Take play dough, for example. In the beginning, you may want to mix the dough and have it ready for the children to explore and experiment with when they come in. Perhaps you'll put out rolling pins and cookie cutters for the children to use by themselves. You can do this for a number of days with different implements, once the children's interest in rolling pins and cookie cutters has waned.

After children have exhausted the possibilities for manipulating the tools and dough, you can involve them in the fun of measuring and mixing the dough themselves before they play with it. Another time you can have them add food coloring of varying colors for an entirely different effect.

At another time, put out colored chalk, dishes of water, and brown paper grocery bags. Children can experiment by drawing on the bags with or without water, for different effects. The chalk can be dipped in water each time the child draws. Another day, bring in chalkboards for the children's chalk-drawing experiments.

No matter what art materials you use, arrange them so that the children can be creative with them on their own. Collage scraps, paste, and backing paper can be waiting for children on one of their tables. What they do with them is up to them. Another day have food coloring, medicine droppers, and jars of water waiting.

Finger painting can be done on smooth paper, on tabletops, on large plastic trays, or on large sheets of butcher paper on the floor. Children can start with shaving cream to get used to the messiness of finger painting but still be able to clean it up easily. The point is to set up art activities so that children can work creatively on their own. Occasionally you may have to get involved to get the children started, but then you can withdraw and let them finish by themselves.

The same principles apply to mixing paint. Let children experiment on their own with two colors at first. Yellow and blue make green; yellow and red make orange; blue and red make purple. After experimenting with each of these pairs of colors for a while, put out three colors for mixing, and then later, four.

Acceptance of Art Products

If freedom is the most important aspect of creativity, then acceptance is the second. You must accept unconditionally whatever the child produces, just as you accept the child unconditionally. Not all children may live up to the standards you expect, but that does not mean you don't accept them and value them as human beings.

The same is true of their creative products. A smudge of brown covering an easel paper may mean a breakthrough to a child struggling to conquer the medium of drippy paint and awkward brushes. You must accept it for what it is—not a painting, but a process, the results of a difficult struggle with the medium. In addition, you must accept it honestly. What should you say? How about: "You surely used a lot of paint in your work today, Charles!" That is an honest appraisal of what happened, and the child can accept that.

However, a child may have done a representational drawing and want your reaction to it. If you are not sure what to say because you are not sure what the drawing represents, you can respond by commenting on the artistic elements of the drawing. Its color, its patterns, its shape, the lines used, the texture of the painting, and the placement of the painting on the paper are all good possibilities. To ask a child "What is it?" may be insulting when the child knows the red blob is a fire engine. Instead, you might say, "I like the way you used the red color. What do you think?" or "I really can see that picture. The color is bright and beautiful."

Some teachers ask children, "Do you want to tell me about your picture?" This is certainly a nonjudgmental comment and may elicit information about the picture that you can then follow up on. However, what the child is showing you may not be a picture at all but the results of the artistic process she was following. She will probably not be able to articulate that. Furthermore, children don't always want to talk about their paintings and drawings. Showing them to you may be only an indication that they are done and want you to see what they did.

To other children, their art is private. They may not want to talk about it or even show it to you. That should be their choice, but give them the opportunity to hang their work on the wall where art is displayed. Let the child place it

This girl seems to be painting a picture of a person and a rainbow.

where she wants, or you may give her the choice of mounting it first on backing paper to show it off better.

In the schools of Reggio Emilia in Italy young children produce artwork of amazing quality. Mulcahey (2009) tells us one of the reasons for this: "Teachers use rich language before and while their children are creating, which stimulates feelings and imagination. Children are often more imaginative and pictorial than adults, and this rich language feeds their thinking, resulting in a qualitatively diverse array of artworks" (p. 37).

What would you say to the girl who did the painting in this photo? What do you think she might answer? Mulcahey warns us not to make assumptions about children's artwork. She says: "There is no one right answer for what to say to children when they show you their artwork. Look at the elements the children have used, such as lines, shapes, colors, and textures. Just saying them out loud is a simple start" (2009, p. 35). As the girl continues her painting, she seems to be covering over everything she originally painted. This may help us understand that the *process* is more important to a young child than the *product*. Whatever you say to her, be sure it is accepting.

Books as Lead-Ins to Art Activities

> *Art* (McDonnell, 2006) is a simple book about a boy, Art, and the art he draws. Some pages show his scribbles or lines; some show splotches and dots. Then he begins drawing objects with a black crayon: a house, a tree, a cool car, stars, a moon. Finally, they all come together as he sleeps in a wonderful full-color picture of Art taking off for the moon. In the end his mother displays his original scribbles and squiggles on the refrigerator.

Keep this book in the art center and read it to individual children there who ask you to. What is their reaction? Does the story encourage them to talk about their own art? Or make their own book?

Children need to become aware of artists as well. In *Through Georgia's Eyes* (Rodriguez, 2006), the life of Georgia O'Keeffe, pioneer American artist, is portrayed in cut-paper collages of Georgia and her paintings. Her giant red poppies nearly pop off the page as do her rusty red canyons and white cow's skull. She saw the world through different eyes and painted what she saw. Be sure to obtain prints of Georgia's flowers for the children to look at. Then bring in bouquets of flowers from time to time for the children to investigate with their senses: sight, smell, touch. Do they see different shapes and colors too? Some children may want to paint their own impressions. Be sure to accept whatever they do.

Other books as lead-ins to talking about art:

Art from Her Heart: Folk Artist Clementine Hunter (Whitehead, 2008)
I'm the Best Artist in the Ocean (Sherry, 2008)

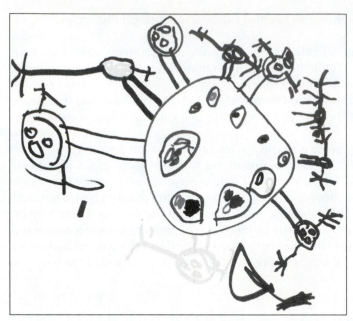

This girl has drawn everyone in her family sitting around a table.

Stages of Art Development

You will become more appreciative of children's art if you understand the various developmental stages children go through in drawing when they are allowed to express themselves spontaneously. (See Figure 7.1.) From 2 to 3 years old, children mainly scribble, which is an important stage that should not be discouraged if we want children to develop drawing skills. Scribbling is to drawing what babbling is to speaking. All children everywhere make these same markings, in the same way, at approximately the same age (Kellogg, 1969).

Sometime between 2 and 4 years old, the scribbles take on outline shapes such as circles, ovals, squares, triangles, and crosses. Between 3 and 5, children begin to make designs from the shapes they have been drawing. Although there are an unlimited number of possibilities, children usually draw only a few favorites over and over, such as "radials" and "suns." Between the ages of 4 and 5, their designs often take the form of a person. These so-called tadpole people grow out of suns, with the rays of the sun becoming the arms, legs, and hair of the person, and the circle becoming the face and the body. All children everywhere seem to make their first people this way.

By age 5, many children are at a pictorial stage, creating representational drawings. Whether they continue developing talent in art during their elementary school years depends as much on freedom and acceptance as it does on inborn skill.

It is important for you and the children's parents to know about the stages of art development in young children so that the next time a 3-year-old shows you a page of art scribbles, you will not be tempted to dismiss it as "only scribbles." Instead, you will know it is the child's first exciting step in the developmental process of learning to draw.

To demonstrate that you really do accept children's artwork, whether scribbles or pictures, make a collection of each child's paintings over a number of weeks or months. You can display children's paintings attractively in your room on backing paper or in frames. You can also take photos of each child working at an easel, as well as photos of his or her completed work to be included in a scrapbook about the child, a portfolio, or in your CDA Professional Resource File.

Figure 7.1   Stages of
Art Development

Source: Adapted from
Analyzing Children's Art by
R. Kellogg, 1969, Palo Alto,
CA: National Press.

2–3 years	<u>Scribble</u>
	Uncontrolled (marks on paper)
	Controlled (control of eye and hand movement)
2–4 years	<u>Shapes</u>
	Circles, squares, ovals, triangles, rectangles
3–5 years	<u>Designs</u>
	Suns (oval or square; short lines extending from sun)
	Radials (lines radiating out from dot or circle)
4–5 years	<u>Humans</u>
	Makes a "sun face"
	Horizontal line from each side as arms; two long lines from bottom as legs; may make circle hands and feet
4–5 years	<u>Pictorial</u>
	Animals with pointed ears
	Houses, cars, trees, flowers

ENCOURAGES CHILDREN TO CREATE AND HAVE FUN WITH MUSIC

Children need adult role models to dramatize to them how we want them to behave. This is as true in the creative arts as it is in eating food at the lunch table. The cliché is true: Children will do as we do, not as we say. If you want your children to be creative with music, then it is up to you to lead the way.

Your creative actions should be as natural and spontaneous as you want the children's to be. In other words, don't direct the children to watch what you're doing and copy you. You want children to take original actions spurred by your leadership, not to imitate you.

Are you afraid to sing in front of others? Many of us are. Could it have something to do with our own improper introduction to music? We owe it to the children in our care to avoid the same mistake with them. Music is essential for children's development. But not every teacher feels this way. As Snyder (1997) notes, "Parents and teachers who don't have a musical background may not perceive the value of early music experiences, or may feel awkward and inadequate to engage in musical activities" (p. 165).

As early childhood professionals in the 21st century, we need to know why it is essential to overcome this reluctance to include music as an important part of the curriculum. If you are one who feels inadequate in music, the following information may make you change your position.

Brain Research Regarding Music

Researchers have found that early exposure to music may be necessary or at least may greatly enhance the development of cognitive processes. "Music is the most direct route to thinking, because it requires neither words nor symbols to be perceived" (Snyder, 1997, p. 165). But early exposure to music is especially essential during the critical period for development of the brain's "music center." This critical period for development takes place during the preschool and beginning elementary years. What Snyder has to say is important news to many early childhood educators: "Music and other arts that evoke emotional response appear to open the gate to the neurocortex and higher level thinking. Music stimulates and motivates critical thinking" (p. 166).

Frank Wilson, a neuroscientist who has registered brain scans of children as they perform certain tasks, reports that when children read words, the language center of the brain lights up on his scanner. But when they read music, the entire brain lights up like a Christmas tree (Snyder, 1997, p. 168). Hap Palmer (2001), a children's music specialist, found that songs not only stimulate children's oral language development, but young children can even learn to read through singing the words in specially written books accompanied by musical tapes. Davies (2000) reports that because music heightens emotional involvement in learning, it makes it easier to remember information: "Music helps us store and retrieve rich, multisensory memories" (p. 149).

Shore and Strasser (2006) emphasize the benefits of infusing music throughout the early childhood curriculum. Figure 7.2 shows some of the benefits.

Chanting

Now that you know how important it is to involve your children in music, you need to make a concerted effort to do so. How will you begin? You don't need to be able

Figure 7.2 Music in the Curriculum

- Helps children synthesize experiences
- Helps children transition into new activities
- Calms down children during nap time
- Helps children share cultural traditions
- Helps children build self-esteem
- Improves academic performance in language and math

Some children clap during a chant.

to carry a tune; many of the children can't either. All that matters is that you have fun with sounds and you get the children involved. If you are having fun, the children will too. Start with a monotone chant. Make up your own if you don't know any.

Hap-py day, Hap-py day,
Let's have a, Happy, happy day!

Clap while you are chanting. Some of the children may follow your lead and clap along with you. Repeat the chant a few times, and perhaps some of the children will join in. This isn't done during a formal "music period." Let's not make music formal. It can be done any time you feel like it. Maybe something makes you feel happy. Maybe everyone is busily working and it makes you feel good. You are doing your song or chant because you feel like expressing an emotion. Whether or not the children respond doesn't matter, but your acting in this spontaneous and creative way sets the stage for children to make up songs or chants when they feel good too.

Books as Lead-Ins to Singing/Chanting a Happy Song

When familiar songs are written as children's picture books, children are getting "two-for-the-price-of-one." That is, they can sing the words to a familiar song while at the same time looking at those words written and illustrated in a book, an effective reading aid. If the song is a happy one, the whole class will benefit by the positive atmosphere it creates.

Song picture books have words to a familiar song written and illustrated in book form. "*If You're Happy and You Know It*" shows a little girl first clapping her hands. On the second verse a brown dog wags its tail. Then an elephant flaps its ears, and so on. Everyone can sing along and imitate the animals. Then have a child choose to be each of the animals and imitate it when her turn comes.

If they want more, have pairs of children each choose an animal to be. Signal them when it's their turn to perform. At the end, be sure to have everyone make their noises and motions all together in a grand finale. (And do it again, teacher!) Finally, have children make up new animals and their noises. If you don't have the book, sing the song anyway.

A new rendition of that old favorite has also made an appearance: *On Top of Spaghetti* (Johnson, 2006). This time the meatball rolls too fast for Yodeler Jones to catch it after somebody sneezes and it rolls out his door. That poor meatball ends up as mush, but the mush is magic and grows into a meatball tree, with the most dee-licious meatballs this side of Sicily. Your children will want to join in the song and laugh themselves silly over the wacky animal illustrations.

Other song picture books as lead-ins to singing:

I Love You a Bushel and a Peck (Wells, 2005)

She'll Be Coming 'Round the Mountain (Emmett & Allwright, 2006)

Children can also act out the words to familiar chants while singing them. If the chants also appear in picture books, teachers can scan the book pages, cut out and laminate the people and animal characters, and have children stand them up in the sand table when their verse is sung. Here are some of the books:

Miss Mary Mack (Hoberman, 1998)

Old MacDonald Had a Farm (Rounds, 1989)

Over the Rainbow (Collins, 2009) [CD included]

Skip to My Lou (Westcott, 1989)

The Wheels on the Bus (Kovalski, 1987)

The Seals on the Bus (Hort, 2000)

What fun children can have acting out the animal antics of seals, tigers, geese, snakes, and skunks in *The Seals on the Bus* as they sing the song to the tune of "The Wheels on the Bus Go Round and Round." Achilles (1999) suggests that individual children can play with the cutout characters in a sandbox cake pan theater while lis-tening to the song on headphones. If you do not have a tape of a particular song, make your own on a blank cassette as the children sing it. As she notes, "Sandbox theater provides an opportunity for an individual child to manipulate characters while listening to a musical story on headphones. The caregiver prepares the theater by filling a rectangular cake pan with sand and gluing pictures of the characters in a song on tongue depressors. The child moves the characters while listening to or singing the song" (p. 24).

Inclusion

Song picture books are valuable aids for helping children with special needs. As Isen-berg and Jalongo (2010) tell us: "For children with difficulty focusing, song picture books provide a concrete prompt; for DLLs song picture books support language learning; for children with visual impairments, song picture books can be sung; and for children with hearing impairments, song picture books can be viewed" (p. 170).

In addition to involving children in musical activities, Barclay (2010) points out: "Song picture books are wonderful tools for fostering emergent literacy skills; they can be used to develop concepts about books and print, language fluency, phonological awareness, vocabulary, comprehension, and emergent writing abilities" (p. 139). All this and they're fun, too!

Directions

Here's another fun musical activity. Instead of giving children directions by speaking them, try singing or chanting directions. It is much more effective. It can apply to any number of situations: putting on outside garments, setting the table, washing hands, or getting out cots for the afternoon nap (when you can whisper the chant). You can sing or chant a welcome to the children in the morning or when using their names through-out the day. Here are some beginning lines to familiar tunes just to get you started:

Where is Carlos? ("Where Is Thumbkin?")

Where, oh where, is nice little Lisa? ("Paw Paw Patch")

Rob, Rob, come to lunch. ("Skip to My Lou")

Here comes Keisha through the door. ("This Old Man")

What other situations during the day can you convert to songs? How about pickup time?

We're picking up the blocks,

We're picking up the blocks,

Clunk, clunk, clunk, clunk,

We're picking up the blocks.

(To the tune of "The Farmer in the Dell")

If the children join in, let them help you invent words for the other items to be picked up.

Creative Movement

You and the children can also enjoy creative movement along with the music you are making. Large-motor movements such as walking, jumping, hopping, running, and leaping can be done to music. Once children have learned a song or chant, you or they can begin to make appropriate movements. If the song expresses happiness, have the children make happy movements. How can they do it? Perhaps by jumping or clapping or hopping in a circle as they sing. Ask the children to show they feel happy with some kind of movement. Each child may express it differently. Using their bodies as well as their voices validates the feeling and increases their enjoyment (see Creative Movement in Chapter 4).

Physical education specialist Rae Pica (2009) also tells us: "Creative movement activities foster imagination. To replicate the movement of a turtle, children must imagine the slowness of that animal. To achieve a certain group shape or act of bal-ance, they must first envision it" (p. 60). These movements, of course, must be theirs alone and not imitations of the teacher.

Using Recorded Music

Even nonmusician teachers can provide a quality music program for young children by bringing in tapes or CDs from lullabies to the classics that children can listen to on headsets in the music center. Some can be instrumentals and others feature vocalists. As Jalongo (1996) notes, "Children respond to different types of music through different types of vocalizations and body movements" (p. 6).

Music can help you set moods in the classroom. Play it softly in the background during the free-choice period or louder during large-motor activities. The songs you sing with the children can come from recorded music. Play them over and over, and soon both you and the children will know the songs by heart. Then when you want to calm down the children before naptime, for example, sing (or chant) calming songs with them. Some CDs that children especially like include these from Constructive Playthings (phone: 1-800-832-0572):

Quiet Places (Hap Palmer)

A Child's Quiet World of Lullabies (Hap Palmer)

Dreamland: World Lullabies (Various Artists)

Songs Children Love to Sing (Ella Jenkins)

You'll Sing a Song and I'll Sing a Song (Ella Jenkins)

Manipulating the Music Medium

What other kinds of creative musical experiences do the children have in your classroom? Children need to play with music as they do with blocks, trying out different combinations, breaking them up, and starting all over. And again, as with art, it is the process, not the product, that is important. Songs and dances may be highly satisfying, but if they are not arrived at in fun, they may never be repeated.

Initially, children will do with music and movement just what they do with art: learn to manipulate the medium. This sounds strange when we talk about music, but it is the natural way young children learn any new skill spontaneously. In other words, they need the chance to play with sounds, rhythm, and movement. According to Kemple, Batey, and Hartle (2004, p. 32), "Most preschool programs offer few opportunities for exploring and experimenting with sound." What about yours?

You can set up a sound-making table in the Music/Listening Center (see Chapter 3). Sound-makers can be a series of small containers, such as empty tuna cans, juice cans, margarine cups and covers, with a collection of seeds, beans, rice, and pebbles the children can place inside the containers to shake. Have a CD player or cassette player on the table that the children can use by themselves, along with several CDs or tapes of rhythmic music. Let them try shaking the containers to music. They may want to record and play back the results.

At another time, use containers as drums. Add a collection of sticks or drumsticks with tape wrapped around the ends to cut down on noise, and let the children practice drumming to music. You can also use metal containers and large spoons with their bowls taped over as drumsticks. Let the children fill a set of jars or glasses with varying amounts of water and tap them with a spoon. Put out a large collection of "junk" items and encourage the children to invent their own music makers. You may call this noise, not music, but don't tell the children that, if you want them to continue creatively.

This stage of music making compares to the scribble stage in art and the babble stage in speaking. After the children have learned to manipulate the medium with ease, they will want to perform it again and again during the *mastery* stage of exploratory play. Be prepared!

Rhythm Instruments

Sometimes a story can stimulate children to create something of their own. *The Banza* (Wolkstein, 1981) tells the Haitian folktale of a little tiger, Teegra, and goat, Cabree, who are best friends. To seal their friendship, the tiger gives the goat a magic "banza," or banjo, to protect her, saying, "The banza belongs to the heart, and there is no stronger protection than the heart." When the little goat finds herself surrounded by 10 hungry tigers, she plays a song on the banjo that finally frightens all the tigers away.

Your children can make their own magic banjos with shoe boxes and long rubber bands. Help them to cut a large heart-shaped hole out of the cover of the box, just like Cabree's, and to cut four grooves at each end of the cover for holding the four rubber bands, which are stretched lengthwise around the cover and box. Children can paint or decorate their banjos to suit themselves before adding the rubber bands. Have them sing or hum as they strum with their thumbs—but not too hard.

Often teachers think of rhythm instruments in plural, that is, as a rhythm band. Children enjoy making music as loud as they can in a rhythm band. But before you begin having children march around the room in a group playing their instruments, be sure that each child first has a chance to make music with a single instrument. Otherwise, individual instruments may not be heard above the sound of an entire band.

That is why it is important to maintain a music center with a CD player or tape player that children can use independently. Rhythm instruments can be hung on a pegboard in the area for use by children during free-choice periods. Encourage children to try out any of the instruments by themselves to see what they sound like. Then have them play their instruments to recordings of background music such as *Get Up and Go* or *African Playground*, CDs from Lakeshore. You can limit the volume on the record player by taping down the knob, if this seems a problem, or have children use headsets with the volume controlled.

After children have had the chance to experiment with the instruments, bring the instruments to circle time and introduce them one at a time to the children. Pass each instrument around and let them give it a try. Then each child who wants to can take an instrument and march around the room with the group to the music of one of the recordings mentioned. Because children often have conflicts about getting a particular instrument when the whole class is involved, have everyone exchange instruments for each march they participate in. Then each child will have a turn with more than one instrument. Later they can practice on their favorite instrument in the music center.

If you bring your own instrument to play, make it one that the children can also try out. Remember, it is the music maker, not the listener, who gets the most out of the experience. Children can strum on your autoharp, for instance, while you press down the chord buttons. Have a child sit next to you and strum as you press the chord buttons and sing a song with the group. They can take turns until everyone gets a chance. Other instruments include guitars, ukuleles, and electric keyboards. A small keyboard brings the piano down to size for preschool children.

Blowing instruments such as harmonicas, kazoos, and plastic flutes have always been popular with youngsters. Unfortunately, most are not really safe for a group of children because of germ transfer through saliva, unless you clean each instrument with a medicated wipe after use.

But children can make their own personal blowing instrument with a long wrapping paper tube, especially after you read them the hilarious *Do You Do a Didgeridoo?* (Page, 2008 [CD included]), about Mr. Music Man who has terrific trouble finding this Australian instrument in his music store.

Books as Lead-Ins to Instrument Playing

A book that describes a girl's whole family playing different music on different instruments in different settings is *My Family Plays Music* (Cox, 2003). The girl's mom plays the fiddle in a country-western band; her dad plays the cello in a string quartet; sister plays the clarinet in a marching band; her brother plays lead guitar in a rock 'n' roll band; her aunt plays the vibes in a jazz combo; her uncle plays the saxophone in a big band; her grandma plays the banjo in a bluegrass band, and on and on. With each family member, the girl also plays a percussion instrument she has made. Look for books with pictures of instruments on the cover. Even a child's toys can play instruments as in *Boom Boom Go Away* (Geringer, 2010)

> In *Boom Boom Go Away* a little boy's toy gnome plays a drum, his elf plays a gong, a prince plays a bassoon, a knight plays bells, a robot plays spoons, and a bear plays a horn. Each blurts out his sound in a cumulative fashion one after the other at bedtime until the boy finally falls asleep. Have each child choose a rhythm instrument to make a sound as you read.

Children do not need outside instruments to make music. They can be an instrument themselves by humming, clapping, or tapping their feet or fingers. You may want to introduce them to rhythm clapping during group time. Let them clap out name chants—"Here-comes-La-ta-sha"—with a clap for each syllable. Or children may want to play "Follow the Leader," with clapping patterns in a rap rhythm. One child claps out a rhythm, and then the other children try to imitate it. These rhythms can be recorded and played back.

Once you realize that many opportunities for individual play and experimentation with instruments are essential at the preschool level, your music program will take on an entirely different character. In addition, you may discover a particular child with an undiscovered musical talent. Sometimes a 3-year-old turns up who is a better autoharp strummer than you! As Jalongo (1996) reminds us, "Music is particularly important in the early childhood program because, as leading theorist and Harvard professor Howard Gardner has concluded, 'Of all the gifts with which individuals may be endowed, none emerges earlier than musical talent'" (p. 11).

Other Creative Activities

Every curriculum area in the classroom can promote creativity in children if you set it up so that children can use it on their own. Sand and water tables are sources for imaginative play when interesting accessories are located within the children's reach. Manipulative materials and table toys also promote creativity when children are free to choose materials they want and use them in imaginative ways.

SUMMARY

This chapter focuses on the goal of promoting children's creativity through playful expression and freedom of activity in the areas of fantasy role play, art, and music. Fantasy role play, an activity new to many preschool programs, asks children to pretend to be a fictitious storybook character or to be themselves in a fantasy setting. By hearing you read a picture book with a fantasy theme, children can talk about what happened and then get involved in fantasizing about "what else would happen if . . . ." Prop boxes containing costumes or miniature figures help children to extend these stories by pretending on their own, an excellent stimulant for creative thinking.

By encouraging children to experiment with materials and colors in art and then by accepting their artistic products, we support children's continued creative development. Although teacher-directed art has a place in the curriculum in promoting children's direction-following and manipulative skills, it should not be confused with creative art in which the child is in control of manipulating the medium her own way to discover what will happen. However, teachers need to know the stages of children's development of drawing skills to support their experiments.

Music can also promote creativity in children when teachers use it themselves in a relaxed and enjoyable manner. To encourage music production in the preschool classroom, teachers must lead the way by chanting, singing, and providing music-making objects and instruments. Children need to become actively involved in creating their own music, and not merely be passive listeners to records and tapes. Rhythm instruments can be made by the children and kept out for their use.

Ethical Dilemma

When a new director came to the preschool where Arlene, a teaching assistant, worked, all of the teaching staff were strongly encouraged to help children become involved in music by being involved themselves. Fun-filled after-school workshops were held to help them develop singing or chanting or rhythm making or simple instrument playing. Arlene would not attend. Arlene, who could not carry a tune, objected strenuously to being forced into doing something she felt she could not or would not do. When her lack of participation in musical activities and her negative attitude toward them affected her teaching performance, she was counseled to look for another position. Arlene responded by threatening to hire a lawyer and sue the director. What would you do?

LEARNING ACTIVITIES

1. Make 10 file cards from ideas obtained from the Suggested Readings or Web sites with specific ideas for developing children's creativity. Include the source on each card.

2. Read one of the suggested fantasy picture books with the children. Talk about it afterward and provide props for their fantasy role play.

3. Talk to a small group about superheroes, what they like about them, or what kind of superhero they would like to be. Read the book *Superhero ABC* or cut out some pictures of comic book superheroes. Bring in some capes, masks, or goggles and have them act out a dilemma of their choice that a superhero might want to solve. Talk to them about it afterward. Write up the results.

4. Make a collection of a child's paintings or drawings over a period of time that illustrates the stages of art children go through. Write up or discuss how your collection illustrates the stages.

5. Bring in a print or two of Georgia O'Keeffe's paintings of flowers. Bring in some real flowers. Read the book *Through Georgia's Eyes* to a small group of children. Talk about how Georgia saw things differently than most people and painted things differently. What do the children see in your flowers? Would they like to try painting them? Anything they painted would be okay, even scribbles. They could use any medium in the art center. See what happens.

6. Do a singing/chanting activity with children using ideas from this chapter. Record the results.

7. Set up a sound or rhythm instrument activity for individuals or small groups to use. Write up the results.

8. Design a new art or music center for your classroom. Make a sketch of it and list what materials you would include in it. Write up how you would want the children to use it, and how you would encourage them to do so.

SUGGESTED READINGS

Beaty, J. J. (2010). *Observing development of the young child*, 7th ed. Upper Saddle River, NJ: Merrill.

Eckoff, A. (2010). Using games to explore visual art with young children. *Young Children, 65*(1), 18–22.

Hoffman, R. (2004). *Magic cape amazing powers: Transforming superhero play in the classroom.* St. Paul, MN: Redleaf Press.

Isbell, R. T., & Raines, S. (2007). *Creativity and the arts with young children.* Clifton Park, NY: Thomson/Cengage.

Kim, J., & Robinson, H. M. (2010). Four steps for becoming familiar with early music standards. *Young Children, 65*(2), 42–46.

Mulcahey, C. (2009). Providing rich art activities for young children. *Young Children, 64*(4), 107–112.

Pica, R. (2010). *Experiences in movement and music: Birth to age 8.* Clifton Park, NY: Wadsworth/Cengage.

Wanerman, T. (2010). Using story drama with young preschoolers. *Young Children, 65*(2), 20–28.

WEB SITES

Arts Education Partnership
http://www.aep-arts.org

Learning by Leaps and Bounds
http://www.naeyc.org/yc/columns

MENC, the National Association for Music Education
http://www.menc.org

Miss Jackie Music
http://www.jackiesilberg.com

National Art Education Association
http://www.naea-reston.org

National Dance Education Organization
http://www.ndeo.org

Start with the Arts
http://www.varts.org

CHILDREN'S BOOKS

Bottner, B. (2010). *Miss Brooks loves books (and I don't).* New York: Knopf.

Collins, J. (2009). *Over the rainbow.* Morganville, NJ: Imagine Publishing. (CD included)

*Cox, J. (2003). *My family plays music.* New York: Holiday House.

*Dorros, A. (1991). *Abuela.* New York: Dutton's Children's Books.

Ellery, T., & Ellery, A. (2006). *If I had a dragon.* New York: Simon & Schuster.

Emmett, J., & Allwright, D. (2007). *She'll be coming' round the mountain.* New York: Atheneum.

Geringer, L. (2010). *Boom boom go away.* New York: Atheneum.

*Hoberman, M. A. (1998). *Miss Mary Mack.* New York: Scholastic.

*Hort, L. (2000). *The seals on the bus.* New York: Henry Holt.

Johnson, P. B. (2006). *On top of spaghetti.* New York: Scholastic.

Kovalski, M. (1987). *The wheels on the bus.* Boston: Little, Brown.

Lord, C. *Hot rod hamster.* New York: Scholastic Press.

McDonnell, P. (2006). *Art.* New York: Little, Brown.

*McLeod, B. (2006). *Superhero ABC.* New York: HarperCollins.

Numeroff, L. (2008). *If you give a cat a cupcake.* New York: HarperCollins.

Orloff, K. K. (2006). *If Mom had three arms.* New York: Sterling.

Ormerod, J. (2003). *If you're happy and you know it.* New York: Star Bright Books.

Page, N. (2008). *Do you do a didgeridoo?* Hertfordshire, England: Make Believe Ideas. (CD included)

*Ringgold, F. (1991). *Tar beach.* New York: Crown.

Rodriguez, R. (2006). *Through Georgia's eyes.* New York: Henry Holt.

Rounds, G. (1989). *Old MacDonald had a farm.* New York: Holiday House.

Sherry, K. (2008). *I'm the best artist in the ocean.* New York: Dial.

Soman, D., & Davis, J. (2008). *Ladybug girl.* New York: Dial.

Soman, D., & Davis, J. (2009). *Ladybug girl and bumblebee boy.* New York: Dial.

*Soto, G. (1993). *Too many tamales.* New York: G. P. Putnam's Sons.

Wells, R. (2005). *I love you a bushel and a peck.* New York: HarperCollins.

Westcott, N. B. (1989). *Skip to my Lou.* Boston: Little, Brown.

Whitehead, K. (2008). *Art from her heart.* New York: Putnam.

Wolkstein, D. (1981). *The banza.* New York: Dial.

*Multicultural

CHAPTER 8

Building a Positive Self-Concept

☐ General Objective

To help children improve their self-concept through your attitude and behavior toward them

☑ Specific Objectives

_____ Accepts self and every child as worthy and uses nonverbal cues to let children know they are accepted

_____ Accepts and respects diversity in children and helps children to respect one another

_____ Helps every child to develop independence and experience success in the classroom

*S*ELF-CONCEPT formation begins at birth and develops throughout a child's preschool years. This sense of self includes both her *self-image* (her inner picture of herself) and her *self-esteem* (her sense of self-worth). A child's self-image includes how she feels about her looks, her gender, her ethnicity, her standing in the family, and her abilities. It is not judgmental but descriptive. Her self-esteem, in contrast, is an evaluation of all of these aspects. As Kosnik (1993) tells us,

"These two areas combine to form our self-concept. Throughout our lives a continuous dialogue exists between these two aspects of self. Our self-concept determines who we are, what we think we are, what we think we can do, and what we think we can become" (p. 32).

How children eventually come to feel about themselves is the result of an accumulation of contacts and experiences with other people and with the environment. If most of these contacts have been positive, children should feel good about themselves. If children are accepted by their families, if they have been loved and cared for, shown affection, fed and clothed properly, and provided with a stimulating environment, then they begin to develop a perception of themselves as likable human beings. If they are not neglected or left alone too much, not scolded too harshly or restricted too severely, and not nagged at constantly, then they in turn will tend to like themselves and other human beings.

You need to send each child a clear message of your positive feelings toward them.

> **NAEYC Criteria for Curriculum Standard**
>
> Describe how you would meet the following standard:
>
> 2.L.01 Children are provided varied learning opportunities that foster positive identity and an emerging sense of self and others.

Marshall (2009) adds that: "Self-concept and factors that affect its development are important areas of concern for early childhood educators because research indicates that young children who have a positive view of themselves are more able to cope with the demands and stresses of school" (p. 19).

If, however, children have accumulated a series of negative responses from other people and the environment, they will come to believe there is something wrong with them. Young children are highly egocentric; they view everything as if they are the source of all happenings around them. If everything they do receives a negative response, they quite naturally assume it is their fault and that they are not good. If the adults around them seldom pay attention to them, they may feel they are not likable. Marshall adds that, according to research, "low self-concept is related to poor mental health, poor academic achievement, and delinquency" (p. 19).

Preschool children are at the stage of making judgments about their worth and competencies. Frost, Wortham, and Reifel (2005) tell us, "They tend to overestimate their mastery of new skills and underestimate how hard new tasks are. They feel that they are liked or disliked depending on how well they can do things and are easily influenced by parental approval or disapproval" (p. 135).

You and your classroom staff must help the children in your care experience as many positive interactions with people and things as possible. You need to be aware, however, that self-concept grows from an accumulation of responses and not just from one or two. You and your coworkers will therefore want to be consistent in your behavior with children so that they receive a clear, ungarbled message of your positive feelings toward them.

ACCEPTS SELF AND EVERY CHILD AS WORTHY AND USES NONVERBAL CUES TO LET CHILDREN KNOW THEY ARE ACCEPTED

Acceptance is an essential component in the development of a positive self-concept. Most people need to feel that they are accepted by those around them to feel good about themselves. Just as important is their acceptance of themselves as worthy persons before they can wholly accept others. It is therefore critical that children accept themselves and feel acceptance *by* others and *for* others.

Adult Self-Acceptance

This role of acceptance applies to adults as well as children. For you as a teacher to accept the children in your program, you also need to feel good about yourself as a person. Are you accepted by the people who are significant in your life? Do you accept yourself? These may be areas you need to work on before you can be a truly effective teacher. What do you like about yourself? List some of the qualities that you think are most positive. Are any of the following qualities on your list?

Positive Qualities List

My love for children
My ability to establish rapport with
  children
My ability to stay with a task until
  it is finished

My dedication to teaching
My sense of humor

Then make a second list. Do not call it your "negative qualities list." Just as with children, we also need to approach things positively. When we use the word *negative* as it concerns ourselves or children, we tend to think in terms of negative, bad, wrong. Instead, label this list "Qualities I Would Like to Possess." Are any of the following qualities on your second list?

Qualities I Would Like to Possess

Confidence that I am doing my job correctly

Better control over my temper

Ability to sing comfortably in front of the children

Better organizational skills

A nicer sounding voice

Choose one of the qualities on the second list and try working on it. What will give you confidence that you are doing your job correctly, for instance? Look at your positive qualities on the first list and think about how they can help you to become confident about doing your job. You may decide that if all of the children accept you and you are able to establish rapport with each of them, then you can feel confident you are doing your job. Your acceptance of every one of the children and their reciprocal acceptance of you thus becomes one of the tasks you should focus on in the days and weeks to come.

Adult-Child Acceptance

Your first step in helping a child accept and feel good about herself is thus to accept the child yourself, totally and unconditionally. This advice may sound obvious to you. Of course you accept the unhappy child—just as you accept all of the children in your classroom. But do you accept her totally and unconditionally? In reality, you may have children you favor above others as well as children you do not like. What about the loud and aggressive child or a child who is never clean, who is overweight, who whines or tattles, or who doesn't speak English? You need to sort out your feelings and change them before you can hope to bring about change in the children's feelings about themselves.

A simple way to start with children is similar to the way you started with yourself: List each of the children in your class. After each name write down, as frankly and honestly as possible, a positive quality you like about each child and why. Also write what you would like to see changed in each child and why. Then write down your reaction to the child in the classroom. (For your eyes only.) For example:

Sarah

What I like: Her quiet way of playing

Why: I like quiet children.

Changes needed: Her uncleanliness

Why: I dislike dirtiness.

My reaction in class: I leave her alone.

Antwon

What I like: When he plays without disrupting others

Why: I like children to be friendly toward each other.

Changes needed: His negative attitude

Why: I don't like the way he often acts toward others.

My reaction in class: I scold him when he misbehaves.

When you have finished, go back through the list and ask yourself the following questions for each child: Do I really accept this child totally and unconditionally? Do my daily reactions convey to the child that I accept him as he is? If not, you may need to change the way you react toward the child so that he knows you accept him.

This does not mean that you must accept disruptive or destructive behavior from a child. You accept the child, not the behavior. You should accept every child as a valuable individual despite the child's appearance or behavior. This acceptance means that you will help each child overcome inappropriate behavior through your behavior toward that child and your respect for him or her as an individual. If you find from your list that you do not do this with certain children, then you need to begin changing your own attitude toward them.

You can start by listing, for three days, positive behaviors that you notice about a child whom you have not accepted totally. Keep a pen and pad handy during the day and make a special effort to observe and record positive things about the child. These notes, like your original set, are for your eyes only or for sharing with your trainer. Keep them in a private place to be disposed of when you finish. Sarah and Antwon are children you have not accepted fully according to your reactions toward them. You might start observing and recording positive behaviors for each of these children.

Starting with Antwon, what did you find? You might have noticed that on the first morning Antwon said "Hi" to Ramon when he came in, that he put his jacket in his cubby without bothering anyone, and that he ate his snack without disturbing his neighbor.

How did you respond to these positive actions? You waved at him from across the room when he came in and said, "Hi, Antwon!" You watched him put his jacket in his cubby, nodding and smiling at him when he turned around. After snack you smiled and said, "That was a good snack time, Antwon, wasn't it?" You already seem to know by intuition that it is always good to call children by name when you speak to them. This is probably part of your ability to establish good rapport with children that you noted under your positive qualities.

Within a few days of similar observing, recording, and responding, you may find that a change has occurred both in the child and in yourself. When you look for positive behaviors in children, you will find them. We see what we look for. The more positive behaviors you notice, the better you begin to feel about the youngster. This often comes across to the child nonverbally, and he in turn begins to act more positively. In the end, both of you feel good about one another—you because the child's behavior seems to have improved and the child because he senses that you approve of him more than you did previously. Try the previous exercise to see how it works for you.

Books as Lead-Ins to Adult-Child Self-Concept Activities

Can books really help children develop a positive self-concept? Feeney and Moravcik (2005) have this to say about it: "Picture books for young children play a major role in shaping their emerging images of themselves, others, and the larger society.

When the story lines and images are positive in the books that they read, children are likely to develop healthy self-concepts and favorable views of others" (p. 22).

> In *Mama, Do You Love Me?* (Joose, 1991), a little Inuit girl asks the title question to her mother. Her mother always answers in a positive manner even when the girl's extreme actions could make her angry. Even if the girl turned into the meanest polar bear you ever saw, the mother would still love her because her girl would be inside the bear.

What about the children you care for? Read this book to a small group and ask them to think of other kinds of mischief they might have done to their mothers (or grandmas or aunts). Would they still accept and love them?

In a follow-up book, *Papa, Do You Love Me?* (Joose, 2005), a little Maasai boy asks his African father this question. In this case the boy continues asking his father what he would do if the boy became hot, or thirsty, or fell asleep while watching the cattle, and other extreme situations. The answer is always a positive one as well. Can the boys in your group think of actions that might annoy their fathers (or grandfathers or uncles)? Would they still accept and love them?

In a third follow-up book, *Grandma Calls Me Beautiful* (Joose, 2008), a little Hawaiian girl asks her Tutu, her grandmother, to tell her the story of why she was named Beautiful. Tropical birds and butterflies flit through an island world filled with color—while she is plain. But not to her Tutu. Hair black like night, snapping with stars. Skin brown like a field kneaded smooth by many feet. Everything about her is beautiful. Ask your listeners to think of things about themselves that are beautiful like their surroundings.

In *Red is Beautiful* (John & Thomas, 2003), a bilingual book in English and Navajo, striking colors sweep across every page as the little girl Nashasha rides home on the school bus in tears, away from her classmates who tease her about her rough skin. Her grandmother lovingly gathers her up into their *hogan* home where she teaches her about the wonders of *chiih*—a red Earth material Navajos use for healing the skin. (Much later when grown Nashasha uses this material in a successful cosmetics business.) What do your listeners know about ways the Earth can heal them?

Nonverbal Cues

In addition to speaking, also demonstrate your acceptance of children through nonverbal cues. Children understand more about how you feel toward them by the way you act than by what you say. Your *tone of voice,* for instance, conveys as much or more meaning than your words. How do you sound to the child you seem to have trouble accepting totally? Switch on your tape recorder when you are in a learning center with the child. After class, play back the tape or CD and listen to yourself. Ignore everything but the tone of your voice. Play it low enough so you cannot even make out the words. Are you satisfied with what you hear? If not, you may want to make a note to yourself about changing the tone of your voice, perhaps making it softer or keeping the scolding tone out of it. This is also another of the qualities from your list that you wanted to develop in yourself.

Another nonverbal cue you should evaluate is your *facial expression*. How does it look to a child? Do you scowl or frown very much? Do you smile a lot? Try smiling at an unhappy child. Children reflect the people around them. If nobody ever smiles at them, why should they feel happy? Be persistent in your smiling. Eventually you will get a smile in return.

Nearness and touch are also important cues of acceptance to preschool children. Affection is usually expressed through hugs, a hand on the shoulder, an arm around the waist, or sitting or standing close to someone. Most children crave this affection. Those who seem not to, who instead withdraw from touch or contact, may indeed have self-concept problems or may be merely shy. Your nonverbal cues of acceptance with these children may have to be smiles and a friendly voice until they feel better about themselves and become more at ease in the classroom. Do not allow the current exaggerated concern about "good touches and bad touches" to alter your display of affection toward the children in your care. Your "good touches" are necessary for the growth of their positive self-concept.

A Favorite Child

It is important for all of the adults in the preschool classroom to behave consistently toward all of the children. If you are the head teacher or team leader, it is your responsibility to make sure this happens. If you notice that a classroom worker seems to have a favorite child or seems to ignore another child, you may want to have a team meeting at which all of you do the exercise of listing the children's names, along with your likes, changes needed, and reactions. The harm created by an adult's showing favoritism lies in the nonverbal cues this action conveys to each of the other children. It says, very clearly, "This favored child is somehow more likable than you are" or "You are not as good as this other child."

Your acceptance of and your positive reactions toward all of the children in your class are thus extremely important in promoting their growth of healthy self-concepts. Just as you assess children's feelings about themselves periodically, you must also constantly check on your own feelings about the children. As Eaton (1997) notes, "Research suggests that an adult's sensitive, personally attentive, genuinely focused relationship with a child increases the child's self-esteem" (p. 44). Be sure every child receives this attention.

Behavior Management Style

What about your behavior management style? Are you strict and controlling of children's behavior in the classroom? Azria-Evans (2004) notes, "Children who are exposed to predominantly controlling adults develop a sense of self that is indecisive and that needs or seeks control from others" (p. 22). But adults who are permissive and set no limits on children's behavior may be saying to the children, "I don't really care about you and your behavior, or I would help you set limits on it." It is important that you help children develop self-control while at the same time finding ways to defuse or redirect their uncontrolled behavior. (See Chapter 10, "Providing Guidance.")

You can observe a child's behaviors to determine his self-concept.

Child's Self-Acceptance

What about the children's own acceptance of themselves? How do children feel about themselves in your classroom? A child's self-concept is elusive to pin down. One way to begin assessing self-concept is through observing children and recording their behavior according to a checklist. The "Self-Concept Checklist" in Figure 8.1 can help you and your colleagues assess a child's self-perception. The behaviors listed should occur consistently; otherwise they may not represent an accurate picture of the child.

Try at the outset to determine how children feel about themselves. Because they often have difficulty expressing this verbally, you can try to determine it through observing and recording children's particular responses or behaviors as they interact with other children and activities. Add this information to each child's records and use it as you make individual plans for the child.

For children who have few check marks, you and your coworkers will need to provide special

---

Child's Name_____ **Date**_____

_____ Looks at you without covering face when you speak to child

_____ Can identify himself or herself by first and last name

_____ Seeks other children to play with or will join when asked

_____ Seldom shows fear of new or different things

_____ Is seldom destructive of materials or disruptive of activities

_____ Smiles, seems happy much of the time

_____ Shows pride in accomplishments

_____ Stands up for rights

_____ Moves confidently, with good motor control

Figure 8.1   Self-Concept Checklist

Source: From Janice J. Beaty, *Skills for Preschool Teachers,* Ninth Edition. Copyright © 2012 by Pearson Education, Inc. All rights reserved.

experiences for strengthening their self-concepts. Perhaps the most critical indicator of a child's self-image is the entry "Smiles, seems happy much of the time." The child who does not smile or act happy seems to demonstrate an obvious evidence of troubled feelings. What can you do to help?

Mirrors, Photos, and Tapes/CDs

Besides accepting the child yourself, the most important role you can play is helping children accept themselves. Children need to know what they look like to accept themselves completely. A full-length mirror is thus a classroom necessity. Children will use it not only in the dramatic play area but also at odd moments during the day. They are curious about themselves. "Is this what I really look like?" You will find that they use mirrors differently from adults who, after all, already know what they look like. Some children may make faces at themselves or pile on hats and dress-up clothes before they face the mirror. Others may stare at their images for quite a while.

Young children are trying to sort themselves out and find out who they are. Hand mirrors serve the same purpose, giving a closeup view of the face for a child sitting at a table. Keep more than one in the classroom.

A digital camera is another good tool for promoting the development of a positive self-concept. Take many photos of each child during the program year when they have just built a block building, completed a science project, or pretended to be a firefighter. Now they can see how they look as builders of tremendous block apartment houses or drivers of zooming fire trucks. As Good (2005/2006) says, "Children are eager to see their achievements, first on the camera's monitor and later on a print posted in the room or in a slide show on the computer" (p. 79).

Take photos of the child and his or her parents when you make home visits, once again to demonstrate your acceptance of both the child and the family. Photograph each child doing an art project, perhaps feeding a classroom pet, participating in a field trip, making a puzzle, going down a slide, or talking with a friend. Display the photos in the center or in a personal scrapbook each child may want to make. Have pictures of individuals laminated and used by the youngsters on an attendance board or job chart. Make photo puzzles by enlarging a photo of each child, gluing it to cardboard, and cutting it into puzzle pieces to be kept in separate manila envelopes in the manipulative area.

A tape recorder may serve the same purpose. Spend time with individuals or small groups, recording each of their voices, playing them back, and discussing them. Children may want to tell something about themselves, their pets, their families, or their homes. Or they may want to tell a story, sing a song, or pretend to be someone else. When they learn to use the tape recorder on their own, they can tape each other's voices.

Self-Concept Name Games and Songs

Children enjoy the same feeling about seeing their names as they do about seeing themselves in a mirror or in a photo. Some children may already know how to print their names. Many will know at least the first letter of their name. Use children's printed names in every way you can think of, not only to help them learn to recognize their names but also to make them feel good about themselves. "A-n-t-w-o-n—those are my letters. That's me!" Play "Find Your Name Card" with a small group of children and place their name cards in a pile on a table. Play "Match Your Name Card" with duplicate name cards and the cards on the attendance chart. Bring in sets of alphabet blocks with duplicate blocks of each letter and let individuals try to make their name out of blocks. Take a photo of the completed names. Use children's name cards on their place at the lunch table. Have mats with children's names on them for their seats on the floor at circle time.

Also use children's names in familiar songs whenever you can. As Warner (1999) notes, "Substituting children's names in familiar songs not only will delight children, but also helps them gain a sense of special recognition. Singing 'Paul Had a Little Lamb' or 'Two Little Blackbirds going to the mall; one named Kelsey and the other named Paul,' makes children giggle with pleasure" (p. 21).

Self-Concept Art and Photography

Children's art creations of all kinds should make them feel good about themselves as they learn to manipulate the many art media successfully. Actual body, hands, and feet tracings make an especially good personal statement. Have each child lie down on a large piece of butcher paper while either you or another child traces around the youngster. The child can then paint in the outline of herself, coloring on clothes, shoes, face, and hair. Body tracings like this can be cut out and mounted on the classroom wall, with the child's name on the painting. Some programs do body tracings at the beginning and end of the year so that children can compare the differences. Did they grow taller? Did their art skills improve?

Hands and feet can also be traced, colored in, and mounted on backing paper for all to see. Some programs do hand and feet stampings instead, using water-soluble paints in a shallow pan. Children dip each hand or foot in the paint and stamp it on a white background. This art creation can be separate for each child or a group mural. Children can also do "sneaker rubbings" by fastening a piece of white paper to the bottom of each sneaker and rubbing the side of a crayon over it until the pattern appears. Children can then cut out and mount the shoe bottoms.

Face tracings are sometimes done by the teacher, tracing lightly on tissue paper held against a child's face. Afterward these are colored in and cut out by each child. Wait until every child's personal art has been completed before displaying it in class so that no one feels left out.

Children can draw or paint their own pictures after hearing a story featuring a boy or girl character they would like to be. Artifact 8.1 shows a boy and girl drawn after hearing the Charlie and Lola story *I Will Never Not Ever Eat a Tomato* (Child, 2000; see Chapter 2). Strongly drawn pictures like this are usually drawn by children who feel good about themselves.

Strongly drawn pictures like this are usually drawn by children who feel good about themselves.

Photos of children taken by you or other children also help them see themselves in different ways. Byrnes and Wasik (2009) suggest: "Have the children take pictures of each other on different days when they are wearing different clothing and when they are dressing up in the dramatic play area. Ask them to identify who is in the picture. Talk about how children can look different depending on what they are wearing" (p. 247).

Books as Lead-Ins to Child Self-Acceptance Activities

In *Freckleface Strawberry* (Moore, 2007) a little red-haired girl is teased by her classmates because of her freckles. They call her Freckleface Strawberry. She tries to scrub them off, cover them up, and hide, but nothing works. So she decides to live with them, and finds that she has lots of friends anyway. Ask your listeners what they would do in each of these situations.

Other child self-concept books include *I Like Myself* and *Incredible Me!* When you read *I Like Myself* (Beaumont, 2004), be sure your several listeners sit close enough to see the wonderfully wacky illustrations. The little dark-skinned girl in her red-and-white "barber pole" dress takes her dog along to show all the things she likes about herself outside and inside—even her skeleton! What can your children show about themselves?

Incredible Me! (Appelt, 2003) has a little girl with two red puffs of hair prancing, dancing, and flitting across the pages of the book telling everyone that nobody but her has a nose, 10 toes, a smile, or kiss, or whistle, anything else like hers. Can your children join in with things they have that nobody else does?

ACCEPTS AND RESPECTS DIVERSITY IN CHILDREN AND HELPS CHILDREN TO RESPECT ONE ANOTHER

The children in your classroom will probably reflect the multicultural, rich, poor, gifted, and differently abled tossed salad of humans that makes America an exciting place to live. Feeney and Moravcik (2005) remind us, "Awareness of ethnicity (race) develops as young children observe attributes such as skin color, hair, and facial features. Three- and four-year-olds are aware of racial differences and are beginning to develop attitudes about these differences" (p. 22). Their attitudes come from the attitudes of the adults around them.

If you as an early childhood professional cherish each youngster as a worthy and special person and treat them all the same, the children in your care will follow your lead in accepting each of their classmates as well. To assist you in this acceptance, keep in mind the following guidelines:

- Stress similarities but honor differences.
- Build on each child's strengths.
- Have high expectations for everyone.

First of all, as previously mentioned, you must accept the child as he or she is: his looks, his language, his culture, her clothing, her disability, her voice. You show your acceptance by your tone of voice, your smile, your words, your actions. Greet each child cheerfully every day. Help each one to feel at home in your class.

Stress Similarities But Honor Differences

Although you may note that certain children have different skin colors, hairstyles, languages, or disabilities, each is a child like the others, with similar needs for your attention, affection, and support. There is no need for you to treat any child as different or to behave differently toward any child.

You are the behavior model the children look to for a cue as to how they should behave toward a child they perceive as different. If the children see that you behave toward that child just as you do toward them, they will feel safe in doing the same.

For instance, if the children discover that Alberto doesn't speak the same way they do, you can agree with them, pointing out matter-of-factly, "Many people in the world speak different languages. Would you like to learn some words from Alberto's language?" Azria-Evans (2004, p. 25) suggests that you could hang a banner in front of the room with the words for "Welcome" on it in each of the languages spoken by the children and their families. Invite a family member from each of the cultures to read or tell a story in their language. Picture books about children from various cultures should be displayed in your book center, whether or not that culture is represented in the class.

Books as Lead-Ins to Different Cultural Activities

In *Drum, Chavi, Drum!* (Dole, 2003) a bilingual book in English and Spanish, Chavi, a Cuban American girl in Miami, loves to drum. But when Chavi wants to play drums at the neighborhood Calle Ocho Festival, everyone tells her that girls don't play drums. When Chavi dresses in a cape, sombrero, and mask, people think she's a boy, and soon congratulate her as the best drummer in the festival.

Drumming is something done in almost every culture. Can you obtain a pair of bongos for your music center and have your children reenact this exciting story using real drums? Perhaps a Spanish speaker can visit and read the Spanish version of the story.

Be sure to have books showing both genders as main characters. A simple English/Spanish book with a boy character is *My Tata's Guitar* (Brammer, 2003), the story of a boy who finds an old guitar in his grandfather's garage. The grandfather tells him how his own grandfather gave it to him. Now it is the boy's turn. Play music from Latin America on a CD from Lakeshore (*Fiesta Musical*), while your children strum on toy guitars or homemade rubber banjos.

Besides music and language, another area in which children can find similarities is food. Although different children and families may eat different kinds of food, they all have to eat. In the book *Everybody Cooks Rice* (Dooley, 1991), a big sister finds out that everyone in her multiethnic neighborhood eats some kind of rice. You can bring in chopsticks and have the children cook and eat their own rice dish for lunch.

Bee-Bim Bop! (Park, 2005) or "mixed-up rice" is a delicious Korean dish made for the family by a little girl and her mother. Every step of its preparation is illustrated in an exciting rhyming beat—from shopping for the ingredients to eating the yummy mixture. Want to make some for your class? The recipe with cooking instructions for child and grownup are given.

Inclusion

In *It's Okay to Be Different* (Parr, 2001), listeners find out through zany cartoons that it's okay to have a different nose (an elephant's), to be a different color (a zebra), to have wheels (child in wheelchair), to come from a different place (Saturn), or to come in last (a turtle). In other words, you should behave the same way with every child.

The child who is overly aggressive and the child who is overweight also need your acceptance. The child with leg braces and the child with a hearing aid are children first of all, not children with disabilities. They need to feel they are not different from the others, because "feeling different" usually means "feeling inferior" and often invites teasing and ridicule on the part of other children.

Clearly, the adults and older children around them are the ones who most strongly influence young children's attitudes about accepting differences in people, places, food, clothing, skin color, hairstyles, and disabilities. Be sure your own attitude of acceptance comes across strongly to the youngsters by the way you treat all of them and their families as *special persons*.

Build on Each Child's Strengths

You can begin to help any children who do not seem to feel good about themselves by identifying their strengths and helping them to build on them. For example, a child who speaks Spanish can help the others learn to count in Spanish. The others can help her learn to count in English. Bring in books and tapes to support this language exchange.

A child with a hearing impairment may be able to show the other children how to sign "hello." *The Handmade Alphabet* (Rankin, 1991) displays a different hand on each page, with fingers showing the sign for a particular alphabet letter from *A* to *Z*. White hands, brown hands, gloved hands, and even the X-ray of a hand demonstrate the letters. Your children can learn to sign their own initials or names.

Everyone can do something well. Help each child discover her particular skill and then build on it. The aggressive child may be an expert climber who can help other less skillful climbers to master the jungle gym. The shy child may turn out to be the class computer expert who can share her skills with the rest.

Perhaps the child with poor motor coordination can grasp a spoon and stir well. It is up to you, then, to provide activities in which that child can experience success: mixing gelatin or powdered drinks or play dough. Add other activities to scaffold the experience. Let children put together a fruit salad with that child in charge of the melon baller. Think of other implements that the child might use successfully: a paper punch to count the number of children in class each day or a food mill to grind up cooked apples or pumpkins. Maybe that child can be a drummer in your music-making activities.

Be sure to read *Cleversticks* (Ashley, 1992), a story about Ling Sung, the Chinese boy who enters preschool but is unable to accomplish tasks the other children complete with ease, for example, tying his shoes, printing his name, buttoning his jacket, or fastening his painting apron. Then by accident he discovers what he is good at: picking up the pieces of the cookie he dropped by using inverted paintbrushes as chopsticks. All the children clap for his accomplishment, and his dad calls him "Cleversticks."

You may want to list such skills on individual Accomplishment Cards for each child, with space for the dates when they accomplish something new. Parents need to know about your goals for their children, and you need to know about their goals as well. Discuss with them what children are able to do by themselves in your classroom, so that parents can encourage them to accomplish similar things at home.

Have High Expectations for Everyone

Inclusion

Finally, have high expectations for everyone in the class. With your support and guidance, each child should be able to participate in most of the activities. A child who must use a wheelchair may not be able to climb the monkey bars but may be able to pull himself *around* them with a rope for physical exercise. A shy child can whisper through a puppet if speaking aloud is too painful. A non-English-speaking child can tape-record her original story of a picture book in her own language for another child to hear.

Whatever the activity, expect and encourage (but not force) everyone to join in. If the children are singing, a child with a hearing impairment can join in by playing a rhythm instrument or beating a drum. A child who doesn't speak the language can hum the song on a comb covered with paper. The shy or withdrawn child can have her puppet sing the words.

Invite the children to set up challenges for themselves. Instead of competing with other children, let them compete with themselves. How far did they jump last week? Can they do better today? Use a tape measure and record the results. Alfredo has learned to count to 10 in English. What would he like to learn next? Counting to 20? The children in the block area are timing their pickup with a stopwatch every day. They are recording their times on a chart and trying to set a new record each time they pick up and stack the blocks accurately. Children and parents, too, may want to suggest new challenges.

Cultural Influences on Children's Self-Concept

As you accept children from a variety of ethnic, cultural, and racial backgrounds, be aware that the cultural values of the children and their families may very well affect how children from different backgrounds tend to feel about themselves. How do you feel about their self-concepts? It is important to realize that many cultures consider self-concept in their children different from our Western model. We look for independence, individuality, and asserting oneself as demonstrating a positive self-concept. Many Asian, African, and Latin American cultures emphasize harmony and interdependent relationships. Many Chinese look for children to be shy, reticent, and quiet. These same children might be considered inhibited and lacking in self-confidence by North American teachers (Marshall, 2009, p. 60).

Preschool teachers need to be aware of these cultural differences when assessing the self-concepts of their children. As Marshall (2001) continues, "Some cultures such as traditional Navajo cultures expect children to observe before attempting to try things. For these children standing back and observing should not be taken as an indication of low self-esteem" (p. 20). Keep this in mind when assessing such children.

Teachers also need to talk with parents and families about what sort of behavior the parents value and expect from their children, as well as discussing your own program's goals. The children themselves tend to be quite resilient about such differences, mainly behaving both at home and at school as expected. Young children are very observant, noting what is going on around them, what is expected of them in different situations, and trying to fit in as best they can.

Help Children Respect One Another

Stay alert for how children interact with one another in classroom learning centers. What should you look for? Does one group dominate a certain center? For example, do boys monopolize the block building center? Ask the children how they want to get others involved. They may want to mix up the boys and girls by turn-taking games if this is a problem. Remember, it is their classroom. They may suggest drawing names out of a hat when necessary. Or they may want to have a girls' building day and a boys' day. Try it and see how it works.

How children behave toward one another may be another problem. Your actions should show how you accept all the children even when you don't accept their aggressive or negative behavior, by helping them find ways to behave otherwise. Your speech should also affirm your acceptance and respect of them. As Roffman and Wanerman (2011) point out: "Children learn how to speak to each other from listening to you. You can also coach them by making suggestions about how to relate to their peers in specific situations." Communication is the key factor in helping people get along, they say. "You can influence how children see each other with what you say about their peers and how you say it" (p. 160).

You can influence children to respect one another by how you talk to their peers.

HELPS EVERY CHILD TO DEVELOP INDEPENDENCE AND EXPERIENCE SUCCESS IN THE CLASSROOM

One of the most important factors influencing the development of a healthy self-concept is success. Children of this age need to experience success to feel good about themselves. The activities and materials you provide can boost the children's positive self-concepts if they find that they can accomplish them successfully. Achieving success outside their home environment is very important for young children. They need to experience success repeatedly to feel good about themselves and to feel confident that they are able to accomplish meaningful things.

Make sure that activities and materials are appropriate for your children's developmental levels. In other words, don't put out the most complicated puzzles, books, and art projects at the beginning of the year. Nor should you stress competition in your classroom. Your children will meet that soon enough in the outside world. Their experience in your classroom should give them breathing space—a time to develop positive feelings about themselves as worthy persons who can accomplish the interesting and challenging activities in your program. Winning or losing can come later in life when their positive self-concept has grown strong.

Although children should be able to choose from among any of the games and materials you provide, you can steer those who have difficulties to the simpler materials and activities. For those who seldom sit still long enough to complete an activity, consider sitting with them and encouraging them to complete it. Make it a game.

Some children are so fearful of failure that they just won't try. You may need to help them to succeed step by step. Hand the puzzle maker a puzzle piece and let him try to find where it goes. Encourage him to try again. "You can find it, Hakeem; look again." Hand him another piece if he doesn't take one on his own. When the puzzle is completed, ask him if he wants a photo of the puzzle for his personal scrapbook. This may be the first time Hakeem has completed a puzzle. He will be proud of his accomplishment if you show him that you are too.

Strengthening a Child's Independence

Children's concepts of themselves receive an additional boost when they learn how to do things on their own. Some preschool teachers do not realize this. They think they are helping children by tying their shoes, zipping their jackets, serving their food, and pouring their milk. They think they are making things easier for the children if they put out art materials, start up computer programs, and have puzzles and table blocks ready and waiting. Children do not protest. After all, they have been little and helpless all those years before coming to preschool.

As children grow and change, the adults around them should change too. They must begin to let go of their children and allow them the freedom to do things independently. Helping young children grow and develop independence should be one of the principal goals for any child development program. In current terms, we call this "empowering children." As Schweinhart and Weikart (1993) say, "Central to this definition is the idea that young children are active learners who can initiate their own learning activities and function as active learners, rather than mere passive recipients of information from others. Such active learning empowers children to assume a measure of control over their environment and develop the conviction that they have some control over their lives" (p. 56).

Control over the Classroom Environment

Think about your own classroom. What control do the children have? You might make a list of the things that children can complete by themselves or that they have personal responsibility for. Such a list might include the items in Figure 8.2.

This is only a partial list. Can the children in your program do these things? More important, are they allowed to? Some teachers say, "I would never allow a 3-year-old to use a sharp knife. He might cut himself." But many other teachers reply, "All my children learn to handle dangerous implements such as knives and saws so that they won't get hurt. If they should ever slip and cut themselves (but none have), that too is a learning experience, and we have bandages and sympathy always at hand."

Some teachers worry about children's using tape recorders, record players, and computers, because they are expensive and may be broken by children. Other teachers report that they purchase only the most durable childproof recorders: those that will best survive children's handling. As for computers, these machines are surprisingly durable as long as they are not dropped and liquid is not spilled on them. A simple chart in the computer area can remind children of these rules:

- Two children at a time
- No liquids
- Wash hands first

Water plants	Operate tape recorder, CD player
Feed fish	Operate computer
Feed and water guinea pig	Use hammer and saw
Set table for snack or lunch	Cut with scissors and knife
Help teacher with cots for nap	Follow recipe chart
Take mail to office	Sign up with name scribble
Choose curriculum area to work in	Help with cleanup, pickup
Get out own art materials, puzzles	Wait for a turn
Help make play dough	Sign out books for overnight

Figure 8.2   Classroom Tasks

Figure 8.3   Self-Help
Skills

- Hang up outer garments in personal cubbies.
- Use the bathroom independently.
- Put on own paint or water play apron and goggles.
- Wash hands and brush teeth.
- Serve own food and pour own milk and juice.
- Clear own table area.
- Get out and put away own sheet and blanket.
- Put on outer garments and tie shoes.

Teachers who give young children adult-type responsibilities believe it is of primary importance for children to use tape recorders, CD players, and computers on their own. They are willing to spend as much time as necessary to instruct young children in their value and proper use and to monitor the children until they are able to use these devices independently. If children are to learn through exploratory manipulation, mastery, and meaning, then they need the freedom to experiment using all the classroom materials and equipment on their own. When children find that they can be successful with adult implements, their concepts of themselves as worthy people improve significantly. Other skills children need to learn to do by themselves in your program include the self-help skills in Figure 8.3.

You can model some of these skills or ask a more experienced child to help a newcomer. Once a child has mastered these skills, his self-concept will receive another big boost.

Children's Activity Choices

Another important ingredient of children's success in early childhood programs is allowing them to choose the learning center of their interest during the free-choice or work/play period. Children need to see what is available and then have the freedom to choose an activity that interests them. If the center they select is full, they can pick another area while waiting for their turn. It is a good idea to have a sign-up sheet for popular centers so that every child who wants one gets a turn.

Make each learning center in the classroom as equally attractive as possible. For example, don't expect children to choose the book center if it contains only a few books on a shelf against the wall and if there is no place to read the book but a wooden chair and table. Instead, fill this area with brightly colored pillows and a throw rug, a new selection of books with colorful covers facing out, a beanbag chair, and a selection of stuffed animals, character dolls, and puppets to go with the books available. You'll soon have children signing up for a turn in this center.

Have something interesting and different going on in each center every week. Put up challenging question signs and directions. For example, in the book center have a sign that asks, "How did Charlie get Lola to eat all the vegetables she hated?"

Children feel good about themselves when they find they can succeed in classroom activities.

Children will first have to figure out what the sign asks them to do. Then they will have to go back through the book and find Charlie's trick. Or put out a shoe box containing cutout pictures of vegetables and put up a sign saying, "Find the vegetable that was Lola's favorite."

In the manipulative/math center have a tape recorder ready with a blank tape and a large sealed clear plastic jar with felt-tip pens inside. Have a sign that says, "How many pens are in this jar? Tell your name and answer to the tape recorder." When children find out what the words say, they will be flocking to this center to try to count the pens and tape-record their answer. In the block-building center, have a box full of little farm animals and a sign that says, "Please build a barn for us."

When every learning center is equally attractive, then children will choose each one eagerly. Be sure it is their choice and not yours. Some teachers assign certain children to particular centers because they feel that the children need experience in the center. This may serve the teacher's purpose but not necessarily the child's. Even when children repeatedly choose the same center, we must remember that young children's learning involves manipulation, mastery (repetition), and meaning. Be sure everyone has plenty of time for the necessary repetition. Only the children know how much time they personally need.

Children's Special Skills

Every child usually has at least one special skill she can accomplish with ease. Some children already know what their best skill is. Omar knows how to build enormous block towers. Dominic is a natural at strumming the teacher's autoharp. But some children seem to spend much of their time observing what others can do, without revealing any special skills of their own. Keep track of these children as they work and play in the different learning centers to see if they also may excel at something in particular. Talk with the children at the lunch table about their interests at home. Leaf through a magazine or toy catalog with a youngster to see if any items seem to attract their interest.

Once you have unearthed a special interest for a child, follow up with books, puzzles, games, and activities that support such an interest. One teacher discovered that Maurice wanted to be an artist like his father but everyone ridiculed his attempts at art. The teacher decided to introduce Maurice to Fred, a storybook boy, who also wanted to be an artist but didn't know how to draw, by reading Maurice the book *The Class Artist* (Karas, 2001). In it Fred's sister shows him a simple way to draw a pilgrim, and Fred is on his way. Several other children joined Maurice in listening to the story, and before long there were a number of new "class artists" practicing their skills in Maurice's class.

Teacher's Role

How can you be sure that children are succeeding? Have Accomplishment Cards on every child and record every day what learning center the child played in and what he or she accomplished. Then at the weekly planning session go over these cards with the team to hear what others have to say and to plan new activities appropriate for this child and the others.

Your primary role in the classroom is to set up stimulating activities that involve every child but also to choose activities that have specific benefits for certain children. Then, by observing how individual children interact with materials and other children, you can plan how to scaffold their learning to help each one move up to the next level.

You are not alone in this role. Whether you are a teacher, a student teacher, an assistant, or a community volunteer, you are part of a team. When one of the team is leading a children's group project, for example, someone else is free to operate on a one-to-one basis with a child who may need special help in improving her self-concept.

SUMMARY

This chapter discusses methods for improving the self-concept of your children through your attitude and behavior. First of all, you must accept yourself by listing your positive qualities and then working to develop other qualities you would like to possess. Next you must accept each of the children unconditionally and show them that you do through nonverbal and verbal cues. Smile at them. Encourage them with words. Let them know how you feel about them. For children you have difficulty accepting, observe and record the positive things they do for three days. Show them that you approve with nonverbal cues, and eventually their attitude should change.

Use the "Self-Concept Checklist" in Figure 8.1 to assess each child's behavior, an indication of how they feel about themselves. Make plans to help individuals feel better about themselves with mirrors, photos, tapes, self-concept name games, self-concept art, and self-concept picture books.

Children begin to accept themselves in the classroom when they find that they can succeed in the activities and tasks they encounter. They begin to accept one another when they see you model unconditional acceptance of all of the other children no matter what their background, appearance, or differences are. By stressing similarities in children and honoring their differences, you can help others develop a similar attitude. Focus on areas such as food or language to demonstrate children's common bonds, but show how interesting different people's language or food can be.

Identify and build on children's strengths to help them feel good about themselves. Everyone can do something well, and you must find out what that is for each child. Then challenge them to use their skills in new ways. Help children to succeed in the learning centers of the classroom by encouraging their independence and allowing them to control their environment and to choose their own activities. Then observe and record their choices and accomplishments to determine your next step in helping them improve their self-concepts.

Ethical Dilemma

The mother of Eugene, a new boy in the class, was very upset about the other boys teasing Eugene in class because he was overweight. They followed him home after school, threw acorns at him, and called him names when he tried to run away. The mother felt the teachers were not doing enough to control the other boys and intended to report the situation to the Policy Council. What would you do?

LEARNING ACTIVITIES

1. Read one or more of the Suggested Readings or view Web sites. Add 10 cards to your file with specific ideas for helping children develop a positive self-concept. Include the reference source on each card.

2. Assess the self-concept of every child in your classroom using the "Self-Concept Checklist" in Figure 8.1.

3. Make a list of all the children in your class. After each name write down frankly and honestly what you like about the child and why, what changes you think are needed and why, and your reaction to the child in class.

4. Choose a child you have perhaps not accepted unconditionally and try to change your attitude by listing for three days all the positive things you see that child do. Show your approval with nonverbal cues and record the results.

5. Plan and carry out several activities, based on ideas in this chapter, with a child who seems to have a poor self-concept. Record the results.

6. Make a list of every child in the class and record what he or she can do well. Choose one of the children who may need special help and use her strengths to help her experience success in a different activity. Record the results.

7. Take digital photos of one of the children who seems to need help with his self-concept as he engages in one of the classroom activities. Ask him to take three pictures with the camera of anything

he likes. Print the pictures and talk about them with him, writing down his comments and helping him start a personal scrapbook if he wants to.

8. Read one of the books mentioned in the chapter to a small group of children and use it as a lead-in to a self-concept activity. Write up the results.

SUGGESTED READINGS

Beaty, J. J. (2010). *Observing development of the young child* (7th ed.). Upper Saddle River, NJ: Merrill.

Espinosa, L. M. (2010). *Getting it right: For young children from diverse backgrounds.* Upper Saddle River, NJ: Pearson.

Gonzalez-Mena, J. (2010). *50 strategies for communicating and working with diverse families* (2nd ed.). Upper Saddle River, NJ: Pearson.

Kemple, K. M., & Lopez, M. (2009). Blue eyes, brown eyes, cornrows and curls: Building on books to explore physical diversity. *Dimensions of Early Childhood, 37*(1), 23–30.

WEB SITES

Mind in the Making
http://www.mindinthemaking.org

National Association for Bilingual Education
http://www.nabe.org

Teaching Tolerance
http://www.tolerance.org

Zero to Three
http://www.zerotothree.org

CHILDREN'S BOOKS

Appelt, K. (2003). *Incredible me!* New York: HarperCollins.

*Ashley, B. (1992). *Cleversticks.* New York: Crown.

*Beaumont, K. (2004). *I like myself.* Orlando, FL: Harcourt.

*Brammer, E. C. (2003). *My tata's guitar.* Houston, TX: Pinata Books.

Child, L. (2000). *I will never not ever eat a tomato.* Cambridge, MA: Candlewick.

*Dole, M. L. (2003). *Drum, Chavi, drum!* San Francisco: Children's Book Press.

*Dooley, N. (1991). *Everybody cooks rice.* Minneapolis, MN: Carolrhoda.

*Jabar, C. (2006). *Wow! It sure is good to be you!* Boston: Houghton Mifflin.

*John, R., & Thomas, P. A. (2003). *Red is beautiful.* Flagstaff, AZ: Salina Bookshelf.

*Joose, B. M. (1991). *Mama, do you love me?* San Francisco: Chronicle Books.

*Joose, B. M. (2005). *Papa, do you love me?* San Francisco: Chronicle Books.

*Joose, B. M. (2008). *Grandma calls me Beautiful.* San Francisco: Chronicle Books.

Karas, G. B. (2001). *The class artist.* New York: Greenwillow.

Moore, J. (2007). *Freckleface Strawberry.* New York: Bloomsbury USA.

*Park, L. S. (2005). *Bee-bim bop!* New York: Clarion Books.

*Parr, T. (2001). *It's okay to be different.* Boston: Little, Brown.

*Rankin, L. (1991). *The handmade alphabet.* New York: Dial.

*Multicultural

CHAPTER 9

Promoting Social Skills

☐ **General Objective**

To help children develop the social skills of interacting in harmony with others

☑ **Specific Objectives**

_____ Helps children learn to work and play cooperatively through sharing and turn-taking

_____ Helps children learn to enter ongoing play without disruptions

_____ Helps children learn to find playmate-friends

L EARNING *social skills* has long been one of the important goals for children in early childhood programs. Early childhood educators understand that young children are highly self-centered beings, a necessary step in the human growth pattern for the individual to survive infancy. But as children grow older, they need to develop into social beings who can get along with others outside their homes. Kemple and Ellis (2009) tell us: "Current research suggests that young children who are more socially competent (i.e., skilled in self-regulation, perspective taking, emotional expression, cooperation, sharing, and problem solving) and engage regularly in meaningful friendships are more likely to make an easier transition to school and to achieve academic success" (p. 6).

Children in your center must learn to work and play cooperatively not only because we expect it of them but also because they are in a group situation that demands it. They need to learn to get along with the other children through sharing and turn-taking, to enter ongoing play without creating a fuss, and to find friends to play with. It may not be easy for some.

HELPS CHILDREN LEARN TO WORK AND PLAY COOPERA TIVELY THROUGH SHARING AND TURN-TAKING

Three-year-olds, for instance, may be more attuned to adults than to other children. After all, they are not far removed from the toddler stage, when they were almost completely dependent on adult caregivers. Now they are thrust into a group, where adults do not have time for them exclusively and where they are expected *not* to act as dependent, self-centered beings. Many young children do not realize that this will happen to them when they go to preschool. It is quite an adjustment for some children.

You and the other staff members should recognize this problem and help ease children into becoming social beings who can work and play happily with other children. This is no chore for some children; they have learned these skills elsewhere. For others, you must work carefully to set up opportunities for them to become part of the group.

To recognize which children already display social skills and which ones may need help in developing these skills, you may want to observe each of your children by using the "Social Skills Checklist" in Figure 9.1. Be as unobtrusive as possible as you observe each child during group play. This information will give you insights into the social development of individual children so that you can determine which ones

Figure 9.1 Social Skills Checklist

Source: From Janice J. Beaty, *Skills for Preschool Teachers,* Ninth Edition. Copyright © 2012 by Pearson Education, Inc. All rights reserved.

Permission is granted by publisher to reproduce this checklist for evaluation and record keeping.

Child's Name_____**Date**_____

_____ Observes others at play as an onlooker

_____ Plays in solitary manner away from a group

_____ Plays parallel to other children, but alone

_____ Seeks other children to play with or joins a group

_____ Enters ongoing play without a fuss

_____ Takes turns with roles, toys, and equipment

_____ Waits for turn without a fuss

_____ Shares toys, materials, and equipment

_____ Solves interpersonal conflicts on own

_____ Makes friends with another child

The teacher's role is to set up situations where children can play together.

are able to share and take turns, gain access to group play, and resolve conflicts on their own.

Children learn these skills by being involved in spontaneous play with other children. These are not skills that are "taught" by a teacher. The teacher's role is to set up situations in which children can play together and to observe each child using a checklist like the one in Figure 9.1 to determine to what extent the child is developing social skills. For those who need special help, the teacher can then help—but not pressure—them to become involved with others. For children who need special help in learning to take turns or to resolve conflicts, for instance, the teacher can set up special situations outside of group play where children can practice the skills they will be learning spontaneously during the play.

Social Play

Play is the primary means through which young children learn: about themselves, about others, and about the world around them. Whereas adults often view play as recreation, play for young children is their work, and they spend a great deal of time, energy, and concentration in their play with the materials and people around them. When children play with other children we call it "social play." Edwards (2006) has this to say about it: "Social play is the 'umbrella' of all play experiences, encompassing several different levels of social interactions. Young children engage in all types of social play, such as when they are playing chase, or sitting side-by-side working on puzzles, or involved in spontaneous play such as playing 'heroes' while running around the playground. These social interactions provide children opportunities to practice and learn self-related and interpersonal related social skills" (p. 192).

The pioneer child development theorists Piaget and Vygotsky were both concerned with young children's social play. Piaget's play theories focused on the child's cognitive development through symbolic play (pretend play), which appears spontaneously in the last months of the sensorimotor stage (see Figure 5.1), and develops into dramatic play in the preoperational period. Games with rules appear in the concrete operational stage and continue through the formal operations period—all without outside help.

Vygotsky's focus, in contrast, was on the development of representational or make-believe play rather than stages of play. He looked at young children's social play as the essential ingredient in the development of their comprehension, but his theories included the assistance of older children and adults to scaffold the play. He noted that play is the source of development and creates the zone of proximal development (Frost, Wortham, & Reifel, 2005, p. 128).

Early childhood researchers have long been interested in learning how children use spontaneous social play to develop the skills needed to get along with one another ever since Mildred Parten published her early study, "Social Participation Among Pre-School Children," in 1932. Parten defined six categories of play behavior:

Parten's Play Categories

1. *Unoccupied behavior:* The child does not participate in the play around him. He stays in one spot, follows the teacher or wanders around.

2. *Onlooker behavior:* The child spends much time watching what other children are doing and may even talk to them, but he does not join or interact with them physically.

3. *Solitary independent play:* The child engages in play activities, but he plays on his own and not with others or with their toys.

4. *Parallel activity:* The child plays independently but he plays next to other children and often uses their toys or materials.

5. *Associative play:* The child plays with other children using the same materials and even talking with them, but he acts on his own and does not subordinate his interests to those of the group.

6. *Cooperative play:* The child plays in a group that has organized itself to do a particular thing, and whose members have taken on different play roles. (pp. 248–251)

As you observe the children in your center at play throughout the year, you may also recognize that many of them progress through this natural sequence of play behaviors from onlooker to solitary play to parallel play to group play. These levels of play seem to be age related, with the youngest, least mature children starting as onlookers, then progressing spontaneously through the other levels until they finally are able to play cooperatively with a group.

Importance of Parallel Play

Because the earlier stages of play seem to be a less mature form of social interaction, many teachers set up the learning environment to encourage cooperative play. Anderson and Robinson (2006) have found that although children do progress through these stages, it is parallel play that plays an important and unsuspected role in this progression. They noted, "Even though the amount of time kindergarten children engaged in cooperative play increased, the amount of time they engaged in parallel play was still substantial and was not significantly less than that of the preschool children" (p. 11).

This did not seem to mean that less mature children still engaged in parallel play. Their research concluded that "Parallel play is pivotal between playing alone and successful peer group entry in school-age children's play" [as it is with preschool children] (p. 11). In other words, parallel play is a bridge between onlooker, solitary, and cooperative play. It works both ways. Children go back and forth, into and out of parallel play. Observe them and you will see it.

Onlooker-to-Parallel-to-Cooperative Play

Anderson and Robinson's (2006) research discovered this important aspect of the play progression: "Preschool children use the onlooker-to-parallel-to-cooperative interaction shift not only to make the initial transition into cooperative play, but they continue to use this strategy to step back out of cooperative play and back into cooperative play many times during a single play scenario" (p. 13). Take every chance you get to do your own observations on children's social play. Record what each player is doing and saying. Are the children following this sequence? Sometimes their actions are so subtle you do not realize they are playing parallel to the others instead of with them.

When we observe children, it is always through the eyes and interpretations of adults. We sometimes miss essential elements about children's own motives and their actions. It is thus important that you and every early childhood teacher spend time observing and recording children's behavior and carefully interpreting what it means. There is much about young children we still do not know. But the more we carefully observe and deeply engage with them, the more we all will learn.

Teacher's Role

- Set up the physical arrangement of the classroom to accommodate small-group activities.
- Schedule enough free-choice time for children to become deeply involved in their play.

- Accept children wherever they are in this developmental sequence.
- Observe and record the social skills being demonstrated by each of the children.
- Help (but not force) them to progress through this sequence of social skill development.

Some of the social skills we will be looking for include those listed in the "Social Skills Checklist," Figure 9.1.

Sharing and Turn-Taking

When young children first enter a preschool program they are often bewildered by the number of toys, games, materials, and pieces of equipment available. Are all of these wonders for them? Because of their egocentric point of view, some children begin to act as if this is the case. These toys are for them alone. If they want a toy another child is playing with, they may simply take it—by force if necessary.

Children who act like this are not trying to be mean. Instead, the social skills of sharing, taking turns, and waiting for turns are simply not yet part of their behavior. The ability to control their impulses, to wait, or to negotiate or bargain for a turn needs to be learned through observation of others or trial-and-error interactions on their part. As noted by Katz and McClellan (1997), "Turn taking involves being able to detect cues in a partner's behavior that indicate that he is about to bring his turn to an end; to discern the moment that would be the most propitious to press for one's own turn; and so forth. Mastery of these skills takes time and lots of experience" (p. 91).

You as a teacher can help by encouraging the child to ask for a turn rather than trying to take the desired toy by force. The following are some additional strategies.

Modeling and Demonstrating Turn-Taking Behavior

Children can learn from your example and that of the other adults in the classroom. Make it obvious that you respect their rights and will stand up for them if necessary. Make it a point to thank children who wait for a turn or who share. Do this again and again, and some of the children will soon imitate your behavior. Thank children for saying thanks. That will help other children to remember. Because children also imitate peer behavior, your modeling will spread throughout the classroom as other children see the original child behaving this way.

Bring in a special toy or activity for sharing and taking turns. For example, to demonstrate taking turns, the teacher can show a small group of children some new toy or stuffed animal that they might all want to play with. How can they decide who will get the first turn, and the next? How long should a child be allowed to play with the toy? These problems can be talked about and decided on at group meeting time. Perhaps the children would like a sign-up list where those who want a turn can sign their own name (even in scribble writing). Or perhaps they would like to regulate turns by drawing tickets out of a hat with numbers on them to determine the order. They can also manage the time with a three-minute egg timer. Then it is up to the children to put these skills to use in the spontaneous group play situations that you promote during free-choice time.

Puppets

For children who still have difficulty sharing toys, you might bring in two puppets, one for you and one for a child who gets involved frequently in sharing conflicts with another child. Ask the child if she would like to play puppets with you. Introduce the puppets. Hers can be "Sadie-Share-the-Toy." Yours can be "Donna-Don't-Give-It-Up." Have your puppet get involved with her puppet over a sharing conflict. For example, you could have your puppet say, "Look what I've got. I found this neat dinosaur over on the toy shelf." (Have a real toy dinosaur to get the child's attention.) Her puppet might respond, "Can I see it? I want to play with it too." Yours can reply, "Nope, it's mine. I found it first. You can't have it."

At this point you can intervene to speak as yourself. Ask the child what Sadie-Share-the-Toy could say to persuade Donna-Don't-Give-It-Up to share the dinosaur toy with her. Also discuss the strategies that probably won't work: getting angry, yelling, or taking the toy by force. Then continue the role play until Sadie finally gets the toy. Getting the real toy when she exhibits the proper behavior reinforces the behavior and helps the child understand what works and what doesn't work in sharing.

Books as Lead-Ins to Sharing and Turn-Taking Activities

Reading a book about a sharing conflict works best *after* the child has experienced the conflict rather than before. Children need real and concrete experiences on which to base the more abstract ideas gained from books. However, stories are an effective follow-up to reinforce the learning children gain from conflicts.

> In *The Boy Who Wouldn't Share* (Reiss, 2008) Edward is the frightful boy who wouldn't share a single toy. Rhyming verses and hilarious illustrations show him grabbing everything away from his sister Claire until he is buried under a pile of toys. When his mother comes with a plate of fudge, she can't see Edward and gives it all to Claire. Have your listeners predict what will happen next.

This story calls out for a reenactment. Have every child who wants to, choose a toy to keep away from the sister. They can stand in a big circle around Edward, seated on the floor. One child can be Claire and another, the mother. As you read the story, point to one child at a time to pile his toy on Edward. The mother's plate can contain pretend fudge (or real fruit slices). Talk about the story afterward. Do the children think that Edward has really learned his lesson?

Other books as lead-ins to sharing activities:

Mine! Mine! Mine! (Becker, 2006)

The Mine-O-Saur (Bardhan-Quallen, 2007)

Computer Turn-Taking

Children learn powerful lessons about cooperating with others when they have direct experience with equipment calling for more than one child to use at a time. The classroom computer, for instance, should be set up for two children to use at a time. Children can choose to use the computer during free-choice time by selecting the two computer area necklaces. Then let the two users work out their own turn-taking scheme for each program.

Observers have noted that computer turn-taking problems are frequently settled through conversation rather than physical struggle, as is often the case with other classroom materials. Because turn-taking has to be worked out for nearly every computer program, computer partners learn lessons about who gets the first choice of a program, who goes first, and how many mouse clicks each person gets. Onlookers learn about waiting for turns, not pushing ahead of someone who was there first, and sharing ideas (through conversation) with someone who has a turn.

For children who have difficulty interacting with others like this, you may need to help them get started, but with great care and without pressure. Petty (2009) points out: "Often, children who have difficulty entering play situations are more successful when an adult or a more accomplished peer guides their participation, especially if their language skills are limited" (p. 82). If a child doesn't seem to participate in group enterprises at all, you will first want to assess the situation by observing and recording.

Have children work out their own scheme for turn-taking.

HELPS CHILDREN LEARN TO ENTER ONGOING PLAY WITHOUT DISRUPTIONS

Children's free-choice play in a preschool setting often ebbs and flows like waves on a beach. No one is still for long. Youngsters come together for a short time in the block area; someone is painting at the easel; a few children wander into the dramatic play kitchen; someone dresses up in high heels and takes the baby doll for a ride in the carriage; two children operate the computer; others are busy at the arts and crafts tables; several are involved with counting blocks and stringing beads; someone is up on the loft listening to a tape with a headset. In the next instant everything changes, and different children are occupied with or trying to gain access to these activities.

You may wonder why children don't stay longer in one place. Then you remember about the short attention spans of children 3 to 5 years of age. You also recognize their boundless energy and endless drive for finding out what is going on everywhere. If you watch long enough, you are sure to encounter one of the common access struggles that arises when someone wants to enter an ongoing play situation. "I want to do what they're doing, and they won't let me!" is a complaint sounded over and over in early childhood programs.

NAEYC Criteria for Curriculum Standard

Describe how you would meet the following standard:

2.B.05 Children have varied opportunities to develop skills for entering into social groups, developing friendships, learning to help, and other prosocial behavior.

If a child has not been invited to join or does not know how to establish contact with the ongoing players, he or she is almost always rejected. As noted by early childhood specialist Ramsey (1991), "Interactions in preschool classrooms are short, so children are constantly having to gain entry into new groups. This process is made more difficult because children who are already engaged with each other tend to protect their interactive space and reject newcomers" (p. 27).

What is a child to do who sees his favorite toy animals being lined up on the floor by two other children but is rejected when he wants to join them? This typical group-entry conflict can be a frustrating dilemma for the child, and he may end up disrupting the play of the other children or coming to you in tears. Your knowledge of group-access strategies can help such a child convert the conflict into a positive social skill learning situation for all involved.

Group-Access Strategies

What do you need to know? You need to be aware of what works for most children who try to enter ongoing play and what does not work. Observers of young children

One of the best ways to gain access to an activity is to hover near the player.

have noted that one of the best strategies for a child who has been rejected is to hover silently near the group, carefully observing what they are doing (i.e., *onlooker behavior*). Once the child knows what the group is doing, he can do *parallel play* with similar materials near them. When the time seems right, he can try again to enter the group.

In this case you could suggest to Antonio, the rejected child, that he get a few more animals from the shelf and line them up on the floor next to the other two children (i.e., *scaffolding*). In a little while they might let him into their play, but if they don't, he can continue playing on his own. Most children who have been rejected don't try to enter the play again. Child observers have noted, however, that youngsters who make a second attempt to gain entry are much more likely to be accepted on the second try.

In the case of ongoing dramatic play, a rejected child should also watch what the others are doing and then begin playing in her own way nearby. For example, if Kaylee has been refused entry into the ongoing doctor's-office play of three other children, she can observe what's happening until she notes that two of the girls are taking their baby dolls to the doctor's for a shot. She might then get a doll of her own and enter the play, saying, "My baby needs a shot too." If a child wants you to intervene, you can suggest, "Why don't you watch what the girls are doing? They may let you play after a while." If the child cannot figure out on her own how to insert herself into the play, you can suggest, "Why don't you get a doll and play too?"

Not all strategies work. Asking the players questions that refer to oneself does not seem to help. For example, "Can I play?" or "Can I have that doll?" almost always results in the answer "no." Children who make aggressive claims against the players are also rejected. For example, saying "I was here first!" or "That's mine!" or "I got it first" only irritates the other players rather than allowing the new child entrance. If rejected children disrupt ongoing play by taking the materials, shouting, or throwing things, they succeed only in stopping the play altogether. Furthermore, the other children remember such actions and may ostracize the outsiders from their further activities. Figure 9.2 lists some of the strategies for entering ongoing play.

Why shouldn't you as the teacher simply tell the players to let the outside child into their activity? You certainly have the authority and power to do this. But should you? A teacher's intervention in an interpersonal conflict that can be resolved by the

Figure 9.2 Entering
Ongoing Play

Strategies that work for young children:

1. Observing silently (onlooker)
2. Mimicking the play (parallel play)
3. Trying again to enter the group

Strategies children should avoid:

1. Asking "I" questions
2. Making aggressive claims
3. Disrupting the play physically

children themselves misses an important point. Children have come to your class-room to learn how to get along with one another. The principal way children can really learn such social skills is *by becoming involved in interpersonal conflicts and attempting to resolve them on their own.*

Your role should be a supportive one in children's conflicts. If someone is hurt or crying or if physical aggression is taking place, you must of course intervene. But if the situation is a common group-access conflict, then give the children a chance to resolve it on their own.

Play access struggles with other children are the most critical learning opportunities that young children must deal with. Such conflicts teach profound lessons in getting along with others: how to watch and wait, when to initiate contact, how to learn what is going on in the play, how to blend in with the group, what to say so you won't be rejected, and what to do in case you are rejected. These crucial lessons are repeated over and over as children ebb and flow during free play.

Books as Lead-Ins to Entering Ongoing Play

The classic book about children's access problems is *This Is Our House* (Rosen, 1996) about a cardboard carton house out on the playground. George quickly climbs in and claims it for his own. He keeps out every child who tries to play in it. At last he has to leave to go to the bathroom. Everyone quickly squeezes in and when George comes back there is no room for him. He finally decides this is a house for everyone. Ask your listeners what they would have done to get into George's house.

Children love playing with cardboard cartons. Bring in a large carton for your children to convert into a playhouse. Have them decide on rules for who can play and how many can play at a time. Can they make up stories about their house like George's? One class illustrated their story with digital photos they took by themselves—another use of their turn-taking rules.

Dramatic Play

One of the most effective opportunities for children to learn and practice social skills of all kinds is through the spontaneous pretend play that takes place in the dramatic play center, sometimes called "sociodramatic play." Edwards (2002) defines it as "play in which children assume roles and act out episodes." Sociodramatic play is also described as play that involves social role-playing with others and refers to children's pretend play when two or more children assume related roles and interact with each other (pp. 194–195).

Most classrooms have a dramatic play center where children are encouraged to pretend and take on roles. Sometimes called the "housekeeping" or "family area," it contains equipment such as a play stove, refrigerator, sink, and table, as well as kitchen equipment and dress-up clothes. These props encourage children to take on spontaneously the family roles they see at home: mother, father, baby, sister, brother. (See Chapter 3, "Dramatic Play Center.")

In a preschool classroom, this kind of activity gives children an opportunity to be part of a group. If they are shy about interacting, they can become acquainted with others through the roles they take on. They can hide behind their roles, so to speak, in the way a shy child hides behind a puppet. Dramatic play is one of the most unique opportunities you can provide for children's learning of social skills. To get along with the other players, children must learn to share, to take turns, to adjust their actions to the group, and to resolve conflicts without an adult's help.

Learning from Peers in Dramatic Play

We know how important peer pressure is with older children. Child development research has now come to recognize how important peers are to younger children as well. They exchange information about the world around them, they offer suggestions to one another on appropriate ways to behave, and some even try to impose their will on others in the group. Children learn what is expected of them and whether or not to conform to this pressure. (See Figure 9.3, "Social Skills Learned in Dramatic Play.")

Children observe how other children are treated by their peers, what works and what doesn't work in interpersonal conflicts, and how far a peer can go in trying to get his own way. Aggressive children learn that others will not accept their

Figure 9.3 Social Skills Learned in Dramatic Play

- How to get along with others
- How to avoid conflicts
- How to negotiate
- How to compromise
- How to take turns

overbearing ways. The group may demonstrate its feelings by stopping the play altogether when things get out of hand or by not allowing their aggressive peer to join them the next time. Not only do aggressive children learn a lesson when such negative peer responses happen again and again, but other child players also learn that similar reactions from the group could happen to them if they behave in this aggressive manner.

Reifel and Sutterby (2009) point out that children observe closely who gets to play and what roles they take. Such negotiating is an important part of social communication. Socially adept children get the best roles while others not so adept get to play only if they take less valued roles such as baby or pet. Over time, they say, "children's play negotiations contribute to their social statuses in the classroom, to how they are valued as playmates, what friendships they form, and who become the leaders and followers in the group" (pp. 246–247).

Learning Real-Life Roles

Besides teaching them social skills, dramatic play also gives children the opportunity to try out the real-life roles they see enacted around them. It helps them understand what it is like to be a mother or a brother. They begin to see things from another perspective, often trying on for size the roles they will eventually play as adults. While they play these roles in the classroom, they are becoming socialized in a much more effective way than any adult could teach them. They learn to follow peer directions, to take leader or follower roles, to compromise their own desires, to resolve interpeer conflict—all through spontaneous play.

Furthermore, dramatic play helps children clarify new ideas and concepts about society and the world around them. As they gain information about unfamiliar people and situations, they are able to make it understandable by incorporating it into their imaginative play. The child who has a plumber come to her house plays out this situation in the housekeeping corner and begins to understand it better. Dramatic play, in other words, gives concrete meaning to abstract ideas.

Dramatic play also helps children master uncomfortable feelings. Adults are sometimes unaware of the frustrations children feel at being small and helpless in a grown-up world. Pretending to be an adult helps them gain some control over their world and helps them work out fears and frustrations. They can pretend about going to the doctor and getting a shot, about going to a strange school next year, or about staying overnight with a babysitter and thus lessen the trauma of the real event.

Finally, such play helps young children develop creative skills by forcing them to use their imaginations. They make up the roles, the rules, the situations, and the solutions. The drama can be as elaborate or simple as the players make it. And strange as it seems, it is through imaginative play like this that children come to understand the difference between fantasy and reality. The real world becomes more real to children who have opportunities to pretend.

Books as Lead-Ins to Dramatic Play

What Shall We Play? (Heap, 2002) shows three multiethnic children playing together: Lily May who always wants to play fairies, Matt who disagrees with the others at first, and Martha who has very definite ideas for pretend play scenarios. How do they resolve their problems?

Have children sit close as you read to a small group. Ask them to discuss what they would have done in each situation. What kinds of pretend play do they like to do? What role is their favorite?

Other books as lead-ins to dramatic play:

Mud Tacos! (Lopez & Lopez-Wong, 2009)

Even Firefighters Hug Their Moms (MacLean, 2002)

Dramatic Play Areas

You will want to have a permanent area in your classroom for this kind of dress-up play, as discussed in Chapter 3. In addition to the permanent household area, other dramatic play areas may also be appropriate from time to time. For example, you may want to set up a supermarket, shoe store, or post office, especially after the children have visited one of these sites on a field trip. Children can bring empty cartons, cans, and boxes to fill the shelves of a store.

Isbell and Raines (2007) suggest using *prop boxes* to store materials for later use. "A large clear plastic container can be used to collect and store props that can be used to encourage play around a specific theme. A beauty salon prop box could contain a blow dryer, combs, brushes, empty spray bottles, hair magazines, appointment book, cape, and hand-held mirror."

Dramatic play can also take place with smaller toys in many other areas of the classroom, and it serves the same socialization purpose. You can encourage dramatic play in the block corner by mounting, at child's eye level, pictures of activities involving the field trip sites the children have visited: stores, farm, zoo, pet store, post office, or park. Then you must provide appropriate toys and props to accompany the play: figures of people and animals, little cars and trucks, string, aquarium tubing, or little boxes. Let the children use these props on their own in any way they want. To be effective, pretend play must be spontaneous.

Do the same near the sand or water table and in the manipulative area. A supply of miniature people, animals, cars, trucks, boats, and doll furniture is essential if you are committed to promoting imaginative play.

Teacher's Role

Your initial role may be as an observer. You will want to determine which children take part in dramatic play and which never do. Can they take turns? Can they resolve conflicts? Who are the leaders? The followers? What other roles do they play? How long can they sustain their roles? Do they allow other children to participate in their play?

Children's fear of going to a doctor or dentist may surface in dramatic play. If you observe that children have mistaken ideas about what doctors or dentists do, do not interrupt the play to "set them straight." Instead, take note of their misconceptions. Later you may want to read them a book about visiting the doctor or dentist. Or you may feel that the children have been able to work out their fears satisfactorily on their own in their dramatic play.

What happens in the dramatic play area is often determined by the way you set it up, what equipment and furniture are available, and what paraphernalia you put out. If the children have expressed fear of police officers, for example, you may want to put out appropriate props—say, a police cap—especially after a classroom visit from an officer.

As a Model

If you observe that certain children are not participating in dramatic play, are not staying with a role, or are not really interacting with others in their roles, you may want to help them get involved by playing a role yourself (i.e., modeling). For example, you might say, "C'mon, Shandra, let's visit Jayce's store. You carry the pretend money. What shall we buy?" When the child seems involved and comfortable, you can ease out of your role the same way you entered.

For new groups of children who seem to have no idea how to get started in dramatic play, you may even have to assign roles and start the play by taking a role yourself. When things are going smoothly, you can withdraw. "Let's go to the beach," you might say. "Does anybody want to go to the beach with me? Okay, let's pack our swimming suits. The bags are on the shelf. Rachel, you bring the picnic basket. Rob, you bring the beach ball. I'll bring the towels. Sharon, would you like to drive the bus to the beach?"

All of this, of course, is pretend. If you happen to have beach bags or picnic baskets for props, all the better. If not, the children can pretend they have them. If going to the beach turns out to be a favorite theme, then create a "prop box" that you fill with necessary props (e.g., beach toys, towels, sunglasses), and store it on a shelf along with other prop boxes in a designated area. Computer paper boxes covered with colored contact paper and labeled with a sign or picture make fine prop storage containers.

Ask the children what other dramatic play themes they would like to try. Some will probably mention places they have visited with their parents or where their parents work: office, restaurant, gas station, convenience store, museum, flower shop, bakery, repair shop, factory, school, hairdresser, or sports shop. Fill the prop boxes with appropriate implements from home, from flea markets, or from the actual sites themselves. Then introduce the boxes one at a time when it seems appropriate.

As a Mediator

When dramatic play begins to get wild or seems to disintegrate, you may need to step in and change its direction. Isenberg and Jalongo (2010) point out that: "teachers of young children frequently encounter children's conflicts and disputes about toys, space, roles to play, or rules. As a mediator, you will want to help children develop peaceful resolutions" (p. 62). For instance, when a race with tiny cars in the block-building center has deteriorated into squabbles and shouting, you might say, "What do race car drivers do when the race is finished?"

If you have the props on hand, you may be able to redirect the children into "washing and polishing their race cars." Children decided to use milk cartons open at both ends as car wash buildings to drive through, old cut-off toothbrushes to clean the cars, and paper tissues to polish them.. Finding a peaceful resolution to conflicts like this can be satisfying to all concerned if children are given a chance to employ their own ideas.

Block Building

Social skills can also be learned and practiced in the block-building center. Children role-play in this center just as in the dramatic play center but in a scaled-down manner. Unit blocks are used realistically to construct roads, bridges, and buildings or more abstractly as cars, planes, spaceships, or anything else a child's imagination can conceive. Children play with the constructions they create both realistically and imaginatively, depending on their experience with life, with blocks, and with pretending.

Occasionally a child does not seem to know how to get started in block building. This is an instance where you might want to intervene. How should you go about it? Sometimes simply your presence in the block corner will entice a shy or insecure child into the area. You might then ask the child to get you a long block from the shelf if she doesn't seem to know what to do. Put the block down and ask her to get another block. Ask the child where to place it. Get her involved in selecting and placing other blocks one by one. Once she is involved, you can withdraw, as in dramatic play. Tell her you'll be back in a few minutes to see how many other blocks she has placed on her structure and what it will look like. Your role should be one of support for the shy or unsure child and that of observer for the rest.

You will soon become aware of which children build by themselves (solitary play), who builds next to the others but independently (parallel play), and finally who is able to build cooperatively with other children (cooperative play), the final step in the socialization process. Keep records of the children's progress on individual Accomplishment Cards along with the results of the "Social Skills Checklist" shown in Figure 9.1.

It is important not to pressure children to socialize. It is not up to you to make Gabriel play with Jake. You may need to provide the opportunity for both, but the children must make the contact on their own. This will often happen automatically after both feel secure in the block area. That means they will have experimented with blocks on their own. Many children need to do a great deal of solitary and parallel block building before they gain the confidence to cooperate with other children.

Handling Interpersonal Conflicts

Frequently, the first social contacts are ones of conflict. "He took my block!" or "She won't let me play!" Often, as a teacher or student teacher, you will be drawn into the situation because the children want you to settle it. Situations of uncontrolled anger, destruction of materials, or harm to other children demand that you step in. Firmly but calmly, you must enforce previously established limits of not letting children hurt one another or harm materials.

However, you can let the children handle many of their own interpersonal conflicts once they feel they have your support. Give them masking tape to mark off boundaries for building, if that seems to help. Help them make a sign that asks others not to knock down the building. Help them set the kitchen timer to five minutes so that they can take turns with a favorite truck in the block area. Let children give out tickets to other builders who would like to join in. Ask the children themselves what they want to do to solve the problem. You and the children can come up with dozens of similar ideas to help them resolve conflicts.

You must remember, of course, that adult direction stifles children's own problem solving. You may need to encourage children at the outset to help them get started, but then you should tactfully withdraw. You may need to help redirect their play when it gets out of hand, but then you should step aside. For group play to be truly effective in promoting the development of social skills, children need to manage their social roles by themselves.

Other-Esteem Conflict Conversion

Children do need to know you will respect each child's rights; then you can help individuals stand up for their own rights. When conflicts arise, it is often impossible for the teacher to determine who was right and who was wrong. Try not to deal with children's conflicts on the basis of right and wrong or blame and shame. Instead, listen to each child in a noncommittal way.

For example, Latasha says Brooke took the toy cash register that she was playing with. She starts to cry. Brooke says that she had it first and left it for only a few minutes to find some toy money. When she came back, Latasha was playing with it, so she took it away from her.

You can best help both children *recognize each other's points of view* and empathize about their feelings by listening to each, thanking them for telling you what happened, and then by asking how each one thinks the other child feels about it. This is quite different from the usual blame and shame approach, or asking a child how she feels. Children are usually surprised to be asked how the *other* child feels. After they finally reply, then you can ask what each one thinks should be done to make the other child feel better. This approach is known as "other-esteem conflict conversion." It is a positive learning approach to handling social conflicts rather than a blame and punishment approach.

For example, Latasha tells the teacher that it's Brooke's fault because she took the cash register away from her. Brooke says that it's Latasha's fault because she was

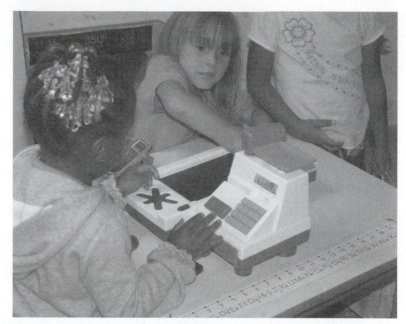

Brooke is taking the cash register Latasha is playing with.

playing with it first and left it for just a minute to get some money. She took it back from Latasha. The teacher listens carefully to each point of view and then says to each child, "Thanks for telling me what happened." She does not blame either child or let the two children get into their own who's-to-blame argument.

Instead, she next asks, "Latasha, how do you think Brooke feels about what happened?" Latasha may be very surprised at this question, and say, "But it's her fault. She took my cash register." The teacher can then reply, "I know, you already told me, but now we're talking about feelings. How do you think Brooke feels? Look at her face."

When Latasha finally is able to answer that Brooke looks mad, then the teacher can ask Brooke how she thinks Latasha feels. She is also surprised at this turn of events and still wants to blame Latasha. But the teacher insists on talking about feelings. Brooke may finally say that she thinks Latasha feels bad because she is crying. This is where the "conflict conversion" happens. Instead of blame and shame, the teacher has converted the situation to feelings: How does the other child feel? Most youngsters can respond honestly to this question. Then the teacher concludes by asking each child what he or she thinks will make the other child feel better.

This is generally a big relief for each child because they are not being blamed or being punished. Furthermore, the children themselves have control over the resolution. This usually means they will abide by whatever they decide to do and not carry on the conflict later. An adult-imposed solution is never that satisfactory and often results in bad feelings or a continuation of the conflict. But children's solutions are often more creative than an adult's might be. Perhaps they decide to take turns with

Figure 9.4 Teacher's Role in Other-Esteem Conflict Conversion

1. Listen to the child.
2. Thank each child for telling you what happened.
3. Do not blame either one or get into a blaming argument.
4. Ask each child how he thinks the *other* child feels.
5. Ask each child what should be done to make the *other* child feel better.
6. Follow the agreed-upon solution.

the cash register using a kitchen timer, or both use the cash register at the same time, or to play a different game altogether; or they might even decide to give each other a big hug! Figure 9.4 outlines the steps the teacher can take in an other-esteem conflict conversion situation.

No matter how you finally handle conflict, be consistent. If you handle interpersonal problems in the same objective manner every time, the children will come to trust you and to understand that you will treat each of them fairly in their dealings with one another. This gives them a good basis for handling problems on their own. Then they can try out different strategies to see which ones work best. Sometimes the only solution is to have the teacher put away the disputed toy until another day.

As these ideas become internalized through the children's experiences in the classroom, their social behavior should also change from self-centeredness to cooperation and other-esteem.

The Shy Child

The shy or unsure child or a dual language learner, however, may need your help to get started, or she may never attempt group entry. One way to help the child is to take a role yourself for a brief period and then extract yourself when the child seems comfortable playing with others. "Shall we visit Rosa's house today, Denise? You knock on the door and see if she is home." If the child lacks the social skills to gain entry to play groups, your modeling of the appropriate behavior and dialogue can help.

Classroom materials can sometimes help such children become involved with others. Materials through which they can project, yet not reveal themselves totally, are best. A toy cell phone, for instance, allows them to talk with other children indirectly, until they feel comfortable enough for a more direct encounter. A teacher can initiate such a pretend phone call. Puppets and dolls or toy animals also allow shy children the same protection. A stuffed animal can act as a security blanket and provide a way for an unsure child to approach someone else.

If a child seems happy in self-contained play, invite but don't push him into a group activity. He may in fact do better on his own. We need to respect these differences in children just as we do in adults. Don't give up entirely on the so-called loner, however. Some children are simply overwhelmed by large groups. You might begin by inviting them to do something with one other friend: look at a book together, help pick up toys together, set the table together, get out the cots for nap time, or go to the office to get the mail. The friends may eventually participate in group activities on their own.

Making friends with the classroom guinea pig or rabbit can be the first step toward making friends with another child. The teacher can help children become involved with a classroom animal like this to get this process started. Find out what shy youngsters are interested in, and use that knowledge to motivate them to become involved with others.

Books as Lead-Ins to Help Children Get Involved with Others

> *Sammy:The Classroom Guinea Pig* (Berenzy, 2005) is a fine book to help get a shy child involved with classroom activities and other children. Sammy lives in a cage in Mrs. B's classroom. On the Monday morning of the story, Sammy interrupts everything with a loud WHEEEP! Then he runs around kicking up wood shavings and wheeping loudly. Finally, Maria figures out he is just lonely after the weekend and wants attention. What do your listeners do when they want attention?

Have a shy child and one other helper be guinea pig caretakers for a week if they agree. Afterward these two can show the next pair of helpers how to feed and care for the little animal. This experience ideally will lead a shy child into other activities as interesting and rewarding.

Other guinea pig books to lead children into pet activities:

Charlie Hits It Big (Blumenthal, 2007)

I Completely Know About Guinea Pigs (Child, 2008)

Patches Lost and Found (Kroll, 2001)

HELPS CHILDREN LEARN TO FIND PLAYMATE-FRIENDS

Friendship among young children is not the same as it is among older children or adults. Preschoolers often value friends for their abilities to meet their (the preschooler's) needs rather than for their personalities. Young children need a friend to help them build a block building, or play firefighter, or push a wagon around. Because young children are self-centered, early friendships are often one sided and fluid. A friend is valued if he satisfies certain needs of the other child. Someone who shares a toy or plays with a preschool child is considered a friend, for the moment at least.

Child psychologist Corsaro (2003) tells us, "Kids come to realize that interaction is fragile and acceptance into on-going activities is often difficult. Therefore, the kids concentrate on creating, sharing, and protecting their play. In short, the kids are more

Figure 9.5 Children's
Friendship-Building
Strategies

1.   Invite another child to play or work together.
2.   Share toys and materials.
3.   Carry on a conversation.
4.   Offer to help.
5.   Exchange play ideas.
6.   Read or listen to a book together.
7.   Follow another child's lead, or lead another.
8.   Walk, eat, play together.
9.   Be partners on a field trip.
10.   Laugh together.
11.   Have fun together.

concerned with 'playing' than 'making friends,' and, anyway, you make friends by playing with other kids—as many as you can" (p. 69).

For a child who has difficulty finding a playmate-friend in the classroom, the teacher can sometimes help by modeling the appropriate behavior. Put on a hand puppet and have the child put on one, if she will. Have your puppet ask the child's puppet to do something. Could they build a tower together? Perhaps this child could also show another child how to do something she is familiar with. Could they use the computer together, make a puppet talk, read a book, or build a Lego building together? These activities can provide the means for a child to enter other group activities where she might form a friendship. Figure 9.5 lists some of the strategies children can use for friendship building.

Listening Partners

You as teacher may have to help. You might start by reading a book about friendship to two children. You can choose the book, pick pairs of children, and invite them to listen to the story. If the book characters are boys, for instance, you may want two boys to listen. *Yo! Yes?* (Raschka, 1993) shows large pictures of two lonely boys, one African American and one Anglo, on opposite pages, standing and looking at one another. One says "Yo!" and the other says "Yes?" as they tentatively approach one another with single words in oversize type. Each is looking for a friend, and when they finally come together, they both say "Yow!"

Ask your listeners what they would say if they met someone they wanted for a friend. What else would they say if the person agreed to be their friend? If your listeners ask you to read the book again, be sure you comply. Then ask if they could "read" it to one another themselves. Tell them to make up their own words for this simple story if they forget the words in the book.

Margaret and Margarita (Reiser, 1993) are two little girls taken to a park by their mothers who end up on the same park bench. Margaret, with her toy rabbit Susan, speaks English, but Margarita, with her toy cat Susana, speaks Spanish. What will they do? While the adults sit with their backs turned, the two little girls make tentative advances toward one another, saying "Hello" and *"Hola"* and finally having their toy pets respond in the opposite language. Soon they are friends, although each is speaking her own language. What would your listening partners do if they were Margaret or Margarita?

Often it is games children play that bring them together. In the Charlie and Lola book *You Can Be My Friend* (Child, 2008), Charlie's friend Marv is bringing his little brother Morten over to play with Lola. She excitedly tries playing tea party with him. He doesn't speak a word. Then dressing up and playing pirate. Nothing. Pretending to be upside down. Still nothing. When they stop for snacks Lola sighs and blows bubbles in her pink milk. Morten giggles! Then more giggles. Outside they blow giant bubbles and pretend to be inside them. He is playing! He is talking! Then he wants to play the board game Round and Round, which Lola hates. But she plays it because Morten is her new special friend.

For children who might be enticed to play a board game after you read them the book it is based on, two listening partners could play the following simple board games from Constructive Playthings (1-800-832-0572):

Green Eggs and Ham Game	*Cat in the Hat Game*
Dr. Seuss's ABC Game	*Goodnight Moon Game*
Eric Carle Animal Game	*Very Hungry Caterpillar Game*

Inclusion

Often children with special needs may have trouble finding friends in the classroom, sometimes because children outside the classroom have not treated them well. As McCay and Keyes (2001/2002) note, "Children with disabilities in the regular classroom tend to have more difficulty building friendships, because they may have learned that other children can hurt them. Children's behavior is guided by their interpretation of social cues based on prior experience" (p. 75).

You as a teacher can help not by scolding others or pointing out the need for special help regarding such children, but by treating children with special needs in the same loving way you treat all of the children. You can help them participate in all of the classroom activities, as well as taking on simple leadership roles such as being in charge of getting out materials and equipment for art or outdoor play, feeding the aquarium fish, or helping to get out naptime cots.

They too can become listening partners when you read appropriate books to two children at a time, or computer partners if they want to take turns on the computer. You can also help them find playmate-friends just as you do with other children who need assistance. Isenberg and Jalongo (2010) point out: "Children with mild disabilities often follow the same stages of play as their non-disabled peers, but their social interaction skills are often delayed. This often leads to more solitary, less cooperative play" (p. 59). Children with Autism Spectrum Disorder, for example, may have difficulty with social skills and may lack mental representations and the language needed for pretend play, say Isenberg and Jalongo. You can teach them the skills needed through your modeling of behavior.

However, teachers need to be aware that friendship evolves and cannot be forced. Talking to the children about who is friends with whom does not help the situation. Some children do seem to prefer the company of a particular child, but this is no reason to point out to the others that Sandra and Rachel are such close friends. Such statements may unknowingly put pressure on children who do not have identifiable friends. *Finding a personal friend is not the point in preschool.* Most children have not yet developed to this level. Having a playmate is more important, but talking about it is not.

Creating a Kindness Class

The class itself can reflect your focus on treating one another with respect and kindness. Friendship grows out of little acts of kindness such as one child helping another to pick up the blocks without being asked, sharing a lunch sandwich with another, or giving up a computer turn to someone else. You can alert the children to these acts of kindness in several ways. For instance, one teacher began by commenting to the children on every kind act she saw and writing it down on a slip of paper that she posted on the bulletin board under the label "Acts of Kindness." Another teacher wrote down acts on cards and put them into a large glass "Kindness Jar."

But that was just the beginning. Soon the children were contributing their own "sightings of kindness." This time the staff members asked the children themselves to record such acts on cards the best way they could by scribbling, printing, drawing pictures, or asking one another to write their names. Such cards could then be put into a jar or a basket, or pasted in a "kindness scrapbook" for everyone to look at in the book center. Some children also wanted to give their "kindness cards" to the children who performed the kind acts to take home or put in their personal journals. The teacher in this class noted, "I realized that, for the children, sharing a personal kind act was not really different from showing one's picture or journal to the class. Telling about their kind acts was a way for them to affirm their growth in thoughtfulness" (Whitin, 2001, p. 20).

Before the year was up some children were also reporting their conflict resolutions as acts of kindness. The teacher was especially gratified to hear "we decided that we would be friends" as the solution to a conflict over a toy. What everyone, including the teaching staff, learned was that when you look for kindness you find it; when you expect children—and teachers—to be kind to one another, it happens. Who else could this class include in their kindness campaign? What about parents? Cooks? Bus drivers? Visitors? Children and teachers from other classes? When will you start your own "kindness class"?

SUMMARY

This chapter discusses ways to promote children's social development by helping them to learn to get along with one another. It is often difficult for children of this age, who are egocentric in nature, to work and play cooperatively in a group setting. To facilitate such play, the teacher needs to observe and record information about individuals and their social skills development, such as who seeks other children to play with, who can take turns, or who can solve interpersonal conflicts on their own. Teachers help children learn turn-taking by demonstrating with toys and puppets, by reading books about sharing and turn-taking, and by setting up turn-taking situations such as partners at the computer.

For children who need assistance in learning to enter ongoing group play, teachers help them to use strategies that have been found to work and to avoid strategies that do not work. Their experiences in the dramatic play and block-building areas can provide opportunities for children to work out relationship problems with their peers. Through dramatic play, children learn to see things from another's point of view. They exchange information with one another, often about appropriate ways to behave. They learn to share, take turns, and wait for a turn.

The teacher's role is to stimulate such play in the first place by helping children become involved in pretend play. When play disintegrates,

she scaffolds it further by posing a question or suggesting a new direction. To help the shy child become involved in such play the teacher may take on a role herself, modeling appropriate dialogue and behavior.

A friend for preschool children is often someone who shares a toy or plays with them. Teachers can help children find playmate-friends through their modeling behavior, use of puppets, and pairing children to listen to books with friendship themes. Toys and play materials can also bring children together as playmates and friends. Children with special needs may need direct help from the teaching staff to find friends. Friendship itself can grow out of little acts of kindness noted by the teaching staff and children as they record and share these acts.

Ethical Dilemma

A new child to the program, Rinaldo, a Hispanic boy, was having trouble getting along with the other children. They would not let him enter their play groups, and when he became aggressive, the teacher made him sit in the time-out chair. His mother was so upset that after talking with the teacher (who claimed Rinaldo was the one who started all the trouble), she wrote a letter to the editor of the town newspaper about the situation. She said the teacher was a racist and treated her child differently from the Anglo children in the class. What would you do if you were the teacher? The mother? Rinaldo?

LEARNING ACTIVITIES

1. Read one or more of the Suggested Readings or view the Web sites. Add 10 cards to your Professional Resource File with specific ideas for helping children develop social skills. Include a reference source on each card.

2. Use the "Social Skills Checklist" in Figure 9.1 to guide your observation of children as they engage in dramatic play or block building. Record and interpret the results, noting children who may need help.

3. Choose one or more of the children who may need help developing social skills and use ideas from this chapter to help them improve.

4. Bring in a prop box with items for children to use in dramatic play or block building based on a new theme from a field trip or other classroom activity. Record the children's use of props.

5. Help children who are having difficulty entering ongoing play to use one or more of the strategies described in this chapter. Record the results.

6. Help shy children to become involved in activities or to find a friend using ideas presented in this chapter. Record the results.

7. Help children resolve turn-taking conflicts by demonstrating with toys or puppets how to take turns, learning how the other child in the conflict feels, and helping the other child feel better. Record the results.

SUGGESTED READINGS

Kemple, M. R. (2004). *Let's be friends.* New York: Teachers College Press.

Nissen, H., & Hawkins, C. J. (2008). Observing and supporting young children's social competence. *Dimensions of Early Childhood, 36*(3), 21–29.

Riley, D., San Juan, R. R., & Ramminger, A. (2008). *Social and emotional development.* Washington, DC: NAEYC.

Roffman, L., & Wanerman, T. (2011). *Including one including all: A guide to relationship-based early childhood inclusion.* St. Paul, MN: Redleaf Press.

Tokarz, B. (2008, May–June). Block play: It's not just for boys anymore. *Exchange,* 68–71.

Tunks, K. W. (2009). Block play: Suggestions for common dilemmas. *Dimensions of Early Childhood, 37*(1), 3–7.

Warner, L., & Wilmoth, L. (2007). Cardboard boxes: Learning concepts galore! *Dimensions of Early Childhood, 35*(1), 11–16.

WEB SITES

The Center on the Social and Emotional Foundations for Early Learning
http://www.csefel.uiuc.edu

The Collaborative for Academic, Social, and Emotional Learning
http://www.casel.org

Teaching Strategies
http://www.teachingstrategies.org

The Technical Assistance Center on Positive Behavioral Intervention and Support
http://www.pbis.org

CHILDREN'S BOOKS

Bardhan-Quallen, S. (2007). *The mine-o-saur.* New York: Putnam.

*Becker, S. (2006). *Mine! Mine! Mine!* New York: Sterling Publishing.

*Berenzy, A. (2005). *Sammy: The classroom guinea pig.* New York: Henry Holt.

Blumenthal, D. (2007). *Charlie hits it big.* New York: HarperCollins.

Child, L. (2008). *I completely know about guinea pigs.* New York: Dial.

Child, L. (2008). *You can be my friend.* New York: Grosset & Dunlap.

*Heap, S. (2002). *What shall we play?* Cambridge, MA: Candlewick Press.

Kroll, S. (2001). *Patches lost and found.* Delray Beach, FL: Winslow Press.

Lipniacka, E. (2003). *Who shares?* New York: Dial Books.

*Lopez, M., & Lopez-Wong, M. (2009). *Mud tacos!* New York: Celebra Children's Books.

MacLean, C. K. (2002). *Even firefighters hug their moms.* New York: Dutton Children's Books.

*Raschka, C. (1993). *Yo! Yes?* New York: Orchard.

*Reiser, L. (1993). *Margaret and Margarita.* New York: Greenwillow.

Reiss, M. (2008). *The boy who wouldn't share.* New York: HarperCollins.

*Rosen, M. (1996). *This is our house.* Cambridge, MA: Candlewick.

*Multicultural

CHAPTER 10

Providing Guidance

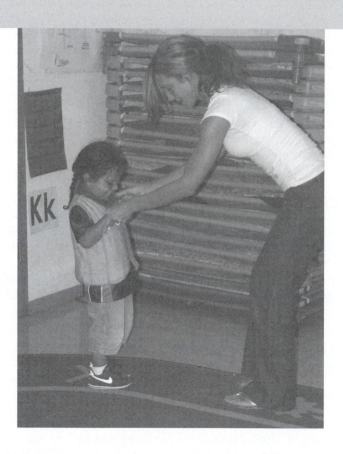

To promote the development of self-control in young children through positive guidance

☑ **Specific Objectives**

____ Uses positive prevention measures to help children eliminate inappropriate behavior

____ Uses positive intervention measures to help children control their inappropriate behavior

____ Uses positive reinforcement techniques to help children learn appropriate behavior

P OSITIVE GUIDANCE that helps children develop control over inappropriate behavior also helps improve their self-esteem. Children who feel good about themselves are less prone to exhibit disruptive, negative behavior. Some children enter your classroom smiling, with good feelings about their self-worth and cooperative behavior that reflects these feelings. Other children come with as many as three or four years of accumulated negative experiences that are reflected in their disruptive behavior. How can you help such children learn appropriate behavior?

Some teachers have long responded with traditional "discipline" for a child's inappropriate behavior. Such discipline usually means punishing, penalizing, correcting, or chastising a child. This kind of behavior management may stop a child's actions, but it creates other serious problems. Because the control comes from outside the child, she fails to develop her own self-control and becomes dependent on the adult to manage her behavior. Second, most discipline makes a child feel ashamed and often angry, ready to strike out again at the next opportunity. The action has been stopped, but the negative feelings created often go on and on.

If you are aware that much of young children's inappropriate behavior stems from insecurities and a negative self-image, you will eventually conclude that punishment, harsh treatment, loud commands, or scolding on your part do not provide solutions. These responses are themselves inappropriate behavior and only reinforce a child's poor self-image. Such discipline does not help the child feel good about herself or build the inner control needed to get along in the world.

Today many preschool teachers are turning instead to guidance, a positive response that keeps the child's self-image in mind. As defined by Gartrell (1997), "Teachers who practice guidance believe in the positive potential of children. . . . Teachers who use guidance think beyond conventional classroom discipline—the intent of which is to keep children in line. Rather than simply being a reaction to crises, guidance involves developmentally appropriate, culturally responsive education to reduce the occurrence of classroom problems. Guidance means creating a positive learning environment for each child in the group" (pp. 34–35).

Preschool children come to your classroom to develop manipulative skills, to improve large-motor coordination, to learn social skills, to develop language, to develop creativity, to learn cognitive concepts, and to improve their self-image. Learning to control their behavior should also be a learning goal. Put this goal at the top of your list for certain children and go about teaching it as you would any skill. Young children need objective, not emotional, guidance in the area of learning appropriate behavior.

USES POSITIVE PREVENTION MEASURES TO HELP CHILDREN ELIMINATE INAPPROPRIATE BEHAVIOR

Learning Environment

First, you need to anticipate problem behavior and set up your learning environment so that it does not happen. Young children may run around wildly if your classroom arrangement gives them the space to do this. Children may squabble over toys and materials if there are not enough for everyone or if toys are not at the appropriate developmental level of the children. Likewise, children may become bored with books and toys if the "same old ones" are always on the shelves, with nothing new ever added or none of the old ones put away.

NAEYC Criteria for Teaching Standard

Describe how you would meet the following standard:

3.A.05 Teachers work to prevent challenging or disruptive behaviors through environmental design and engaging activities.

Some of the causes for disruptive behavior in a preschool classroom can be corrected by rearranging the room and providing more materials as described in the Room Arrangement Checklist in Figure 10.1. By setting up your classroom as shown in this checklist, you will go a long way toward reducing friction between children, in addition to freeing yourself to work with small groups and individuals

Figure 10.1 Room Arrangement Checklist

General Room Conditions

_____ Learning centers separated with low dividers or shelves

_____ Centers located to avoid large empty spaces

_____ Enough centers to keep children engaged

_____ Room in centers for several children at a time

_____ Light and sunny, sound-proofed

Accessibility

_____ Space to enter and leave centers easily

_____ Accessible to children in wheelchairs, walkers, braces

_____ Materials on low shelves, facing out

_____ Traffic patterns wide for free movement

_____ Traffic patterns short to prevent running

Materials

_____ Enough for several children at once

_____ More than one of favorite toy

_____ Outlets for expressing feelings

_____ Colored to create emotional tone

_____ Changed as interests change

Private Spaces

_____ Cubbies, shelves, boxes for possessions

_____ Floor pillows in quiet corner

_____ Overstuffed chair or couch

_____ Small inflated pool with pillows

_____ Large carton with door cut out

_____ Card table covered with blanket

who need special help. The way space is used to define learning centers, to allow for pathways between areas, and to prevent overcrowding can help prevent disruptive behavior before it starts. Hearron and Hildebrand (2005) point out: "Crowding violates the individual's social space and is likely to trigger aggression" (p. 135).

Ratcliff (2001) explains, "Research shows that placing young children in relatively small areas may increase aggressive behavior. More accidental physical encounters—head bumping and fingers getting stepped on—occur in crowded areas, and children's play and/or creations can be interrupted or accidentally destroyed. Young children often don't see a difference between accidental and intentional actions and respond with aggression" (p. 84).

Colors to Create Emotional Tone

The colors you use in your wall hangings, curtains, carpets, and equipment can create whatever emotional tone you desire in the classroom. For example, red-checkered tablecloths on tables at lunchtime invite children to sit down for a happy meal. Colored plates and napkins add to the festive mood. Yellow curtains at windows give off a sunny, happy-day feeling. Pastel throw rugs and colored burlap wall hangings make a reading center calm and peaceful. Put a colored light bulb in a dramatic play center lamp from time to time. Ask children what colors they want, and take them along to help you buy beanbag chairs for the reading center or the children's private place.

As child development specialist Clare Cherry (1972, p. 34) tells us in one of her now-classic books, "Color is magic, readily available to all and free for use by the young child. Experience it with him. Take him by the hand and plunge headlong into the very essence of its feelings and its affects. You can afford to be generous. Dish it out in liberal portions and let him know that it thrills you. Share with him its sparkle and its gloss, its quietness and its music, its smell and its touch. And watch him grow."

New Materials

Teachers can also help reduce disruptive behavior by introducing new toys or equipment to the entire class during morning group time, by passing around the new materials and later storing them on a labeled shelf or location that everyone recognizes. If teachers anticipate conflicts over the new material, they can ask youngsters ahead of time how they would like to set up a turn-taking arrangement for the new object. Another method for preventing possession squabbles is to obtain at least two of the favorite toys. In the case of dinosaurs, always a favorite, two is never enough.

If conflicts over toys and materials occur regularly in your classroom, read books with this theme to individuals or small groups. Then discuss what your children would have done in the same situation.

Book as a Lead-In to Preventing Possession Squabbles

> *But Excuse Me That Is My Book* (Child, 2005) is another Charlie and Lola book with little Lola being unable to find her best-book-in-the-whole-world in the library. Then she sees another girl taking out *her* book. If your children are familiar with the Charlie and Lola books, ask them to predict how you think Charlie will solve this problem.

Discuss this story with the children. How would they change Lola's point of view about the library book being her book? How are books and toys in your classroom in the same situation for the children? Can you resolve possession disputes over a toy the way Charlie did?

Encouraging Environment for Boys

Some teachers say it is the boys who cause the most disruption. Or is it? Classrooms not set up to accommodate highly physically active children may be to blame. King and Gartrell (2003) note, "Many boys do need more physical activity and may be developmentally younger by 6 to 18 months than girls. Active, energetic children, notably boys, seem to spend a lot of time engaged in off-task behavior, looking for and finding mischief" (p. 33). How is it in your classroom?

If you have such physically active children (both boys and girls), why not set up an indoor physical fitness learning center? Have beanbags for throwing at a cardboard carton target; carpet squares for jumping; boards for walking and balancing; a floor mat for calisthenics; a mini–exercise bike (put a trike on blocks); and a CD player and CDs for exercising (e.g., *Preschool Aerobic Fun, Exersongs,* or *Good Morning Exercises for Kids* from Lakeshore 1-800-778-44560.)

Inclusion

Here's an idea: Children with physical impairments who are having difficulty handling a trike on the playground can be helped onto the stationary trike in your indoor physical fitness center. Strap on a seat belt on the trike and see if they can pedal. Have them wear a bike helmet just like your outside riders to make the experience as real as possible. They can ride to faraway places in their imaginations just like the characters in the bike-riding books in Chapter 1. If it is that much fun, everyone will want a turn.

Orderly Sequence of Events

Another positive measure you can take to prevent disruptive behavior among children is to maintain a stable and orderly sequence of events each day. The daily schedule should be maintained in the same order so that children feel secure in knowing what will occur and what comes next. Although the home life of some of your children may be chaotic, their classroom life should be stable enough to have a calming influence on their behavior. Have an illustrated daily schedule chart mounted at the children's eye level. Refer to it daily so that children begin to feel comfortable with the sequence of events.

The sequence should be a balanced one. For example, active play should be followed by quiet activities. Have a quiet or rest period after vigorous outdoor play. But do not force children to rest if they have not been active enough to make this necessary. If you do schedule a mid-morning rest period but the children are not tired, you may spend the whole time trying to force the children to rest.

A Minimum of Waiting

Don't keep children waiting. You can anticipate that some youngsters will act disruptively if you make them stand or sit for long periods while waiting to go out or if you make them sit at tables with nothing to do while waiting for lunch. If inappropriate behavior occurs, it is your fault, not the children's. Plan your schedule so that long waits are unnecessary. However, if unanticipated waiting should occur, be prepared with a transition activity to hold the children's interest and attention. Read them a story, do a fingerplay, sing a song, or play a guessing game or a name game.

A Maximum of Time

Giving children plenty of time is another trick of the trade that experienced preschool teachers have found to be valuable in preventing inappropriate behavior. Give them time to choose activities, time to get involved, time to talk with friends, time to complete what they are doing, and time to pick up. (See Figure 10.2.) Your program should be relaxed and unhurried. Young children take longer to do everything than we often anticipate. They need this time to accomplish things on their own. If they feel pressured because you impose your own time limits on them, they may be disruptive.

Pickup time is often a period of disruptive behavior on the part of some children. If this is the case in your classroom, you can anticipate this behavior and diffuse it. Some teachers inform the class: "It's five minutes to pickup time." This direction is not always effective. Most preschool children have a poor concept of five minutes, or any length of time, for that matter. For certain children, it may be the signal to leave their learning center quickly so that they won't have to pick it up! Try it and see how it works.

Figure 10.2 Time for Preschoolers

- Time to choose an activity
- Time to get involved
- Time to talk with friends
- Time to complete the activity
- Time to pick up

It may be more effective for you to go to certain areas and tell the children quietly, "You can finish playing now. I'll be around in a few minutes to help you get started picking up." It is important for adults to contribute to pickup. Some children are too overwhelmed with all of the blocks or toys scattered across the floor to know how to get started. Involve them in a pickup game, such as, "Let's use a big block as a bulldozer to push all the little blocks over to the shelf." Once they get started, you can leave and go to another area. Or play a peppy CD and see how much they can get picked up before the CD finishes. Pickup should be fun, not a chore.

Child Involvement in Rules

Another positive measure for preventing negative behavior is to involve the children in making classroom rules. If children have a role in deciding what is expected of them, they are often better behaved and more cooperative in complying with the rules. At meeting time, talk to the children about rules. Ask what kind of rule they should have about the toys and materials. Rules such as "the children who got materials out should help pick up" and "use materials carefully" may be the rules that evolve from this discussion. Have the children help you make a few simple rules about materials and equipment. You may want to post these rules, illustrated with stick figures, in the appropriate learning centers:

Block Center: "Build Only as High as You Can Reach"

Computer Center: "Wash Hands Before Using Keyboard"

"Two Children at a Time on Computer"

"Sign Up on Clipboard for Turn"

Children can then help regulate themselves. Even preliterate children will soon be interpreting these signs if they are read aloud and referred to by the teacher and other children. Children can regulate their own turns in learning centers, as well as with favorite toys and activities. (See Chapter 9 for discussion on turn-taking.) Some of the self-regulating devices children can use include those that are listed in Figure 10.3. The children themselves can help to decide which of these devices they want to use to control access to learning centers, to using the computer, to taking turns with the tricycle, or to borrowing a favorite book.

Epstein (2009) points out: "Merely having rules will not change preschoolers' behavior overnight; so don't expect that by making rules you will no longer have to deal

Figure 10.3 Self-Regulating Devices

- Learning center necklaces or tags
- Tickets for popular centers or toys
- Drawing names out of a hat for a turn
- Sign-up sheets or clipboards for turn-taking
- Kitchen timer or egg hourglass for controlling amount of time

with typical and recurring problems" (p. 128). But she believes that when invented rules come from concerns voiced by the children, the children have a personal stake in solving the problem.

When teachers make all the rules and children have no voice at all, classrooms often become tense and children uncomfortable. Some children may try to break the rules just to test the teacher. A hilarious picture book to illustrate wild rule problems addresses this problem.

Book as a Lead-In to Rule-Making Problems

> In *The Hair of Zoe Fleefenbacher Goes to School* (Anderson, 2009) Zoe's immense mop of red hair has a life of its own, as whoever tries to control it soon finds out. There is no trouble in kindergarten but the first-grade teacher has RULES. The hair finally overcomes her rules, and the teacher even learns a few things.

Talk with the children after reading this book. Can they tell from the illustrations who was really in control of the hair? Why did the hair act differently in kindergarten and first grade?

Setting Limits

When children clearly understand the limits to their behavior in the classroom, they are more inclined to accept them. This means that the limits should be simple and few in number. You and your coworkers need to agree ahead of time on the behavior limits that you will enforce firmly, consistently, and without shame or blame on the children. Many programs subscribe to the following behavior limits:

Children will not be allowed

to hurt themselves,

to hurt each other,

or to damage materials.

These are not rules to be posted in the classroom but limits that everyone has agreed on and all will enforce. Without such limits, children may frequently test you to see how far you will let them go. They need to be satisfied that you will not allow destructive things to happen. They need to feel secure in the classroom environment so they can expend their energies on constructive activities.

Your coworkers also need to keep these limits clearly in mind because they too will be responsible for enforcing them firmly, consistently, but not sternly. Other rules regarding the number of children in activity areas, taking turns, and sharing materials can be regulated mainly by the children themselves through the physical arrangement of the classroom and turn-taking methods previously set up.

Knowing the Children

If you know your children well and how they act in different situations, you may be able to intervene before disruption occurs. As Loomis and Wagner (2005) tell us, "When a teacher knows a child well enough to read the cues, responding is easier. An observant teacher who knows what to watch for may even be able to prevent certain behaviors" (p. 95). For example, keep your eyes open for children who suddenly disengage in the activity they are involved with. Jose, whose short attention span sometimes set in with an abrupt halt, would get up, look around, and proceed to cause as much mischief as he could in other children's activities before a teacher intervened. Once the teachers understood what was happening, they kept an eye on Jose, and when he made his abrupt shift, one of them would quickly engage him in another activity or read him a story.

Force Unacceptable

Finally, do not force young children to participate in group activities. Some are not ready to be involved with large and, to them, overwhelming groups. Others may not feel secure enough in the classroom environment to join a group. You should invite but not pressure such children.

A child who doesn't join in can read a book or watch.

Figure 10.4 Strategies for Preventing Inappropriate Behavior

- Set up classroom in well-defined spacious learning centers.
- Provide enough materials and activities at appropriate developmental levels.
- Introduce new materials to everyone and set up turn-taking arrangements.
- Maintain a balanced daily schedule.
- Minimize length of children's waiting time.
- Allow children time to choose and become deeply involved in activities.
- Involve children in making their own rules and choosing their own self-regulating devices.
- Know your children well and anticipate any disruptive behavior.
- Set a few simple behavior limits and enforce them consistently.

If you anticipate that certain children who do not join in will instead be disruptive, then have an activity or task ready for them. Give them a choice: "If you don't want to join us, Dantrell, here is a storybook for you to read. When you're finished, you may want to join us. If not, you can watch what we are doing."

These, then, are a few of the preventative steps you and your coworkers can take to decrease inappropriate behavior by the children (see Figure 10.4). What other strategies have you used?

USES POSITIVE INTERVENTION MEASURES TO HELP CHILDREN CONTROL THEIR INAPPROPRIATE BEHAVIOR

Accepting Negative Feelings

What will you do when children become angry or upset and begin to act out their feelings? First of all, don't wait for this to happen and then be forced to react inappropriately yourself. Anticipate the children's behavior and be prepared for them to be out of sorts, as you yourself are from time to time.

Once you acknowledge that negative feelings are a natural part of a young child's growth and development, you will be able to take the next step more readily, that is, accepting these feelings. It is natural for children to feel angry, frustrated, or upset. Acceptance does not mean approval; it means only that you recognize that children have both negative and positive feelings. Acceptance is the next step in helping children control the inappropriate aspects of their behavior.

In addition, accepting a child's negative feelings helps to diffuse them. You need to display your acceptance by not becoming angry or upset yourself. You need to stay calm and respond to the child in a matter-of-fact tone of voice. Your unruffled behavior is another step in calming the child. Your actions say, "If the teacher doesn't get upset, then it can't be so bad."

Helping Children Verbalize Negative Feelings

Next, you need to help children express their negative feelings in an acceptable manner. Helping them find a harmless way to express these feelings diffuses them. Otherwise, they may burst out again as soon as you turn your back.

Verbalizing feelings, that is, expressing them in words, is one of the most effective ways to resolve them. Expressing anger, jealousy, or frustration in words helps to relieve these negative emotions. Your calm voice saying, "How do you feel, Jennifer? Tell me how you feel," may be all it takes to calm down the child. If the child will not talk directly to you, she may talk to a hand puppet you hold or through a hand puppet she holds. Be patient. A child caught up in an emotional outburst often needs time to calm down enough to talk.

Books as Lead-Ins to Verbalizing Feelings

For the youngest children who do not know enough words to express their feelings, you can read them a book about children expressing their feelings in words when the time is right.

> In the simple book *I Am a Rainbow* (Parton, 2009), children's feelings are shown as six different colors, which can come together as a rainbow. The way you act can be different from the way you feel.

After reading the book to a small group at a time, have the children tell what made them feel the way the children in the book felt. How were they able to change negative feelings?

Other books as lead-ins to discussing feelings:

How Are You Peeling? Foods with Moods (Freymann, 1999)

John Denver's Sunshine on My Shoulders (Canyon, 2003) [with CD]

The Story of My Feelings (Berkner, 2007) [with CD]

That Makes Me Mad! (Kroll, 2002)

When Sophie Gets Angry—Really, Really Angry (Bang, 1999)

Yesterday I Had the Blues (Frame, 2003)

You can mount pictures of children laughing, crying, or feeling lonely in your total-group area for a talk at meeting time. If you have no pictures, simply scan pictures of the characters in these books to motivate your children to talk about their own feelings. Constructive Playthings (1-800-832-0572) also has a set of Emotion Photo Cards with 22 pictures of children's faces showing different emotional expressions for your children to talk about. Then when children burst out with actions instead of words during an emotional situation, remind them gently but firmly, "Tell him how you feel, Calvin. Don't hit him," or "Use words, Natalie, not fists." If you are consistent with your reminders, children will eventually learn to speak first, rather than act. When you hear them reminding each other to "Tell her. Don't hit her," you will know that verbalizing feelings has finally become a habit with the children.

Redirecting Inappropriate Behavior

A hostile, crying child may not be able to respond verbally, however. Instead, a classroom activity may help him calm down and regain control of himself. Water play is an especially soothing activity. If you don't have a water table, you can fill the toy sink in the housekeeping corner or a plastic basin on a table for an upset child to play with. To redirect inappropriate behavior is a strategy to steer children away from a behavior by getting them involved in an appropriate activity. Sometimes a book will do it.

Clay and dough are also excellent for children to use in working out frustrations. Encourage them to knead the material or pound it with their fists or a wooden mallet. Beanbags serve the same purpose. Let children expend their negative energy constructively by throwing beanbags or a foam ball at a target.

Finger painting also helps children release negative energy. Consider setting up a quiet corner with a comfortable rocking chair and space for water play, dough, or finger painting. If children know you will help and support them in releasing negative feelings nondestructively, they will begin to assume more control themselves.

Sometimes a book will help redirect children into an appropriate activity.

No Time-Out Chair

One of the intervention methods frequently used in early childhood classrooms for out-of-control children has been the time-out chair. No longer. The time-out chair is out in many classrooms today, as far as positive intervention methods are concerned. Most teachers heave a sigh of relief when they hear about its demise. It was always a struggle for teachers to make out-of-control children sit in it in the first place. Their noisy protests and crying tended to disrupt the entire classroom.

The more submissive children allowed themselves to be placed in the chair, but at what cost to their self-concept? They were not supposed to be isolated because the chair was within the classroom, but the other children kept away anyway. It was not supposed to be a punishment, just a time-out for disruptive children to calm down. Nevertheless, their peers treated them as being punished and shunned them, a particularly unpleasant punishment. It was not supposed to be a threat, yet there it sat, a definite threatening presence in an otherwise pleasant environment—like a dunce's chair from an old-time schoolroom waiting to be occupied. We are glad to see it go, along with other negative intervention techniques that tend to insult children instead of teaching them appropriate behavior.

As Gonzalez-Mena and Shareef (2005) report from an overheard conversation, when one teacher called the time-out chair a gift for children who need to get away from the group to control themselves, another responded, "It's not a gift—it's a punishment. And a harsh one at that. Besides, the misbehaving child needs the group to help him change his behavior. Isolation is the last thing he needs" (p. 34).

How do you feel about this problem? Gartrell (2001) notes, "When used as a discipline, the time-out is one of a group of techniques—including name-on-the-board, an assigned yellow or red 'light,' and the disciplinary referral slip—that still rely on blame and shame to bring a child's behavior 'back into line.' This is the modern equivalent of the dunce stool" (p. 9).

Out-of-Control Children

Still, a question remains. What about out-of-control children who are not calm enough to rejoin the group or respond to any verbal interchange? They may be running wildly about, screaming or destroying another child's property. First of all, you must stop them—calmly, firmly, and dispassionately. Many teachers find that their most effective action is to take such children aside—but not to a designated time-out chair—*and remain with them* until they are calm enough to talk. It may mean holding the crying child on your lap or sitting close by. It may mean waiting quietly until the child feels better. Talking to out-of-control children is usually futile and often provokes further outbursts from them. What they need is the time and space to recover their control. A quiet adult nearby shows them you care about them and are there to help when they are ready. Volunteers such as Foster Grandparents from the Foster Grandparents program are especially effective at holding and calming such upset children.

Remain with upset child until he is calm enough to talk.

Temper Tantrums

If the child in question is having a temper tantrum on the floor of the block area, you may need to direct other children away from the area while the tantrum runs its course. At the appropriate time, you can speak calmly and softly to the child, redirecting his attention to some activity you wish him to do to take his mind off the tantrum. For example, you can say, "Rodney, when you feel that you can, would you please bring me the truck over by the block shelf." Once Rodney brings the truck, you can talk to him softly about feelings, telling him that you want him to feel better or asking what might help him to get over feeling so upset. When he has finally regained control, he can choose to rejoin the others.

Biting and Hitting

Biting and hitting are impulsive behaviors that originate in infancy as exploratory behaviors. For some children they continue on into the preschool years to express the child's frustration or to get a caregiver's attention. Brazelton and Sparrow (2001) say that impulsive behavior like this is frightening to the child. She doesn't know how to stop it, so she repeats it over and over because it produces such a powerful response. "When adults overreact or disregard the behavior, the child will repeat the behavior as if to say, 'I'm out of control. Help me!'" (p. 49). Teachers in toddler programs also observe, "Biting occurs more frequently when children experience stress such as changes in their environment or a lack of adult attention" (Ramming, Kyger, & Thompson, 2006, p. 18).

As a teacher in a preschool program you must, of course, stop such behaviors, but do it in a way that is quick, firm, and to the point—not harsh, blaming, and punishing. You may need to hold the child firmly or take her to one side and tell her you don't allow children to hurt other children. Do this every time it happens to break the cycle. At the same time you and she need to have in mind an immediate substitute she can resort to once she has calmed down. For biting, think of a material that involves the mouth. What could she bite on whenever she feels this way? One teacher suggested a rubber animal stamper (a tiger or shark) that she put a hole through and strung on a string to be worn around the child's neck if she agreed.

What about hitting? Have the child help you decide what she could hit to release this strong anger energy harmlessly. One teacher tells about filling a sponge with water, placing it in a shallow pan, and having the child punch the water out of it. If it makes a mess, that can remind the child of how much anger energy flies around when she hits someone—and this time she gets to feel it herself (Beaty, 2006, pp. 71–72).

Intervening in Interpersonal Conflicts

Child development researchers have discovered that more than 90 percent of the interpersonal conflicts that occur in preschool programs involve squabbles over possessions. Young children with their self-centered point of view often start out by thinking that the toys and activities in the classroom are for them alone, as discussed in Chapter 9. "It's mine!" or "He took my toy!" are frequently heard complaints in many preschool programs. It takes young children a great deal of time and much hands-on experience before they can learn to share and take turns with their classmates. As children grow older, however, the number of possession conflicts seems to decrease, although conflicts over materials are still the most frequent cause for dissension in the classroom.

Most of these conflicts are brief interruptions in play, resolved by the children themselves. One or the other gets the toy or gives up a turn. Sometimes they come running to you to resolve their dilemma. Your response should be one that helps children solve the problem on their own.

Occasionally, however, the conflict becomes so overpowering that you must intervene. When children are hitting, fighting, throwing materials, or crying, it is time for you to take action. What will you do? One of the most effective forms of intervention is known as "conflict conversion" as discussed in Chapter 9. Take the children in conflict aside, usually two youngsters. When they are calm enough to talk, ask each to tell you what happened. Accept whatever they say. Then ask each to tell *how they think the other child feels.* Finally, ask each child to tell what would make

These children are trying to solve their own problem of the boy's dinosaur knocking down the girl's building.

the other child feel better. Conflict conversion like this helps each child look at the conflict from the other child's point of view, something quite different for them.

Many children are surprised to find that there is another side to the conflict. Most youngsters have never been asked to consider the feelings of the other child, in other words, to take the other child's perspective. But most children are able to consider the other child's feelings when they understand about it. They are relieved to find that you do not blame them for the conflict and you are not going to punish them. Instead, you are asking each one to think about how the other child feels, and then to help decide what can make the other child feel better.

Finding out about the feelings of the other person is often a great revelation to them. It is something most preschoolers had not considered before. But when asked how they think the other person feels, they can respond with accuracy. Lillard and Curenton (1999) point out that even very young children "show surprising awareness of what other people feel, want, and know. By the time they are seven or eight months old babies pay special attention to the emotional expressions of adults. By the second year of life, toddlers are beginning to know when others are feeling happy, angry or sad. They may even comfort someone in distress" (p. 52).

When children are directed to look at the other child in the conflict situation and tell how she feels, it is as if a light bulb turns on in the first child's head. She was so focused on herself she had no idea that the other child was feeling bad. This is where the "conflict conversion" takes place. Now the children themselves can reach a resolution when you ask each one to tell what would help the other child to feel better. Sometimes it is giving up the wanted toy or having you put it away. Just as often it is giving the other child a big hug. It is a satisfying way to end a conflict, especially when children have control of the solution.

Other children also notice what is happening and may even change their behavior as a result of it. Learning about "the other person's feelings" is indeed an important contribution to the preschool classroom in these turbulent days. Positive intervention methods like this to help children develop self-control include those listed in Figure 10.5.

Figure 10.5 Strategies for Intervening in Inappropriate Behavior

- Accept children's negative behavior.
- Remain calm and unruffled.
- Help children to verbalize their feelings.
- Read and discuss books about feelings.
- Redirect inappropriate behavior.
- Use time-out only when an adult can share the time-out.
- Use conflict conversions in children's out-of-control interpersonal conflicts.

USES POSITIVE REINFORCEMENT TECHNIQUES TO HELP CHILDREN LEARN APPROPRIATE BEHAVIOR

Positive Reinforcement

Positive reinforcement helps the teacher focus attention on a child's desirable behaviors and ignore the inappropriate behaviors. Too often teachers focus on inappropriate behavior because it is so attention getting. The disruptive child is frequently crying out for adult attention, even if it means punishment. When we respond to such misbehavior, even with punishment, we do not change it—although we may stop it temporarily. Instead, we reinforce it in a negative way. A response of any kind leads a child to believe, "If I do this, they will pay attention to me."

Therefore, we must shift our attention from the undesirable to the desirable behavior. This is no simple task. It will take a concerted effort on your part and that of the other staff members to shift attention to the positive and ignore the disruptive behaviors of the children. This kind of shift requires the changing of a mind-set. You must take a definite action to bring about the change in yourself first before you can expect a child to change.

You can begin to accomplish this change by making a list of the positive behaviors that a disruptive child exhibits during the day. Share the list with other staff members. Each time the child displays a positive behavior, reinforce her with a smile, a nod, or a word of encouragement. Each time she displays a disruptive behavior, try to ignore it. If you must stop it because it involves harm to another child or damage to a material, simply remove the other child or the material. Do not make eye or verbal contact with the disruptive child at this time. But as soon as the child exhibits desirable behavior, go to her and express your pleasure. Do this as soon as possible so the child receives the message that you will respond to her positive behavior but not to her undesirable actions.

Be sure the other adults in the classroom respond to the disruptive child in the same way. There is no need to get angry or upset, to speak loudly, or to punish the child. You and your coworkers need to keep in mind that "discipline" for young children should be "guidance," which means "learning appropriate behavior" or "learning self-control." For young children to learn self-control means that you and your staff must provide them with many, many such learning opportunities.

You may have to practice this new way of responding a number of times before you can expect results from the children. Have another staff member watch you do it, then talk about what you did and how it worked. Let that person try it, too, with the same child. Work on this method until you make it work for you. It takes more time to get results than does forcing a child to stop his misbehavior. In the end, however, it is more worthwhile because the behavior control comes from within the child rather than from the outside. Such efforts take the child one step closer to developing self-control and another step away from depending on the adults around him to control his behavior.

Focus on Injured Child, Not on Aggressor

When things get out of hand and one child hurts another, your first concern should be for the injured child rather than the aggressor. You must, of course, stop the unacceptable behavior, but you do it by removing the injured child. This is contrary to the ordinary actions of most adults in cases of aggressive child conflict. Ordinarily the teacher rushes to the aggressor to stop her and may even punish her. This reaction, however, tends to reinforce the aggressor's misbehavior by giving her the first attention. If you go first to the injured child, the surprised aggressor will get the message that she cannot gain your attention with such misbehavior.

Do not forget, however, to respond to the aggressor as soon as he or she displays positive behavior. Tell her how you appreciate the way she is behaving now and ask her if there is a different way she can handle her anger in the future so that no one gets hurt. If the child does not seem to know, you might try using puppet role plays. As Adams and Wittmer (2001) note, "Puppets can be used to role-play problems on common classroom situations (such as name calling, lack of sharing, or difficulty in taking turns), or in response to actual conflicts (such as two children arguing over who gets to use the watering can to water the plants)" (p. 12).

When using puppets with one child, the teacher can play the role of one conflictee and the child the role of the other. If the child refuses, the teacher can put a puppet on each hand and play both roles, acting out the conflict while the child watches. Afterward the teacher and child can discuss what happened, what caused it, and how the puppet handled it. Would the child now like to be one of the puppets and try a different resolution? Keep at least two "problem-puppets" in a small box to be used by the children or the teacher with individuals or the whole class at a class meeting when conflicts arise.

Model Appropriate Behavior

How can a disruptive child learn acceptable, appropriate behavior? You and your coworkers need first to explain and then to model this behavior. Children learn a great deal by example. Say to a child, "When you are angry with another child, you need to tell that child how you feel. What could you say to her? Try it." If the child does not know how to express anger in words, you can demonstrate. Tell him, "Say to Sharon: 'Sharon, you spilled paint on my paper. That makes me upset!'"

You need to model this behavior. You need to express your own feelings to the child: "Rob, I am really upset that you hit Sharon instead of talking to her. You need to tell her in words how you feel, and not hit her." If you model this advice again and again, children will notice. Eventually you will hear the children saying to one another, "Tell her in words. Don't hit her."

You also need to maintain your own self-control. When you become angry with children, you need to calm down first before talking to them. Yelling at children puts you in the same position as the child who is out of control. Anger is not helpful to either of you. Children are in your program to learn how to handle their own strong emotions. They want someone to prevent them from getting out of control. They look to you to model this controlled behavior. As Marion (1997) notes, "Adults who are most effective in helping children manage anger model responsible anger management by acknowledging, accepting, and taking responsibility for their own angry feelings and by expressing anger in direct and nonaggressive ways" (p. 65).

You can say, "That really made me upset when the paint was spilled this morning. People need to watch what they are doing."

Or together you could make "mean soup." Save the mean soup activity for a day when everyone is out of sorts. Then read the book *Mean Soup* (Everitt, 1992) to the group, about Horace who has such a bad day at school that he comes home feeling really mean. His mother suggests they make "mean soup" and proceeds to put on a pot of water to heat up. Then each of them takes turns screaming into the pot until they feel better and can stir their troubles away.

You can plug in a hotpot, fill it with water and canned vegetables or vegetable soup, and have every child who wants to participate come up and scream into the pot and stir it for a bit. Afterward serve it for lunch or for a crackers-and-soup snack. Leave the book out for everyone to look at, and be prepared to repeat this activity every week or so.

Other Books as Lead-Ins to Children's Out-of-Control Behavior Activities

Here are several books you should consider keeping in the classroom to be read and discussed before or after behavior problems occur:

Kapow! (O'Connor, 2004)   *No, David!* (Shannon, 1998)

The Dinosaur (Milbourne, 2004)   *Sometimes I'm Bombaloo* (Vail, 2002)

I Dreamt I was a Dinosaur
(Blackstone, 2005)

Be sure you also model courteous behavior. Treat children with the same respect as you would treat a friend. Don't yell across the room at a child who is demonstrating inappropriate behavior. Walk over to the child and talk to her quietly, in a

Figure 10.6 Strategies for Reinforcing Appropriate Behavior

- Shift your attention from inappropriate to appropriate child behavior.
- Look for and reinforce the positive actions of children who disrupt.
- Focus on the injured child, not the aggressor at first.
- Make eye or verbal contact with disruptive children only after their inappropriate behavior has ceased.
- Model appropriate classroom behavior yourself.

courteous but firm manner: "Brenda, you took the paintbrush away from Rachel before she was finished. She is really upset about it. You will need to give it back to her now. If you want to paint, you can sign up for a turn."

You may also need to let a child practice or role-play her actions or words: "Rachel, let's go over to Brenda, and you tell her how you feel. What are you going to say to her?" In this way you model for the children how they should act. Figure 10.6 summarizes some of these reinforcement methods.

Such on-the-spot teaching strategies can be thought of as Vygotskian *scaffolding,* that is, providing and then gradually removing external support for children as they are able to take on more responsibility for their own actions.

Your efforts to improve the children's self-control will be rewarded as they learn to control their behavior in the classroom. Parents, too, may notice their children's growth in this regard and help support your efforts at home. A child with special behavior problems may require concerted and cooperative effort on the part of both home and school to effect a change. It is surely worth the effort.

SUMMARY

The goal of guidance should be to promote the development of self-control in young children. This is accomplished through positive prevention measures such as arranging the learning environment to prevent disruptive behavior, by offering an orderly sequence of daily activities to promote feelings of security, by minimizing the length of time that children have to wait, by maximizing the length of time allowed for children to accomplish things, and by involving children in making classroom rules and setting their own limits.

Positive intervention techniques that help children control out-of-bounds behavior no longer include the time-out chair because of its detrimental effects on children. Instead, teachers intervene first by accepting children's negative feelings, then by helping children verbalize their feelings, and finally by redirecting children's inappropriate behavior into constructive activities such as finger painting and using play dough, water play, and beanbags. Your own calm but firm modeling of appropriate behavior should also help children feel less upset and more in control during times of stress.

For out-of-control children involved in interpersonal conflicts, a new and effective technique called conflict conversion is helpful. By taking the two children with the conflict aside and asking each what happened, you allow them to state their position without being blamed. Then they must think about how the other child feels and consider what will make the other child feel better. Children find themselves in control of the solution and therefore begin to develop better self-control over their own actions.

In addition, children learn self-control by being reinforced positively for their appropriate behavior. For example, each time disruptive children display a positive behavior you can give them a smile, a nod, or a word of praise. Their inappropriate behavior can be ignored as much as possible or responded to matter-of-factly without making eye contact. Focusing on the injured child rather than the aggressor also helps children realize that inappropriate behavior will not get your attention. Little by little the youngsters begin to develop control over their own behaviors and a concern for the feelings of their peers.

Ethical Dilemma

Rhonda, a new teacher in a Head Start program, was having difficulty with two of the girls in the class. They were always fighting, taking things from one another, and telling on each other. These girls lived near Rhonda, and both told their mothers the ways Rhonda disciplined them. The mothers reported Rhonda to the program director, who was already considering letting Rhonda go based on other complaints. Rhonda heard rumors of the contemplated firing and told the director she would show that she was a victim of discrimination if she was fired. What would you do?

LEARNING ACTIVITIES

1. Read one or more of the Suggested Readings or view the Web sites. Add 10 cards to your Professional Resource File with specific ideas for helping children develop self-control. Include reference source on each card.

2. Observe in a classroom for three different days noting children's behavior. If any disruptive behavior is noted, try to determine if it may be caused by the way the room is arranged. (See Figure 10.1, "Room Arrangement Checklist.") Tell how you would eliminate this kind of disruption.

3. Make a list of the rules, limits, and self-regulating devices used in your classroom. Tell how they were arrived at, how they are used, and what difference they make in children's behavior.

4. Observe a disruptive child for a day and write down all of the positive behaviors he or she displays. Show that you approve by smiling or giving a word of praise. Record the results.

5. Read one of the books about feelings to children who display negative feelings. Help them to verbalize their feelings. Record the results.

6. Use the conflict conversion method with two children involved in an interpersonal squabble over possession of a toy or piece of equipment. Record the results.

7. Use one or more of the methods discussed for reinforcing the appropriate behavior of one or more of your children. Why did you choose the method and how did it work?

SUGGESTED READINGS

Carlson, F. M., & Nelson, B. G. (2006). Reducing aggression with touch. *Dimensions of Early Childhood, 34*(3), 9–15.

Gartrell, D. (2007). *A guidance approach for the encouraging classroom.* Clifton Park, NY: Thomson/Delmar/Cengage.

Lamm, S., Grouix, J. G., Hansen, C., Patton, M. M., & Slaton, A. J. (2006). Creating environments for peaceful problem solving. *Young Children, 61*(6), 22–28.

Tunks, K. W. (2009). Block play: Practical solutions for common dilemmas. *Dimensions of Early Childhood, 37*(1), 3–7.

Wheeler, E. J. (2004). *Conflict resolution in early childhood.* Upper Saddle River, NJ: Pearson/Merrill.

WEB SITES

The Technical Assistance Center on Social Emotional Intervention
http://www.challengingbehavior.org

The Center for the Study and Prevention of Violence
http://www.colorado.edu/cspv

The Technical Assistance Center on Positive Behavioral Intervention and Supports
http://www.pbis.org

CHILDREN'S BOOKS

Anderson, L. H. (2009). *The hair of Zoe Fleefenbacher goes to school.* New York: Simon & Schuster.

Bang, M. (1999). *When Sophie gets angry—really, really angry.* New York: The Blue Sky Press.

Berkner, L. (2007). *The story of my feelings.* New York: Orchard Books. [CD included]

Blackstone, S. (2005). *I dreamt I was a dinosaur.* Cambridge, MA: Barefoot Books.

Canyon, C. (2003). *John Denver's sunshine on my shoulders.* Nevada City, CA: Dawn Publications. [CD included]

Child, L. (2005). *But excuse me that is my book.* New York: Dial Books.

Everitt, B. (1992). *Mean soup.* San Diego: Harcourt Brace.

*Frame, J. A. (2003). *Yesterday I had the blues.* Berkeley, CA: Tricycle Press.

Freymann, S. (1999). *How are you peeling? Foods with moods.* New York: Arthur A. Levine Books.

Kroll, S. (2002). *That makes me mad!* New York: SeaStar Books.

Milbourne, A. (2004). *The dinosaur.* London: Usborne Publishing.

*O'Connor, G. (2004). *Kapow!* New York: Simon & Schuster.

Parton, D. (2009). *I am a rainbow.* New York: Putnam.

Shannon, D. (1998) *No, David!* New York: The Blue Sky Press.

Vail, R. (2002). *Sometimes I'm Bombaloo.* New York: Scholastic Press.

*Multicultural

CHAPTER 11

Promoting Family Involvement

☐ **General Objective**

To encourage family involvement in center activities to promote their children's positive development

☑ **Specific Objectives**

____ Involves families in participating in children's programs

____ Recognizes and supports families of different makeups

____ Builds teacher-family relationships through family meetings

*F*AMILY INVOLVEMENT has long been a part of most preschool programs, but only in recent years have we come to realize just how important this involvement can be. Research shows us that programs in which families are highly involved have the longest lasting positive effects on children. Not only do children change their behavior and improve their skills because of their preschool experience, but their families change as well. As Eldridge (2001) reports, "Parents

Figure 11.1 Benefits of Family Involvement

For Children:	Enhanced emotional security
	Easier learning at home and at school
For Teachers:	Deeper understanding of children
	New behavior management strategies
	Understanding of different cultures
	Becoming part of local community
For Families:	Enhanced security about child's education
	New behavior management strategies
	Knowledge of resources available
	Becoming part of school community

involved with school in parent-related activities show increased self-confidence in parenting, more knowledge of child development, and an expanded understanding of the home as an environment for student learning" (p. 66).

Gonzales-Mena (2009) discusses research that tells us: "When parent involvement takes the form of family support, there is evidence that it can lower stress levels in parents and make their lives easier" (p. 371). One of the effects of providing support and relieving stress is to decrease the risk of child abuse. To make such involvement work families must be listened to and have a say in what they need.

Parents and families who are directly involved in their children's preschool programs are much more likely to encourage their children's development at home and to support their learning during the later school years. And parents who are not directly involved but show enthusiasm for their children's preschool programs promote their children's self-esteem and reduce discipline problems both at home and at school. Some other benefits Gonzales-Mena found of family involvement are shown in Figure 11.1.

Most families will not become involved automatically. Teachers must take the initiative, letting them know they are welcome and helping them find a comfortable way to contribute to their child's welfare while in your program. They may not realize how important their role is for their child's success in the classroom. Parents of preschool children are their child's most important role model. If parents ignore or downplay their child's school experience, then the child may not take it seriously as well. Furthermore, if parents do not know what kind of learning is going on in the preschool, they can hardly support or extend that learning at home.

NAEYC Criteria for Relationships Standard

Describe how you would meet the following standard:

1.A.01 Teachers work in partnership with families, establishing and maintaining regular, ongoing, two-way communication.

Thus it is vital for teachers to find ways to involve the parents and families of each child in some aspect of the program. Gaining the support and involvement of parents may not be easy, especially with parents who work during the day or with parents whose own school experience has left them with negative feelings about classrooms and teachers. Nevertheless, if you are committed to family participation, then you can find ways to bring family members into your program.

INVOLVES FAMILIES IN PARTICIPATING IN CHILDREN'S PROGRAMS

Families can be involved at many different levels in their children's programs. Figure 11.2 lists several family involvement possibilities.

Focus on the Child

The most effective approach to parent involvement is to focus on the child, not the program. What is the child like? What kinds of activities are his or her favorites? Does she like to sing or color? Have books been read to the child? Which ones? Should the program know anything special about the child and his needs? Parents are concerned about their children's welfare, and if you focus on this from the beginning, you will quickly capture their attention.

At the intake interview or enrollment process at the beginning of the year, you or another program member can invite parents to become involved and offer them several

---

- Visit the program.
- Have lunch in the program.
- Attend the classroom team meeting to help plan for your children.
- Volunteer as a teacher's assistant.
- Receive training and work as a paid classroom assistant.
- Help the classroom staff on a field trip.
- Visit the program to read a story or sing a song with the children.
- Make equipment, materials, or toys for the program.
- Bring something of your culture or language to the program (stories, songs, dances, foods)
- Put on a fund-raising project for the class.
- Visit the classroom as a community helper or to demonstrate your occupation.
- Become a member of the board or policy council or other decision-making body.
- Carry out at home a children's activity you have learned at the center.
- Join the program's parent club and participate in activities.
- Take instruction in nutrition, cooking, guidance, or another topic in a workshop sponsored by the program.
- Become involved in an early childhood reading group.

Figure 11.2   Family Involvement in Children's Programs

choices. For example, a parent could eat lunch with her or his child once a month, read a story to a small group at "story time" on any Friday, walk to the park with the group any time they go, be the librarian for the parent group in charge of child-care magazines and pamphlets, be a "telephone parent" and call other parents when it is time for the monthly parent meeting, be the "transportation parent" and bring to the meetings parents without cars, or gather news from parents for the parent newsletter. Parents also may have ideas for the monthly workshops, perhaps something they would like to learn about topics such as low-carb eating, shopping on a tight budget, games to make from throwaway items, or positive guidance techniques for the hard-to-manage child.

You may not meet the parents of the children until school actually begins. Some teachers, however, visit the children's homes before school begins and take a picture of the child and family by their front door to include in the child's own personal book he will be making in school. Children not only need to make a transition from home to school but also need to be assured that the teacher and the program accept and respect their home and parents. Try to learn the names of the family members, what grades the children are in, or an interesting fact or two about the infants or toddlers—not to be nosy but to become personally acquainted with each family and have them get to know you. You will want to be able to talk with their child later on about his or her family and how they are doing.

If you are uncomfortable about making a home visit, consider taking a coworker along. If you feel the parent is not comfortable with a home visit, Balaban (2006) suggests, "consider an alternative such as meeting the child and parent at a playground, park, or local ice-cream shop (teacher's treat)" (p. 88).

Building Trust in Parents and Parent Trust in the Program

Just as the parents of the children need to build confidence in you and the program, you also must come to trust the parents. After all, parents, not teachers, are the children's most influential adult guides. Your role is secondary. The parents or guardians of the children are their most important teachers. However, you must be the one to initiate a relationship with these significant people. You must find out what parents expect of the program and then convey to them how the program operates to support their children's growth and development. As Workman and Gage (1997) explain, "We have come to believe that trust between family members and staff is the single most important factor in promoting individual growth, involvement, and the development of self-sufficiency. Establishing relationships and developing trust involve entering into a dialogue to explore issues together and offer information, resources, and personal assistance" (p. 11).

Not every parent may understand or agree with "what" or "how" you are teaching their child. "I want my child to learn her ABCs," a parent may tell you. "She needs to learn to read. Where are the worksheets she should be doing?" Parents who say this may expect you to stand in front of the whole class and "teach." To argue with parents that "young children learn through play" or "young children learn best as individuals" is unproductive and, in the end, unnecessary.

Instead, start your relationship with parents by asking them what they want their children to accomplish during the year. Some may have very specific ideas. Others may not have a clue. Take seriously whatever parents have to say about their children because they are expressing what they think and what they want. It is important to write down parents' goals for their children, as well as their ideas and suggestions. Parents need to know that you are concerned about their children, that you will listen to them, and that you will take them seriously.

Some programs ask parents to fill out a list of learning goals for their children. This not only helps you to determine what areas are important to them but also helps parents to realize how broad and rich the program is. Furthermore, such a list does not indicate "how" you will help their children to accomplish each goal. Thus you need not debate with parents about self-learning versus direct teaching or play versus worksheets. A list like this also gives you a basis for talking with the parents about what they want for their children and why certain items are important (see Figure 11.3).

Child's Name_____**Age**_____

Your Name_____**Date**_____

(Fill in the number that tells how important each goal is for you and your child)

Very important............1

Somewhat important...2

Not important..............3

I WANT MY CHILD TO LEARN THESE SKILLS:

Physical

       1. To climb up and down a climber   _____

       2. To balance on a balance beam   _____

       3. To throw and catch a ball   _____

       4. To put on a jacket and zip it   _____

       5. To tie or fasten shoes   _____

       6. To cut with scissors   _____

       7. To pour without spilling   _____

Cognitive

       8. To identify colors and basic shapes   _____

       9. To sort things that are alike   _____

     10. To count   _____

     11. To understand that numbers represent objects   _____

     12. To care for plants   _____

     13. To care for animals   _____

     14. To care for the environment   _____

Figure 11.3   Parents' Learning Goals for Children

Language

    15. To speak clearly   _____

    16. To say words in another language   _____

    17. To enjoy a storybook   _____

    18. To pretend with puppets and dress-up clothes   _____

    19. To use words for rhymes and fingerplays   _____

    20. To write his or her name   _____

    21. To use a computer learning game   _____

Creativity

    22. To make up a story   _____

    23. To sing a song   _____

    24. To play a rhythm instrument   _____

    25. To use a tape recorder   _____

    26. To paint at an easel   _____

    27. To use play dough and clay   _____

Social Skills

    28. To get along with other children   _____

    29. To take turns   _____

    30. To share toys and materials   _____

    31. To play cooperatively   _____

    32. To make friends   _____

    33. To control inappropriate behavior   _____

    34. To settle conflicts over toys   _____

    35. To talk about feelings   _____

Self-Esteem

    36. To feel unafraid of people or things   _____

    37. To be successful in classroom activities   _____

    38. To be happy in preschool   _____

    39. To like the other children   _____

    40. To feel good about himself or herself   _____

Other

_____

_____

_____

_____

Figure 11.3   *(continued)*

You can use a list, such as the one shown in Figure 11.3, at the beginning of the year, just as you use an intake interview to give you information about families and their goals for their children. Make the list personal for parents. Go over it together with them; don't just mail it to them and ask them to return it. It can be a focus for conversation about their children and your program. Make a second list for yourself at the same time so that both you and the parents have a record of the goals they list as important.

Once parents understand the scope of the program, they may be more willing to contribute by helping their children to accomplish these goals both at home and in the classroom. Ask them if they would also consider volunteering to help other children in the classroom in one of the six areas listed. You can start a sign-up sheet for parent volunteers. Tell parents you will contact them when the children are involved in the area they have signed up for.

Be sure to add to the list the parents' own learning goals for their children. Later, when you communicate with the parents, be sure to refer to the goals that parents consider most important. Discuss with them how their children are doing in these areas.

However, do not use such a goals list later as a report card for children's accomplishments. Their children may not, in fact, accomplish all of the goals, nor should they be expected to. Instead, you can talk to parents about their children's positive accomplishments without using the list when you see them from time to time throughout the year. File the list away for your own further reference.

Beginning School

Many programs begin the school year with a staggered entrance process so that all the parents and children do not come on the same day at the same time. Half the children, for instance, may come on the first day and half on the next, or half in the morning and the other half in the afternoon. On those first days, each half of the class stays only part time. Parents or other family caregivers can be invited to bring their children and stay themselves for the brief class session. You and your coworkers can then better divide your time between the parents and their children. The children and parents should be invited to explore the room. You can set up a water table for them, and look over the other curriculum areas. They may even want to read a book to their child or make a puzzle.

In the meantime, one of you can talk with the parents, asking them about some of the things their child likes to do at home and more about what the parents hope to see the child accomplish in the program. Jot down this information on a file card for each child. The parents may have already talked with the program's parent worker about this, but it is still a good idea for the classroom staff to reinforce the notion that the program cares about them and their child and wants their input. This may be the time to go over with each family the "Parents' Learning Goals for Children" (Figure 11.3) they filled out earlier.

Invite parents to stay until the child feels comfortable without them. This may take several days for some children. If parents work, they may be able to visit the program and come to work late on the first day of the program. If not, they may be able

A parent may want to read a book to the children.

to send another family member. Family members who have difficulty knowing when to leave after staying with a child for several days can be assisted by the staff. Let parents know from the beginning that they should plan to stay a shorter time every day as their child becomes more involved in the classroom activities. In the meantime, a staff member needs to make sure the child does become busily engaged so that she can signal to the family member when it is a good time to leave.

Books to Help Children Become Accustomed to School

In See *You Later, Mom!* (Northway, 2006) William goes with his mom to his first day in a noisy class of multiethnic preschoolers and an East Indian teacher. He watches but doesn't join in and doesn't let go of his mother. Each day he tries another activity but still doesn't let go of his mother, until the last day when he finds a friend to play with. Then he can finally say, "See you later, Mom."

Many children are like William at first who needs his mother to stay awhile until he gets used to a rather large, overpowering group. Reading books like this and those that follow help children understand that their parents haven't abandoned them and will come back for them.

Other books about first days at school:

I Am Too Absolutely Small for School (Child, 2004)

My First Day at Nursery School (Edwards, 2002)

My Somebody Special (Weeks, 2002)

Two-Way Communication

We often pay mere lip service to the notion that the child's parents are his first and most important teachers, yet it is true. To recognize this fact, we must turn our parent-involvement effort into a reciprocal process in which we are not the only ones speaking and telling our story. Parents also need to communicate to us how their children are doing and what is happening in the family that may affect their children. This does not mean we should pry into family matters. Again, the focus is on the child. It means we try to come together on common ground regarding what is best for the child. We will support parents in their efforts and will expect them to support us in ours.

If we find that the two sets of goals for children are different, we need to find ways to communicate to parents about why we are doing what we are doing and to elicit the same information from them. Parents need to know that their youngster's preschool program will support their efforts to help their child grow and learn. Parents also need to know that the program wants their support too. The program's child-rearing techniques may, indeed, be different from their own, but they need to understand that both are acceptable.

Sometimes the differences in expectations focus on behavioral goals. A parent may expect her child to play quietly, to sit still and listen to the teacher, or to keep her clothes clean. The program, however, may expect the same child to become involved with all activities—both quiet and noisy ones—to become independent of the teacher, to make her own choices, and to be less concerned about keeping clean when it is more important to experience all the activities.

Teachers and parents need to talk about these goals face to face if at all possible. Set up a time when you can meet with each family. Can one of the parents visit the class, perhaps on a lunch hour if both are working? Can you visit a child's home in the evening? Can parents come to an evening, early morning, or weekend parent group meeting? Can the group meeting be held in an informal location, such as a restaurant, where parents may feel more at ease?

If parents are unaware that young children learn best through exploratory play, you might consider showing a videotape to illustrate such activities. But if you learn from a parent how important they feel that their child keep clean because of limited clothing resources at home, you will need to find ways to make sure that the child's clothing will not be damaged. A collection of men's shirts for wearing over good clothes may do the trick.

Methods for Two-Way Communication

How to keep families informed about how their child is doing in the program can be accomplished in several of the ways listed in Figure 11.4, Two-Way Communication Methods. It is important that these methods also allow an opportunity for the family to respond.

One of the most popular methods used by one program was *digital photos*. At least once a month one of the staff members took a photo of each child working in a learning center. These were downloaded into the computer, one to a page, with a

- Telephone
- E-mail
- Digital photos
- Notes carried by child
- Tapes or videotapes
- Newsletters
- Bulletin boards
- Two-way journals
- Lending library (book packs)
- Drop-off and pick-up time
- School visits
- Home visits
- Parent conferences; meetings
- Parent workshops

Figure 11.4   Two-Way Communication Methods

brief message on what the child was accomplishing. A second page asked the parents to write what the child was doing at home.

These two pages were sent to parents via e-mail if they had it. If not, children carried their photo pages home in an envelope. Both parents and children loved the photos and the information. All of the parents with e-mail responded about their children's home activities. Most of the other parents wrote a brief note or called the teacher in response. Most of the families made scrapbooks of their year-long collection of photos. At school the staff maintained a bulletin board showing copies of the photos called "This Month in Our Class" and later put the photos in the children's portfolios. The teachers decided it was surely a lot of work, but worth it.

Gonzales-Mena (2010) describes another clever idea used in a kindergarten called "Traveling Teddy Bear." The teddy bear and a two-way journal to record his adventures were sent home in a backpack with a different child every weekend. The teacher wrote something about the child in the journal and asked the parents and child to respond about the teddy bear and child at home.

Books and Materials as Connectors

For some families, materials make the best connector between home and school. Parents can understand the purpose for bringing home a book or for sending to school some empty containers for use in the dramatic play area. Again, the focus is on the child. Keep a duplicate collection of children's books in paperback to be loaned daily and taken home. Children can sign out for one book at a time at the end of the day. They can return it in the morning. If they forget, they will need to wait until they return it before taking out another book. In the same manner, you can have a toy lending library of a duplicate set of the same little toys you use in the classroom, with, for example, cars, trucks, figures of people, animals, and doll furniture. Children can sign out their favorite toy and keep it overnight.

This is a good time for you to exchange notes with a parent. Put a file card in the book the child is borrowing. On it you can write a brief message about the child or the program and ask the parent to reply on the back of the card.

One exciting school-home project involved a teacher taking daily photos of children engaged in various classroom activities with a digital camera. The teacher then scanned them into the computer and the children made up captions for each one, to be used as a PowerPoint slide show when parents came to visit. Then the children asked if they could take home their pictures to show their family. One child suggested they make a scrapbook to share all the pictures with their families. They did it—with space at the back of the book for the families to write a note back to the children. The children could hardly wait to hear what the families wrote about the pictures when they had the book overnight. Every week they added new photos to the book and kept it circulating to the parents. This exciting two-way conversation between children in school and their families at home brought both home and school closer together as families really saw firsthand what their children were doing and learning in preschool (Gennarelli, 2004).

At home, parents can be asked to collect and send to school empty containers to be used for the children's pretend supermarket or shoe boxes for mailboxes. They can also be asked to send dress-up clothes such as hats, shoes, belts, wallets, and purses. Scraps of cloth, scraps of wood, plastic foam containers, margarine cups, and paper towel tubes are other useful items to be saved for the classroom.

Home Visits

The beginning of school may be the time to arrange home visits. You can mention to parents that you want to drop by in a few weeks to let them know how their child has adjusted to the center and that you plan to visit all the parents to give them this information. Plan it for a mutually agreeable time. Mention your intention to have this visit at the beginning of the program; otherwise parents may feel threatened by a home visit later on, fearing that their child has done something wrong. You must, of course, follow up with the visit once you have mentioned it.

Some parents may not be at ease with a teacher visiting their home if they think their home doesn't measure up to the teacher's expectations. Some teachers may not be at ease with home visits because they find themselves out of their own comfortable classroom "territory." Both teachers and parents will feel more at ease with each other if the meeting focuses on the child. The purpose of the home visit is to see the child in the home setting and talk with the parents about how their child is getting along in preschool.

The teacher should take along a photo of the child taken in the classroom engaging in a favorite activity, for example, a block building he has made, a dress-up role she has taken, an art project he is engaged in, or a puzzle she is making. The teacher may also want to take some of the child's artwork to share or a book the child particularly likes.

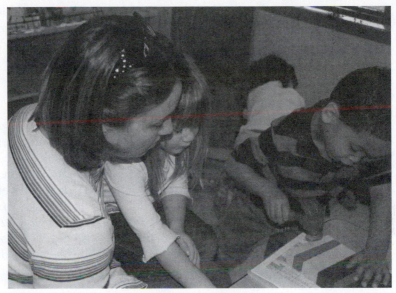

A parent can watch an activity with her child.

The teacher could also talk about the scribbles on the child's paper as being the first step in a child's development of drawing or writing skills. She could leave the favorite book behind for a family member to read to the child. Before leaving, the teacher can invite family members to visit the school at a particular time to watch or participate in some activity.

A home visit like this is important not only for the teacher to gain a feeling for the child's home and family background but also for the family to learn that the program and teacher care enough about their child to take time to visit his home.

Family Members' Classroom Visits

What should a family member do during a visit to the child's classroom? Sit and watch? Join in their child's activity? You can greet visitors at the door and let them know what they can do. They may want to sit and watch at first. Later they can participate in some way if they want. Raymond's father was invited to stir the instant gelatin the children were making for a snack. Michelle's grandmother read the children a story on the day that she came. Mike's mother went with the class on a nature walk as they gathered colored leaves.

Parents need to be aware that some children may act up when they are in the classroom. This is not unusual nor is anything wrong. To distract such children from the discomfort of having their parents present in school or having to share their parents with other children, you might give such children a special role to play, an errand to do, or something to be in charge of to take their minds off their parents. Or you might also give such parents a teacher's role, for example, reading a book to a small group, overseeing the woodworking area, or being in charge of playing a CD or tape.

For some children, the best way to calm them down is for them to work with their parents on an activity. Perhaps they can make a puzzle with their parent, do an easel painting, or build with blocks. Or you might invite the child and parent to look at the classroom book collection and to select a book to sign out and take home.

Parents as Classroom Volunteers

Parents can be encouraged to volunteer in the classroom regularly if they feel comfortable in this role. Parents who interact successfully with the children when they come for a visit may want to return as volunteers. You will need to talk with such parents about program goals, your goals for individual children, and what the parents themselves would be comfortable doing during their stay in the classroom.

It is important to stress teamwork and how they will be a part of the classroom team. The roles of the other team members also need to be addressed so that parents understand what their own role will be and how they should carry it out. Remember, it takes time and effort on the part of the classroom staff to have a successful volunteer effort.

You can post signs in each activity area to tell volunteers and visitors what the children are doing and what the volunteers' roles can be. For example, in the book area, the sign might say, "Children are free to choose any book to read during free-choice period. Volunteers and visitors may want to read a book to a child if the child is interested." In the art area, the sign might say, "Children are encouraged to try out art materials on their own. Volunteers and visitors may want to observe the children and encourage them, but let them do art activities without adult help."

In the beginning, you may want the parent volunteers to observe both children and teachers, focusing on certain areas of the "Teacher Skills Checklist" (see this checklist in the Introduction), so that they have a better understanding of how staff members carry out program goals. The area of guidance is one that often needs an explanation. Let each parent spend time observing how staff members "use positive intervention methods to help children control their inappropriate behavior" or how they "use positive reinforcement techniques to help children learn appropriate behavior." At the end of the observation time, you or another staff member will want to sit down with the parent and discuss what she or he observed. Discuss the methods for guiding children and also explain why certain methods are used. Ask the parent how she handles the same behavior at home.

At first you may want volunteers to work in only one or two learning centers of the classroom, until they become used to the children and the program. You or one of your team members needs to give help and support to the volunteer or to intervene with sensitivity when things do not go well. Have how-to booklets available to lend to volunteers or suggest that they view a videotape about the learning center or guidance method they are working with. Invite volunteers to planning sessions and in-service training programs. When they have acquired enough contact hours in your program, certain volunteers may want to prepare for CDA (Child Development Associate) assessment (see Chapter 13).

You will soon recognize which volunteers are most helpful. Make rules governing classroom volunteers so that the program is not overwhelmed with them. Select one day a week for one volunteer at a time if you find there are too many. You may need to regulate the number of times a person can volunteer if this becomes a problem. Remember, volunteers should be a help in the program, not a hindrance.

Parent Conferences

You will want to have parent conferences at least twice during the year. Most of them will be called by you to speak positively with parents about how their child is doing. A few conferences may be called by the parents to discuss a particular issue. All parent conferences can be satisfying for everyone concerned if you plan for them ahead of time. If the parent speaks a different language, be sure an interpreter is present, perhaps an older child.

The physical space should be comfortable for both you and the parents. Don't sit behind a desk. Sit around a table instead. A table for displaying materials, along with adult-size chairs, does away with barriers. Set up any audiovisual equipment ahead of time for playing audiotapes, videotapes, or DVDs of the child's accomplishments. Have your computer nearby for the children's slide show if the parents have not seen it.

Because both you and the parents are busy people, be sure to schedule the conferences for a certain time period, say thirty minutes, and then keep to the schedule. State at the outset that you want to spend as much time as necessary, but that for today you need to finish as close to your allotted time as possible. This statement gives both you and the parent the knowledge that the conference will not drag on and on and that you will need to focus clearly on the topic at hand.

Relax and enjoy yourself. Your relaxed manner will also put the parent at ease. Many parent conferences start off a bit strained because both of you may be ill at ease with one another. You need not be. You are going to be talking about a fine child and a good program. Focus enthusiastically on these positive things and the conference will take on an affirmative tone. If the parent sounds intimidating, listen carefully and take notes. You do not need to be defensive. When it is your turn to speak, do so with confidence and with facts, not with an argument.

When necessary, give up your own agenda and listen to the parent, suggests Gonzales-Mena (2010). "When it's your turn, instead of arguing, educating, or responding from your own perspective, try to state the perspective of the other person. Put the spirit of what you heard into words. Be prepared to make mistakes. Regard each one as a learning situation rather than a failure on your part" (p. 91).

Parent conferences are most successful when you are able to establish rapport with the parent. To do so you need to plan the conference around the parents' needs and concerns, rather than yours. Duffy (1997, p. 41) suggests structuring the conference in three parts:

1. Listening and sharing stories
2. Discussing child's school performance
3. Preparing for the future

Parent conferences are most successful when you establish rapport with the parent at the outset.

Let the parent talk first and listen carefully to what she or he has to say. If she has trouble getting started, you can prompt her with an anecdote about her child and her involvement with activities and peers. Perhaps she can reply with an anecdote of her own. As Duffy notes, "When parents and children separate for long periods each day, there is a tremendous need to hear stories about each other. What did you eat today? Did you learn a new song, or were you sad, mad, glad over something? Parent conferences are a formal time for parents and teachers to share stories" (p. 40).

After sharing stories you can discuss the child's school performance. You may want to use the "Parents' Learning Goals for Children" (see Figure 11.3) as your guide, sharing with the parent what skills the child has accomplished. Mention at least one accomplishment under each of these headings:

Physical   Cognitive
Language   Creativity
Social Skills   Self-Esteem

Many programs keep portfolios to document each child's learning with examples of her writing; lists of books, songs and games she knows; samples of her art; and photos showing social, physical, and self-esteem. Some programs keep children's scrapbooks with photos of the child in each learning center described in captions by the children themselves. Other programs use digital cameras to document as many of the "Parents' Leaning Goals for Children" as possible with photos of the child involved in each skill.

Next you can ask the parent to describe any specific concerns about the child. Come prepared with child observation notes, individual plans you have used, photos of the child and his accomplishments, and art or writing products the child has done. Share these with the parent. Talk in specifics, not in vague generalities about the child. Not "Oh, he's doing fine" but "Yesterday Josh joined us in singing for the first time. Did you know how well he could sing?" If problems arise, do not be defensive but listen carefully to what parents have to say.

Koch and McDonough (1999) suggest that teachers have "collaborative conversations" with parents in which they examine solutions rather than focusing on problems. Such conversations focus on multiple solutions to problems and treat parents as partners in arriving at solutions. Both parents and teachers should share with each other their personal experiences and possible solutions. Neither one needs to try to convince the other that they are right, but instead, "to ask questions and understand experiences in ways that illuminate resources and spur people to action" (p. 11). However you do it, make sure the conversation is two-way, and not just a monologue on your part (Gonzales-Mena, 2010, p. 88).

Often it is good to have a facilitator who understands about problem-solving conversations to facilitate the meeting. If parents do not speak English, the facilitator should speak their language. She or he will welcome everyone and establish rapport among them with small talk at first. The conversation should begin with trying to define a mutual goal that they all share. Participants can then describe what they have noticed about the child's behavior, both the inappropriate behavior, but also the acceptable behavior—even the smallest thing. How can this acceptable behavior be encouraged? What can each of the participants do to help?

When the time is up, you or the facilitator can conclude the meeting by summarizing what has been discussed and describing any future actions you and the parents plan to take. Be sure to make the meeting positive and reciprocal. Both of you have concern for the child, and both of you need to be specific about future plans. If you need to follow up on the concerns expressed by either of you, now is the time to decide when and what will be done. Finally, thank the parent for coming and invite her to the classroom to see how things are working out.

Inclusion

When preparing for a conference with parents of a child with disabilities, you need to be aware that grief issues may arise. Parent reaction to a handicapping condition may be emotional. Wright, Stegelin, and Hartle (2007) say, "Teachers may encounter states of emotional responses among families, including denial, anger, grief, and shame. These stages are often ongoing, with feelings resurfacing in reaction to changes, needs, and developmental milestones of the child" (p. 293).

RECOGNIZES AND SUPPORTS FAMILIES OF DIFFERENT MAKEUPS

Lifestyles and family styles of the 21st century are far different from those of the traditional American family of the past. Even as recently as 20 years ago, many families consisted of mother as homemaker, father as breadwinner, and children whose first group experience occurred in public school kindergarten. Today's families, however, may be blended, extended, single-parented, bilingual, culturally diverse, and dependent on child care, often from infancy on.

Single-Parent Families

A tremendous increase in the number of single-parent families occurred between 1970 and 2000. The increased divorce rate along with the increase of births among single teenage girls was partly responsible. Adoption of children by single parents was also on the rise. Early deaths of one of the parents also contributed. Although women head most single-parent families, more men have joined the ranks.

Early childhood programs need to recognize and accept such families. Single parents can maintain strong, functioning families with the proper support. Teachers must be aware, though, that children need special support during the turmoil of family breakup, and parents may need special arrangements to meet with preschool teachers. Some early mornings, evenings, or weekends may need to be set aside for parent-teacher meetings. It is your professional responsibility to make the initial contact and arrange your schedule to meet that of a family member.

Books About Single-Parent Families

Some single children may be upset when they find themselves with only a single mother while other children they know have both a mother and father and other siblings. Be sure to read them some of the following books:

> In *Love Is a Family* (Downey, 2001) Lily complains to her mother that she wants a real family like Melissa, who has four brothers and two sisters and whose house is never quiet and neat. Her mother tells her that love is what makes a family. Lily sees this is true at the Family Fun Night at her school, full of stepdads, stepmoms, half-sisters and brothers laughing and showing love.

How do your children respond? Other single-parent books include:

Just the Two of Us (Smith, 2001)

Did I Tell You I Love You Today? (Jordan & Jordan, 2004)

Fred Stays with Me! (Coffelt, 2007)

Mixed/Blended/Adopted Families

Many single parents eventually remarry. In situations where both parents bring with them children from a previous marriage, the new family is often referred to as "mixed" or "blended." Blended families can offer their children the same kind of support as their primary families did. Often, however, it takes time for families and children to build secure relationships with one another, especially if the original family breakup was difficult. Young children seem to suffer most immediately from this stress, often taking on feelings of guilt, shame, and rejection.

Preschool teachers need to be aware of the stress factors possible in mixed and adopted families and show both children and their parents that they are accepted and cherished by the program. Again, it is up to the teacher to make the initial contact and set up parent-teacher meetings at the convenience of the family.

Many programs find that having children's picture books available on the themes discussed here makes a difference with children. You can read the books in class or put them out for children to look at, but especially have them available for families to borrow and read together.

More and more families are turning to adoption, especially when they are unable to have a child of their own. Many of these adopted children come from Asia, Central America, or South America. They may find it difficult to blend in with their brothers and sisters or with other children when they go to preschool. Sometimes reading books to these children and others in your class lend them support.

Books About Adoption and Mixed Families

> In *We Wanted You* (Rosenberg, 2002) the simple story told by the parents of Enrique, the adopted boy, tells how much they wanted him; how they fixed up his room and waited, and how he finally came. But most of all—how much they loved him and still do. How do your children respond?

Other books about adoption include:

Families Are Different (Pellegrini, 1991)

Families Are Forever (Capone & Sherman, 2003)

Happy Adoption Day (McCutcheon, 1996)

Gay and Lesbian Families

As Tracy Burt and colleagues (2010) remind us: "Children's identities and sense of self are inextricably tied to their families. The experience of being welcome or unwelcome, visible or invisible begins in early childhood. Early childhood settings should recognize, value, and include every child and family they serve" (p. 97). Yet children from gay and lesbian families are often treated as if there is something wrong with them or their families.

Children who have two dads or two moms should be accepted and treated the same as all the other children and their families. Books about families should include gay and lesbian families. You may want to read and talk about some of the following:

Books About Gay and Lesbian Families

> The book *And Tango Makes Three* (Richardson & Parnell, 2005) tells the true story of two male penguins, Roy and Silo, who play together, swim together, and build a nest together. When the zoo keeper in the penguin house notices this, he finds an extra egg and puts it in their nest. They take turns sitting on it till it hatches, and out comes Tango, their baby—the only animal in the Central Park Zoo in Manhattan to have two dads!

Children love the story about Tango and his two dads. If you have penguin dolls they may want to reenact the story. Or they may want to dress up in white shirts and black capes and play the parts themselves as you read the story.

Other books about gay and lesbian families:

The Family Book (Parr, 2003)

Molly's Family (Garden, 2005)

The White Swan Express (Okimoto & Aoki, 2002)

Grandparents Raising Grandchildren

Some children are living with grandparents rather than their biological parents. This may be a temporary or permanent situation. No matter. It is up to the preschool program to give its all-out support to both the grandparents and the children. Birckmayer and colleagues (2005) tell us the incredible fact that "More than 2.5 million grandparents now raise grandchildren without a biological parent present in the home" (p. 100).

The reasons for this situation are varied. Some are as simple as taking over the care of a teenage daughter's child or a daughter or son's children after a divorce. Other reasons include parental drug or alcohol abuse, mental or physical illness, child abuse and neglect, incarceration, or death. As Birckmayer continues, "Helping children feel secure and loved while simultaneously dealing with special needs and challenging behaviors can be an overwhelming responsibility for grandparents" (p. 101). Your program can do its part by getting to know and respect these grandparents and providing them with whatever support you can. Birckmayer suggests,

- Listen empathically.
- Introduce them to others in the same situation.
- Introduce them to aging services, food banks, and clinics.
- Provide information on resources for children with special needs. (p. 102)

You can also invite them to visit your program. Perhaps they would like to tell a story, sing a song, or prepare a snack with the children. Grandparents can also be a "surprise reader" who appears once a week to read a story about children and their grandparents.

Books About Grandparents

Many fine books about grandparents and their grandchildren are available today. The following are a few of the multicultural/multiethnic books your children will want you or their visiting grandparents to read over and over:

Alice Yazzie's Year (Maher, 2003). Alice Yazzie and her Navajo grandfather live in a hogan where her everyday life experiences are played out month by month.

Full, Full, Full of Love (Cooke, 2003). Jay Jay visits his African American Grannie every Sunday and helps her cook a scrumptious meal for all the relatives.

Grandma Calls Me Beautiful (Joose, 2008). Beautiful's Hawaiian grandmother, Tutu, tells her the story of her birth.

I Love Saturdays y domingos (Ada, 2002). A little girl visits her Anglo grandparents every Saturday and her Mexican American grandparents every Sunday, enjoying similar but culturally different experiences in this bilingual book.

Pablo's Tree (Mora, 1994). Pablo's Mexican American grandfather Lito plants a tree for him on the day his mother adopts him. On every birthday afterward he puts clever homemade decorations on the tree for Pablo's excitement.

Visiting Day (Woodson, 2002). A little African American girl and her grandmother take the long bus trip up to the prison where the girl's daddy is "serving a little time."

Culturally Diverse Families

Families from cultures different from that of the majority of classroom parents are referred to as culturally diverse. They may be recent immigrants to the United States from Haiti, Cuba, Dominican Republic, Puerto Rico, Mexico, South or Central America, Vietnam, Pacific islands, India, Japan, China, Korea, or other areas of the world. The families may be ethnic minorities such as Hispanics, Asian Americans, Native Americans, or African Americans. They may speak only their native language or be bilingual.

Most immigrants come to this country for economic opportunities as well as political refuge. This has always been the case in the United States. These families expect that a program like yours will help their children to become adjusted to their new country, its language, and its customs. They also expect that their own culture and language will be respected, and not ignored or ridiculed.

You or a member of your classroom team needs to make the initial contact with these families. If the parents do not speak English, then take with you a native language speaker or arrange for an older sibling who speaks English to be present. Initial meetings

Family members can choose a book to take home for their children.

must be face to face at a location convenient to the parents. It is important also that you establish rapport with the parents. As Lee (1997) notes, "When a parent speaks another language, it is important to establish a relationship which is one of equality and respect from the start, setting the tone for the future. If parents feel embarrassed about their English skills, it is sometimes helpful for [care] providers to share how frustrated they feel at not being able to communicate in the parents' language" (p. 58).

Have one of the other parents invite them to a session on "picture books for English language learners." They can look over the colorful books and choose one to take home for their children.

Try to get the immigrant parents involved in their child's program just as you have all of the other families. Go over with them the "Parents' Learning Goals for Children," and invite them to observe how their children are doing and what they can do at home to support this learning. Ask for their input, and list the things that are important to them about their child in the space provided on the goals form. Would any of them like to volunteer in the program? As Brown, Fitzpatrick, and Morrison (2004) note, "Involving parents in their children's education often enables everyone to get beyond cultural stereotypes and helps alleviate any fear parents may have of losing their children to someone else's cultural values" (p. 13).

Some of the activities you, the children, and their families could participate in include singing a song in the child's home language, creating a family picture gallery with pictures from home and school, enlarging family pictures to poster size (take a field trip to a copy center), and making a family-centered library to be shared at home with such family-centered books as these:

Amazing Grace (Hoffman, 1991)
Dim Sum for Everyone (Lin, 2001)
Ella Sarah Gets Dressed Chodos-Irvine, 2003)
Homemade Love (Hooks, 2002)
Hush! A Thai Lullaby (Ho, 1997)
Jingle Dancer (Smith, 2000)

Mama Zooms (Cowen-Fletcher, 1996)
Oonga Boonga (Wishinsky, 1998)
Please, Baby, Please (Lee & Lee, 2002)

Too Many Tamales (Soto, 1996)
What a Family! (Isadora, 2006)

Brinson (2005) reminds us, "It is essential for early educators to promote family participation and complement the diverse learning styles and cultures of all young children." Pena (2000) notes that "children who were enrolled in schools that favored family involvement had higher achievement levels than children in schools with little family involvement" (p. 24).

Working Parents

No matter what the makeup of the family, it is to be expected that the parents will be working and not at home during the day. This means that they depend heavily on their child's preschool for quality care, concern, and support for their children. Help your children's parents to be assured that this is the case. Take the initiative to contact the parents and arrange for meetings at their convenience. This should be an important part of the job description of every teacher and early childhood caregiver.

As a child caregiver, you need to recognize and support every type of family that your children represent. Families set the stage for their children's successes or failures in life. Thus early childhood programs must be deeply involved in supporting the families of their children.

BUILDS TEACHER-FAMILY RELATIONSHIPS THROUGH FAMILY MEETINGS

Family Support of Program

It is just as important that the children's families support your program. This, in fact, seems to be the key to child gains in preschool. If parents show enthusiasm for their children's preschool program, then children profit greatly from it. In cases where parents do not show enthusiasm or may be negative about the program, children do not seem to gain in self-esteem or behavior improvement. Thus it is up to you to get across to parents and families your program's message: The program can help children to grow and develop emotionally, socially, physically, intellectually, creatively, and in language skills if parents and families support what you are doing.

You, in turn, must recognize and support the families in their role in raising their children. How do you do this? First, you must recognize the families of your children by accepting them, just as you accept their children. You may not understand or even agree with their lifestyles. However, that is their business, not yours. Your particular role in accepting your children's families is to support them in their child rearing. To do this, you must develop a two-way communication with parents and families, as previously noted. You must not only communicate to parents what is happening with their children in your program but also elicit from them what their expectations are and how you can support what they are trying to achieve.

Monthly Family Meetings

Monthly family classroom meetings have proved to be the most successful family involvement activities that many programs have attempted. Parents often find these family meetings less intimidating than other kinds of school meetings. They are different from one-on-one parent conferences in which parents only hear about their own child or all-school meetings where parents may not know anyone else. As Diffily (2001) has found, "An investment of 2 hours per month—in a family meeting—cultivates relationships among teachers and families, which in turn promotes family involvement in children's daily activities" (p. 5).

Such meetings are usually held in the early evening and should be set up in a special way that also includes the preschool children. At first the children can become involved in the classroom activities just as they were during the day while their parents get better acquainted with the staff and each other. Then it is the parents' turn in the classroom while the children go to another room to listen to storytelling, story reading, or for quiet play with little toys. Parents are given name tags, sit in an opening circle to introduce themselves, and then choose a learning center to work in for a brief period. It is helpful to have signs in each center telling what academic and developmental skills the children learn in that particular center. You and your coworkers can circulate to the various centers, acting as you would with children. At the end of a brief period, the parents can rotate to another center until they have visited as many centers as time allows.

At the end of the meeting, bring the parents back together for a closing circle where they will sing a song, hear a story, and report on what they did in the various centers. Be sure to have a take-home handout for parents that lists the learning center activities they experienced, tells what children learn from each one, and gives suggestions on how parents can follow up with similar learning activities at home. As you note, the focus here is on how and what their children learn in the various learning centers, rather than on their children's behavior problems.

Activities in Learning Centers

Each monthly meeting can focus on different issues or topics. Emergent literacy is one. Have the classroom full of signs and labels. Put picture books with character cutouts or dolls in certain learning centers. Have new computer literacy programs available, along with follow-up activities in the various centers. For instance, you might have the CD-ROM alphabet program *Chicka Chicka Boom Boom* on the computer, the book *Chicka Chicka Boom Boom* (Martin & Archambault, 1989) in the book center, a broom "tree" wrapped in burlap with foam letters that can stick to it standing up in the loft, alphabet songs on tapes in the music center along with headsets for listening to them, alphabet matching games with plastic letters in the manipulative center, alphabet beanbags and a target in the large-motor center, alphabet dough stampers and play dough in the art center, and so on.

Staff members can help parents get involved in the activities the various centers offer, as well as posing other problems they must solve, just as they would with the children: "Find the magnetic letter your name starts with." "See how many of that same letter you can find in this box of magnetic letters, and put them on the magnet board." "Look at the name cards of all the people in the room. Find what names start with the same letter as yours." "Can you paint your name on the easel?" "Can you stamp your name in the play dough?" "Can you climb all the letters up to the top of the alphabet tree? Which ones fall off?" Afterward, when the parents come together to discuss what they have done, you can talk to them about how children teach themselves to recognize certain letters, how children first learn letters that are important to them, how it is not necessary to learn to name all the letters of the alphabet at first, why children may first write letters backward or upside down, and what letter games children might play at home.

At another meeting you may focus on the social skills of turn-taking, waiting for a turn, making friends, entering ongoing play, or getting along with others. Be sure to have picture books with stories featuring these topics available. Afterward, have parents talk about their own and their children's experiences. How can they help their children at home with follow-up activities? Parents also have a chance to express concerns and get answers to their questions.

Relationships also develop among families. As Diffily (2001) notes, "Simply getting to know other parents who have children of the same age, and being able to talk about their children, is reassuring to many parents" (p. 8). Family classroom meetings soon take on the characteristics of friends getting together. Teachers benefit by finding that parents who attend are often more willing to share books and materials from home and to become directly involved in helping in the program.

Motivating Family Attendance

It is important to have regular family classroom meetings so that parents get used to the idea. They can select the best evening to meet and also telephone one another to remind them to come. Parents who speak little English can be encouraged to come if you or they can provide a translator, perhaps even one of their older children. If the activity is enjoyable and useful to them and their children, they will come. Soon the word will get around and most of the other parents may join in. Be sure to ask for and act on parents' ideas for topics to feature and for children's activities they know about. It can be an exciting learning get-together for everyone. Always provide a take-home sheet with ideas for families to follow up with their children.

Some programs use the last meeting of the year as a potluck supper with everyone contributing a dish. By now people know one another and can plan together what to bring. You will want to prepare the children by reading one of the potluck stories. Can they help prepare any of the food?

Books About Potluck Suppers

Alligator Arrived with Apples: A Potluck Alphabet Feast (Dragonwagon, 1987) is a feast with an alphabet of animals bringing a fabulous food of their letter: bear brought banana bread, but flamingo fixed flambé; llama lugged lemons, limes, and lingonberries.

The Beastly Feast (Goldstone, 1998) is a wild rhyming alphabet of beasts and their foods: bears bring pears, and parrots bring carrots. Have your children try to guess what puffins bring (muffins), or what mosquitoes bring (burritos). After a few times hearing this story, they will soon have every food memorized.

Potluck (Shelby, 1991) is a child potluck with an alphabet of multicultural children bringing yummy-looking alphabetical foods: Lonnie brings lasagna, Quincy brings quiche, and finally Zeke and Zelda zoom in with zucchini.

SUMMARY

Families can be involved in program activities in a variety of ways. They can visit the classroom to assist the staff in daily activities, field trips, or making materials. They can share with the children a song, a story, or a cultural practice. They can serve on committees or policy councils. The classroom staff should make the initial contact with families and arrange for them to visit or participate. The focus should be on the child and should be a positive one. Teachers can get parents' input about goals for their children if they fill out the "Parents' Learning Goals for Children," as shown in Figure 11.3. Family members also can be encouraged to volunteer their services, but then they need to be assisted and supported by the staff by being given specific tasks.

The program and staff need to recognize and support nontraditional families such as single-parent families, blended families, gay and lesbian families, and culturally diverse families. When both parents work, teachers need to arrange meetings at times convenient for the family. Two-way face-to-face communication is important for both the program and the family to understand the goals each has for the child involved. It is just as important for the child's development to have his family support the program with enthusiasm as it is for the program to support the child.

One of the most successful family involvement activities is often a monthly family classroom meeting where parents take the roles of their children and learn how children learn in the various classroom centers.

Ethical Dilemma

Can there be too much parent involvement? Yes. In one situation, one of the mothers persisted in coming into the program daily, interfering with the teacher, staff, and children. She lived nearby, and because her only child was in the program she seemed to have nothing to do but visit the class. The teacher at first tried to have her read a book to the children, but none of them would listen. Meanwhile, her son was running wildly around disrupting the other children and their activities. Finally, the teacher told her that parents were asked to do classroom volunteering only by invitation, and they thanked her for completing her share. Now it was someone else's turn. She came the next day anyway. What would you do?

LEARNING ACTIVITIES

1. Read one or more of the Suggested Readings or view the Web sites listed. Add 10 cards to your Professional Resource File with specific ideas for promoting parent involvement. Include reference source.

2. Communicate with a parent using the "Parents' Learning Goals for Children" (Figure 11.3) or another idea from this chapter that focuses on their child.

3. Get a parent involved in the program as a classroom volunteer and work with her in a classroom learning center in which she feels comfortable.

4. It is important to talk face to face with family members from culturally diverse, single-parent, or blended families about their children. Find out what the family member's goals are for the child, and discuss the program's goals with him or her.

5. Plan a program at the school that parents can attend; get their input into what should be presented and get them involved in working on the program in some way.

6. Help to set up the classroom learning centers for a family classroom meeting, printing signs that tell what and how children learn in each center, making handouts for the parents, participating in the meeting, and talking with the parents who come about their children.

7. Set up a classroom lending library for parents with adult books and pamphlets about child care and education, as well as picture books for them to read to their children.

SUGGESTED READINGS

Halgunseth, L. (2009). Family engagement, diverse families, and early childhood education programs: An integrated review of the literature. *Young Children, 64*(5), 56–58.

Kersey, K. C., & Masterson, M. L. (2009). Teachers connecting with families—In the best interest of children. *Young Children, 64*(5), 34–38.

Mitchell, S. M., Foulger, R. S., & Wetzel, K. (2009). Ten tips involving families through Internet-based communication. *Young Children, 64*(5), 46–49.

Nagel, N. G., & Wells, J. G. (2009). Honoring family and culture: Learning from New Zealand. *Young Children, 64*(5), 40–44.

Okagaki, L., & Diamond, K. (2009). Cultural and linguistic differences in families with young children: Implications for early childhood teachers. In Essa, E. L., & Burnham, M. M. (Eds.), *Informing our practice: Useful research on young children's development.* Washington, DC: NAEYC.

Raikes, H. H., & Edwards, C. P. (2009). Staying in step: Supporting relationships with families. *Young Childen, 64*(5), 50–55.

Rowell, E. H. (2007). Missing! Picture books reflecting gay and lesbian families. *Young Children, 62*(3), 24–30.

Souto-Manning, M. (2010). Family involvement: Challenges to consider, strengths to build on. *Young Children, 65*(2), 82–88.

WEB SITES

American Association of Retired Persons Grandparent Information Center
http://www.aarp.org/life/grandparents

Center on School, Family and Community Partnerships
http://www.csos.jhu.edu

Families and Community Initiatives
http://www.naeyc.org/ecp/trainings

Harvard Family Research Project
http://www.hfrp.org/family-involvement

National Council for Community and Education Partnerships
http://www.edpartnerships.org

The SEDL National Center for Family & Community Connections with Schools
http://www.sedl.org

Teachers and Families
http://www.teachersandfamilies.com

CHILDREN'S BOOKS

*Ada, A. (2002). *I love Saturdays y domingos.* New York: Atheneum.

*Capone, D., & Sherman, C. (2003). *Families are forever.* Montauk, NY: Simple as That.

Child, L. (2004). *I am too absolutely small for school.* Cambridge, MA: Candlewick Press.

*Chodos-Irvine, M. (2003). *Ella Sarah gets dressed.* San Diego, CA: Harcourt.

Coffelt, N. (2007). *Fred stays with me!* Boston: Little, Brown.

*Cooke, T. (2003). *Full, full, full of love.* Cambridge, MA: Candlewick Press.

Cowen-Fletcher, J. (1996). *Mama zooms.* New York: Scholastic Press.

*Downey, R. (2001). *Love is a family.* New York: Regan Books.

Dragonwagon, C. (1987). *Alligator arrived with apples.* New York: Macmillan.

Edwards, B. (2002). *My first day at nursery school.* New York: Bloomsbury.

Garden, N. (2005). Molly's family. New York: Farrar Straus Giroux.

Goldstone, B. (1998). *The beastly feast.* New York: Henry Holt.

*Ho, M. (1997). *Hush! A Thai lullaby.* New York: Orchard Books.

*Hoffman, M. (1991). *Amazing Grace.* New York: Dial Books.

*Hooks, b. (2002). *Homemade love.* New York: Hyperion.

*Isadora, R. (2006). *What a family! A fresh look at family trees.* New York: G. P. Putnam's Sons.

*Joose, B. M. (2008). *Grandma calls me Beautiful.* San Francisco: Chronicle Books.

*Jordan, D., & Jordan, R. M. (2004). *Did I tell you I love you today?* New York: Simon & Schuster.

*Lee, S., & Lee, T. (2002). *Please, Baby, please.* New York: Simon & Schuster.

*Lin, G. (2001). *Dim sum for everyone.* New York: Knopf.

*Maher, R. (2003). *Alice Yazzie's year.* Berkeley, CA: Tricycle Press.

Martin, B., & Archambault, J. (1989), *Chicka chicka boom boom.* New York: Simon & Schuster.

*McCutcheon, J. (1996). *Happy adoption day!* Boston: Little, Brown.

*Mora, P. (1994). *Pablo's tree.* New York: Macmillan.

*Northway, J. (2006). *See you later, Mom!* London, England: Francis Lincoln Children's Books.

*Okimoto, J. D., & Aoki, E. M. (2002). *The White Swan Express.* New York: Clarion.

*Parr, T. (2003). *The family book.* Boston: Little, Brown.

*Pellegrini, N. (1991). *Families are different.* New York: Scholastic Press.

Richardson, J., & Parnell, P. (2005). *And Tango makes three.* New York: Simon & Schuster.

*Rosenberg, L. (2002). *We wanted you.* Brookfield, CT: Roaring Brook Press.

Shelby, A. (1991). *Potluck.* New York: Orchard Books.

*Smith, C. (2000). *Jingle dancer.* New York: Morrow.

*Smith, W. (2001). *Just the two of us.* New York: Scholastic.

Weeks, S. (2002). *My somebody special.* San Diego, CA: Harcourt.

Wishinsky, F. (1998). *Oonga boonga.* New York: Dutton Children's Books.

*Woodson, J. (2002). *Visiting day.* New York: Scholastic Press.

*Multicultural

Providing Program Management

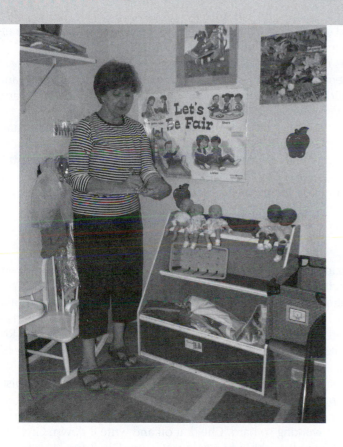

P ROGRAM MANAGEMENT for an early childhood teacher involves four broad functions: observation, planning, implementing, and assessment. Because such a program focuses on young children, the management component must also use children as its basis. Beginning with a needs assessment of the children through observing, recording, and interpreting the results, you and your staff are then able to plan for individuals and the group, implement the plans,

Figure 12.1 Program
Management Skills

- Observing and recording children's needs and interests
- Interpreting results
- Planning curriculum to meet needs
- Implementing plans
- Assessing outcomes and follow-up

assess the outcomes, and decide on the necessary follow-up. The skills needed for effective program management thus include those in Figure 12.1.

Although these skills may seem obvious, the way you and your staff carry them out makes all the difference. Do you view them with excitement, enthusiasm, and pleasure? Or do you avoid them until you can no longer put them off, and then carry them out halfheartedly? What will it take to make you as eager to observe young children and plan for them as it is to work with them? Think of the children: enthusiastic, smiling, rambunctious, and ready to burst into the classroom and get their hands on the wondrous array of materials and activities you have provided. Remember, it is the children who deserve the most exciting program you can create for them. Pretend you are an artist at an easel and design their program with brilliant brushstrokes and vibrant colors.

Make Your Design Colorful

If you know that organizing things is not one of your strengths, make it one of your special missions to correct this insufficiency and bring it up to par with the rest of your child-care skills. For instance, buy file folders in your favorite colors instead of vanilla manila. Use a rainbow of self-stick notes to remind you to stay on task. Keep children's records on colored rather than white paper with their photos at the top. Remember you have a digital camera you can plug into your computer, and print all kinds of pictures any time for any use.

For instance, print each youngster's "Learning Center Involvement Checklist" (Figure 12.2) on colored paper with his or her photo at the top. After you've made an observation of the child in one of the learning centers, find a moment to tell her how happy you were to see her working so hard. Check it off and write it down. Give her a colored sheet of her choice to scribble her own notes on. Don't forget to take a photo or two when she is not looking your way.

OBSERVES, RECORDS, AND INTERPRETS THE NEEDS AND INTERESTS OF THE CHILDREN

Before you can make plans for any kind of program, carry out a *needs assessment*. For a program like yours based on young children, it is the children whose needs should be assessed. Are they developing as they should be physically, cognitively,

Figure 12.2 Learning Center Involvement Checklist

Name _____   **Date** _____

Observer _____   **Time** _____

1. **Child in block-building center**
   _____ Carries blocks, fills and dumps, doesn't build
   _____ Builds in flat rows on floor or stacks vertically
   _____ Makes bridges with block across two parallel blocks
   _____ Builds buildings
   _____ Names buildings, plays with them

2. **Child in book center**
   _____ Shows interest in pictures in books
   _____ Talks about the pictures
   _____ Pretends to read
   _____ Can retell a story
   _____ Recognizes some words

3. **Child in dramatic play center**
   _____ Plays a role (pretends to be someone)
   _____ Pretends about a thing
   _____ Pretends about a make-believe situation
   _____ Stays with role for five minutes or more
   _____ Uses verbal communication during play

4. **Child in large-motor center**
   _____ Balances on a board
   _____ Climbs easily
   _____ Gets down from high places easily
   _____ Jumps with both feet over an object
   _____ Hits a target throwing a beanbag or ball

5. **Child in manipulative/math center**
   _____ Sorts, matches objects by color
   _____ Sorts, matches objects by shape, size
   _____ Counts number of objects in a set
   _____ Threads objects on a string
   _____ Makes puzzles easily

6. **Child in art center**
   _____ Paints with brushes
   _____ Plays with play dough/clay
   _____ Cuts with scissors
   _____ Uses paste or glue appropriately
   _____ Creates images of people, things

(*Continued*)

Figure 12.2   *continued*

7. **Child in music center**
   _____ Uses tape player without help
   _____ Sings/makes up songs by self
   _____ Sings songs with others
   _____ Does creative movement
   _____ Plays a rhythm or toy instrument

8. **Child in science center**
   _____ Explores materials in center
   _____ Uses senses to examine new things
   _____ Uses science tools (magnets, etc.)
   _____ Asks questions about materials
   _____ Takes care of plants, animals

9. **Child in sand/water center**
   _____ Spends time playing in sand/water
   _____ Uses tools, toys appropriately
   _____ Respects rules, limits
   _____ Shares or takes turns with materials
   _____ Pretends with materials creatively

10. **Child in woodworking center**
   _____ Handles tools with confidence
   _____ Pounds in nails
   _____ Saws wood
   _____ Makes things out of wood
   _____ Respects rules, limits

11. **Child in writing center**
   _____ Does scribble writing
   _____ Makes mock letters
   _____ Uses computer alphabet program
   _____ Prints name, some letters reversed
   _____ Prints name, some words accurately

socially, emotionally, in language and creativity? Does this mean giving them a test? No, not with 3-, 4-, and 5-year-olds who are notoriously poor test takers. You need to see them in action. This means much of your assessment will be done by observing, recording, and interpreting the results of your observations, and the rest by interviewing parents and the children themselves.

Jones (2004) explains, "Assessment may be defined as the ongoing process of gathering evidence of learning in order to make informed judgments about instructional practice. This process occurs continually in almost every early childhood classroom

Teachers should observe children to determine their needs.

as teachers listen to children's conversations, observe their actions, and make judgments about the progress of an individual child or a group of children" (p. 15).

Observing

A simple way to keep track of a child's progress in your program is to make ongoing observations of each child using a checklist that helps you focus on what it is you need to know. Most teachers want to know how the child is developing physically, cognitively, socially, emotionally, in language, and creativity. If you have set up your classroom as suggested in Chapter 3, "Establishing a Learning Environment," then you already have learning centers that can provide this knowledge about the children who use them. Figure 12.2, the "Learning Center Involvement Checklist," looks at each learning center, listing five actions the child may be performing.

Mindes (2007) points out: "Observations of the children in the program inform the decisions of teachers. Observations are the most important assessment tool, more so than any book or set of packaged tests. Teachers who regularly and systematically observe young children use the soundest informational basis for curriculum and instructional planning. By knowing what to look for and how to observe children, teachers make accurate inferences regarding the needs of children" (p. 60).

Inclusion

Although this particular assessment looks at children in learning centers, observers must be sensitive to the requirements of children with special needs and children from different cultures. Lopez, Salas, and Flores (2005) remind us, "To truly provide an assessment that is culturally sensitive, practitioners must address much more than just language and consider children's families and cultural experiences" (p. 49). It is always important to invite family members to participate in the assessment and ask for their input when you are planning.

Recording

You and your staff need to spend time observing and recording the actions of each child during the free-choice period at the beginning of the program year. Some teachers also make a *running record* of each child's actions during a specified period of time. A running record is a detailed narrative of behavior recorded in a sequential manner as it happens. The observer stands or sits apart from the child and writes down everything she sees happening with a particular child. The recording may be as short as several minutes or from time to time during a full day (Beaty, 2010, p. 28).

Many teachers use a checklist such as the "Learning Center Involvement Checklist" in Figure 12.2. Teachers who have set up learning centers like the ones described in Chapter 3 want to know what is happening with children within each learning center. How are they using the centers? Are any centers overcrowded? Are any being ignored? Can the children handle the self-directed activities within the centers without adult help? Do they stay with the activities until they are finished, or do they wander from center to center? Most important of all, how are children developing and what are they actually learning in these centers?

To make such an assessment, gather as much data as possible for each child at the beginning of the year. Then an emergent curriculum can be planned and implemented based on the children's needs. Ask your own staff how they want to gather this information. They may agree that the best way is to combine a checklist with a running record. The checklist helps the observer to focus on what may be happening in each center, and the running record fills in the details of what a child is actually doing and saying. Sound overwhelming? It's not. Try it and see.

Have each staff member (teacher, assistant, and student intern) be responsible for five or six children. They can then observe these children for five minutes or so during the free-choice period on several days, checking off their actions and jotting down running record notes. At the end of the week, they summarize what they have found out. During the next week they can then fill in the gaps about children for whom they have little or no information.

When enough data are gathered and summarized, put it all together. What will you have? For individuals, you should be able to tell which learning centers each child spends the most time in, which ones are avoided, and what his favorite activities are. For the class as a whole, you should be able to tell which centers and which activities are the most popular and whether the activities are developmentally appropriate (not too easy or not too difficult).

Interpreting Results

For example, three observations for Marsella showed that she spent the most time in the book center, had fun playing roles in the dramatic play center, did some matching and puzzle making in the manipulative/math center, painted at the easel in the art center, used the tape player and made up songs in the music center, asked questions and fed the guinea pig in the science center, and made strings of letters and printed her name in the writing center. She was not involved in the other centers. A number of the girls had similar observation results. They seem to avoid block building, large-motor activities, some science activities, and woodworking.

A number of boys spent most of their free-choice time in similar activities: building roads for little cars in the block center, climbing on the climber in the large-motor center, making astronaut puzzles in the manipulative/math center, using the tape player or toy guitar in the music center, using the microscope in the science center, playing with water toys at the sensory table, using the computer in the writing center, and pounding nails into stumps in the woodworking center. Many boys avoided books, dramatic play, art, and writing. Sound familiar? Because it was early in the year, a few children were still onlookers or wanderers. All of the children, however, participated in a morning circle, a total-group activity, and a story reading just before lunch. What did the teaching staff finally learn from these observations?

1. Children knew how to use the learning centers during free-choice period and could regulate the number of children in each center by themselves.

2. All of the learning centers were being used but not by all of the children.

3. To attract both boys and girls to all of the centers, they needed to find an activity that would be enticing to both.

4. Certain children needed help getting involved and staying involved in activities.

5. Some children were unable to complete certain activities.

6. The program as a whole was doing fine, but now it was time to bring it all together with an integrated learning curriculum.

PLANS AND IMPLEMENTS AN EMERGENT CURRICULUM BASED ON CHILDREN'S NEEDS AND INTERESTS

Team Planning

Program management in an early childhood classroom requires planning on the part of all those who will carry it out, that is, teachers, assistants, student teachers, and volunteers. Even the children themselves are part of the planning process. As Patricia Berl (1998), an early childhood administration specialist, points out, "Ask any director, stop any teacher, and he will tell you that planning makes the difference. With time to plan, chaos can become calm, tension can give way to decent relations, seat-of-the-pants classroom management can become quality education" (p. 61).

If you don't plan for something to happen, nothing will happen, say knowledgeable teachers. This is only common sense. Yet for some early childhood teaching teams, very little planning takes place. In many instances the teacher decides what art project to put out, what science activity to pursue, or what material to fill in the sensory table. Other staff members merely go along with whatever the teacher decides. The daily activities may or may not interest the children but seldom have any connection with one another or with whatever activities are available next week.

How can you tell what children have accomplished in your program if you have not planned for them to accomplish anything? How will you know what concerns staff members may be harboring if they have no forum for expressing their concerns? Where is the excitement that new ideas generate if there is no time to brainstorm? Without a specific time for planning, you and your team members will miss the great

Figure 12.3 Advantages of
Team Planning

- All team members have the opportunity to give input and help plan the curriculum.
- Team members better understand their responsibilities.
- Team members are more eager to carry out activities with children because they have helped to plan them.
- Team members are better able to build on what they have done in the past because there is continuity in the planning.
- Team members feel an ownership in the program and a sense of accomplishment in their work.

satisfaction of working together, creating new plans to help children grow and learn. You may also miss the pride and satisfaction of having your own ideas accepted by the others and put into practice with great enthusiasm by the children.

Classroom planning is not just an exercise to satisfy your administration. It is a necessity for everyone involved in a quality early childhood program. Figure 12.3 lists the advantages of team planning.

Team Planning Sessions

For programs to operate smoothly and with continuity, weekly planning sessions for all team members must be held regularly. Some programs choose a portion of Friday afternoons for planning time. They may call in a substitute while the team carries out its planning, schedule a senior volunteer to read to the children, or dismiss the children early if they are not involved.

Everyone on the classroom team must be aware of how plans are made, when they are made, and who is involved. If you are the lead teacher, you realize that for plans to be made and carried out, everyone on the team must participate. Carrying out plans is much more effective if the participants take part in planning for them. If you are an assistant, a student teacher, or a volunteer, you realize that the effectiveness of your contribution to the program depends on your own input in planning the activities you are responsible for.

Weekly team sessions should be threefold. Everyone needs to contribute to the discussion of these three questions:

1. Where are we now?

2. Where do we want to go?

3. How can we get there?

A *summary* of what has been happening in the classroom during the week can be led by the teacher, who will record the information from others on newsprint or a chalkboard for all to see. Observation records, data about group and individual accomplishments, and how particular activities worked out can be part of the summary. The needs assessment previously discussed will be the biggest contribution to planning at the beginning of the program year.

Plans for the following weeks will be based on what has been happening, as well as certain individual and group goals everyone has been working on. Brainstorming can help to generate new ideas as well as follow-ups for ongoing activities. Tasks and duties for every team member are then determined.

No single person in an early childhood classroom can or should do everything. But successful management of the program depends as much on staff interpersonal relations and cooperation as on any other single element. Balance is the key here as the entire staff becomes involved in planning.

Team Roles and Responsibilities

The teacher, of necessity, is the leader and therefore needs to take the lead in encouraging expression of ideas and concerns of other team members. This lead teacher must not dominate nor allow others to dominate. She should ask for suggestions from the others and then either ask them to volunteer or give them the responsibility to carry out classroom activities without interference from her. Other team members should also be willing to offer suggestions and take on responsibility. Classroom duties, for example, can be rotated throughout the team. Assistants, student teachers, and volunteers, as well as the lead teacher, can be responsible for most of the following on a rotating basis as shown in Figure 12.4.

Everyone can observe individual children and record pertinent information. Everyone can be involved in reading to individuals and attending meetings. Each should also have a chance to be in charge of a small group as well as working with individuals. Teachers need to join with other team members in classroom setup and cleanup. This should not be relegated to an assistant while the teacher occupies herself with more "important" activities. All classroom activities are important for everyone involved.

Teamwork means that everyone on the teaching team shares *all* the responsibilities of the classroom. When teamwork operates effectively, a visitor to the classroom will not be able to tell who is the teacher and who are the assistants.

Figure 12.4 Classroom Duties

- Participating daily in setup and cleanup of the classroom
- Being in charge of a small group
- Working with individual children
- Reading books to individuals and small groups
- Observing and recording children's behavior
- Attending and participating in weekly classroom planning sessions
- Attending family classroom meetings

Good interpersonal communication makes teamwork possible. The team recognizes that the leader has overall responsibility but is willing to work together toward a common goal. Each member trusts and respects the others, so when things go wrong, team members are able to communicate problems and resolve them in the friendly atmosphere of team meetings.

Overcoming Team Problems

Problems do occur from time to time. When more than one person is involved in working closely in the same room with the same children and staff members for long periods of time, it is only natural that conflicts arise. It is the team's responsibility to take time to resolve such problems. When problems arise, the team should choose someone from the program to lead an informal dialogue. This could be the program director, the educational coordinator, the family worker, or anyone else the team agrees on. Figure 12.5 lists the guidelines for conducting such a meeting.

Programs that schedule monthly team sessions like this are often able to resolve problems successfully. At these sessions, all of the team members are asked to contribute in a positive manner, following the guidelines. The leader reads the notes that have been written and prepares for the session, keeping in mind the necessity for a positive orientation. These sessions are not only follow-ups of concerns that surfaced the month before but also general problem-solving and brainstorming sessions.

To set the tone, the leader begins the session by sharing the positive accomplishments that were stated through writing. Participants add any additional achievements that come to mind. The leader then chooses one area of concern and opens it for discussion. Whatever resolution is finally agreed can be recorded on the newsprint or chalkboard.

Figure 12.5 Guidelines for Team Problem-Solving Meetings

1. Choose someone from the program but outside the classroom to be the team leader.

2. Have each team member write a brief note to include the following:
   a. A positive action or accomplishment of the team during the past month
   b. An area of concern needing discussion or action
   c. Any questions regarding the team approach.

3. Have the team leader collect and read from these notes, and then conduct the meeting as an open discussion, using good listening and communication skills.

4. Have the leader summarize:
   a. What has been said
   b. What has been agreed upon
   c. What will be done and by whom.

Teams that have used this approach find that writing down "areas of concern" in their initial notes to the leader helps to diffuse emotional issues and lets them state their case objectively. Having meetings like this every month rather than only when problems arise also helps to prevent interpersonal problems from developing into major communication breakdowns. Once these are settled, it is time to get down to the actual planning of the curriculum.

Employing an Emergent Curriculum

What is an *emergent curriculum,* and how does it differ from the traditional curriculum often planned for the preschool classroom? An emergent curriculum grows from the ideas, activities, and interests of both the teachers and the children as they happen, rather than being planned ahead of time by teachers alone as in the traditional sense. As Buell and Sutton (2008) tell us: "Emergent curriculum builds on the interests of children, is often spontaneous and responsive to the immediate interests of a group of children, and is driven by children's ideas, excitement, information, and questions" (p. 100).

The educational plan and how it is carried out is often referred to as the "curriculum" in early childhood programs. But as Jones and Nimmo (1994) note, "In early childhood education, curriculum isn't the focus, children are. It's easy for teachers to get hooked on curriculum because it's so much more manageable than children. But curriculum is *what happens* in an educational environment—not what is rationally planned to happen, but what actually takes place" (p. 12).

Programs based on an emergent curriculum often start with general or specific themes the staff and children have brainstormed together and go on from there, responding to children's interest and concerns as they evolve over the course of time. Such curriculum themes are broad topics that give the program an overall learning focus. They are concerned with the child and her world rather than academic subjects such as social studies and language arts. To support each theme, the learning centers of the classroom contribute specific learning activities for individuals and small groups, thus giving the program an integrated approach.

Curriculum themes can emerge from many sources: teachers' or children's expressed interests, science projects, a favorite book, a news item, a holiday, family concerns, or child development topics. A popular overall theme currently used by many programs concerns the environment and our use of it. Translated into children's terms, one such theme might read "The Earth cares for us; we must care for the Earth." How could you and your team translate that into appropriate ongoing activities for the children?

Using Curriculum Webs in Planning

Many programs are currently using a process known as *webbing* to explore broad curriculum ideas and convert them into activities. Team members (and, in most instances, children) brainstorm ideas at a planning session. The team leader writes words to represent these ideas on easel paper or a chalkboard, connecting each word with a line to any other words deriving from it, eventually creating what looks like a spiderweb of topics. Jones and Nimmo (1994) discuss webs: "A web is a tentative plan. It doesn't tell you exactly what will happen or in what order. That depends in large part on the children's response. So, first you plan and then you start trying your ideas, paying attention to what happens, evaluating, and moving on with further activities" (p. 11).

What is the advantage of doing webbing to help plan your curriculum? Buell and Sutton say that "webbing enables teachers to brainstorm and record ideas in an organized way" (2008, p. 100). Jones and Nimmo feel that "it gives a staff of adults a chance to explore the possibilities of any material or idea in order to make decisions about use" (1994, p. 11). This process can and should invite children and even parents to brainstorm ideas. The results are known as an "emergent curriculum," one that evolves from the needs and interests of the adult-child classroom community.

For example, to make a web of topics about the curriculum theme "we must care for the Earth," the leader writes "Caring for the Earth" in the middle of a sheet of newsprint and asks the group to brainstorm ideas about this theme. As the leader enters the topics mentioned, she draws lines from the initial topic words to subtopics leading from it. This first rather informal web might look like Figure 12.6, "Curriculum Web—Caring for the Earth."

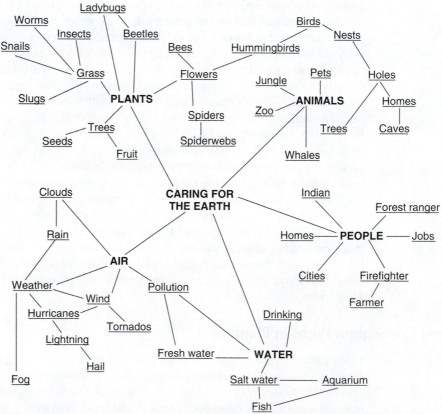

Figure 12.6   Curriculum Web—Caring for the Earth

Next, the team considers all of the ideas generated to decide where to start with plans for actual classroom activities. Do any of these topics or subtopics strike a chord with the planners? What about the children? Have any of them shown a strong interest in any of these topics? You may not know much about a particular topic yourself, but if it seems important to the children, you can learn about it along with them. Listen to what they have to say at the planning session and be sure to record their ideas on the web.

Children's Response to Curriculum Webs

Teachers are often surprised at children's excited response to webbing. When the youngsters find they can contribute words themselves, they think of all sorts of off-beat things. Other children who understand what it is all about soon set everyone straight. "You have to say words that can be joined to other words. You can't say *volcano* because there are no words it can be joined to."

Then Marsella spoke up. "I've got a book at home that shows a real web. It's about a spider building a web. I'll bring it tomorrow." And she did. She brought in Carle's (1984) classic *The Very Busy Spider*, which became a wonderful lead-in to an exploration of spiders, then insects, then butterflies, and finally worms, snails, and slugs for weeks to come. This topic was not one that the teachers would have considered for building their curriculum around. But when they noted the children's tremendous excitement generated by the idea of collecting spiders, insects, and butterflies out in the yard, they joined in.

Converting Children's Interests into a Theme-Based Curriculum

Now what? Now that you have tapped into a topic of great interest to children (spiders), how do you convert it into a theme-based curriculum? This teacher liked to involve children in a new topic by taking them on a field trip to investigate it. She felt that seeing and touching real things was the way to engage their deep interest in a topic. Bugs look fascinating as pictures in books, but what are they like in real life?

Field Trips

Marsella's class took several field trips outside to experience the living Earth. Five or six children at a time went outside in the yard to look for spiders and insects while the others spent time inside looking at books or listening to stories about them until it was their turn. One of the staff members checked out the yard ahead of time to make sure there was no broken glass or any unsafe animal around. Then they provided each child with a plastic jar and a hand net for collecting insects. They stayed away from wasps and bees. Once they were finished, the next group went out.

Observing and Recording Their Discoveries

Altogether they found many ants, two spiders, a cricket, and a ladybug. Before the children put their insects into the terrarium they had prepared, they tried to find out what they could about each one by observing it in its collecting jar. A staff member helped them label each jar with the name of the insect. Then the collector added her name.

Each child had a notebook to record what her bug looked like and anything else about it she observed. The teacher called this *documenting*. Drawing a picture of a bug turned out to be simple: a circle or oval with six legs sticking out (eight for spiders), and eyes or antennas at one end. Writing about it was harder. Some could print words, but most dictated a sentence or two for the teacher to record in their notebooks.

How could they find out more about their insects? The teacher told them that the longer they observed each one, the more they would find out. Also the closer they looked, the more they would see. She put out several magnifying glasses for the children to use. At first no one knew what to look for. Then Damon found out his ladybug could fly. Its back shell (wing case) split in two and wings came out. Everyone had to see. That made all of them look more closely at their insects and spiders. Now what?

Picture Books as Lead-Ins to an Entire Curriculum

Once again the making of another curriculum web gave everyone a chance to brainstorm ideas that could then serve as the basis of the curriculum. Because this teacher liked to use picture books as lead-ins to curriculum activities, she decided to ask the staff and children to brainstorm the use of a book on spiders as the center of the web. Ideas that they gained from the book could then come under each of the learning centers in the classroom.

To use a book as a lead-in to an entire curriculum as this class did, and not just for one activity, you need to choose a book you feel would hold the children's attention, contain appropriate information presented in an original manner, and be one the children would want to hear again and again. An entire series of natural history books speaks to children in this manner about spiders, insects, and other crawling creatures, the Backyard Books by Allen and Humphries (2000):

Are You an Ant?	*Are You a Grasshopper?*
Are You a Bee?	*Are You a Ladybug?*
Are You a Butterfly?	*Are You a Snail?*
Are You a Dragonfly?	*Are You a Spider?*

Each book is written as a simple story telling how you (the insect) were born, and what you would look like, eat, do, or look out for, if you were that creature. Children can, in fact, pretend to be that creature in their dramatic play. This is as personal as it gets for young children, and this is what makes learning real. As you plan your emergent curriculum activities, be sure to:

1. Make your plans personal for the children involved.

2. Set up your learning centers as self-directed discovery centers for the children.

3. Listen to what the children have to say about what they are doing so you will know what should happen next.

Before this staff went any further, they gathered together several other books they planned to use on the topic of spiders and insects:

Are You a Ladybug? (Allen & Humphries, 2000)	*Diary of a Worm,* (Cronin, 2003)
	Under One Rock (Fredericks, 2001)

Are You a Spider? (Allen &
    Humphries, 2000)
The Very Busy Spider (Carle, 1984)
Diary of a Spider (Cronin, 2005)
I Love Bugs! (Dodd, 2010)

Aaaarrgghh! Spider! (Monks, 2004)
Face-to-Face with the Ladybug
    (Tracqui, 2002)
Itsy Bitsy Spider (Toms, 2009)
Beetle Bop (Fleming, 2007)

The hands-down favorite of all the books was *I Love Bugs!* Children love to scare themselves!

I Love Bugs! is a rhyming, swinging, say-the-words-out-loud book that the whole class learned almost by heart about the "flouncy, frilly, flutter bugs, and silly clitter-clutter bugs" with huge, comical pictures. But they couldn't wait till the last black pages with the hairy, eight-legged bug hanging from the ceiling! Then they would all get up and run away squealing like the boy in the book.

After listening to the book *Are You a Spider?* the children were ready to brain-storm again about how this book could lead into learning center activities and what these activities would be. Figure 12.7 shows the results.

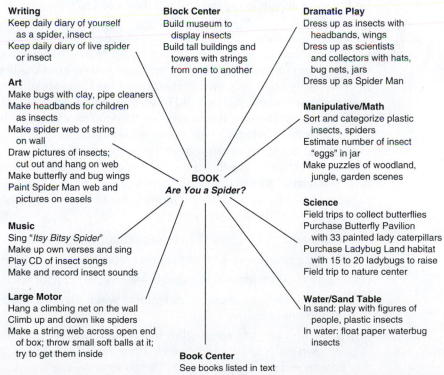

Writing
Keep daily diary of yourself
    as a spider, insect
Keep daily diary of live spider
    or insect

Art
Make bugs with clay, pipe cleaners
Make headbands for children
    as insects
Make spider web of string
    on wall
Draw pictures of insects;
    cut out and hang on web
Make butterfly and bug wings
Paint Spider Man web and
    pictures on easels

Music
Sing "*Itsy Bitsy Spider*"
Make up own verses and sing
Play CD of insect songs
Make and record insect sounds

Large Motor
Hang a climbing net on the wall
Climb up and down like spiders
Make a string web across open end
    of box; throw small soft balls at it;
    try to get them inside

Block Center
Build museum to
    display insects
Build tall buildings and
    towers with strings
    from one to another

BOOK
Are You a Spider?

Book Center
See books listed in text

Dramatic Play
Dress up as insects with
    headbands, wings
Dress up as scientists
    and collectors with hats,
    bug nets, jars
Dress up as Spider Man

Manipulative/Math
Sort and categorize plastic
    insects, spiders
Estimate number of insect
    "eggs" in jar
Make puzzles of woodland,
    jungle, garden scenes

Science
Field trips to collect butterflies
Purchase Butterfly Pavilion
    with 33 painted lady caterpillars
Purchase Ladybug Land habitat
    with 15 to 20 ladybugs to raise
Field trip to nature center

Water/Sand Table
In sand: play with figures of
    people, plastic insects
In water: float paper waterbug
    insects

Figure 12.7   Learning Center Curriculum Web for *Are You a Spider?*

As the staff and children brainstormed ideas, the teacher wrote down their words on the chalkboard without placing them under topics. Afterward, she sorted them out and listed them under the learning centers shown in Figure 12.7. These ideas would get them started, and later they could generate other activities as they learned more about spiders and insects. The teacher was also careful to write down questions the children asked as they became more deeply involved in the topics. For example, after hearing *Are You a Ladybug?* the children wanted to know why ladybugs are so colorful and aphids are not. This question led to a whole range of new activities. This time the teacher wrote out a more formal *lesson plan* for a unit asking "Why Are Ladybugs So Colorful and Aphids Are Not?" (see Figure 12.8).

Managing Time

Teachers often want to know how long they should keep an activity going or how much time they should spend on a particular topic. As you make team plans for what will occur daily, take special note of the longest and most important activity periods of the day: the free-choice periods. It is here that the children will spend the majority of their time, working and playing in the learning centers, listening to books being read, and participating in art, crafts, science, cooking, and manipulative activities on the activity tables. How long should these periods be? Should they be the same length every day, or will they need to change in length depending on circumstances?

You must be aware of the responses of the children. As long as they show interest and enthusiasm, keep the activities going. Make changes in the various learning centers when interest lags, using other ideas gained from the brainstorming, but especially using children's own suggestions. One thing should lead to another in an emergent curriculum, just as it did in your planning.

The learning centers themselves are the framework for an integrated curriculum if you stock them with materials and activities to support the theme or topic you have chosen. It is not necessary to change the entire classroom at once. Instead, try adding new insect activities to each of the centers as the need and interest arises. What we have discovered about young children's learning through brain research, the study of European preschools, and our own observations of children's behavior in the classroom leads us to these conclusions:

1. Real learning takes time (much longer than we realized).
2. Real learning involves continuity and repetition (much more than we realized).
3. Young children learn best through self-directed playful discovery.
4. Young children have problems learning when they are under pressure to hurry up and finish.
5. Young children can accomplish much more than we ever realized if we raise our own expectations and give children the time, freedom, and opportunity to choose and pursue activities on their own.

Figure 12.8 Lesson Plan for "Why Are Ladybugs So Colorful and Aphids Are Not?"

Topic:	**Insect colors as signals or camouflage**
Theme:	Why are ladybugs so colorful and aphids are not?
Objective:	Children will learn why ladybugs have red colors and aphids are green or colorless
Materials:	Red construction paper, black markers, sheets of see-through plastic, scissors
Lesson:	Read the story *Are You a Ladybug?* to one small group at a time. Have them look closely at the pictures. What does the baby ladybug look like? What makes it change to its red and black-dotted shell? What do the aphids look like? Do they change colors? Now have children play the ladybug-aphid game called "I can find you." Have one group be ladybugs and another one be aphids. The ladybugs should trace little circles on the red paper, cut them out, and put dots on them. The aphids should trace little circles on the see-through plastic sheets, and cut them out. Count to make sure you have the same number of each. Now each group should go around the classroom without the others looking, hiding their paper insects in plain sight. Don't put them under anything, but keep them out in the open. Now give each group a basket and ask them to go around the classroom and collect as many of the opposite insects as they can. Do they find more ladybugs or aphids? Is there a reason for finding more ladybugs? What is it? Yes, the ladybugs are easier to see because of their bright color. The aphids are harder to find because they are colorless or green like the plants they suck on. We say that they are "camouflaged," or hidden by their color. But ladybugs can find them by smelling them and seeing them. Ladybugs don't need to be camouflaged. Their bright colors have another message: Red means "Stop; stay away!" to the other insects or birds that would eat them because they taste terrible. What other colors have meanings? What about green?
Follow-up:	Another day read the book *Face-to-Face with the Ladybug*. What new things about ladybugs do they learn? Would they like to raise some ladybugs as this book describes and then give them to people with flower or vegetable gardens to eat any aphids? Aphids especially like roses. Would they like to make ladybug wings like the first book shows and make up a game, "Ladybug, ladybug, fly away home"?

Managing Time Blocks

A simple but effective way many programs schedule activities is in the form of time blocks. Time blocks are labeled periods of time of *unspecified length* that occur in approximately the same order every day, but within which there is flexibility for many things to happen. The time blocks used in many programs include the following:

1. Arrival
2. Opening circle
3. Free choice (A.M.)
4. Snack time (A.M.)
5. Playground
6. Story time
7. Lunchtime
8. Nap time
9. Snack (P.M.)
10. Free choice (P.M.)
11. Closing circle
12. Departure

If yours is a half-day program, the children's departure could occur after lunch. If lunch is not included in your half-day schedule, you could add a closing circle, after which the children would depart. The length of each time block and the order in which you schedule it depends on your goals, your children's needs, and daily circumstances.

One advantage of using time blocks is flexibility. The length of time blocks can vary according to circumstances, although their order will remain the same. For example, arrival usually takes about 15 minutes every morning. But occasionally the bus will be late, so arrival time may stretch to 30 minutes or more. You may decide to omit the free-choice period entirely that morning and go immediately out onto the playground because the children have been cooped up on the bus so long that they need to get out in the open, where they can release their pent-up energy. Another day you may find the children are just too restless for circle time. What they really need is a run around the playground.

In other words, time blocks do not tie you to specific times. Rather, they refer to activities and their sequential order. Their flexibility frees you and your staff to plan for a variety of activities within a certain block. It does not lock you into the kind of schedule that dictates, for example, that snack time must occur at 10 A.M. All you know about snack time is that it precedes the playground time block, and that snack time and playground time could occur simultaneously if you decide to serve the juice for a snack outside on a hot day.

Another advantage of time blocks is their built-in balance. You can easily alternate contrasting kinds of activities simply by the order in which you schedule the particular time blocks. Just as important is the stability your program acquires through the use of time blocks. The same periods tend to occur in about the same order every day. This promotes a sense of security among the children. To enjoy a variety of activities, young children need this kind of structure that they understand and within which they feel comfortable. Once you have determined your general time block order, make a simple illustrated chart showing each time block so that children, volunteers, and visitors can tell at a glance what is going on and when.

Finally, time blocks provide a simple system of program management for classroom workers. Student teachers, Foster Grandparents, and other volunteers are much more at ease if they too can readily understand a daily schedule and become comfortable with it.

Time Management in the Preschools of Reggio Emilia

American educators have visited preschools throughout the world to gain new ideas about what works best with young children and to compare our preschools with those of other countries. American visitors to the Reggio Emilia preschools in Italy were at first astounded at the high level of art and writing accomplishments of very young children. Then they discovered that the children are allowed to work on their self-chosen projects for as long as they want or need to—sometimes for days or even weeks. As Seefeldt (1995) notes, "Time is used differently in Reggio preschools than in preschools in the United States. Experiences and themes last months, as opposed to the one- or two-week units typical in the United States. And children are never expected to move on to something new until they have exhausted their own ideas fully. Often, in Reggio, children were observed painting at easels for an entire morning or working with clay for hours" (p. 42).

Does this mean that American preschools should abandon the idea of time blocks altogether and open the days to long work/play periods during which children pursue a certain project to its conclusion? Not necessarily. As the observers came to realize, it is not the children's products that are important, but the process the child goes through to produce the art or the writing. Because this process is treated so seriously and given so much time in the Reggio preschools, the children's products are extraordinary. Observers also found many Europeans to be more relaxed about time than their American counterparts.

Perhaps, instead of lengthening or eliminating time blocks, American preschool teachers should consider keeping the same activities going in the time blocks for more than one or two days because they realize that children's experiences need to be repeated over and over for them to learn from the process.

Gandini (2002) has more to say about time in Reggio Emilia schools: "Time is not set by a clock, and continuity is not interrupted by the calendar. Children's own sense of time and their personal rhythm are considered in the planning and carrying out activities and projects. Teachers get to know the personal time of the children and each child's particular characteristics because children stay with the same teacher and the same peer group for three-year cycles. This process of looping further promotes the concept of *an education based on relationships*" (pp. 17–18).

No matter how you finally decide to schedule time in your classroom, observe carefully how your children use the time. When programs force children to stop what they are doing and move on to something else, they may be short-circuiting the children's learning process. You will know this is happening when the children show great reluctance to stop or change what they are doing. Does this happen in your program? Conversely, some time periods may need to be cut shorter than the time allotted because the children are finished with their activities and seem to be milling around looking for something new.

How you schedule time in your program should be based on the children's interests and needs rather than on the convenience of the teacher. Careful observation of the children's behavior can help you determine how long or short the time periods need to be.

ASSESSES OUTCOMES AND ARRANGES FOLLOW-UP

Child Observation

How can you tell if your program is successful? Evaluating program outcomes requires you to collect information about the children and their actions just as you did for the needs assessment. Which learning centers are they involved in? Which ones do they avoid? What do they have to say about the activities available? Are they able to complete them with ease? Do the activities hold their interest for long? What do they seem most enthusiastic about? What are they learning from these activities? These questions are the same ones you asked during the initial assessment.

Information about the success of the activities can be gathered during weekly team meetings. Team members can report on the activities they were responsible for, how they worked out, and what the children accomplished. The lead teacher usually jots down notes after each daily closing circle when different children tell what they did and what they liked that day. She can share such information with the team as they plan for the next week. If problems arise about individual children, team members can plan to observe and record the child for brief time periods on several days.

Someone on the staff must step back unobtrusively and observe the child, giving special attention to the identified needs. This observation of the child's interactions with materials and other children can be recorded as a running record of the child's actions and words as they occur or as a checking off of behaviors on a checklist. You will be gathering observational data just as you did at the outset, not only to help the child but also to assist the staff in evaluating the emergent curriculum. Be sure to take enough time in observing.

NAEYC Criteria for Assessment of Child Progress Standard

Describe how you would meet the following standard:

4.D.02 Teaching teams meet at least weekly to interpret and use assessment results to align curriculum and teaching practices to the interests and needs of the children.

Observing Marsella with the Learning Center Involvement Checklist

One of the staff members observed Marsella to see if she worked in any of the learning centers she had avoided before the theme of spiders and insects was introduced. Yes. She was one of the leaders in most of the centers. Figure 12.9 shows what the staff recorded.

Once again staff members needed to observe and record Marsella's actions in the various centers over a few days. After meeting with the staff, additions to the various centers were made based on the assessments of the children and the new curriculum theme they were following. Figure 12.9 shows what they recorded about Marsella. The list of learning centers, their new additions, and Marsella's involvement in them follows.

Figure 12.9 Marsella's
Learning Involvement
Checklist

Name ___Marsella M___   Date _5/14;15_
Observer _____selma_____   Time _9-12_

1. Child in block-building center

_____ Carries blocks, fills and dumps, doesn't build

___✓___ Builds in flat rows on floor or stacks vertically

_____ Makes bridges with block across two parallel blocks

___✓___ Builds buildings

___✓___ Names buildings, plays with them

2. Child in book center

___✓___ Shows interest in picture books

___✓___ Talks about the pictures

___✓___ Pretends to read

___✓___ Can retell a story

___✓___ Recognizes some words

3. Child in dramatic play center

___✓___ Plays a role (pretends to be someone)

___✓___ Pretends about a thing

___✓___ Pretends about a make-believe situation

___✓___ Stays with role for five minutes or more

___✓___ Uses verbal communication during play

4. Child in large motor center

_____ Balances on a board

___✓___ Climbs easily

___✓___ Gets down from high places easily

___✓___ Jumps with both feet over an object

___✓___ Hits a target throwing a beanbag or ball

5. Child in manipulative/math center

___✓___ Sorts, matches objects by color

___✓___ Sorts, matches objects by shape, size

___✓___ Counts number of objects in a set

___✓___ Threads objects on a string

___✓___ Makes puzzles easily

6. Child in art center

___✓___ Paints with brushes

___✓___ Plays with play dough/clay

___✓___ Cuts with scissors

___✓___ Uses paste or glue appropriately

___✓___ Creates images of people, things

(Continued)

Figure 12.9   *continued*

7. **Child in music center**
   ___✓___ Uses tape player without help
   ___✓___ Sings/makes up songs by self
   ___✓___ Sings songs with others
   _____ Does creative movement
   ___✓___ Plays a rhythm or toy instrument

8. **Child in science center**
   ___✓___ Explores materials in center
   ___✓___ Uses senses to examine new things
   ___✓___ Uses science tools (magnets, etc.)
   ___✓___ Asks questions about materials
   ___✓___ Takes care of plants, animals

9. **Child in sand/water center**
   _____ Spends time playing in sand/water
   _____ Uses tools, toys appropriately
   _____ Respects rules, limits
   _____ Shares or takes turns with materials
   _____ Pretends with materials creatively

10. **Child in woodworking center**
   _____ Handles tools with confidence
   _____ Pounds in nails
   _____ Saws wood
   _____ Makes things out of wood
   _____ Respects rules, limits

11. **Child in writing center**
   _____ Does scribble writing
   ___✓___ Makes mock letters
   ___✓___ Uses computer alphabet letters
   _____ Prints name, some letters reversed
   ___✓___ Prints name, some words accurately

ADDITIONS TO LEARNING CENTERS

Block-Building Center

(Additions to center: small plastic insects, vehicles, people figures; dollhouse furniture; posters of gardens, farms, jungles). Marsella hurried to this center every morning, often bringing little containers from home. She was building a hospital with rooms and beds for injured insects. She used the little vehicles as ambulances to carry plastic bugs that she transported in the containers. Several girls and boys joined her in this elaborate drama.

Book Center

(Additions to center: spiderweb on back wall; names of insect books attached to web; insect books displayed; puppet tree and glove puppets of ladybug, spider, bee, and butterfly). More children looked at books in this center and played with the puppets than ever before. Teachers spent more time here reading to individuals. Marsella's favorite book was *Are You a Ladybug?* (Allen & Humphries, 2000).

Dramatic Play Center

(Additions to center: dress-up props for scientist; desk with microscope, science tools; child-size wings of ladybug, monarch butterfly, and bee). Marsella used this center for her "base of explorations" for insect collecting. Other children buzzed around playing bug roles.

Large-Motor Center

(Additions to center: play tunnel; colored hopping sacks). More boys still used the center than girls, but Marsella got everyone interested in her new drama of hatching out of a chrysalis (the hopping sack), or sometimes crawling out through the tunnel.

Manipulative/Math Center

(Additions to center: eight-piece bugs puzzle set; bugs jigsaw puzzle; *Bugs on Parade* counting book, and 175 bug counters). Marsella didn't do the counting, but she loved the challenge of making the bugs jigsaw puzzle.

Art Center

(Additions to center: posters of insects and flowers; giant insect stampers; large collage set). Everyone loved the insect stampers and went around stamping everything they could find (their writing paper, journals, envelopes; not books!). Marsella got the idea of decorating her stamped bugs with glitter, sequins, mini pom-poms, pipe cleaner antennas, and wiggly eyes. The teacher finally put the stampers away and encouraged the children to draw and decorate their own insects.

Music Center

(Additions to center: *Bugs: Read It Sing It Big Book* and cassette; *Bugs, Bugs, Bugs,* a sing-along CD; a classroom Song Bank and CD with 40 songs and pictures of their titles). Marsella liked "Shoo Fly, Don't Bother Me" the best. She also sang and recorded her own bug songs.

Science Center

(Additions to center: Ladybug Land with 20 live ladybugs, magnifier, and guide; Lakeshore Exploring Bugs Center). Marsella still fed the guinea pig, but her main interest was the ladybugs. She also pestered the teachers to go out in the yard on more collecting trips (which they did).

Sand/Water Center

(Additions to center: none). Marsella still did not play in this center. The staff realized they needed to add something related to insects to attract her and others.

Woodworking Center

(Additions to center: none). Marsella still did not play in this center, although she talked to the staff about building a butterfly habitat, but that would have to wait.

Writing Center

(Additions to center: new writing center desk with cubbies for storing supplies and a fold-down desktop; small insect stampers; blank write-and-draw journals; write-and wipe lapboards and crayons; magnetic letters and board). Everyone flocked to this center and signed up for the two desk chairs. Marsella took her lapboard to another table and filled it with drawings of bugs and their names.

Observations of Marsella with the "Learning Center Involvement Checklist" (Figure 12.9) found that she was indeed involved in most of the centers. Only centers where no new materials or equipment had been added failed to attract her. But there was still an important program outcomes assessment to be made: What were she and the other children learning? One of the program themes had been "The Earth cares for us; we must care for the Earth." Did the children understand how they cared for the Earth when they learned about insects, or how the insects also cared for the Earth? How could the staff find out?

Assessment Interviews

The program director gave them the idea of interviewing the children directly. She said that either interviewing single children singly or in pairs while they played with materials could often elicit important information not available by other means. Seefeldt (1998) has this to say: "Interviews possess a number of virtues that make them an ideal tool for assessing young children. They are flexible. The interviewer can go over the same questions, probe others more intently, and direct and adapt the interview until clarity is reached and as much information as possible has been collected" (p. 321).

The teacher decided that reading a picture book to an individual or small group and then asking them about it might be the way to go. Books were important as lead-ins to many activities in the program, and how children understood them would help to answer questions about whether the children really knew what caring for the Earth was all about. They wanted to interview Marsella, especially, but wondered if she would respond openly to their questions. She wasn't as open with the staff members as she was with the other children. Could they read a particular

The teacher interviews a child after reading a book with a bug theme.

book to a small group that included Marsella and then ask their questions to all of the children?

The teacher decided to conduct an interview with Marsella and two peers by reading them a book. She understood that there was a protocol to be followed even in an informal interview (see Figure 12.10). The teacher chose the book *Are You a Ladybug?*,

Figure 12.10 Protocol for Book Assessment Interview

1. Select a book with a character the child/children can relate to.
2. Read the book ahead of time and decide on a few key questions.
3. Establish a good rapport with the child/children.
4. Read the story in an exciting and enjoyable manner.
5. Use natural conversation that will elicit answers to key questions.
6. Probe in nonthreatening ways.
7. Follow unexpected leads.
8. Listen closely and carefully.
9. Record results afterward.

Marsella's favorite, but one the other two children did not know. Here are the questions she asked afterward along with some of the children's answers:

- What did you like about being a ladybug in this story?

  I liked turning red with black spots.
  Flying.
  Keeping the birds away.
  Living on flowers.
  I didn't like it.

- What did you not like?

  Having my skin split.
  Tasting terrible.
  Eating aphids.
  I'm never gonna be a bug!

- Why did you have to eat aphids?

  I don't know.
  Because you live on them.
  That's all there was.
  They taste yummy to ladybugs.
  Yuck!

- What are aphids?

  I don't know.
  They look terrible.
  They're all over the rose plant.
  They eat plants.

- How do ladybugs like you help the Earth?

  I don't know.
  They kill the aphids.
  They make plants grow.
  People like them.

The teacher was more than happy with the answers. She felt the children listened closely to the story and understood what it was about. Even the children who responded "I don't know" nodded when the other children answered and afterward wanted to hear the story again. They all did. This showed the teacher that *a follow-up reading* was both necessary and helpful for the children's understanding. They made her stop when they came to the pictures that answered her questions. She found there was some confusion about the ladybug larva and the aphids but was able to clear it up. Now they all wanted to be ladybugs!

Team Planning for Follow-Up

Marsella's checklist results put her ahead of many of the others in her development. Each of the children should be observed and recorded in the same manner. Then you will need to summarize and interpret the findings with members of the classroom team. Remember that you are looking at one child's accomplishments: how he or she uses the learning centers you have set up. What are the child's strengths? Jot down several. What are his areas that need strengthening? Jot them down too. Is there a way you can help the child improve in the areas where you have left blanks? Are there other activities that would suit this child better? Team members can give their input as you plan the activities for the weeks ahead—not to single out this child but to integrate his special requirements into the plans for everyone. Follow-up can be part of the team planning as you assess the outcomes for each child.

If this process seems too complex and time consuming, remember that you are looking at only one child at a time. This is the kind of information you need to be able to help in the child's development and in the staff's future planning. Start by first observing children who are having problems in the classroom learning centers. Later as you involve them in activities to improve their skills, you can begin to observe the other children, one at a time, as well. Have more than one team member use the same observation form to look at and record his or her views of the child. They can then present their findings to the rest of the team at the weekly meetings. There is still one more step.

Documentation

Programs that base their planning on an emergent curriculum and use children's input on the project design also document the ongoing accomplishments and final outcomes of their plans. Lewin-Benham (2006) states, "Documentation is the process of recording children's thoughts and actions on a topic to maintain their focus and expand their interest" (p. 31). Such documentation is not difficult when all of the learning centers can contribute to its overall design just at they did to the project theme.

Teachers, staff, and children need to document the experience as each step happens and to record the project as it emerges. Children will be recording their own experiences in their journals or daily "Diary of a Ladybug." When the project is finished, an overall record of the project can be kept and displayed on a Documentation Panel. As Lewin-Benham tells us, "A finished documentation panel should convey what started the experience, how it developed and why, and its outcome or the open-ended questions that sparked it" (p. 31). It is important to use the children's own words, photos of them, pictures and artwork they have made, names of books read, and any other appropriate information.

One class used the "Learning Center Curriculum Web" (see Figure 12.7) for a documentation panel based on a different book each week or so. They covered a large bulletin board with colored paper and mounted a dust jacket of the book in the center. A black web (string) was then strung out to each learning center, and children mounted a contribution from each center that was involved with that particular book. For example, for the book *Aaaarrgghh! Spider!* (Monks, 2004), the children helped to make or photograph the following examples from each of the learning centers that contributed:

Writing Center

Signs hanging from web:

"I want to be your pet"

"Please make me your pet!"

"I'm a good family pet!"

Music Center

Photos of children with spider glove puppets dancing

Water Table

Photos of plastic spiders floating on sponges

Dramatic Play

Photos of plastic flies on a dish with plastic spider ready to pounce

Block Building

Photos of plastic spider riding in vehicle to block buildings

Large Motor

Little three-dimensional swing with plastic spider in it

Art Center

Silver spider webs on black backing paper; made from glue-stick-drawn webs covered with silver glitter

The documentation panel was labeled "Can a Spider Be a Pet?" Under this heading was a subheading reading, "Reasons for Making This Spider a Pet." Children's dictated comments were also listed on why people are afraid of spiders, how spiders help people, and why you shouldn't be afraid of spiders. The teacher photographed each of these panels to be kept as a record for outcomes of the spider/insect project.

The teacher of this class understood the important role of assessment in her management of the program. She agreed with Sorrels, Norris, and Sheehan (2005) who say, "Teachers who 'curriculum' begin by assessing children's strengths and weaknesses, their prior knowledge and experiences, their needs and interests, and their ethnic and cultural backgrounds. 'Curriculuming' continues with assessment as teachers identify gaps in children's knowledge, development, and understanding, and determine whether or not local, state, and national standards have been met" (p. 9).

SUMMARY

Program planning starts with a needs assessment of children in which staff members and family members observe, record, and interpret children's needs. Then the teacher and staff can plan for individuals and the group, implement the plans, assess the outcomes, and decide on follow-up. A simple way to observe and record is by using a checklist such as the "Learning Center Involvement Checklist" both at the beginning and ending of the year. Staff members then interpret the results and make plans at team planning sessions. All members of the classroom team, including volunteers, should be involved in the planning process. Then they will be more committed and willing to carry out the plans.

Regular weekly planning sessions should address where the group is, where it wants to go, and how it can get there. Team members need to share responsibility for managing various tasks and duties. When team members encounter interpersonal problems, a leader can bring them together using verbal and nonverbal communication, as well as writing and listening skills, to resolve the problem.

An emergent curriculum helps teams focus on children and respond to their needs and interests, often using curriculum webs to explore topics and ideas. Everyone, including children, brainstorms possible ideas to be explored. Children also observe and record their discoveries.

Managing time and how it is spent is another important aspect of planning. Using time blocks to indicate the order of the various activities is more helpful than schedules that set specific times for activities. Children should not be forced to hurry up and finish. Instead, the time blocks themselves can be lengthened. The curriculum itself can be planned using emergent themes derived from children's or teachers' interests or needs, science projects, popular children's books, or child development topics. Learning centers are then stocked with materials to support the curriculum topic and to integrate the activities being planned. New curriculum topics often emerge naturally as follow-ups of activities the children show interest in.

Assessing the outcomes of the curriculum activities requires the staff to collect data about the children just as they did for the initial needs assessment using observing and recording, but also requires assessment interviews and documentation panels. Sharing this information at team meetings helped the team to plan follow-up activities for individuals and the group.

Ethical Dilemma

One parent was outraged that the class was studying spiders because her child was deathly afraid of them. This parent made a scene at a parent meeting and threatened to take her child out of the program unless the project was dropped. What would you do?

LEARNING ACTIVITIES

1. Read one or more of the Suggested Readings or view Web sites and add 10 file cards to your file with specific ideas for daily, weekly, monthly, or yearly plans. Include the source.

2. Participate in a team planning session. Take notes on the topics discussed and resolved.

3. Write out suggestions for meeting with and helping two team members with interpersonal problems.

4. Brainstorm with others about a particular topic and make a curriculum web on the topic. Choose one of the subtopics from the web and work up a plan for activities in each of the learning centers to support the subtopic

5. Observe and record a child using the "Learning Center Involvement Checklist" (Figure 12.2). Interpret the results and decide on activities to help the child become involved in particular learning centers.

6. Use a children's book as the focus and develop a curriculum web for the various learning centers with activities based on the book.

7. Make an evaluation of the present curriculum using data gathered from observations using the "Learning Center Involvement Checklist." How can the curriculum be changed to respond to any concerns?

SUGGESTED READINGS

Hearron, P. F., & Hildebrand, V. (2003). *Management of child development centers* (5th ed.). Upper Saddle River, NJ: Merrill/ Prentice Hall.

Scheinhat, L. J. (2009). Designing a curriculum for ec teachers and caregivers. *Exchange, 31*(2), 34–37.

Seitz, H. (2008). The power of documentation in the early childhood classroom. *Young Children, 63*(2), 88–93.

Whaley, C. (2007). Emergent, integrated curriculum: Meeting standards in meaningful ways. *Dimensions of Early Childhood, 35*(2), 3–10.

WEB SITES

Center for Performance Assessment
http://www.makingstandardswork.com

Center for the Study of Testing, Evaluation, and Educational Policy
http://www.csteep.bc.edu

Critical Issue: Assessing Young Children's Progress Appropriately
http://www.ncrel.org

Early Childhood Educational Assessment Consortium
http://www.ccsso.org/projects

KidsSource Online
http://www.kidssource.com

Reggio Emilia
http://www.reggioemilia.com

CHILDREN'S BOOKS

Allen, J., & Humphries, T. (2000). *Are you a butterfly?* Boston: Kingfisher.

Allen, J., & Humphries, T. (2000). *Are you a ladybug?* Boston: Kingfisher.

Allen, J., & Humphries, T. (2000). *Are you a snail?* Boston: Kingfisher.

Allen, J., & Humphries, T. (2000). *Are you a spider?* Boston: Kingfisher.

Carle, E. (1984). *The very busy spider.* New York: Philomel Books.

Cronin, D. (2003). *Diary of a worm.* New York: Joanna Cotler Books.

Cronin, D. (2005). *Diary of a spider.* New York: Joanna Cotler Books.

Dodd, E. (2010). *I love bugs.* New York: Holiday House.

Fleming, D. (2007). *Beetle bop.* Orlando, FL: Harcourt.

*Fredericks, A. D. (2001). *Under one rock: Bugs, slugs, and other ughs.* Nevada City, CA: Dawn Publications.

Monks, L. (2004). *Aaaarrgghh! Spider!* Boston: Houghton Mifflin.

Toms, K. (2009). *Itsy bitsy spider.* Berkhamsted, Hertforshire, England: Make Believe Ideas.

Tracqui, V. (2002). *Face-to-face with the ladybug.* Watertown, MA: Charlesbridge.

* Multicultural

CHAPTER 13

Promoting Professionalism

☐ **General Objective**

To continue professional growth as a teacher of young children

☑ **Specific Objectives**

____ Makes a commitment to the early childhood profession

____ Behaves ethically toward children, families, and coworkers

____ Takes every opportunity to improve professional growth

W̲hat is a *PROFESSIONAL* in the early childhood field, and what behaviors make a person a professional? Whether you are a college student, a teaching assistant, a parent volunteer, a Child Development Associate (CDA) candidate, or a teacher, this is an important question for you to consider carefully. What qualities do professionals in this particular field possess? What will be expected of you that is different from what you are already doing?

Our professional organization, the National Association for the Education of Young Children (NAEYC), announced in 2005 the revised standards for professional preparation of early childhood professionals. In 2009 these standards were again revised for certifying early childhood professional preparation. The standards can be summarized as follows:

1. Promoting child development and learning
2. Building family and community relationships
3. Observing, documenting, and assessing
4. Using developmentally effective approaches to connect with children and families
5. Using content knowledge to build meaningful curriculum
6. Becoming a professional

The NAEYC Web site (http://www.naeyc.org) describes these standards as "offering practitioners a framework for applying new knowledge to critical issues. They support important *early learning* goals across settings serving children from birth through age 8. They support critical *early childhood policy* structures including professional credentialing, accreditation of professional preparation programs, state approval of teacher education programs, and state professional development systems. Preparation for *inclusion* and *diversity* is required to meet each of these standards."

Becoming a Professional

To become a professional "candidates identify and conduct themselves as members of the early childhood profession. They know and use ethical guidelines and other professional standards related to early childhood practice. They are continuous, collaborative learners who demonstrate knowledgeable, reflective, and critical perspectives on their work, making informed decisions that integrate knowledge from a variety of sources. They are informed advocates for sound educational practices and policies" (Hyson, 2002, p. 78).

Hyson explains that these standards offer "a *shared vision* for the future preparation of *all* who work with young children and their families. The details may differ, but at every level and in every setting the focus is the same. Competent early childhood educators need knowledge, skills, and professional dispositions in the five [now six] core areas" (p. 78). The complete document "NAEYC Standards for Early Childhood Professional Preparation: Baccalaureate or Initial Licensure Level" may be downloaded from http://www.naeyc.org.

This chapter discusses three important categories of professional development that many early childhood professionals themselves agree on. To be considered a professional in the field of early childhood you must do the following:

1. Make a commitment to the profession.
   a. Gain a knowledge base in the field.
   b. Complete some type of training.
   c. Complete some type of service.

2. Behave ethically toward children, their families, and your coworkers.
   a. Show respect for all.
   b. Demonstrate caring for all children.
   c. Respect privacy.

3. Continue to improve your professional growth.
   a. Become involved in ongoing training.
   b. Join a professional organization, read its publications, and network with colleagues.
   c. Contribute something of value to the field.

Early Childhood Programs

The early childhood field is broad, with its principal components including infant care, child care, child teaching, teacher training, health care, children with special needs, family involvement, and administration of programs. The children referred to include infants and toddlers (birth to 3 years old), preschoolers (3 to 5 years), prekindergartners (4 to 5 years), kindergartners (5 to 6 years), and sometimes early elementary children (up to 7 or 8 years).

The programs designed for such children include child care in homes, centers, business and industrial settings, churches, hospitals, senior citizen centers, universities, and military bases. They also include Head Start programs, nursery school and preschool programs, prekindergarten and kindergarten school programs, and before- and after-school programs. These programs are operated by a variety of organizations including private individuals and companies, parent groups, community groups, service organizations, business and industry, public and private schools, religious organizations, the military, colleges and universities, health care facilities, and local, state, and federal government agencies.

The early childhood field is expanding rapidly to meet the needs of the increasing number of working parents, children at risk, and children with special needs because of the growing realization that early childhood education can benefit all young children. With the increased demand for such services comes a growing concern about the quality of care and education offered to children and the qualifications of the caregivers and teachers involved.

Concerns

Parents are concerned about the lack of full-day programs, the character and training of those who are caring for their children, the activities offered during the program day, and how they will be able to afford the care. Teachers and caregivers are concerned about low salaries, how to better themselves in this field, and how they will be able to meet new job qualifications or licensure.

Government regulatory agencies are concerned about how to ensure that all programs meet minimum standards. Professional groups are concerned about how to maintain quality programs when various state licensure regulations for both early childhood facilities and their teaching staffs vary so widely. College and universities are concerned about how to change their course offerings and degree requirements to meet new state regulations and national standards. These are a few of the issues facing this rapidly expanding field that is struggling to become a recognized profession.

A Helping Profession

The commitment that an early childhood worker makes to this exciting new profession is an important one. Ours is a helping profession, which means that we must put our clients—the children and families we serve—first in our professional lives. Translated into practical terms, our commitment means that we may have to come in early and stay late to make sure that classes are covered and children are served, that we may have to take children home if the bus breaks down or a parent fails to come, that we may miss coffee breaks or even lunch if a classroom emergency demands our attention, that we may have to spend many hours at home preparing activities for the following day.

In other words, our own needs are secondary when it comes to our professional lives. A professional commitment in any of the helping professions requires us to give of ourselves without expecting to be paid for every hour we contribute. Such a commitment means investing time and energy. We may have to work extra hours or even come in when we are not feeling up to par because a particular situation demands it of us. This behavior is often quite different from that of the paraprofessional or nonprofessional.

Often people working part time or paid hourly look at their work in terms of the hours they put in. They may be reluctant to respond to demands made on them outside of their normal working hours. The professional, in contrast, must take a broader view of program demands and be willing to sacrifice time and energy if the need arises. *Giving of oneself without expecting a particular reward marks the true professional in fields such as early childhood education.*

MAKES A COMMITMENT TO THE EARLY CHILDHOOD PROFESSION

Knowledge Base in the Field of Early Childhood

Professionals in every field must have a familiarity with and understanding of the knowledge on which the field is founded. In early childhood education, this includes familiarity with the foundations of early childhood education and its principal contributors such as Rousseau, Pestalozzi, and Froebel, from the 18th and 19th centuries; Montessori, Pratt, and Mitchell, from the early 20th century; the contributions from the field of psychology by Freud, Gesell, Erikson, Piaget, Vygotsky, and Gardner; the kindergarten and nursery school movements in the United States at the turn of the century; the day-care movement given impetus during World War II; the Head Start and the compensatory education movement born during the War on Poverty of the 1960s and 1970s; particular curriculum models in vogue today such as those developed by High/Scope, Montessori, or Reggio Emilia; and current research with implications for early childhood development such as brain research, developmentally appropriate practice, and emergent literacy.

In addition, professionals in the field must have a knowledge of child development, health, psychology, sociology, education, literacy, children's literature, art, music, dance, physical education, special education, multicultural education, and English-language learning because these fields affect young children and their families.

Professionals also need to understand conflicting child development theories such as the maturational theory, the cognitive-development theory, the behaviorist theory, the social learning theory, and the constructivist points of view. They should examine Bronfenbrenner's ecological theory, Gardner's theory of multiple intelligences, and Reggio Emilia's "hundred languages of children." They should be familiar with learning practices such as discovery or exploratory play, the project approach, emergent literacy, and the emergent curriculum as they apply to young children, to design what is termed "developmentally appropriate practice" for the children in their care (Wortham, 2006).

Developmentally Appropriate Practice (DAP)

It is especially important that professionals in the field be aware of the guidelines for developmentally appropriate practice (DAP), as spelled out by our professional organization, the National Association for the Education of Young Children (NAEYC), and discussed in the Introduction.

It is a never-ending task to keep up with developments in this dynamic field. True professionals make the effort to keep abreast of this knowledge by taking college courses and workshops, attending in-service training, reading textbooks and journal articles, inviting knowledgeable guest speakers to their programs, attending local, state, and national conferences where such information is disseminated, and visiting other early childhood programs that feature particular curriculum ideas.

Reading Early Childhood Journals

Castle (2009) tells us: "The knowledge base of the early childhood profession is constantly growing. To keep up, read professional literature at least once a week. Choose articles in respected professional journals, program documents, or information from credible Web sites" (p. 8). Some of the most respected journals are:

Childhood Education (Association for Childhood Education International)

Dimensions of Early Childhood (Southern Early Childhood Association)

Exchange (Child Care Exchange)

Young Children (National Association for the Education of Young Children)

New Knowledge

In addition to the commonly recognized knowledge about child development and learning, professionals must always be open to new knowledge as it is discovered by research and technology, developed by professionals in the far corners of the Earth, or even revealed by the children themselves through our observation of them. What a surprise it was for literacy specialists from Argentina to discover that young children could emerge into reading and writing without being formally taught (Ferreiro & Teberosky, 1982). Children themselves were actually teaching the professionals what they could do by coming into kindergarten programs already knowing how to read. Then it was up to literacy specialists to discover how this had happened and what they could do to support this development of "emergent literacy." For example, is learning to write largely an act of discovery on the part of children, or does it have to be taught? Often it takes many years for professionals to convert such theory into practice.

We must be ever vigilant to new ideas that may emerge and new ways of doing things that may come forth. The door to understanding child development has not been closed. What we know about young children is perhaps only the tip of the iceberg. Not so many years ago we believed that infants and young children were blank slates waiting to be filled by us with knowledge. Now we realize that children come into this world with the ability to create their own knowledge. Today we talk about six areas of child development that need to be considered: physical, cognitive, language, social, emotional, and creative. Is that all there is? Or might there be undiscovered aspects in the development of the human being that we may not yet have recognized? You, as a new student in this dynamic field, may be the one to discover an entirely overlooked aspect of young children's development.

We need to learn much more about how young children initially operate from the right hemisphere of the brain that controls visual perception, sensory stimulation, emotions, holistic thinking, imagination, humor, art, music, and creativity, and how to help them cross over to adult thinking modes using the left hemisphere of the brain controlling analytic, logical, sequential, and abstract thinking, reading, writing, and math. Or should we first consider the opposite: How can adults regain right hemisphere functions in their own lives? Perhaps the children can teach us. We need to examine the current rise of hyperactivity in children from a positive point of view. How can it help them? Perhaps it is us that are out of sync with the world, not them. How can we change the way we act toward children with attention-deficit hyperactivity disorder (ADHD) to make a positive difference in their lives?

What about brain research? Findings by neuroscientists about brain development, brain chemistry, the origins of intelligence and of language need to be translated into how we should teach young children and how they learn. We need to consider the enormous amount of new knowledge that is surfacing about human development in every field to determine how and whether it can be applied to child development, teaching, and learning. For instance, as Greenspan (1997) notes, "In recent years, through our research and that of others, we have found unexpected common origins for the mind's highest capacities: intelligence, morality, and sense of self. We have charted critical stages in the mind's early growth, most of which occur even before our first thoughts are registered. At each stage certain critical experiences are necessary. Contrary to traditional notions, these experiences are not cognitive but are types of subtle emotional exchanges. In fact, emotions, not cognitive stimulation, serve as the mind's primary architect" (p. 1).

How can such new knowledge be used in the early childhood classroom? Professionals in the field will be the ones applying such information now and in the future. Professionals should be persons who do not close their minds to new concepts. They understand that *teaching and learning are reciprocal functions*: Teachers teach children, but at the same time they learn from children. Children learn from teachers, but at the same time they also teach teachers things about themselves. All professionals can help to expand this knowledge base in the field of early childhood education by keeping alert for new ideas and sharing their inspirations, aspirations, and experiences with others in the field.

Training Opportunities in the Field of Early Childhood

Professionals in every field must complete some type of formal training. The field of early childhood requires various types and levels of training or education depending on the position and state requirements. Child-care workers are often required to have 12 to 18 credit hours of courses in early childhood. Teachers may be required to have a two-year or four-year college degree.

Many child-care providers, however, may have started their early childhood careers informally as babysitters in their own homes. Then as their own children enter a child-care program, those that show interest or promise may be asked to volunteer in a classroom. If the program has an in-service training component, they may be able to receive training and eventual certification through a Head Start Program, a local social services department, or a Military Family Child Care Program. As one director of a Marine Corps Family Care Program reports, "It has taken quite a while to move providers from seeing themselves as babysitters to looking upon themselves as child care professionals. They are there now. Our next task is to help parents understand the difference" (Nielsen, 2002, p. 13).

Technology-Based E-Learning

With today's focus on high-tech teaching and learning in schools, colleges, and universities throughout the country, it is only natural that e-learning should also be available to students preparing for early childhood teaching positions. The author of this text was involved for three years in a highly successful distance learning Child Development Associate (CDA) training program out of Columbia, South Carolina, called Early Childhood Professional Development Network (ECPDN), now completed. Weekly TV satellite broadcasts on topics from the book *Essentials for Child Development Associates Working with Young Children* (Day, 2004) were both live and interactive between Head Start viewers and early childhood experts in the TV studio. Follow-up weekly conference calls gave participants the opportunity to discuss what they had viewed. Participants were required to do written assignments as well as to apply what they were learning in their classrooms. Head Starts throughout Indian reservations in the American West as well as on Pacific islands throughout Micronesia benefited from this kind of training that was otherwise unavailable in their distant locations.

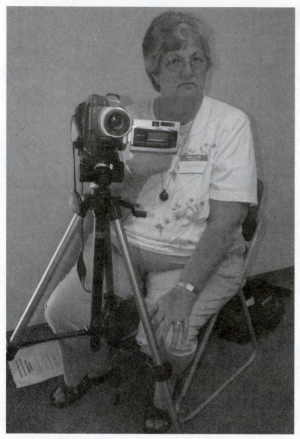

Many programs use their own video photography for training.

Donohue and Neugebauer (2004) tell us, "From our experiences with e-teaching, and what we have learned from others in distance learning programs and those who teach courses on-line, we have identified elements of successful e-learning programs, innovative uses of technology, and promising technology tools and applications that support professional growth and development" (p. 22). Because these programs change frequently over the years, it is necessary to contact them directly to learn more.

A few of those offering degree programs in early childhood include Concordia University-Saint Paul in Minnesota, Kansas State University, Northhampton Community College in Pennsylvania, Nova Southeastern University in Florida, and Pacific Oaks College in California. States that have also developed virtual universities that allow students to take e-courses from a number of institutions within the state include Colorado Community Colleges Online, Kentucky Virtual University, E-Lect E-Learning for Early Childhood Teachers from Minnesota State Colleges and Universities, and New York State Early Childhood Education Online (pp. 22–23).

Many distance learning programs use traditional correspondence courses, but more rely on TV broadcasts via cable or satellite, computer-based learning, and Web-based training (streaming, message boards, interactivity, animation, and database). Virtual reality simulations are also popular. One such program, the ChildCare Education Institute, is a distance learning institution offering over 100 on-line courses in English and Spanish, including CDA coursework (1-888-418-5358). Before becoming involved in these programs, participants need to check the quality of their content for

- Ideas and strategies leading to positive outcomes for young children.
- Professionally recognized authors.
- Widely accepted, research-based information. (Harvey, 2004, pp. 35–36)

Child Development Associate

In addition to the traditional modes of training for early childhood education, there is another increasingly popular national program for developing the necessary competence to teach throughout the country in the field: Child Development Associate

(CDA) training, assessment, and credentialing. CDA training is competency-based and performance-based, which means that a certain percentage of the training must occur *in* the early childhood classroom and that the trainee must demonstrate competence with children in such a setting.

Because many CDA candidates use this text, *Skills for Preschool Teachers,* for their training, a separate section of the text, Appendix A: "Becoming a CDA: Child Development Associate," has been included. Candidates will find information relating to the methods of preparation for three different types of credentials: center based, family child care, and home visitor. In addition, more in-depth information on developing the Professional Resource File and how to prepare competency statements is given. Future plans call for CDA online application and assessment in addition to traditional processes. Check the Council's website: http://www.cdacouncil.org for more information.

Why Become a CDA?

Why should you become a CDA? First, it will help you in your work as a classroom teacher or assistant. It will help you improve your skills in working with young children and their families; in setting up appropriate physical environments; in keeping the children in your care safe and healthy; in providing opportunities for them to improve their physical, cognitive, language, and creative development; and in planning activities and managing individuals and groups.

It will also help you to assess your strengths and areas needing strengthening so that you will be able to make the necessary improvement. You will do this not only through self-evaluation and preparation, but also through the eyes of an early childhood professional, your adviser, whom you will come to know as a friend.

Receiving the CDA credential will elevate your status in your program and enhance the program's status in the community. In some instances, you may receive a promotion or salary raise. This credential may be worth college credit at various institutions. Because the CDA is a national credential, your talents will also be more marketable in other states if you should move.

Finally, the CDA credential will induct you as a professional into the field of early childhood education. Some professions require a bachelor's degree for entry. The early childhood field is coming more and more to recognize the CDA as the first professional step in an ever-expanding career. Bredekamp (2000) collected a great deal of evidence of the individual impact of the CDA. Frances Pryor, who is now director of an NAEYC-accredited Head Start program in Florida, had this to say about receiving her CDA: "It was the most exciting day of my life. It helped me in all areas and motivated me to want to do more" (p. 18).

To encourage students and child-care workers to take the training and go through the credentialing process, financial assistance is provided by many states. TEACH Scholarships and the Child Care and Development Block Grant (CCDBG) can provide funding for the CDA assessment fee and other costs of earning or renewing the credential. To find out if your state provides this assistance, contact the state child-care licensing agency or your local resource and referral agency about free or low-cost CDA training.

Licensing and Credentialing

Another important mark of professionals in any field is a credential. Professionals need a degree, license, or credential to certify that they are qualified in the field. Credentials of various kinds can be awarded to qualified individuals based on college courses or programs completed, workshops taken, training completed, tests taken, or types and amounts of experience. Licensing or credentialing bodies may be colleges and universities, state departments of education, local programs, or state or national agencies. Types of credentials vary from college degrees to workshop completion certificates. The NAEYC lists six levels of early childhood professional categories (see Figure 13.1).

Service Requirements in the Field of Early Childhood Education

All professions require their members to complete a certain amount of service to be recognized. Taking classroom courses or obtaining general college degrees does not totally qualify a person as a professional in early childhood. Field experience in an early childhood program or classroom is necessary for all credentials or degrees. The amount of experience varies according to the professional level as indicated in Figure 13.1. Although the levels reflect a conceptual framework rather than standard requirements, many certificates, degrees, or positions do require such service. Just to enter CDA training, for instance, a candidate must have completed 480 hours of direct experience working with children in a child-care setting.

Most child-care programs offer opportunities for students or volunteers from the community to gain work experience with children as teacher assistants, one of the first steps up the early childhood career ladder. Colleges and universities require early childhood majors to work a certain number of weeks as student teachers in nursery schools, prekindergartens, preschools, or child-care facilities.

Parents of preschool children often work as volunteers in their child's program to gain necessary experience that can lead to training or job placement in the field. Some training workshops or seminars are held on site for participants to gain firsthand experience with children. Local child-care agencies can inform you of job opportunities that require specific amounts of training and can often direct you to the training opportunities available in the community.

BEHAVES ETHICALLY TOWARD CHILDREN, FAMILIES, AND COWORKERS

Shows Respect for All

A second important area of professionalism in early childhood education is that of ethical behavior, including confidential treatment of information about children and families. In addition to putting children and families first, professionals also demonstrate a positive attitude toward their clients at all times. No matter what the family

Professional Level I

Individuals employed in an early childhood professional role working under supervision and participating in training designed to lead to assessment of competencies or a degree

Professional Level II

Successful completion of CDA Professional Preparation Program or completion of systematic, comprehensive training program leading to CDA Credential through direct assessment

Successful completion of one-year early childhood certificate program

Professional Level III

Successful completion of associate degree from a program conforming to NAEYC guidelines, or

Successful completion of associate degree plus 30 units of professional studies in early childhood development or education including 300 hours of supervised teaching experience in an early childhood program, or

Successful demonstration of the knowledge, performance, and dispositions expected as outcomes of an associate degree program conforming to NAEYC guidelines

Professional Level IV

Successful completion of a baccalaureate degree from a program conforming to NAEYC guidelines, or

State certificate meeting NAEYC/NCATE certification guidelines, or

Successful completion of a baccalaureate degree in another field with more than 30 professional units in early childhood development/education including 300 hours of supervised teaching experience, including 150 hours each for two of the following three age groups: infants and toddlers, 3- to 5-year-olds, or the primary grades, or

Successful demonstration of the knowledge, performance, and disposition expected as outcomes of a baccalaureate degree program conforming to NAEYC guidelines

Professional Level V

Successful completion of a master's degree in a program that conforms to NAEYC guidelines, or

Successful demonstration of the knowledge, performance, and disposition expected as outcomes of a master's degree program conforming to NAEYC guidelines

Professional Level VI

Successful completion of a Ph.D. or Ed.D. in a program conforming to NAEYC guidelines, or

Successful demonstration of the knowledge, performance, and disposition expected as outcomes of a doctoral degree program conforming to NAEYC guidelines

Figure 13.1 Early Childhood Professional Categories

Source: Adapted from "NAEYC Position Statement: A Conceptual Framework for Early Childhood Professional Development" by the National Association for the Education of Young Children, 1994, *Young Children, 49,* p. 74. Copyright 1994 by NAEYC. Reprinted by permission.

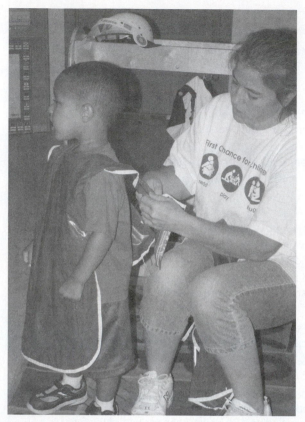

You must demonstrate to every child every day you care about him.

background, no matter how serious the problems faced by the family, no matter what the past behavior of the child and family, true professionals retain an objective view of the situation and treat the child and family in a positive manner.

Parents who abuse their children need your help just as much as or more than parents who treat their children positively. Low-income families deserve the same treatment as affluent families. Children from families of racial, ethnic, or religious backgrounds different from that of the teachers should be treated in the same respectful manner as all others. In other words, children are children—to be accepted, respected, and cherished along with their families by true professionals in the early childhood field.

Demonstrates Caring Toward All Children

Behaving ethically toward children includes relating to them in emotionally positive ways. Figure 13.2 lists positive traits every early childcare professional should exhibit. The original CDA program included these same personal capacities as part of the competencies that early childhood workers need to develop.

Figure 13.2 Personal Capacities of Early Childhood Professionals

- Is sensitive to children's feelings and the quality of young thinking
- Is ready to listen to children to understand their feelings
- Uses nonverbal forms of communication and adapts adult language to maximizing communication with children
- Protects orderliness without sacrificing spontaneity and childlike exuberance
- Accepts children's individuality and makes positive use of individual differences within the child's group
- Exercises control without being threatening
- Is emotionally responsive, takes pleasure in children's successes, and is supportive during times of trouble
- Brings humor and imagination into the group
- Is committed to maximizing the child's and family's strengths and potentials

Your job is to demonstrate to every one of the children in your class every day that you care about them. Nonverbal cues such as smiling, laughing, talking to them, joking with them, putting a hand on a shoulder, giving them a hug, sitting close to them, or holding them on your lap let children know you care for them personally. You must demonstrate this feeling to every child, not to one or two special children. Picking out a favorite child and lavishing attention on her is unethical. Rejecting a child because he is whiny or aggressive or wears dirty clothing is also unethical. Ethical behavior requires you to respond with positive feelings to every child in your class.

Respects Privacy of Children, Families, and Coworkers

As a preschool teacher, you are probably very much a "people person." You are undoubtedly interested in every aspect of the children and their families. Your position allows you to find out all kinds of information about them. You'll know good things and bad—about health problems, family problems, promotions, firings, new babies, new husbands or wives, and gossip.

As an early childhood professional, you have an ethical duty to treat all such information confidentially. If you hear other staff members gossiping, do not join in, but remind them as tactfully as possible that this kind of information is confidential. If parents ply you with gossip about other parents or children, let them know in a diplomatic way that this information should not be shared.

Ethical behavior of this type also applies to the children. For example, do not talk with parents about their children when the children are present. These conversations are confidential and can damage a child's self-concept. If parents start talking to you about their child while the child is standing nearby, tell them you prefer to talk at another time or that perhaps their child can play in another room while you chat. Parents who understand how professionally you treat information about them and others are bound to respect both you and your program.

NAEYC's Code of Ethical Conduct

The National Association for the Education of Young Children's Code of Ethical Conduct from 1997 has been brought up to date by a 2005 revision (NAEYC, 2005). This code offers guidelines for responsible behavior in early education and sets forth a common basis for resolving the principal ethical dilemmas encountered in early childhood care and education. The primary focus of the code is on the teacher's daily practice with children and their families in programs for children from birth through 8 years of age. Figure 13.3 lists the core values on which the code is based.

All professions have ethical standards. In a new and expanding profession such as early childhood, it is important for practitioners to have such a code as a standard for behavior involving difficult moral actions and decisions. Copies of the complete *Code of Ethical Conduct and Statement of Commitment* can be obtained from NAEYC on their Web site, http://www.naeyc.org, or in the book *Ethics and the Early Childhood Educator: Using the NAEYC Code* (Feeney & Freeman, 2006). Applying such standards in the day-to-day life of the classroom can be made easier if your staff

Figure 13.3   Core Values

Appreciate childhood as a unique and valuable stage of the human life cycle	Respect the dignity, worth, and uniqueness of each individual
Base our work on knowledge of how children develop and learn	Respect diversity in children, families, and colleagues
Appreciate and support the bond between the child and family	Recognize that children and adults achieve their full potential in the context of relationships that are based on trust and respect
Recognize that children are best understood and supported in the context of family, culture, community, and society	

explicitly addresses them as part of your preservice and inservice training. As noted by Brophy-Herb, Kostelnik, and Stein (2001), "Ethical concepts and skills are best taught as part of a planned, multilevel approach that includes ample opportunities for facilitated discussions, personal reflections, examinations of professional codes of conduct, and explorations of systematic decision-making models for making ethical judgments" (p. 81).

For many early childhood practitioners, this may be the first time they have dealt with a formal code of ethics. You and your staff should read through the code to become familiar with it. You may be surprised to find that the code does not tell exactly how to handle every case. Instead, the guidelines are general rules of conduct that may be applied to different situations. The idea of the code is to help professionals determine broad categories of ethical and unethical behavior. As Brophy-Herb et al. (2001) note, "Adherence to a code of ethics distinguishes early childhood professionals from lay persons with no commitment to the field" (p. 81).

If you consider each of the guidelines carefully, you may find that there is a difference between personal morality and professional ethics. For example, you may need more than a simple knowledge of right and wrong (personal morality) when dealing with a group of people from diverse backgrounds. What makes sense for an individual may not be in accord with agreed-upon professional standards. As a professional you must act in accordance with the standards.

Training About Ethical Conduct

From staff training you may be surprised to learn that not all dilemmas are ethical. For instance, determining whether to decide a conflict in favor of the child involved or to follow the teacher's previous direction is not an ethical dilemma but one that may reflect educational practices, priorities, convenience, or personal preference. Many ethical dilemmas have no clear-cut straightforward solution but only a choice between two relatively undesirable ethical choices. In other words, there is not only one correct ethical response (Brophy-Herb et al., 2001, p. 82). Nevertheless, having

Ethical Responsibilities to Children

P. 1.1 Above all, we shall not harm children. We shall not participate in practices that are emotionally damaging, physically harmful, disrespectful, degrading, dangerous, exploitive, or intimidating to children. This principle has precedence over all others in this code.

P. 1.2 We shall care for and educate children in positive emotional and social environments that are cognitively stimulating and that support each child's cultural, language, ethnicity, and family structure.

P. 1.3 We shall not participate in practices that discriminate against children by denying benefits, giving special advantages, or excluding them from programs or activities on the basis of their sex, race, national origin, religious beliefs, medical condition, disability, or the marital status/family structure, sexual orientation, or religious beliefs or other affiliations of their families.

P. 1.4 We shall involve all those with relevant knowledge (including families and staff) in decisions concerning a child, as appropriate, ensuring confidentiality of sensitive information.

Ethical Responsibilities to Families

P. 2.1 We shall not deny family members access to their child's classroom or program setting unless access is denied by court order or other legal restriction.

P. 2.2 We shall inform families of program philosophy, policies, curriculum, assessment system, and personnel qualifications, and explain why we teach as we do—which should be in accordance with our ethical responsibilities to children.

P. 2.3 We shall inform families of and, when appropriate, involve them in policy decisions.

P. 2.4 We shall involve the family in significant decisions affecting their child.

*Abbreviated overview.

Figure 13.4   Ethical Responsibilities to Children and Families*

Source:. NAEYC Early Childhood Program Standards and Accreditation Criteria, (2005), Washington, DC: Author, pp. 119–121.

the NAEYC guidelines is a valuable starting point. Using the Activity Sourcebook *Teaching the NAEYC Code of Ethical Conduct* (Feeney, Freeman, & Moravcik, 2000) is another helpful resource. An abbreviated overview of the Code's Ethical Responsibilities to Children and Families is shown in Figure 13.4.

Use these principles to help you resolve the ethical dilemmas found at the end of each chapter. Are these real *ethical dilemmas,* or could they instead be based on *personal values and morality* rather than ethics? A dilemma involves a choice between values and responsibilities. Which of the ethical principles in Figure 13.4 might apply to "ethical dilemmas" in the text?

You may want to discuss any of the real ethical problems that have arisen among your teachers, your colleagues, the children, their families, the sponsoring agency, the school, and even the community. Keep alert for such problems and discuss them at the next staff meeting. Did they really involve ethical problems? How were they resolved? In what way did the NAEYC Code help you to make the decisions? How would you handle such problems in the future? What other similar ethical problems can you foresee happening in the future? How will you handle these? Having a professional Code of Ethical Conduct to fall back on helps everyone take an objective view of sensitive situations that may arise. Persons with no commitment to the early childhood field should feel relieved that our profession has come forward with a definite set of guidelines for responsible behavior. You as a new professional in the field should feel more confident that your decisions are in line with those of other professionals in the field.

Two excellent articles to read and discuss with all of your colleagues are "Ethical Dilemmas for Early Childhood Educators: The Ethics of Being Accountable" (Israel, 2004, pp. 24–32) in *Young Children* (November 2004) and *The NAEYC Code Is a Living Document* (Freeman & Feeney, 2004, pp. 12–16) in the same journal.

TAKES EVERY OPPORTUNITY TO IMPROVE PROFESSIONAL GROWTH

Ongoing Training

As you become more professional in your outlook, early childhood training should become an ongoing part of your life. Like Head Start, many programs have in-service training programs built into their schedules. The year begins with a preservice workshop for all teachers and assistants and continues with on-site or regional workshops in the various program component areas such as curriculum, nutrition, health, mental health, career development, and parent involvement.

Ongoing training alerts staff members to current developments in the early childhood field such as the new brain research and its impact on child development. Teaching skills are also sharpened when specialists offer workshops on topics important to the curriculum. Staff members are able to share ideas with one another about what works and what doesn't work.

Volunteers attend workshops such as those on emergent literacy.

Figure 13.5   CDA
Credential Renewal
Criteria

1. Documented proof of a current Red Cross or other agency First Aid Certificate.

2. Documented proof of at least 4.5 Continuing Education Units (CEUs) or a three-credit-hour course in early childhood education/child development, principles of adult learning, mental health counseling, etc.

3. Documented proof of recent (within past year) work experience with young children or families of young children (a minimum of 80 hours).

4. A completed Letter of Recommendation Form regarding the CDA's competence with young children prepared by an Early Childhood Education Professional.

5. Documented proof (within current year) of membership in a national or local early childhood professional organization.

CDA Credential Renewal

Recognizing the necessity for ongoing training, the Child Development Associate (CDA) program requires that CDAs renew their credential three years after its receipt and every five years thereafter. Renewal candidates must meet the following criteria (*CDA Renewal: Procedures for renewing the CDA Credential,* http://www.cdacouncil .org/cda_renew. 3/13/2010) (See Figure 13.5)

Join a Professional Organization, Read Its Publications, Network with Colleagues in the Field

The number of professional organizations concerned with young children increases every year. Some of the largest and most important to teachers include the following national organizations:

American Montessori Society (AMS)

150 Fifth Avenue

New York, NY 10011

(*Montessori Life,* quarterly journal)

Association for Childhood Education International (ACEI)

17904 Georgia Avenue, Suite 215

Olney, MD 20832

(*Childhood Education,* journal published six times a year)

National Association for the Education of Young Children (NAEYC)

1509 16th Street, NW

Washington, DC 20036–1426

(*Young Children,* bimonthly journal)

Southern Early Childhood Association (SECA)

8500 W. Markham Street, Suite 105

P. O. Box 55930

Little Rock, AR 72215–5930

(*Dimensions of Early Childhood*, quarterly journal)

These national organizations also have state offices and local chapters holding regular meetings. All teachers of young children should join one of these organizations, read its publications, and attend its meetings. Attending local meetings is important for teaching staff to meet and network with other teachers working nearby. Attending state and national meetings can expand participants' points of view, give them the latest information on topics of interest to them, as well as introduce them to leaders in the field.

Every professional field reaches its members through such organizations, publications, and meetings. Early childhood teaching staffs need to become members of such a professional organization in order to become recognized members of the profession. CDAs are required to join a professional organization in order to renew their certificates. For others it is imperative that they join an organization in order to keep up with current issues, trends, and ideas in this ever-expanding field.

Professional Publications

Exchange
    http://www.childcareexchange.com
Children and Families Magazine
    http://www.nhsa.org
Childhood Education
    http://www.acei.org
Dimensions of Early Childhood
    http://www.southernearly
    childhood.org
Head Start Information & Publication Center
    http://www.headstartinfo.org

MenTeach
    http://www.MenTeach.org
National Association for Bilingual Education News
    http://www.nabe.org
Young Children
    http://www.naeyc.org
Young Exceptional Children
    http://www.dec-sped.org

Career Opportunities

If you are interested in finding career opportunities in the early childhood education field, check Figure 13.1, "Early Childhood Professional Categories," to determine your current level of professional development. Job openings in early childhood education field are on the rise. Some of the programs looking for teachers, teaching assistants, substitutes, and volunteers include the following:

Before- and after-school care   Mall care centers
Cooperative preschools   Military child-care centers

Community and church-sponsored centers	Montessori Schools
Head Start centers	Neighborhood playgroups
Hospital child-care centers	Private sector preschools
Industry-sponsored centers	Public school prekindergartens
Infant-and-toddler centers	Residential treatment child-care centers
	University preschools

Machado and Reynolds (2006) have published a comprehensive guide to finding a position in the field that includes a CD-ROM: *Employment Opportunities in Education: How to Secure Your Career.* For those interested in working with infants and toddlers, the Teacher Skills Checklist on which this text is based has been converted by Polk Community College in Florida into a "Teacher Skills Checklist for Infants and Toddlers" (see Appendix B).

Professional Portfolio

It is important you have documentation that illustrates your philosophy, professional growth, and experiences to share with other professionals or for job interviews. Such a collection, often referred to as a *professional portfolio,* illustrates your accomplishments as an early childhood professional in a clear and understandable fashion. CDA training requires their candidates to create such a Professional Resource File to serve as their portfolio. (See Appendix A.)

Although there is no preferred form for a portfolio, many professionals use a three-ring binder with clear plastic sleeves for inserting the materials. Contents can be divided into sections and can include: a table of contents, your resume, a statement of your philosophy, and references in the first section; professional memberships, certificates of achievement, transcripts or courses and training completed in the next section; classroom experience showing lesson plans, daily schedule, floor plan, family communications, observation checklists, and samples of children's work in a final section. Several photographs and sample letters can illustrate this section (Priest, 2010, pp. 94–95). The professional portfolio is not a scrapbook or photo album, but a clear and concise representation of you as a professional, which showcases your skills in this special and important field.

Personal Contribution

In becoming a professional in the early childhood field, you have committed yourself to a career of giving to children, to their families, to your team members, and to your program. In addition, you may be called on to share your knowledge and skills with others in the community and even further afield. As a professional, you should welcome this opportunity. The growing need for qualified early childhood personnel puts special demands on all of us. Spreading the good news about quality programs for young children, helping paraprofessionals in the field to become credentialed, and helping to start new programs are a few of the ways you might contribute. For specific ideas, consider the contributions listed in Figure 13.6.

Figure 13.6 Personal
Contributions of Early
Childhood Professionals

- Serve on board of community child-care program
- Become CDA adviser for another candidate
- Speak at a community group about your program
- Show slides/PowerPoint to parents about how children learn through exploratory play
- Share knowledge and skills with children in another classroom (play instrument, do art project, tell story)
- Submit child-care topic for presentation with team member at a state or national conference
- Advise community librarian about good picture books to purchase
- Volunteer in child-care resource center
- Appear as guest speaker at college class
- Write to early childhood textbook authors about successful ideas you have tried with children

The list could go on about the many possibilities for sharing your early childhood skills and knowledge with others. The topic of early childhood education is of paramount importance to everyone in the community these days, especially for families with young children. How are these youngsters to grow up in health and happiness, surrounded as many are by dysfunctional families, street violence, and environmental destruction?

Simple gifts are just as important to the people you interact with daily as your contributions to the field as listed in Figure 13.7. Jacobs (2001) discusses several other simple gifts that early childhood practitioners can give to children and other teachers in their program (pp. 77–78).

Figure 13.7 Simple Gifts

Share yourself (give yourself to your children every day).

Share your interests (bring in your special talent, hobby, or interest).

Help children look at life through the eyes of a photographer (you, if you are one).

Help children and others use computer graphics (if you know how).

Read a picture book to several children every day.

Bring in a personal collection of dolls, teapots, pins, magnets, spoons, postcards.

Sew something with your children; help them create something with their hands.

Explore science and nature with others (share a pet, do an experiment, take a walk outdoors, make recycled paper).

Bake; write out a recipe and bake something familiar with the children.

Think about the gifts you bring each time you come to the center. It may be the precious moments in which you give the gift of who you are that makes all the difference.

As Jacobs reminds us, "Take a few moments from your busy day to think about the gifts you bring each time you walk into the room. Doing this may help you recognize the special strengths in your children as well. When your children and students look back to remember what made an impact in their lives, it may well be the time spent with you as you opened new doors to them, sharing unique talents and interests. It may be the precious moments in which you gave the gift of who you are, and the gift of your time, that made all the difference" (p. 79). Does this make you a professional? You know it does.

Early childhood professionals can lead the way with a positive vision of the future for young children. The exuberance of the youngsters, their energy and creativity, and their drive to discover what makes the world tick are topics you are intimately familiar with. You can share this with others. You can help make a difference in the children's world to come when you touch others with your newly acquired knowledge and skills about children and families. For a new professional in the early childhood field, your contribution is no longer an option but a necessity. Children, parents, community members—all of us—we need you!

SUMMARY

To become a professional in the early childhood field, you must first make a commitment to the field by putting children and families first in your professional life. This often means sacrificing time and energy to make sure children and families are served by your program as they should be. It may mean coming to the program early and leaving late. It also means providing services yourself when no one else is available.

To be considered a member of the early childhood profession, you must also gain a knowledge base in the field through workshops, courses, college and university programs, or CDA training. Your training should lead to some sort of credential, certificate, or degree. One of the important methods for acquiring competence as well as being credentialed in the field is by becoming a CDA. This training, assessment, and credentialing program requires trainees to complete a course of study, to perform competently in an early childhood setting, to assemble a Professional Portfolio, and to complete a written and oral situational assessment. (See Appendix A.) In addition, a professional is generally required to complete a period of service in the field as a volunteer, teaching assistant, teacher, or caregiver, using developmentally appropriate practices with children.

A professional also treats information about children and families confidentially. When parents or staff members begin gossiping about children, a professional should not participate and should help others to understand why this behavior is not acceptable. Other ethical behaviors toward children involve being sensitive to their feelings, adapting your language to their understanding, being emotionally responsive, and bringing humor and imagination into the classroom.

To continue your professional growth as a teacher of young children, take every opportunity to gain knowledge and skills in the field by joining a professional organization such as the National Association for the Education of Young Children, reading its journal, *Young Children*,

and attending local, state, or national meetings. Many early childhood workers also find networking with other professionals to be especially helpful.

Finally, as a professional, you need to make your own ongoing contribution to the field, perhaps in the form of a presentation to a parent group, a college class, or an early childhood conference; by helping a coworker become a CDA; by giving a librarian information on children's picture books to order; or by sharing one of your skills with the children or another early childhood class. As a new professional in this expanding field, you can truly make a difference with the skills you have developed and are ready to share with others.

LEARNING ACTIVITIES

1. Read one of the Suggested Readings or view one of the Web sites listed and make 10 file cards with specific ideas for professional development.

2. Make a self-assessment using the "Teacher Skills Checklist," as discussed in the Introduction. Discuss the results with your trainer or college instructor and together make a training plan for you to follow.

3. Choose three of the ethical dilemmas at the ends of the chapters and write out which of the Ethical Responsibilities to Children in Figure 13.4 might apply to each of these dilemmas.

4. Make a list of organizations or agencies in your community (or county) that are concerned with young children and their families. Attend one of their meetings and write a summary.

5. Write to the Council for Early Childhood Professional Recognition for a packet of information on obtaining a CDA credential. Find out where you can obtain CDA training locally.

6. Join an early childhood organization, obtain a copy of an early childhood professional journal such as *Young Children,* and write a summary of interesting ideas from the articles in one issue.

7. How has this reading of *Skills for Preschool Teachers* and your training program changed you as a person and as a teacher or teacher-to-be of young children? Be specific.

8. Make a Professional Portfolio as described in this chapter.

SUGGESTED READINGS

Armstrong, L. J., Kinney, K. C., & Clayton, L. H. (2009). Getting started: Leadership opportunities for beginning early childhood teachers. *Dimensions of Early Childhood, 37*(3), 11–17.

Barbour, N., & Lash, M. (2009). *The professional development of teachers of young children.* In S.

Feeney, A. Galper, & C. Seefeldt (Eds.), *Continuing issues in early childhood education* (3rd ed.). Upper Saddle River, NJ: Merrill.

Castle, K. (2009). What do early childhood professionals do? *Dimensions of Early Childhood, 37*(3), 4–10.

Copple, C., & Bredekamp, S. (Eds.). *(2009). Developmentally appropriate practice in early childhood programs.* 3rd ed. Washington, DC: National Association for the Education of Young Children.

Feeney, S. (2010). Ethics today in early care and education: Review, reflection, and the future. *Young Children, 65*(2), 72–77.

Gronlund, G., & James, M. (2008). *Early learning standards and staff development.* St. Paul, MN: Redleaf Press.

Jones, M., & Shelton, M. (2006). *Developing your portfolio: Enhancing your learning and showing your stuff.* New York: Routledge.

Pierce, D. (2008). *The CDA prep guide: The complete review manual.* St. Paul, MN: Redleaf.

Priest, C. (2010) The benefits of developing a professional portfolio. *Young Children, 65* (1), 92–96.

WEB SITES

Alliance for Childhood
http://www.allianceforchildhood.org

Association for Childhood Education International
http://www.acei.org

Child Care Exchange
http://www.childcareewxchange.com

Council for Professional Recognition
http://www.cdacouncil.org

Heads Up! Network: National Head Start Association
http://www.heads-up.org

National Association for the Education of Young Children
http://www.naeyc.org

National Board for Professional Teaching Standards
http://www.nbpts.org

Southern Early Childhood Association
http://www.southernearlychildhood.org

The Center for Career Development in Early Care & Education, Wheelock College
http://www.wheelock.edu

Becoming a CDA: Child Development Associate

I n addition to the traditional modes of training for early childhood education, another increasingly popular method for developing the necessary competence to teach in the field is Child Development Associate (CDA) training, assessment, and credentialing. CDA training is based on competency and on performance, which means that a certain percentage of the training must occur *in* the early childhood classroom and that the trainee must demonstrate competence with children in such a setting.

The Child Development Associate program emerged in the 1970s as a collaborative effort on the part of early childhood professionals and the federal government to create a new category of early childhood professional: the Child Development Associate. From the beginning the program had two separate parts: training done by local colleges or early childhood programs and credentialing done by the national office (Child Development Associate National Credentialing Program). Today that program has consolidated both training and credentialing under a CDA Professional Preparation Program offered by the Council for Professional Recognition, 2460 16th Street, NW, Washington, D.C., 20009-3575. (See also http://www.cdacouncil.org.)

CDA training programs may enroll candidates for different types of credentials: center- based, family child care, or home visitor. Candidates may also choose a bilingual credential if they work in a program that requires them to use a second language as well as English in any of these settings. (Council for Professional Recognition, 2006, p. 3).

STEPS TO OBTAINING A CDA CREDENTIAL

Steps to obtaining a CDA credential include four components:

- Determining eligibility
- Meeting training requirement
- Purchasing application packet
- Completing assessment requirement

Eligibility Requirement

Candidates seeking to apply for CDA assessment may work in any of three settings: center-based, family child care, or home visitor. They must meet the eligibility requirements shown in Figure A.1.

Settings

All candidates must also be able to identify an appropriate setting where they can be observed working as the lead caregiver. They include:

- Center-Based CDA
- Family Child Care CDA
- Home Visitor CDA

Training for *Center-Based CDA* must include a state-approved child development center where the Candidate can be observed working as a lead teacher with a specific group of children. Two different endorsements are available: "Preschool," for Candidates working with 3- through 5-year-old children, and "Infant/Toddler," for candidates working with children from birth up to 36 months.

Training for *Family Child Care CDA* must include a family child-care home that meets minimum state and local regulations, where Candidates can be observed working as primary providers with at least two children, 5 years old or younger and not related to the candidate.

Figure A.1   Eligibility
Requirements

- Be 18 years of age or older
- Hold a high school diploma or GED
- Have 480 hours of experience working with children within the past five years
- Have 120 clock hours of formal child care education within the past five years.

Figure A.2   Training
Content Areas

1. Planning a safe, healthy, learning environment.
2. Steps to advance children's physical and intellectual development.
3. Positive ways to support children's social and emotional development.
4. Strategies to establish productive relationships with families.
5. Strategies to manage an effective program operation.
6. Maintaining a commitment to professionalism.
7. Observing and recording children's behavior.
8. Principles of child development and learning.

Training for *Home Visitor CDA* must include an established program of home visits to families with children 5 years old or younger to meet the needs of their young children. Candidates can be observed working in the home as an adult educator with the parents. The *Bilingual Specialization* can apply to training in any of these settings. (Council for Professional Recognition, 2006, p. 3).

Training Requirement

The eligibility requirement for CDA Candidates to have 120 clock hours of formal child care education may be met through participation in the wide variety of training available in the field, including in-service training. While the formal education hours can be credit or noncredit, the hours must be through an agency or organization with expertise in early childhood teacher preparation. The agency or organization must provide verification of the Candidate's education in the form of a transcript, certificate, or letter.

The 120 clock hours of education must be documented, with no fewer than 10 hours in each of the following content areas (See Figure A.2):

(http://www.cdacouncil.org/cda; 3/13/2010)

Using Skills for Preschool Teachers in CDA Training

This textbook, *Skills for Preschool Teachers,* is designed to be used in CDA training programs either by individuals who prefer the In-Service Training Option or by colleges or training programs who prefer the classroom or seminar approach. The "Teacher Skills Checklist" (see Introduction) can be used by any CDA trainee or adviser as an initial assessment tool. Then a training prescription can be developed for the trainee to follow as he or she proceeds through the training. Each chapter of this book represents one of the 13 CDA Functional Areas from 6 of the CDA Training Content Areas discussed in the Training Requirement. (See Figure A.3.)

As Candidates read the chapters and complete the learning activities, they will also be producing evidence for the 13 Functional Area sections of a Professional

Figure A.3 Training Content Areas with *Skills for Preschool Teachers* Chapters

1. *Planning a safe, healthy, learning environment*
   Chapter 1 Maintaining a Safe Classroom
   Chapter 2 Maintaining a Healthy Classroom
   Chapter 3 Establishing a Learning Environment

2. *Advancing children's physical and intellectual development*
   Chapter 4 Advancing Physical Skills
   Chapter 5 Advancing Cognitive Skills
   Chapter 6 Advancing Communication Skills
   Chapter 7 Advancing Creative Skills

3. *Supporting children's social and emotional development*
   Chapter 8 Building a Positive Self-Concept
   Chapter 9 Promoting Social Skills
   Chapter 10 Providing Guidance

4. *Establishing productive relationships with families*
   Chapter 11 Promoting Family Involvement

5. *Managing an effective program operation*
   Chapter 12 Providing Program Management

6. *Maintaining a commitment to professionalism*
   Chapter 13 Promoting Professionalism

Resource File. Observation checklists, file cards of activities, and lists of children's books are products they can use. Photographs of children using learning centers as suggested in the chapters can be accompanied by descriptions and write-ups of competence. Other resource materials candidates can use in their training include those listed under References, Suggested Readings, and Web Sites. When Candidates are ready they can purchase an Application Packet.

Application Packet

Individuals who meet all the Candidate eligibility requirements and who can be observed in an eligible setting can purchase an application packet appropriate for the types of credential they wish to receive. Four types of packets include (See Figure A.4):

These packets contain all the documents Candidates will need to apply for CDA assessment. Each packet is customized for the selected child care setting and contains two copies of the *CDA Competencies Standards Book,* instructions and instrument for the observation, scholarship information, parent questionnaires, and the application form.

(http://www.cdacouncil.org/cda)

Figure A.4 Application Packets

- *Preschool Packet* for Candidates working in a center-based setting with children 3-5 years old.
- *Infant Toddler Packet* for Candidates working with children from birth to 36 months of age.
- *Family Child Care Packet* for Candidates working with one or all age groups in a family child care home
- *Home Visitor Packet* for Candidates working with parents of young children.

Assessment Requirement

Once Candidates have received the Application Packet they can begin assembling the requirements for CDA assessment. These requirements are completed in three phases:

- Preparation of necessary materials
- Filing of application
- Verification of competence and knowledge

Preparation of Necessary Materials

Professional Resource File

Candidates must prepare a Professional Resource File that can be arranged like a portfolio, either in a bound notebook, inside file folders in a box, or in other creative ways. The candidate must be able to carry the Professional Resource File from a work site, on a home visit, or to a meeting. The file must contain 17 items based on the 6 CDA Training Content Areas. It must show evidence of what the candidate finds valuable in her or his work. The Resource File has three major sections: Autobiography, Statements of Competence, and Resource Collection.

Autobiography Candidates must write a 300-word autobiography that tells who they are and the things that influenced their decision to work with young children. Some candidates may feel uncomfortable with writing about themselves. They may first want to discuss what they should say with their trainer. Then they may want to jot down a few reasons they began their work with children, how they felt about it once they started, and what obtaining a CDA credential could mean to them in the future. Although the trainer can lend support in this writing, the ideas and words should be the candidate's own. Such an autobiography should help them sort out their own feelings about working with children and what it has meant in their lives.

Statements of Competence An in-depth statement of the candidate's competence in each of the 13 CDA Functional Areas under the 6 CDA Competency Goals should be written out. Figure A.5 provides an example of the competency statements for Mary Jones for the CDA Area "Safe."

CANDIDATE'S NAME <u>Mary Jones</u>   **DATE** _____

COMPETENCY GOAL #1: *To establish and maintain a safe, healthy, learning environment*

INTRODUCTORY PARAGRAPH: (Write Introductory Paragraph *only at the beginning* of each Competency Goal).

    I maintain a safe, healthy learning environment by keeping the indoor and outdoor areas well-organized with enough space for children to move safely from one activity to another. I promote good health and nutrition and provide an environment that encourages play, exploration, and learning.

FUNCTIONAL AREA: SAFE

DEFINITION: Candidate provides a safe environment to prevent and reduce injuries.

GOAL FOR CHILDREN: *My goal for children is that they will learn fire safety procedures.*

STATEMENT OF COMPETENCE: *I plan and practice fire drills monthly.*

SPECIFIC EXAMPLES OF WHAT YOU DO TO ACHIEVE YOUR GOAL FOR CHILDREN:

    I plan with my classroom team and other building personnel the specific time and procedures for each fire drill. My planning includes a circle time discussion of fire drills and how to leave the classroom safely and quickly when the fire drill alarm sounds. We listen to the sound of the fire alarm so the children will not be afraid. We practice leaving the building following arrows on the floor leading out the door to our classroom's designated location on the lawn. I take the daily attendance sheet with me so I can be certain all children are out of the building. I praise the children for a job well done to encourage future appropriate fire drill behaviors.

Figure A.5   Professional Resource File, Safe

Resource Collection   The bulk of the material in the Professional Resource File is the material the candidate has collected to show competence in each of the 13 Functional Areas: Safe, Healthy, Learning Environment, Physical, Cognitive, Communication, Creative, Self, Social, Guidance, Family, Program Management, and Professionalism.

    It can contain items such as file cards with children's activities for each of the 13 Functional Areas; pamphlets or brochures from early childhood education association meetings; booklets on how children grow and learn that would be appropriate for parents; observation tools, such as checklists for recording information they have gathered about children; lists of agencies in the community that provide help for children with developmental disabilities; emergency telephone numbers; Red Cross certificates; titles of children's books dealing with development of gender identity, separation, family diversity, or multicultural backgrounds; goals of your program; favorite poems and songs for children; file cards from the chapters of this text; or a list of Web Sites you have used on parenting.

Parent Opinion Questionnaires

The Application Packet also contains Parent Opinion Questionnaires in English or Spanish, which the Candidate must distribute to parents of the children in the class. The Questionnaire contains 27 positive statements about the Candidate to which the parent must respond by marking yes, no, or does not apply. The Questionnaires are confidential with no one but officials authorized by the Council for Professional Recognition permitted to read them. They must be returned to you in a plain sealed envelope for you to include with the materials you will be giving to the Council Representative. The Council requires that you collect the completed forms from at least 75 percent of the total number of your children's parents.

CDA Assessment Observation

You will need a CDA advisor to observe you as you work with children in your classroom. Training programs usually provide an advisor. The Council can also be contacted for a listing of registered CDA advisors in your area. Make a copy for yourself of the CDA Assessment Instrument booklet you received in your application packet. Give the original to your CDA advisor for her/him to fill out when she visits your classroom. Go through the booklet, doing a self-evaluation of your work with children and becoming familiar with the things your advisor with be looking for and for which you will be rated.

Your CDA advisor needs to visit you in your classroom at least once before conducting an official assessment observation. She/he will then share with you the results, indicating problems areas and methods for improving them. The final observation is a formal one by your advisor, and the results cannot be shared. She will be rating you on items according to the CDA Competency Goals and Functional Areas. The formal observation may take as long as three hours, after which her filled out Assessment Observation Instrument booklet will be placed in an envelope and sealed.

Application

When all of the documentation is complete, the Candidate and CDA advisor sign the application form and send it to the Council along with an assessment fee and training documentation. The Council assigns a Council Representative to conduct the Verification Visit.

Verification Visit

The Council Representative will contact the Candidate at least twice to introduce herself and explain how the Verification Visit will take place; also to go over a checklist to make sure all the required materials are ready. The Candidate must arrange for a quiet room where the visit can take place. During the first part of the visit the Candidate will take an Early Childhood Studies Review exam consisting of 60 multiple choice questions. The Candidate is allowed two hours to complete the exam, but most finish sooner. After this the Council Representative will administer an Oral Interview in which the Candidate discusses and gives own ideas about 10 different early childhood scenarios shown on 10 illustrated cards. All of the verification materials and testing results are then sent to the Council for Professional Recognition, which will award the CDA Credential if the Candidate's work is satisfactory. (http://www.cdacouncil.org/cda; 3/13/10)

REFERENCES

Council for Professional Recognition. (2006). *The child development associate assessment system and competency standards; preschool caregivers in center-based programs.* Washington, DC: Author. http://www.cdacouncil.org/cda (3/13/10)

SUGGESTED READINGS

Bredekamp, S. (2000). CDA at 25: Reflections on the past and projections for the future. *Young Children, 55*(5), 15–19.

Day, C. B. (Ed.). (2006). *Essentials for child development associates working with young children* (2nd ed.). Washington, DC: Council for Professional Recognition.

Pierce, D. (2008). *The CDA prep guide; the complete review manual.* St. Paul, MN: Redleaf Press.

Teacher Skills Checklist for Infants and Toddlers

(From the Polk Community College, Lakeland, Florida, faculty members)

Teacher Skills Checklist for Infants and Toddlers

Student _____

Observer _____

Program _____

Visit Date _____

Job Title _____

Visit Hours _____ to _____

 ## DIRECTIONS

Please put a "Y" on the line in front of the items you see the student/teacher perform regularly. Put an "N" on the line in front of the items you do not see the student/teacher perform regularly. Please leave blank all items where there is no opportunity to observe.

Area #1

SAFE—Maintaining a Safe Classroom
To be able to set up and maintain a safe classroom environment and to reduce and prevent injuries.

_____ Promotes toy and material safety within each learning center. (Locks cribs, no choking hazards)

_____   Plans and implements necessary emergency procedures. (Cribs on wheels for evacuation drills, updated parent contact information)

_____   Provides a safe classroom atmosphere through teacher behavior.

Area #2

HEALTHY—Maintaining a Healthy Classroom
To be able to set up and maintain a healthy classroom that promotes good child health and nutrition and is free from factors contributing to illness.

_____   Encourages children to follow common health and nutrition practices. (Both teacher and infant hand washing following diapering, before meals, a variety of age-appropriate food)

_____   Recognizes unusual behavior or symptoms of children who may be ill and provides for the children.

_____   Supports the mental and emotional health of every child. (Comforts, soothes, encourages new exploration)

Area #3

LEARNING ENVIRONMENT—Establishing a Learning Environment
To be able to set up and arrange an early childhood classroom so that children will become self-directed in their learning.

_____   Separates and places learning centers in appropriate spaces. (Enough open space to crawl, practice walking, and explore a variety of toys)

_____   Provides appropriate materials for children's self-directed play and learning. (Variety of toys to choose from, encourage reaching, grasping, babbling)

_____   Changes materials periodically to meet children's developmental needs. (Enough toys to meet different areas of stimulation, outdoor experiences)

Area #4

PHYSICAL—Advancing Physical Skills
To promote children's physical development by determining their needs and providing appropriate materials and activities.

_____   Assesses children's large-motor skills and provides appropriate equipment and activities. (Encourage rolling over, crawling, pulling up, and safe space to practice these skills)

_____   Assesses children's small-motor skills and provides appropriate materials and activities. (Variety of rattles, kick toys, toys to push, etc.)

_____   Provides opportunities for children to engage in creative movement. (Holding, rocking, dancing)

Area #5

COGNITIVE—Advancing Cognitive Skills
To promote children's cognitive development by involving them in exploring their world.

_____ Helps children develop curiosity about their world through sensory exploration. (Sensory books, toys that move, play music, talking to them, singing, touching)

_____ Helps children develop basic concepts about their world by classifying, comparing, and counting objects in it. (Explore the room, look at/talk about colors, shapes, describe objects to them)

_____ Helps children apply basic concepts about their natural world through hands-on experiences. (Exploration of teacher's face, play beside other infants)

Area #6

COMMUNICATION—Advancing Communication Skills
To promote children's communication skills through listening, speaking, emergent reading, and emergent writing.

_____ Talks with individual children to encourage listening and speaking. (During routine care, talk back in response to their coos and babbles)

_____ Uses books and stories to motivate listening, speaking, and emergent reading. (Encourage them to hold the book and explore it, use expression when reading)

_____ Provides materials and activities to support emergent writing. (Crushing and tearing paper, picking up with two fingers, grasping)

Area #7

CREATIVE—Advancing Creative Skills
To promote children's creativity through playful expression and freedom of activity.

_____ Gives children time, opportunity, and freedom to do pretending and fantasy role play. (Give them floor play time, tummy time, and free movement areas)

_____ Provides a variety of art materials and activities for children to explore on their own. (Pudding painting, crushing paper, etc.)

_____ Encourages children to create and have fun with music.

Area #8

SELF—Building a Positive Self-Concept
To help children improve their self-concept through your attitude and behavior toward them.

_____ Accepts self and every child as worthy and uses nonverbal cues to let children know they are accepted.

_____ Accepts diversity in children and helps children to accept one another. (Meets their needs consistently and quickly)

_____ Helps every child to experience success in the classroom. (Encourages exploration, have pictures of their face and others for them to see)

Area #9

SOCIAL—Promoting Social Skills
To help children develop the social skills of interacting in harmony with others.

_____ Helps children learn to work and play cooperatively through sharing and turn-taking. (Teacher is a consistent social partner, warm, loving, and dependable)

_____ Helps children learn to enter ongoing play without disruptions.

_____ Helps children learn to make friends.

Area #10

GUIDANCE—Providing Guidance
To promote the development of self-control in young children through positive guidance.

_____ Uses positive prevention measures to help eliminate inappropriate behavior in the classroom. (Quick response to their needs, enough open floor space)

_____ Uses positive intervention methods to help children control their inappropriate behavior. (Redirection to another toy or area of the room for stimulation)

_____ Uses positive reinforcement techniques to help children learn appropriate behavior. (Praise for their efforts, for touching with soft touches, etc.)

Area #11

FAMILIES—Promoting Family Involvement
To encourage family involvement in center activities to promote their children's positive development.

_____ Involves parents in participating in children's program.

_____ Recognizes and supports families of different makeup.

_____ Builds teacher-family relationships through family classroom meetings.

Area #12

PROGRAM MANAGEMENT—Providing Program Management.
To develop an effective early childhood classroom program based on the needs and interests of the children.

_____ Uses a team approach to plan a flexible curriculum.

_____   Plans and implements an emergent curriculum to assure a quality program.

_____   Evaluates curriculum outcomes through child observations and team conferences.

Area #13   **PROFESSIONALISM—Promoting Professionalism**
            To continue professional growth as a teacher of young children.

_____   Makes a commitment to the early childhood profession.

_____   Behaves ethically toward children and their families.

_____   Takes every opportunity to improve professional growth.

Final Notes (Observations, Comments, Questions, Follow-Up Plans)

_____

_____

_____

_____

_____

_____

_____

Name of Visiting Instructor   Date of Visit

Location of Visit   Age of Children   Times of Visit

References

Achilles, E. (1999). Creating music environments in early childhood programs. *Young Children, 54*(1), 21–26.

Adams, S. K., & Wittmer, D. S. (2001). "I had it first." Teaching young children to solve problems peacefully. *Childhood Education, 78*(1), 10–16.

Althouse, R., Johnson, M. H., & Mitchell, S. T. (2003). *The colors of learning: Integrating the visual arts into the early childhood curriculum.* New York: Teachers College Press.

American Academy of Pediatrics and American Public Health Association. (2002). *Caring for our children, national health and safety performance standards: Guidelines for out-of-home child care programs.* Elk Grove Village, IL: American Academy of Pediatrics.

American Cancer Society. (2000). *Kids' first cookbook.* Atlanta, GA: Health Contents Products Publishing Group.

Anderson, G. T., & Robinson, C. C. (2006). Rethinking the dynamics of young children's social play. *Dimensions of Early Childhood, 34*(1), 11–16.

Appleton, J., McCrea, N., & Patterson, C. (2001). *Do carrots make you see better? A guide to food and nutrition in early childhood programs.* Beltsville, MD: Gryphon House.

Aronson, S. S. (Ed.). (2002). *Healthy young children: A manual of programs.* Washington, DC: National Association for the Education of Young Children (NAEYC).

Azria-Evans, M. (2004). Self-esteem and young children: Guiding principles. *Dimensions of Early Childhood, 32*(1), 21–26.

Balaban, N. (2006). *Everyday goodbyes: Starting school and early care; A guide to the separation process.* New York: Teachers College Press.

Barclay, K. H. (2010). Using song picture books to support early literacy development. *Childhood Education, 86*(3), 138–145.

Beaty, J. J. (2006). *50 early childhood guidance strategies.* Upper Saddle River, NJ: Merrill/Prentice Hall.

Beaty, J. J. (2010). *Observing development of the young child* (7th ed.). Upper Saddle River, NJ: Merrill/Prentice Hall.

Beaty, J. J., & Pratt, L. (2011). *Early literacy in preschool and kindergarten: A multicultural perspective* (3rd ed.). Boston, MA: Allyn & Bacon.

Bellows, L., & Anderson, J. (2006). The food friends: Encouraging preschoolers to try new foods. *Young Children, 61*(3), 37–39.

Berl, P. (1998). Becoming planners: Finding time and insight. *Exchange,* 61–63.

Bernath, P., & Masi, W. (2006). Smart school snacks: A comprehensive preschool nutrition education program. *Young Children, 61*(3), 20–24.

Birckmayer, J., Cohen, J., Jensen, I. D., & Variano, D. A. (2005). Supporting grandparents who raise grandchildren. *Young Children, 60*(3), 100–104.

Bloom, F. E., Nelson, C. A., & Lazerson, A. (2001). *Brain, mind, and behavior* (3rd ed.). New York: Worth.

Bodrova, E., & Leong, D. J. (2007). *Tools of the mind: The Vygotskian approach to early childhood education* (2nd ed.). Upper Saddle River, NJ: Merrill/Prentice Hall.

Brazelton, R. B., & Sparrow, J. D. (2001). *Touchpoints three to six: Your child's emotional and behavioral development.* Cambridge, MA: Perseus Publishing.

Bredekamp, S. (2000). CDA at 25: Reflections on the past and projections for the future. *Young Children, 55*(5), 15–19.

Bridge, C. A. (1986). Predictable books for beginning readers and writers. In M. R. Sampson (Ed.), *The pursuit of literacy: Early reading and writing.* Dubuque, IA: Kendall/Hunt.

Brinson, S. A. (2005). R-E-S-P-E-C-T for family diversity. *Dimensions of Early Childhood, 33*(2), 24–30.

Brophy-Herb, H. E., Kostelnik, M. J., & Stein, L. C. (2001). A developmental approach to teaching about ethics using the NAEYC Codes of Ethical Conduct. *Young Children, 56*(1), 80–84.

Brown, K., Fitzpatrick, T. S., & Morrison, G. S. (2004). Valuing diversity in classrooms through family involvement. *Dimensions of Early Childhood, 32*(3), 11–16.

Buell, M. J., & Sutton, T. M. (2008). Weaving a web with children at the center: A new approach to emergent curriculum planning for young preschoolers. *Young Children, 63*(4), 100–105.

Bullard, J. (2010). *Creating environments for learning.* Upper Saddle River, NJ: Merrill.

Bunnett, R., & Davis, N. L. (1997). Getting to the heart of the matter. *Child Care Information Exchange, 114,* 42–44.

Burt, T., Geinaw, A., & Lesser, L. K. (2010). Do no harm: Creating welcoming and inclusive environments for lesbian, gay, bisexual, and transgender families in early childhood settings. *Young Children, 65*(1), 97–102.

Burton, S. J., & Edwards, L. C. (2006). Creative play: Building connections with children who are learning English. *Dimensions of Early Childhood, 34*(2), 3–8.

Byrnes, A., & Wasik, B. A. (2009). Picture this: Using photography as a learning tool in early childhood classrooms. *Childhood Education, 85*(4), 243–248.

Caples, S. E. (1996). Some guidelines for preschool design. *Young Children, 51*(4), 14–21.

Castle, K. (2009). What do early childhood professionals do? *Dimensions of Early Childhood, 37*(3), 4–9.

Cherry, C. (1972). *Creative art for the developing child.* Belmont, CA: Fearon.

Clements, D. H., & Sarama, J. (2003). Young children and technology: What does the research say? *Young Children, 58*(6), 34–40.

Clements, R. L., & Schneider, S. L. (2006). *Movement-based learning for children: Academic concepts and physical activity for ages three through eight.* Reston, VA: National Association for Sport and Physical Education.

Copple, C., & Bredekamp, S. (Eds.). (2009). *Developmentally appropriate practice in early childhood programs* (3rd ed.). Washington, DC:

National Association for the Education of Young Children.

Corsaro, W. A. (2003). *We're friends, right?* Washington, DC: Joseph Henry Press.

Curtis, D., & Carter, M. (2005). Rethinking early childhood environments to enhance learning. *Young Children, 60*(3), 34–38.

Davies, M. A. (2000). Learning . . . the beat goes on. *Childhood Education, 76*(3), 148–153.

Day, C. B. (2004). *Essentials for child development associates working with young children* (2nd ed.). Washington, DC: Council for Professional Recognition.

Deiner, P. L. (1993). *Resources for teaching children with diverse abilities* (2nd ed.). Fort Worth, TX: Harcourt.

Diffily, D. (2001). Family meetings: Teachers and families build relationships. *Dimensions of Early Childhood, 29*(3), 5–10.

Dixon-Krauss, L. (1996). *Vygotsky in the classroom: Mediated literacy instruction and assessment.* White Plains, NY: Longman.

Donohue, C., & Neugebauer, R. (2004). Innovations in e-learning: New promise for professional development. *Young Children, 59*(3), 22–26.

Duffy, R. (1997). Parents' perspectives on conferencing. *Child Care Information Exchange, 116,* 40–43.

Eaton, M. (1997). Positive discipline: Fostering the self-esteem of young children. *Young Children, 52*(6), 43–46.

Edwards, L. C. (2006). *The creative arts: A process approach for teachers and children.* Upper Saddle River, NJ: Merrill/Prentice Hall.

Eldridge, D. (2001). Parent involvement: It's worth the effort. *Young Children, 56*(4), 65–69.

Epstein, A. S. (2009). *You, me, us: Social-emotional learning in preschool.* Ypsilanti, MI: High Scope Press.

Espinosa, L. M. (2010). *Getting it right for young children with diverse backgrounds: Applying research to improve practice.* Upper Saddle River, NJ: Pearson.

Evans, M. (1993). *Pet care guides for kids: FISH.* New York: Dorling Kindersley.

Farish, J. M. (2001). Helping young children in frightening times. *Young Children, 56*(6), 6–7.

Feeney, S., & Freeman, N. K. (2006). *Ethics and the early childhood educator: Using the NAEYC code*. Washington, DC: National Association for the Education of Young Children.

Feeney, S., Freeman, N. K., & Moravcik, E. (2000). *Teaching the NAEYC code of ethical conduct*. Washington, DC: National Association for the Education of Young Children.

Feeney, S., & Moravcik, E. (2005). Children's literature: A window to understanding self and others. *Young Children, 60*(5), 20–28.

Ferreiro, E., & Teberosky, A. (1982). *Literacy before schooling*. Exeter, NH: Heinemann.

Fischer, M. A., & Gillespie, C. W. (2003). Computers and young children's development. *Young Children, 58*(4), 85–91.

Flynn, L. L., & Kieff, J. (2002). Including everyone in outdoor play. *Young Children, 57*(3), 20–26.

Fox, J. E., & Diffily, D. (2000). Integrating the visual arts—building young children's knowledge, skills, and confidence. *Dimensions of Early Childhood, 29*(1), 3–10.

Freeman, N. K., & Feeney, S. (2004). The NAEYC code is a living document. *Young Children, 59*(6), 12–16.

Friedman, S. (2005). Environments that inspire. *Young Children, 60*(3), 48–55.

Frost, J. L., Wortham, S. C., & Reifel, S. (2005). *Play and child development* (2nd ed.). Upper Saddle River, NJ: Merrill/Prentice Hall.

Frost, L. A., & Bondy, A. S. (1994). *The picture exchange communication system training manual*. Cherry Hill, NJ: Pyramid Education Consultants.

Fulmore, J. S., Geiger, B. F., Werner, K. A.,Tallbot, L. L., & Jones, D. C. (2009). Sun protection education for healthy children. *Childhood Education, 85*(5), 293–299.

Fye, M. A. S., & Mumpower, J. P. (2001). Lost in space? Designing learning areas for today. *Dimensions of Early Childhood, 29*(2), 16–22.

Gallagher, K. C. (2005). Brain research and child development: A primer for developmentally appropriate practice. *Young Children, 60*(4), 12–20.

Gandini, L. (2002). The story and foundations of the Reggio Emilia approach. In R. Fu, A. J. Stremmel, & L. T. Hill (Eds.), *Teaching and learning: Collaborative exploration of the Reggio Emilia approach*. Upper Saddle River, NJ: Merrill/Prentice Hall.

Gardner, H. (1993). *Frames of mind: The theory of multiple intelligences*. New York: Basic.

Gartrell, D. (1997). Beyond guidance to discipline. *Young Children, 52*(6), 34–42.

Gartrell, D. (2001). Replacing time-out: Using guidance to build an encouraging classroom. *Young Children, 56*(6), 8–16.

Gellens, S. (2005). Integrate movement to enhance children's brain development. *Dimensions of Early Childhood, 33*(3), 14–21.

Gennarelli, C. (2004). Communicating with families: Children lead the way. *Young Children, 59*(1), 98–99.

Goldberg, E. (1994). Including children with chronic health conditions: Nebulizers in the classroom. *Young Children, 49*(2), 34–37.

Gonzales-Mena, J. (2009). Family-centered early care and education. In Feeney, S., Galper, A., & Seefeldt, C. (Eds.), *Continuing issues in early childhood education* (3rd ed.). Upper Saddle River, NJ: Merrill.

Gonzales-Mena, J. (2010). *50 strategies for communicating and working with diverse families* (2nd ed.). Upper Saddle River, NJ: Pearson.

Gonzalez-Mena, J., & Shareef, I. (2005). Discussing diverse perspectives on guidance. *Young Children, 60*(6), 34–38.

Good, L. (2005/2006). Snap it up! Using digital photography in early childhood. *Childhood Education, 82*(2), 79–85.

Goodwin, W. L., & Goodwin, L. D. (1996). *Understanding quantitative and qualitative research in early childhood education*. New York: Teachers College Press.

Green, C. R. (1998). This is my name. *Childhood Education, 74*(4), 226–231.

Greenman, J. (2005). *Caring spaces, learning places: Children's environments that work*. Redman, WA: Exchange Press.

Greenspan, S. I. (1997). *The growth of the mind: And the endangered origins of intelligence*. Reading, MA: Addison-Wesley.

Greenspan, S., & Lewis, N. B. (2000). *Building healthy minds: The six experiences that create intelligence and emotional growth in babies and young children*. Cambridge, MA: Perseus.

Harvey, C. E. (2004). Technology-based professional development: A meaningful alternative. *Young Children, 59*(3), 34–40.

Hearron, P. F., & Hildebrand, V. (2005). *Guiding young children* (7th ed.). Upper Saddle River, NJ: Pearson/Merrill.

Hirsh-Pasek, K., & Golinkoff, R. M. (2003). *Einstein never used flash cards: How our children really learn—and why they need to play more and memorize less.* New York: Rodale.

Holland, M. (2004). "That food makes me sick!" Managing food allergies and intolerances in early childhood settings. *Young Children, 59*(2), 42–46.

Holt, B. G. (1992). In M. Rivin (Ed.), Science is a way of life. *Young Children, 47*(4), 4–8.

Hoffman, E. (2004). *Magic capes, amazing powers: Transforming superhero play in the classroom.* St. Paul, MN: Redleaf Press.

Huetting, C. I., Sanborn, C. F., Dimarco, N., Popejoy, A., & Rich, S. (2004). The O generation: Our youngest children are at risk for obesity. *Young Children, 59*(2), 50–55.

Hull, K. (1986). *Safe passages: A guide for teaching childhood personal safety.* San Diego, CA: Dawn Sign Press.

Humphryes, J. (2000). Exploring nature with children. *Young Children, 55*(2), 16–20.

Hyson, M. (2002). Preparing tomorrow's teachers: NAEYC announces new standards. *Young Children, 57*(2), 78–79.

Isbell, R. T., & Raines, S. C. (2007). *Creativity and the arts with young children.* Clifton Park, NY: Delmar/Cengage.

Isenberg, J. P., & Jalongo, M. R. (2010). *Creative thinking and arts-based learning; preschool through fourth grade.* Upper Saddle River, NJ: Merrill.

Ishee, N., & Goldhaber, J. (1990). Story re-enactment: Let the play begin! *Young Children, 45*(3), 70–75.

Israel, M. S. (2004). Ethical dilemmas for early childhood educators: The ethics of being accountable. *Young Children, 59*(6), 24–32.

Jacobs, G. M. (2001). Sharing our gifts. *Young Children, 56*(1), 77–79.

Jalongo, M. R. (1995). Promoting active listening in the classroom. *Childhood Education, 72*(1), 13–18.

Jalongo, M. R. (1996). Using recorded music with young children: A guide for nonmusicians. *Young Children, 51*(5), 6–14.

Jalongo, M. R., & Ribblett, D. M. (1997). Using song picture books to support emergent literacy. *Childhood Education, 74*(1), 15–22.

Jensen, E. (1998). *Teaching with the brain in mind.* Alexandria, VA: Association for Supervision and Curriculum Development.

Jones, E., & Cooper, R. M. (2006). *Playing to get smart.* New York: Teachers College Press.

Jones, E., & Nimmo, J. (1994). *Emergent curriculum.* Washington, DC: National Association for the Education of Young Children.

Jones, J. (2004). Framing the assessment discussion. *Young Children, 59*(1), 14–18.

Kalmar, K. (2008). Let's give children something to talk about! Oral language and preschool literacy. *Young Children, 63*(1), 88–92.

Katz, L. G., & McClellan, D. E. (1997). *Fostering children's social competence: The teacher's role.* Washington, DC: NAEYC.

Kellogg, R. (1969). *Analyzing children's art.* Palo Alto, CA: National Press.

Kemple, K. M., Batey, J. J., & Hartle, L. S. (2004). Music play: Creating centers for musical play and exploration. *Young Children, 59*(4), 30–36.

Kemple, K. M., & Ellis, S. M. (2009). Peer-related social competence in early childhood: Supporting interaction and relationships. In E. L. Essa & M. M. Burnham (Eds.), *Informing our practice: Useful research on young children's development.* Washington, DC: NAEYC.

King, M., & Gartrell, D. (2003). Building an encouraging classroom with boys in mind. *Young Children, 58*(4), 33–37.

Koch, P. K., & McDonough, M. (1999). Improving parent-teacher conferences through collaborative conversations. *Young Children, 54*(2), 11–15.

Kordt-Thomas, C., & Lee., I. M. (2006). Floor time: Rethinking play in the classroom. *Young Children, 61*(3), 86–90.

Kosnik, C. (1993). Everyone is a V.I.P. in this class. *Young Children, 49*(1), 32–37.

Kratcoski, A. M., & Katz, K. B. (1998). Conversing with young language learners in the classroom. *Young Children, 53*(3), 30–33.

Lee, L. (1997). Working with non-English-speaking families. *Child Care Information Exchange, 116,* 57–58.

Lewin-Benham, A. (2006). One teacher, 20 preschoolers, and a goldfish: Environmental awareness, emergent curriculum, and documentation. *Young Children, 61*(2), 28–34.

Leithead, M. (1996). Happy hammering . . . a hammering activity center with built-in success. *Young Children, 51*(3), 12.

Lillard, A., & Curenton, S. (1999). Do young children understand what others feel, want, and know? *Young Children, 54*(5), 52–57.

Lim, J., Wood, B. L., & Cheah, P. (2009). Understanding children with asthma. *Childhood Education, 85*(5), 307–312.

Lind, K. K. (1996). *Exploring science in early childhood: A developmental approach.* Albany, NY: Delmar.

Loomis, C., & Wagner, J. (2005). A different look, a challenging behavior. *Young Children, 60*(2), 94–99.

Lopez, E. J., Salas, L., & Flores, J. P. (2005). Hispanic preschool children: What about assessment and intervention? *Young Children, 60*(6), 48–54.

Macarina, M., Hoover, D., & Becker, C. (2009). The challenger of working with dual language learners. *Young Children, 64*(2), 27–34.

Machado, J. M., & Reynolds, R. E. (2006). *Employment opportunities in education: How to secure your career.* Clifton Park, NY: Thomson/Delmar Learning.

Marion, M. (1997). Guiding young children's understanding and management of anger. *Young Children, 52*(7), 62–67.

Marin Child Care Council. (2000). *Childhood emergencies: What to do.* Boulder, CO: Bull Publishing.

Marshall, H. H. (2001). Cultural influences on the development of self-concept: Updating our thinking. *Young Children, 56*(6), 19–25.

Marshall, H. H. (2009). The development of the self-concept. In E. L. Essa & M. M. Burnham (Eds.), *Informing our practice: Useful research on young children's development.* Washington, DC: NAEYC.

Maxim, G. W. (1989). *The very young child* (3rd ed., p. 261). Upper Saddle River, NJ: Merrill/Prentice Hall.

McCay, L. O., & Keyes, D. W. (2001/2002). Developing social competence in the inclusive primary classroom. *Childhood Education, 78*(2), 70–77.

McDevitt, T. M., & Ormrod, J. E. (2007). *Child development: Educating and working with children and adolescents* (3rd ed.). Upper Saddle River, NJ: Merrill/Prentice Hall.

Miller, S. E. (1999). Balloons, blankets, and balls: Gross-motor activities to use indoors. *Young Children, 54* (5), 58–63.

Mindes, G. (2007). *Assessing Young Children* (3rd ed.). Upper Saddle River, NJ: Merrill/Prentice Hall.

Morrison, K. L. (2004). Positive adult/child interactions: Strategies that support children's healthy development. *Dimensions of Early Learning, 32*(2), 23–28.

Morrow, L. M. (2009). *Literacy development in the early years: Helping children read and write.* Boston: Allyn & Bacon.

Morrow, L. M., Freitag, E., & Gambrel, L. B. (2009). *Using children's literature in preschool: Comprehending and enjoying books.* Newark, DE: International Reading Association.

Mulcahey, C. (2009). *The story in the picture: Inquiry and artmaking with young children.* New York: Teachers College Press.

National Association for the Education of Young Children. (2004). Child care health and safety. *Young Children, 59*(2), 49. Washington, DC: Author.

National Association for the Education of Young Children. (2005). *NAEYC early childhood program standards and accreditation criteria.* Washington, DC: Author.

Nemeth, K. (2009). Meeting the home language mandate: Practical strategies for all classrooms. *Young Children, 64*(2), 36–42.

Neuman, S. B., & Roskos, K. A. (1993). *Language and literacy in the early years.* Fort Worth, TX: Harcourt Brace.

Newberger, J. J. (1997). New brain development research—a wonderful window of opportunity to build public support for early childhood education. *Young Children, 52*(4), 4–9.

Nielsen, D. M. (2002). The journey from babysitter to child care professional: Military Family Child Care providers. *Young Children, 57*(1), 9–14.

Page, B. (2006, Spring). Use your head—wear a helmet. *Children Our Concern,* p. 18.

Palmer, H. (2001). The music, movement, and learning connection. *Young Children, 56*(5), 13–17.

Parten, M. B. (1932). Social participation among preschool children. *Journal of Abnormal and Social Psychology, 27,* 243–369.

Pena, D. (2000). Parent involvement: Influencing factors and implications. *Journal of Educational Research, 94*(1), 42–54.

Petrakos, H., & Howe, N. (1996). The influence of the physical design of the dramatic play center on children's play. *Early Childhood Research Quarterly, 11,* 63–77.

Petty, K. (2009). Using guided participation to support children's social development. *Young Children, 64*(4), 80–85.

Pica, R. (2006). Physical fitness and the early childhood curriculum. *Young Children, 61*(3), 12–19.

Pica, R. (2008a). Why motor skills matter. *Young Children, 63*(4), 48–49.

Pica, R. (2008b). *Physical education for young children: Movement ABCs for the little ones.* Champaign, IL: Human Kinetics.

Pica, R. (2009). Can movement promote creativity? *Young Children, 64*(4), 60–61.

Priest, C. (2010). The benefits of developing a professional portfolio. *Young Children, 65*(1), 92–96.

Ramming, P., Kyger, C. S., & Thompson, S. D. (2006). A new bit on toddler biting: The influence of food, oral motor development, and sensory activities. *Young Children, 61*(2), 17–23.

Ramsey, P. G. (1991). *Making friends in school: Promoting peer relationships in early childhood.* New York: Teachers College Press.

Ratcliff, N. (2001). Use the environment to prevent discipline problems and support learning. *Young Children, 56*(5), 84–88.

Reifel, S., & Sutterby, J. A. (2009). Play theory and practice in contemporary classrooms. In S. Feeney, A. Galper, & C. Seefeldt (Eds.), *Continuing issues in early childhood education.* Upper Saddle River, NJ: Merrill.

Reimers, C., & Brunger, B. A. (2006). *ADHD and the young child* (p. 7). Plantation, FL: Specialty Press.

Rike, C. J., Izumi-Taylor, S., & Moberly, D. (2008, May-June). We grow brains! *Exchange,* 22–28.

Riley, J. G., & Boyce, J. S. (2007). Buddying or bullying? A school-wide decision. *Dimensions of Early Childhood, 35*(1), 3–9.

Robertson, C. (2003). *Safety, nutrition, and health in early education.* Clifton Park, NY: Delmar/Thomson/Cengage.

Roffman, L. O., & Wanerman, T. (2011). *Including one including all.* St. Paul, MN: Redleaf Press.

Roskos, K. A., Tabors, P. O., & Lenhart, L. A. (2009). *Oral language and early literacy in preschool:* *Talking, reading, and writing.* Newark, DE: International Reading Association.

Rushton, S. P. (2001). Applying brain research to create developmentally appropriate learning environments. *Young Children, 56*(5), 76–82.

Sanders, S. W. (2002). *Active for life: Developmentally appropriate movement programs for young children.* Washington, DC: National Association for the Education of Young Children.

Schickedanz, J. A., & Casbergue, R. M. (2009). *Writing in preschool: Learning to orchestrate meaning and marks.* Newark, DE: International Reading Association.

Schiller, P., & Willis, C. A. (2008). Using brain-based teaching strategies to creative supportive early childhood environments that address learning standards. *Young Children, 63*(4), 52–55.

Schweinhart, L. J., & Weikart, D. P. (1993). Success by empowerment: The High/Scope Perry Preschool study through age 27. *Young Children, 49*(1), 54–58.

Seefeldt, C. (1995). Art—a serious work. *Young Children, 50*(3), 39–45.

Seefeldt, C. (1998). Assessing young children. In C. Seefeldt & A. Galper (Eds.), *Continuing issues in early childhood education* (pp. 314–338). Upper Saddle River, NJ: Merrill/Prentice Hall.

Seefeldt, C. (2002). *Creating rooms of wonder: Valuing and displaying children's work to enhance the learning process.* Beltsville, MD: Gryphon House.

Selman, R. (2001). Talk time: Programming communicative interaction into the toddler day. *Young Children, 56*(3), 15–18.

Shepherd, W., & Eaton J. (1997). Creating environments that intrigue and delight children and adults. *Child Care Information Exchange, 117,* 42–47.

Shore, R., & Strasser, J. (2006). Music for their minds. *Young Children, 61*(2), 62–67.

Snyder, S. (1997). Developing musical intelligence: Why and how. *Early Childhood Education Journal, 24*(3), 165–171.

Sorrels, B., Norris, D., & Sheehan, L. (2005). Curriculum is a verb, not a noun. *Dimensions of Early Childhood, 33*(2), 3–10.

Sprenger, M. (2008). *The developing brain: Birth to eight.* Thousand Oaks, CA: Corwin Press.

Sprung, B., Froschl, M., & Campbell, P. B. (1985). *What will happen if . . . young children and the scientific method.* Beltsville, MD: Gryphon House.

Staley, L., & Portman, P. (2000). Red rover, red rover: It's time to move over. *Young Children, 55*(1), 67–72.

Stoll, B. H. (2000). *A to Z health and safety in the child care setting.* Minnestrista, MN: Health Consultants for Child Care.

Stone, J. (1993). Caregiver and teacher language—responsive or restrictive? *Young Children, 48*(4), 12–18.

Sundem, G., Krieger, J., & Pikiewicz, K. (2008). *10 languages you'll need most in the classroom: A guide to communicating with English language learners and their families.* Thousand Oaks, CA: Corwin Press.

Taylor, B. J. (2002). *Early childhood program management.* Upper Saddle River, NJ: Merrill/Prentice Hall.

Texas Child Care. (1994). The doctor is in: Medical offices for dramatic play. *Texas Child Care Quarterly, 18*(3), 22–27.

Thompson, D., & Hudson, S. (2003). The inside information about safety surfacing. *Young Children, 58*(2), 108–111.

Tunks, K. W., & Giles, R. M. (2009). Writing their words: Strategies for supporting young authors. *Young Children, 64*(1), 22–25.

Unglaub, K. W. (1997). What counts in learning to count? *Young Children, 52*(4), 48–49.

U.S. Consumer Product Safety Commision. (1997). *Handbook for public playground safety.* Washington, DC: Government Printing Office.

Vygotsky, L. S. (1981). The genesis of higher mental functions. In J. V. Wertsch (Ed.), *The concept of activity in the Soviet psychology* (pp. 144–188). Armonk, NY: Sharpe.

Warner, L. (1999). Self-esteem: A byproduct of quality classroom music. *Childhood Education, 76*(1), 19–23.

Watt, M. R., Roberts, J. E., & Zeisel, S. A. (1993). Ear infections in young children: The role of the early childhood educator. *Young Children, 49*(1), 65–72.

Wadsworth, B. J. (1989). *Piaget's theory of cognitive and affective development.* New York: Longman.

Wellhousen, K., & Crowther, I. (2004). *Creating effective learning environments.* Clifton Falls, NY: Thomson/Delmar/Cengage.

Werner, P., Timms, S., & Almond, L. (1996). Health-stops: Practical ideas for health-related exercise in preschool and primary classrooms. *Young Children, 51*(6), 48–55.

Whitin, P. (*2001*). Kindness in a jar. *Young Children, 56*(5), 18–22.

Wien, C. A., Coates, A., Keating, B-L., & Bigelow, B. C. (2005). Designing the environment to build connection to place. *Young Children, 60*(3), 16–24.

Wilkes, A. (1991). *My first green book: A life-size guide to caring for our environment.* New York: Knopf.

Willis, C. (2009). Young children with autism spectrum disorder: Strategies that work. *Young Children, 64*(1), 81–89.

Winter, S. W. (2009). Childhood obesity in the testing era. *Childhood Education, 85*(5), 283–287.

Woolf, A. D., Kenna, M. A., & Shane, H. C. (Eds.). (2001). *The children's hospital guide to your child's health and development.* Cambridge, MA: Perseus Publishing.

Wortham, S. C. (2006). *Early childhood curriculum: Developmental bases for learning and teaching* (4th ed.). Upper Saddle River, NJ: Merrill/Prentice Hall.

Workman, S. H., & Gage, J. A. (1997). Family-school partnerships: A family strengths approach. *Young Children, 52*(4), 10–14.

Wright, K., Stegelin, D. A., & Hartle, L. (2007). *Building family, school, and community partnerships* (3rd ed.). Upper Saddle River, NJ: Merrill/Prentice Hall.

Index